D0023034

www.wadsworth.com

wadsworth.com is the World Wide Web site for Wadsworth Publishing Company and is your direct source to dozens of online resources.

At *wadsworth.com* you can find out about supplements, demonstration software, and student resources. You can also send e-mail to many of our authors and preview new publications and exciting new technologies.

wadsworth.com
Changing the way the world learns®

Law and Contemporary Corrections

Christopher E. Smith
Michigan State University

West/Wadsworth Publishing Company
I⊕P® An International Thomson Publishing Company

Belmont, CA • Albany, NY • Boston • Cincinnati • Johannesburg
London • Madrid • Melborne • Mexico City • New York
Pacific Grove, CA • Scottsdale, AZ • Singapore • Tokyo • Toronto

Criminal Justice Editor: Sabra Horne
Senior Development Editor: Dan Alpert
Assistant Editor: Shannon Ryan
Editorial Assistant: Ann Tsai
Marketing Manager: Christine Henry
Project Editor: Jennie Redwitz
Print Buyer: Karen Hunt
Permissions Editor: Susan Walters
Production: Strawberry Field Publishing

Interior Design: Carolyn Deacy
Copy Editor: Tom Briggs
Cover Design: Joan Greenfield
Cover Image: Barbed wire image © Bruce
   Forster/Tony Stone Images; cell and shadow
   man images © 1999 Photodisc, Inc.
Compositor: TBH Typecast, Inc.
Printer: R. R. Donnelley & Sons, Crawfordsville

*This book is printed on acid-free
recycled paper.*

For permission to use material from this text, contact us:
   web   www.thomsonrights.com
   fax   1-800-730-2215
   phone   1-800-730-2214

Printed in the United States of America
1 2 3 4 5 6 7 8 9 10

Wadsworth Publishing Company
10 Davis Drive
Belmont, CA 94002

International Thomson Publishing Europe
Berkshire House
168-173 High Holborn
London, WC1V 7AA, United Kingdom

International Thomson Publishing Asia
60 Albert Street #15-01
Albert Complex
Singapore 189969

International Thomson Publishing Southern Africa
Building 18, Constantia Square
138 Sixteenth Road, P.O. Box 2459
Halfway House, 1685 South Africa

International Thomson Editores
Seneca, 53
Colonia Polanco
11560 México D.F. México

Nelson Canada
1120 Birchmount Road
Scarborough, Ontario
Canada M1K 5G4

Nelson ITP, Australia
102 Dodds Street
South Melbourne
Victoria 3205 Australia

International Thomson Publishing Japan
Hirakawa-cho Kyowa Building, 3F
2-2-1 Hirakawa-cho, Chiyoda-ku
Tokyo 102 Japan

Library of Congress Cataloging-in-Publication Data

Smith, Christopher E.
    Law and contemporary corrections / Christopher E. Smith.
       p.   cm.
    Includes index.
    ISBN 0-534-56628-6
    1. Correctional law—United States.   2. Prisons—Law and
legislation—United States.   3. Prisoners—Legal status, laws, etc.—
United States.   I. Title.
KF9728.S63   1999
344.73'035—dc21   99-13587

DEDICATION

For Charlotte Long
A Trailblazer for Women in Corrections

BRIEF CONTENTS

CONTENTS

CHAPTER 3

Decision Making in Prisoners' Cases 55

The Decision-Making Process 56

Prisoner Litigation in the Federal Courts 56

A Picture of Habeas Corpus Cases 60

A Picture of Prisoners' Section 1983 Civil Rights Lawsuits 61

Corrections Law in Action 64

> **BOX 3-1** Actual Prisoner's Claim in a Civil Rights Lawsuit 65
>
> **BOX 3-2** Actual Report and Recommendation of the U.S. Magistrate Judge 67
>
> **BOX 3-3** Actual District Court Order 71

Summary 72

Key Terms 72

Additional Readings 72

Notes 72

CHAPTER 4

Access to the Courts and Communication Rights 75

Access to the Courts 76

Access to Legal Communications 76

Access to Legal Resources 79

> **BOX 4-1** *Johnson v. Avery,* 393 U.S. 483 (1969) 79
>
> **BOX 4-2** *Bounds v. Smith,* 430 U.S. 817 (1977) 81
>
> **BOX 4-3** Prison Law Libraries 83
>
> **BOX 4-4** *Lewis v. Casey,* 116 S.Ct. 2174 (1996) 84

Mail and Telephones 86

Nonlegal Correspondence 86

> **BOX 4-5** *Procunier v. Martinez,* 416 U.S. 396 (1974) 87
>
> **BOX 4-6** *Turner v. Safley,* 482 U.S. 78 (1987) 89
>
> **BOX 4-7** *Thornburgh v. Abbott,* 490 U.S. 401 (1989) 90

Telephone Contacts 92

> **BOX 4-8** Actual Prisoner Mail Policy 93

Contact with Visitors 93

Visitors and Rights 94

> **BOX 4-9** Actual Prison Visitation Rules 95
>
> **BOX 4-10** Actual Policy on Searching Visitors 97

APPENDICES

Since the 1960s, law has become increasingly important for corrections. Court decisions shaped the policies and practices in corrections institutions and, in some states, helped to transform prisons and jails into new organizational entities. As a result, people in the corrections environment—both personnel and prisoners—look to those decisions to define their rights and obligations. Thus, law influences the daily procedures and interactions that affect corrections personnel and prisoners. As the size of both prison populations and prison staffs has grown, the importance of corrections law has increased in corresponding fashion to touch the lives of more and more people. As of 1997, more than 1 million people were incarcerated in prisons and an additional 4 million were under other forms of correctional supervision in the United States. An additional 350,000 people were employed at corrections facilities nationwide, and tens of thousands more worked in probation, parole, and other aspects of corrections.

The goal of this book is to make important aspects of corrections law accessible to nonlawyers. Current and future corrections officers need to gain an understanding of how law affects the corrections environment. Students of criminal justice need to see the impact of law on an important institutional segment of the criminal justice system. Citizens and voters need to understand the issues and problems affecting this growing segment of government in order to see how their tax dollars are being spent and, simultaneously, to understand how the law serves as one accountability mechanism to keep prisons operating according to constitutional standards.

SPECIAL FEATURES

To fulfill the foregoing needs for information about corrections, this book has several important features that distinguish it from comparable texts:

- This is not a book about "prisoners' rights," but a book about *corrections law*. Discussions of prisoners' rights make up a significant portion of the book, but the book includes other important—and neglected—topics, such as decision-making processes affecting corrections cases and the impact of law on corrections personnel.
- This book does not rely exclusively on descriptions of legal cases. Instead, actual *case excerpts* enable students of corrections law to read and analyze the judges' rulings that have shaped law and policy. Also, *hypothetical cases* challenge readers to think about how to apply legal doctrines to situations that may arise in the environment of corrections.
- This book does not limit its discussion to legal doctrines. It presents contemporary examples drawn from news sources that illustrate how corrections law affects the lives of prisoners and staff. It discusses the details of the litigation process and the decision-making processes within courts. And it examines the impact of prison reform litigation on corrections institutions and the debates about the propriety of judges' involvement in prison reform issues.
- This book does not aspire to be a comprehensive encyclopedia of corrections law cases. Instead, cases, statutes, and hypothetical issues have been carefully selected and developed to provide a broad understanding of the subject without overwhelming students with the kind of details that only active litigators and experts need to know.
- This book does not treat the U.S. Supreme Court as the sole source of law affecting corrections. For many issues, the U.S. Supreme Court has declined to rule and has let lower court decisions stand as the governing case law. Thus, this volume contains case excerpts and examples from state courts and the lower federal courts. In addition, there are extended excerpts from key recent statutes, such as the Prison Litigation Reform Act and the Antiterrorism and Effective Death Penalty Act, to demonstrate how statutes also help shape corrections law.
- The book is up to date because of its inclusion of judicial cases from 1998 as well as the most recent federal statutes.

My hope is that the book's organization, design, and special features will help to provide a broad understanding of the significant legal issues affecting the corrections environment and the key legal doctrines developed by courts and legislatures.

ACKNOWLEDGMENTS

Many people helped to build my interest in and knowledge about corrections and corrections law over the past fifteen years—perhaps without even realizing how they contributed to my education. Because this book represents a culmination of my efforts to understand and organize the important aspects of corrections law, I feel obligated to acknowledge my many debts to the people who assisted me—in both large and small ways—to comprehend how corrections law extends beyond formal legal doctrines to affect the lives of millions of people. Although I am solely responsible for any errors in this book, I am grateful for the assistance and contributions of Neil Cohen, University of Tennessee College of Law; The Hon. Richard Enslen, Chief Judge, U.S. District Judge, Western District of Michigan, Kalamazoo; The Hon. James Carr, U.S. District Judge; Northern District of Ohio, Toledo; The Hon. Doyle Rowland, U.S. Magistrate Judge, Western District of Michigan, Kalamazoo; The Hon. Virginia Morgan, U.S. Magistrate Judge, Eastern District of Michigan, Detroit; The Hon. F. Owen Eagan, U.S. Magistrate Judge (ret.), District of Connecticut, Hartford; Larry Yackle, Boston University School of Law; Thao Tiedt, Law Firm of Ryan, Swanson and Cleveland, Seattle; Pamela Withrow, Michigan Department of Corrections; Erik Walter, Ingham County Circuit Court, Lansing; Susan Herman and Donald Kall Loper, Michigan State University; Black Prisoners' Caucus of the Washington State Reformatory, Monroe; Prison Education Program of Asnuntuck Community College, Enfield, Connecticut; Michigan Attorney General's Office; and Court Clerk's Office, U.S. District Court, Lansing, Michigan.

I owe a special debt to my mentor, George F. Cole of the University of Connecticut, for cultivating my interest in this subject and for commenting on an early manuscript.

I am also grateful to my editor, Sabra Horne, and the staff at West-Wadsworth/ITP for their support and assistance on this project.

Reviewers made invaluable contributions to this project by making helpful suggestions and saving me from several errors. Thus, I am grateful for the contributions of Susan F. Brinkley, University of Tampa; George F. Cole, University of Connecticut; Tom Durkin, University of Florida; Louis Holscher, San Jose State University; Frank Mardavich, Virginia Commonwealth University; Robert D. Mendelsohn, South Dakota State University; Patrick A. Mueller, Stephen F. Austin State University; Tom Petee, Auburn University; Gregory J. Petrakis, University of Missouri, Kansas City; Robert Snow, Florida International University; and Michael S. Vaughan, Georgia State University. If this book succeeds in providing a broad understanding of important issues, its success will be due to the contributions of these people.

This book is dedicated to Charlotte Long, my wife's grandmother—and my grandmother for the past fourteen years, too. In light of this book's subject matter, I believe that this dedication is most appropriate. Charlotte Long was one of the first female corrections officers to work behind the walls at Southern Michigan Prison in Jackson, a high-security institution for male offenders that is well known as the largest walled prison in the world. Like other African-American women of her age, for much of her life she faced difficult obstacles and persistent discrimination during decades in which jobs as cooks and housecleaners were virtually the only employment opportunities available. She persevered during difficult years of limited opportunity until she had the chance to be in the first wave of female corrections officers at male institutions. In corrections, she was able to serve the public, earn a decent wage, and gain promotions to higher ranks. All the while, she endured and overcame harassment and hostility from both prisoners and male corrections officers. To me, she represents the courage and persistence that are characteristic of all trailblazers, and therefore she embodies and represents individuals throughout the country who carried the day-to-day burden of introducing equal employment opportunity into the criminal justice system.

Christopher E. Smith
Michigan State University

CHAPTER ONE

Law and Corrections

Corrections. The word calls to mind images of prisons with high walls and iron gates, housing the worst criminal offenders, who receive what they deserve: punishment under harsh conditions. There is a gap, however, between image and reality. Prisons vary in their harshness, and many provide various education, job training, and drug treatment programs. In addition, corrections includes many more activities and programs than merely prisons, such as probation, parole, halfway houses, and community service. These examples represent some of the ways that we punish offenders in the American criminal justice system. As we increased the number of people under correctional supervision during the 1980s and 1990s, we found new ways to punish offenders, especially through community-based programs.

Although some corrections programs emphasize rehabilitation or the reintegration of offenders into the community, punishment is an essential element of all corrections programs. People in such programs are not enthusiastic volunteers. Rather, they are forced to participate by the judge who sends them to prison or places them in another corrections setting as a result of their violation of criminal law. But punishment is not the only essential element in corrections. All corrections programs are also guided by law. Judges and corrections officials cannot do whatever they want to criminal offenders. Instead, they must obey the law in punishing offenders and running corrections programs. Law also provides protections for individuals in their contacts with government. Criminal suspects receive protections during investigation, arrest, and pretrial processes, including time spent in jail. After conviction, offenders receive legal protections against improper or abusive actions by officials in corrections institutions and programs. However, offenders are not the only individuals concerned about legal protections. Employees in prisons and other corrections programs also look to the law to protect themselves against employment discrimination and improper disciplinary action. In fact, legal rules guide nearly all aspects of corrections policies and practices.

LAW AND THE CONTEXT OF CORRECTIONS

The Need for Legal Rules

What if there were no laws governing corrections? What if corrections officials had complete authority to treat prisoners as they pleased without worrying about violating any legal rules? Many members of the public might respond, "So what? Criminals deserve the harshest treatment possible because of the harm they have caused." While we may sympathize with such sentiments, we must also consider what could happen if there were no legal rules governing corrections. The risk is that some corrections officials would undertake cruel practices and create inhumane conditions that might shock even the staunchest law-and-order advocates, as the account in Box 1-1 suggests.

Of course, not all criminal offenders are murderers. Indeed, relatively few people who are convicted of crimes are the murderers and rapists that society hates and fears the most. People are sentenced to correctional institutions and programs for committing a variety of offenses, not all of them violent. As you can see in Table 1-1, many people in jails and prisons are serving relatively short sentences for nonviolent offenses. While some people may be unconcerned at the prospect of a murderer or rapist being beaten, tortured, or deprived of food and medicine by a prison warden, they likely would be disturbed by such treatment of a teenager convicted of stealing a car. Should someone sentenced to serve six months in jail for theft risk illness, permanent injury, or death because he or she has no legal protections against whatever harsh actions a corrections official wishes to take? By looking back only a few decades in the history of corrections, we can find examples of the risks posed by permitting American corrections officials to do as they please. As you read the U.S. Supreme Court's description of conditions in Arkansas prisons in the 1960s and early 1970s, which is excerpted in Box 1-2, imagine the other kinds of situations that could arise when there are no legal rules to guide corrections.

Offenders serving sentences in prisons and jails are completely at the mercy of the policies and practices of the administrators who run those correctional

BOX 1-1	**What Would a Justice System Be Like Without Rights? Trials and Prisons in Peru, 1997**

In waging its war against rebel guerrillas, Peru uses tough measures—so tough that many critics accuse the country of violating basic human rights. Consider the following:

- Antiterrorism trials are conducted by "faceless" courts in which judges' and prosecutors' faces are not seen; the decision makers cannot be identified. Defendants often do not receive a lawyer until the day of the trial, the trials sometimes last only ten minutes, and there is no cross-examination of witnesses or police.

- A journalist was convicted on suspicion of being a terrorist. He was confined with two other prisoners in a six-foot by six-foot cell that contained only two cement beds. They were permitted to leave the cell for only thirty minutes each day. After four years, his wrongful conviction was overturned, and he was released.

- His pregnant wife also was convicted on suspicion of being a terrorist. She, too, lived in a six-by-six cell, living on only one meal a day. She received no medical attention for seven months, and her daughter was born with a brain lesion. After one year, the government admitted its mistake and released her.

- In the special prisons for suspected terrorists, infectious tuberculosis is a significant problem because of the living conditions. Furthermore, many inmates go insane because of their isolation, and many others attempt to kill themselves, often by banging their heads against the walls. Conditions are also harsh in regular prisons, where it is extremely difficult for prisoners to obtain adequate food and the level of personal hygiene necessary to maintain good health.

- Peru's national coordinator of human rights estimates that 1504 of the estimated 5000 people jailed for terrorism or treason since 1992 are probably innocent. Most of these wrongly convicted people have been released, usually after spending at least three years in prison. However, 598 of these "probably innocent" people remain in prison while trying to get their cases reviewed.

Source: Adapted from Douglas Farah, "In Peru, the Jails Have Few Defenders," *Washington Post National Weekly Edition,* 13 January 1997, pp. 16–17; Catherine Elton, "Jailed by Mistake, Peru's Innocents Stuck with Terrorist Label," *Christian Science Monitor,* 5 March 1998, p. 8; Mike Dorning, "Congressmen Told About Woman's Plight; Illinois Dad Hits Peruvian Jail Conditions," *Chicago Tribune,* 2 May 1997, p. 11.

institutions. Inmates have no ability to obtain food, water, heat, or medical care on their own. For the length of their incarceration, they are dependent on corrections officials within the confines of sealed institutions that control every aspect of their lives. In the absence of legal rules or some other form of outside supervision to prevent abuses, if corrections officials wanted to kill inmates or otherwise abuse them, they could easily do so.

The situation for jail inmates provides an even stronger case for the rule of law. Only about half of the inmates in local jails have been convicted of criminal offenses. The rest of the inmates have been arrested but have not yet been convicted of any offense. In the U.S. legal system, they are presumed to be innocent until they are convicted. Some of them are indeed innocent and will

TABLE 1-1   Most Serious Offenses of Jail and Prison Inmates

Offense	Jail Inmates, 1989 (344,535 inmates)[a]	State Prison Inmates, 1991 (704,181 inmates)[b]
Murder	2.9%	10.6%
Negligent manslaughter	0.5	1.8
Rape	0.9	3.5
Other sexual assault	2.8	5.9
Robbery	7.0	14.8
Assault	7.4	8.2
Burglary	11.4	12.4
Larceny/theft	7.4	4.9
Motor vehicle theft	3.0	2.2
Arson	0.7	0.7
Fraud	3.2	2.8
Drug possession	9.2	7.6
Drug trafficking	11.5	13.3
Public order offenses (weapons, drunk driving, indecency, escape, etc.)	23.2	6.9

[a] Charges against male inmates only.
[b] All inmates.

Source: Kathleen Maguire and Ann L. Pastore, eds., *Sourcebook of Criminal Justice Statistics—1993* (Washington, DC: U.S. Department of Justice, Bureau of Justice Statistics, 1994), pp. 593, 612.

have their charges dropped or will be found "not guilty" after a trial. In 1996, only 49 percent of the 582,300 people in U.S. jails had been convicted of crimes; the other 51 percent were still presumed to be innocent because they had not been convicted of a crime.[1] Should these presumably innocent inmates be subject to abuses at the whim of jail officials? Should they be deprived of food or medical care when they have not yet been convicted of any crime? Anyone in the United States could be arrested for something, including innocent people whom witnesses have mistakenly identified as a criminal offender. Laws governing corrections help to protect unconvicted citizens who have been drawn into the criminal justice system.

The Growing Importance of Corrections Law

Law continues to grow in importance as a means to guide and control corrections officials. The growth in prison populations and other correctional programs means that many thousands more Americans have come into contact with the correctional system over the past two decades. As Table 1-2 shows, in

BOX 1-2   *Hutto v. Finney*, 437 U.S. 678 (1978)

[*This case concerned the Cummins Farm, a prison in Arkansas that employed only eight corrections officers to handle a thousand prisoners. Most of the "guards" at the prison were actually inmates, called "trusties," who had been issued guns and given authority to control—and victimize—other prisoners as they wished. Inmates were beaten, raped, and killed by the trusties, as well as by other prisoners. They also were subjected to beatings with leather straps, and "a hand-cranked device was used to administer electrical shocks to various sensitive parts of an inmate's body" (Hutto v. Finney, p. 682 n. 5). In its 1978 decision, the U.S. Supreme Court focused its attention on the isolation cells that were used to punish prisoners accused of breaking prison rules.*]

Confinement in punitive isolation was for an indeterminate period of time. An average of 4, and sometimes as many as 10 or 11 prisoners were crowded into windowless 8' by 10' cells containing no furniture other than a source of water and a toilet that could only be flushed from outside the cell [when guards chose to do so]. At night the prisoners were given mattresses to spread on the floor. Although some prisoners suffered from infectious diseases such as hepatitis and venereal disease, mattresses were removed and jumbled together each morning, then returned to the cells at random in the evening. [Although the National Academy of Sciences recommends that the average male consume 2700 calories per day and an inactive person will expend 2000 calories in a day just lying, sitting, and standing,] [p]risoners in isolation received fewer than 1,000 calories a day; their meals consisted primarily of a 4-inch square of "grue," a substance created by mashing meat, potatoes, oleo, syrup, vegetables, eggs, and seasoning into a paste and baking the mixture in a pan. . . . Prisoners were sometimes left in isolation for months, their release depending on "their attitudes as appraised by prison personnel" (pp. 682–684).

1968, there were fewer than 188,000 inmates in U.S. prisons, but by the end of 1997, there had been a *650 percent increase* in prison populations. Another 4 million or so people were under other forms of correctional supervision in jails, community-based corrections programs, and probation. In 1980, there were 1.8 million people under correctional supervision in all settings, but by 1995, this number had climbed to nearly 5.4 million people.[2] Thus, hundreds of thousands of additional Americans now are completely dependent on corrections officials for their health and survival in prisons and jail, and millions of additional Americans have their daily lives affected by the decisions of judicial and corrections officials in other corrections settings. Because corrections programs affect the lives of so many more people, it is more important than ever to have legal rules to guide corrections practices.

The increase in the prison population stems, in part, from tougher sentencing policies. Through mandatory sentencing laws and sentencing guidelines, Congress and state legislatures have directed federal and state judges to send more offenders to prison, instead of placing them on probation, and these prisoners often serve longer sentences. As a result, states and the federal government have built many new correctional institutions to house the growing prison

TABLE 1-2	State and Federal Prison Populations, by Year

Year	Number of Inmates
1968	187,914
1972	196,092
1976	262,833
1980	315,974
1984	443,398
1988	603,732
1992	847,271
1997	1,244,554

Source: Kathleen Maguire and Ann L. Pastore, eds., *Sourcebook of Criminal Justice Statistics—1993* (Washington, DC: U.S. Department of Justice, Bureau of Justice Statistics, 1994), p. 600; Darrell K. Gilliard and Allen J. Beck, "Prisoners 1997," *Bureau of Justice Statistics Bulletin* (August 1998): 1–5.

populations. They also have hired thousands of additional corrections officers and administrators, who look to the law for guidance in their treatment of inmates. Law also guides the relationships between management officials in corrections departments and the many employees within those departments. Law helps to protect corrections workers against employment discrimination, unsafe working conditions, and other factors affecting employment in corrections.

In some states, the construction of new prisons has not kept pace with the increase in offenders sentenced to incarceration. Thus, many prisons have become overcrowded. Crowding can make it difficult for officials to maintain sanitary and safe prisons and to provide adequate programs and services. The crowded conditions, in turn, can cause prisoners to file lawsuits claiming that their constitutional rights are being violated.

THE FORMS OF LAW

What is law? In essence, law is the body of authoritative rules for society. These are the rules that are backed up by the power of the American people and their government. In other words, these rules tell everyone, including government officials, what they can and cannot do, and what will happen if someone violates these rules. Rule violations in criminal law—such as murder, rape, assault, or burglary—may result in offenders being sent to prison. Rule violations in civil law may result in court orders that individuals or corporations pay money to compensate people injured by improper actions or dangerous products. This would arise, for example, when someone was injured in an automobile accident caused by negligent driving or a defective car. Other kinds of laws define the rights of individuals, describe the processes the government must follow before taking certain actions, or design government programs affecting criminal justice, health, education, and other policy issues.

We can look to several sources to find the law, including constitutions, statutes, case law, judicial opinions, and regulations. Each produces different forms of law, and each has its own law-making processes.

Constitutions

Constitutions contain the fundamental laws for the United States and for individual states. Constitutions describe the design and powers of government and list the rights possessed by individuals. **Constitutional rights** are basic protections possessed by individuals to guard them against improper government interference with their liberty. For example, the U.S. Constitution, which was ratified in 1788, describes the structure and powers of Congress, the presidency, and the Supreme Court. Similarly, each state has its own constitution describing the design and powers of its legislature, governor, and courts. Because the framers initially were concerned that the U.S. Constitution granted too much power to the federal government, they added a series amendments that, among other things, list the rights possessed by individuals to protect them against abusive actions by government. State constitutions also contain lists of rights applicable to people within their state boundaries. These rights were often included at the time that each state constitution was written rather than added later, as was the case with the U.S. Constitution.

Because constitutions provide the fundamental law of the nation or a state, we do not want constitutions changed without strong reasons. Therefore, the processes for amending constitutions usually require that an amendment enjoy significant popular support before it becomes law. In most states, the voters must approve constitutional amendments. For the U.S. Constitution, amendments can be initiated either by a two-thirds vote in Congress or by a two-thirds majority of state legislatures. However, to be added to the U.S. Constitution, the amendment must subsequently be approved by the legislatures or by constitutional conventions in three-fourths of the states. Each state consitution has its own amendment procedures, such as Michigan's requirement that two-thirds of the state legislators endorse amendment proposals that are subsequently placed before the voters in a statewide referendum. Because it is extremely difficult to gain such levels of support for constitutional provisions, relatively few amendments are added to constitutions.

The first ten amendments to the U.S. Constitution, known as the "Bill of Rights," were ratified in 1791. These amendments contain the most famous and important rights, such as freedom of speech and religion, that Americans learn about as schoolchildren. These amendments also serve as a central focus of legal issues in corrections because of questions about the extent to which convicted offenders continue to possess the protections enjoyed by other individuals in the United States. An additional amendment ratified in 1868, the

Fourteenth Amendment, provides other rights that affect convicted offenders and corrections institutions. As you read the Bill of Rights and portions of the Fourteenth Amendment in Box 1-3, try to identify which rights are most likely to affect how corrections officials are permitted to run their institutions and programs.

States have their own constitutions, which provide the basis for state courts' decisions overseeing corrections policies and practices. Many rights in state constitutions are based on the wording of the federal Bill of Rights. Note, for example, how closely Section 16 of the Michigan Constitution follows the Eighth Amendment of the U.S. Constitution:

> Section 16: Bail; fines; punishments; detention of witnesses. *Excessive bail shall not be required; excessive fines shall not be imposed; cruel or unusual punishment shall not be inflicted; nor shall witnesses be unreasonably detained.*

Although the parallels between Section 16 and the Eighth Amendment are evident with respect to bail, fines, and punishment, there are important differences. Michigan's Section 16 contains an additional constitutional protection not provided by the Eighth Amendment: prohibition against the unreasonable detaining of witnesses. Section 16 also differs from the Eighth Amendment in its coverage of improper punishments. The Eighth Amendment bans "cruel *and* unusual punishments" while Section 16 prohibits "cruel *or* unusual punishment." In this sense, the Michigan Constitution seems to provide greater protection to criminal offenders. That is, it forbids punishments that are either cruel or unusual, whereas the Eighth Amendment seems to cover only those that are both cruel and unusual. In practice, the two phrases could be interpreted in a similar fashion, but the wording differences create the opportunity for Michigan's courts to make broader interpretations.

Statutes

Statutes are laws enacted by elected representatives in legislatures at all levels of government: city, county, state, and national. Congress bears responsibility for statutes governing the entire country. Each state has a legislature to enact statutes. Examples of lower-level legislatures would be county commissions and city councils, whose enactments generally are called *ordinances*. At any given moment, a person in the United States is simultaneously subject to the legal rules enacted by the legislative bodies of these multiple levels of government. The legislature for each level of government may possess the authority to enact laws governing various matters. However, the most significant statutes affecting criminal justice and corrections come from state legislatures and Congress.

State legislatures use statutes to define crimes and punishments within their borders. They enact statutes to determine how citizens will be taxed and how tax money will be spent. Their statutes define what corrections programs will exist and how much money will be spent on each program or prison. Laws

BOX 1-3   The Bill of Rights and the Fourteenth Amendment to the U.S. Constitution

First Amendment: Congress shall make no law respecting an establishment of religion, or prohibiting the free exercise thereof; or abridging the freedom of speech, or of the press; or the right of the people peaceably to assemble, and to petition the Government for redress of grievances.

Second Amendment: A well regulated Militia, being necessary for the security of a free State, the right of the people to keep and bear Arms, shall not be infringed.

Third Amendment: No Soldier shall, in time of peace be quartered in any house, without the consent of the Owner, nor in time of war, but in a manner to be prescribed by law.

Fourth Amendment: The right of the people to be secure in their persons, houses, papers, and effects, against unreasonable searches and seizures, shall not be violated, and no Warrants shall issue, but upon probable cause, supported by Oath or affirmation, and particularly describing the place to be searched, and the persons or things to be seized.

Fifth Amendment: No person shall be held to answer for a capital or otherwise infamous crime, unless on a presentment or indictment of a Grand Jury, except in cases arising in the land or naval forces, or in the Militia, when in actual service in time of War or public danger; nor shall any person be subject for the same offence to be twice put in jeopardy of life or limb; nor shall be compelled in any criminal case to be a witness against himself, nor be deprived of life, liberty, or property, without due process of law; nor shall private property be taken for public use, without just compensation.

Sixth Amendment: In all criminal prosecutions, the accused shall enjoy the right to a speedy and public trial, by an impartial jury of the State and district wherein the crime shall have been committed, which district shall have been previously ascertained by law, and to be informed of the nature and cause of the accusation; to be confronted with the witnesses against him; to have compulsory process for obtaining witnesses in his favor, and to have the Assistance of Counsel for his defence.

Seventh Amendment: In Suits at common law, where the value in controversy shall exceed twenty dollars, the right of trial by jury shall be preserved, and no fact tried by a jury, shall be otherwise re-examined in any Court of the United States, than according to the rules of the common law.

Eighth Amendment: Excessive bail shall not be required, nor excessive fines imposed, nor cruel and unusual punishments inflicted.

Ninth Amendment: The enumeration in the Constitution, of certain rights, shall not be construed to deny or disparage others retained by the people.

Tenth Amendment: The powers not delegated to the United States by the Constitution, nor prohibited by it to the States, are reserved to the States respectively, or to the people.

Fourteenth Amendment

Section 1: All persons born or naturalized in the United States, and subject to the jurisdiction thereof, are citizens of the United States and of the State wherein they reside. No State shall make or enforce any law which shall abridge the privileges or immunities of citizens of the United States; nor shall any State deprive any person of life, liberty, or property, without due process of law; nor deny to any person within its jurisdiction the equal protection of the laws.

Section 5: The Congress shall have the power to enforce, by appropriate legislation, the provisions of this article.

passed by Congress define federal crimes and punishments and provide money for federal law enforcement agencies, courts, and prisons.

While many provisions in constitutions are written in general terms, statutes are often very detailed and specific. In addition, statutes may change frequently. Legislatures regularly write and enact new statutes or modify existing statutes. It normally takes only a majority vote by elected representatives within a legislature to change a statutory law or to enact a new statute. Congress enacts statutes covering the entire country, but states have their own statutes to handle most matters related to criminal justice. As you read the portions of the two statutes in Box 1-4, take note of the detailed language. Both the federal and state statutes appear to be more detailed than the constitutional provisions we previously examined. Is it easy to read and understand the statutes? What are they about? Try to imagine all the statutes that legislatures might enact that affect criminal justice and corrections.

Legal issues often are raised concerning statutes. Judges may be petitioned to interpret a statute and to provide clearer definitions of the statutory law's meaning. Alternatively, someone might claim that a statute should be invalidated because it violates some provision of the constitution. Constitutional provisions are more important than statutes, and judges possess the power of **judicial review,** which permits them to determine if a law passed by a legislature and signed by a president or governor violates a state or federal constitution. In still other cases, individuals or groups might seek to have statutes enforced—for example, when prisoners or corrections employees believe that corrections officials are not properly following the rules created by the legislature.

Case Law

Case law is produced through judges' decisions. In deciding the cases presented to them, judges frequently interpret constitutional provisions, legislative statutes, and other judges' decisions in prior cases. By interpreting law and applying it in deciding cases, judges create new laws or modify existing ones. To illustrate, suppose corrections officers are conducting a "sweep" of the prison, searching all cells to look for weapons, and an inmate struggles with officers as they try to look under his mattress. If the inmate is shoved to the floor and bumps his head during the altercation, has there been a violation of his constitutional protection against "cruel and unusual punishments"? In the case of legal action, the judge would have to interpret the Eighth Amendment's words ("cruel and unusual punishments") in order to decide the case. In making a decision, the judge would be creating case law in the form of a legal rule concerning whether the ban on cruel and unusual punishments applies to injuries suffered by inmates who resist a cell search. The judge's decision would be guided by prior judicial decisions, if any, concerning similar situations.

The United States inherited the **common law** process developed in England. Under the common law process, judges use judicial decisions in prior cases to help them decide new cases. In the case of the prisoner injured resisting a cell search, the judge would not start from scratch in deciding whether such injuries are covered by the ban on cruel and unusual punishments. Instead, the

BOX 1-4   **Sample Federal and State Statutes**

PRISON LITIGATION REFORM ACT
OF 1996, TITLE 18 OF U.S. CODE,
SECTION 3626(b)(2)

Immediate Termination of Prospective Relief

In any civil action with respect to prison conditions, a defendant or intervener shall be entitled
to the immediate termination of any prospective
relief if the relief was approved or granted in the
absence of a finding by the court that the relief
is narrowly drawn, extends no further than necessary to correct the violation of the Federal
right, and is the least intrusive means necessary
to correct the violation of the Federal right.

MICHIGAN COMPILED LAWS,
SECTION 800.284

Searching of Visitors

Sec. 4: The chief administrator of a correctional
facility may search, or have searched any person coming to the correctional facility as a visitor, or in any other capacity, who is suspected
of having any weapon or other implement
which may be used to injure a prisoner or other
person or in assisting a prisoner to escape from
imprisonment, or any alcoholic liquor, prescription drug, poison, or controlled substance upon
his or her person.

judge would first examine prior case decisions about search situations within
prisons and about the meaning of "cruel and unusual punishments." If there
were prior decisions concerning such situations, the judge would likely follow
the rules established by the judges involved—especially if the prior decisions
came from the U.S. Supreme Court or a federal court of appeals. If there were
no prior decisions on the issue, then the judge would use prior interpretations
of the phrase "cruel and unusual punishments" and prior decisions on arrestees' injuries to see if the rules from those cases ought to apply in some form
to the case at hand. Judges can use their judgment about whether and how a
prior decision should apply, but the prior cases provide important guidance. In
the case of a completely new situation, with no legal precedents, the judge has
an opportunity to create a completely new rule that will help to provide guidance in any similar cases that arise later.

In relying on prior judicial decisions, judges use **case precedent.** In the common law, this is known as following *stare decisis*—that is, adhering to decisions
that have come before. The common law process of relying on case precedent
or *stare decisis* benefits the legal system in several ways. The use of case precedent in judicial decisions provides consistency and stability in law. The same
legal principles are applied to similar cases, so that people in one situation are
treated in the same manner as other people who find themselves in a similar situation. Case precedent also increases efficiency in the administration of justice.
Judges do not have to start from scratch in deciding each case, but rather look
to prior case decisions for guidance. Consistency in a judges' decisions helps to
maintain a positive image of justice, and it discourages judges from appearing
to make up their own legal rules—even if they sometimes do just that.

Cases presented in court require judges to interpret constitutions and
statutes. Constitutions often contain general phrases that lack clear, definite

meanings. For example, the meaning of the phrase "cruel and unusual punishments" is not obvious, so judges must use their judgment, in light of case precedent, in determining its meaning. Judges are the ultimate authorities over the
meaning of constitutional language. Lower court judges must obey the constitutional decisions of higher courts, but the **courts of last resort**—namely, state
supreme courts and the U.S. Supreme Court—enjoy significant freedom to create new interpretations of constitutional phrases. If new justices are appointed
to the U.S. Supreme Court or elected to a state supreme court, they can help
make new law by reinterpreting constitutional provisions.

By contrast, legislatures are supposed to be the ultimate authorities over the
meaning of statutes. Despite legislatures' control over statutes' meaning, judges
have significant power to determine the meaning of statutory law. When cases
raising questions about the meaning of statutes are presented in court, judges
must decide what the words of the statute mean and how those words apply to
the specific situation. Again, they look to prior judicial decisions for guidance.
With statutes, however, they also look to discussions in legislative hearings and
published statements by legislators to help them decide what the words of a
statute mean.

For example, look again at the sample segment of the Prison Litigation
Reform Act of 1996 contained in Box 1-4. If a state prison is ordered by a federal judge to reduce the number of prisoners placed in each cell in order to
eliminate overcrowding, the prison may challenge the judge's order in a higher
appellate court. The court will be required to determine whether the lower
court judge's order is "narrowly drawn" and thereby consistent with the
statute. It is not obvious what the phrase "narrowly drawn" means. Clearly,
the phrase is intended to keep judges from going too far in ordering remedies in
prison cases. However, the statute itself does not define when a remedy goes
too far. Thus, the judges on the appellate court must use any prior judicial decisions plus their own judgment to determine whether the lower court judge has
violated the language of the statute.

Judges determine the meaning of statutory law in the cases presented to
them, but legislatures are the ultimate authorities because they can rewrite the
statute's wording if they do not like judges' interpretations. In most instances,
however, legislatures do not enact new statutes to clarify the meaning of
statutes or to override judges' decisions. Legislatures are too busy with a variety of pressing issues to closely monitor and control judges' statutory interpretations. When a majority of legislators strongly object to a judge's decision,
they will take the time to enact corrective legislation. Usually, however, judges'
interpretations control the meaning of statutes because legislatures have moved
on to other issues.

Judicial Opinions

Judges' decisions, which are written in the form of **judicial opinions,** are not
easy to read. They are written not in plain English, but in the language of
lawyers. They are crafted to give guidance to lawyers and judges who will look

to the case as a precedent in preparing arguments or deciding future cases. Judicial opinions provide detailed reasons for the rule of law developed or endorsed by the court to decide the case at hand. They do not get right to the point. Nor do they always announce the rule of law in a clear, straightforward manner. Often, the rule of law established by a judicial opinion is itself subject to interpretation by judges and lawyers in subsequent cases.

To illustrate, read the portion of the U.S. Supreme Court's judicial opinion in *Rummel v. Estelle* (1980) which is excerpted in Box 1-5, and try to pick out the important elements of the judicial opinion. First, look for the **facts**—that is, for a summary of the events and circumstances that produced the court case. Who did what to whom? Why is someone so unhappy with the situation that he or she brought the case to court? The facts in court cases may not include all actual events. Only matters that can be established through admissible evidence will count as legal facts to be included in making decisions. Second, try to identify the **issue** in the case, or the question being addressed by the appellate court. Unlike trial courts, which in criminal cases hear testimony and examine other evidence before a jury or judge determines whether the defendant is guilty, appellate courts focus on narrow questions of law. Generally, appellate courts decide whether the trial court made an error in interpreting some aspect of law or court procedure. In most of the cases presented in this book, the issue will involve someone's claim that a constitutional provision or statute was violated. In *Rummel v. Estelle,* which part of the U.S. Constitution is being examined by the Supreme Court? Third, find the **holding,** which is the answer to the question posed by the issue. In other words, the holding is the rule of law established or endorsed in the judicial opinion. Technically, it is the only aspect of the judicial opinion that other courts are required to apply in subsequent cases concerning the same kind of issue. Fourth, look for the **reasoning,** which is essentially the list of reasons given by the court for deciding the case as it did. Finally, identify the reasoning in any concurring or dissenting opinions. **Concurring opinions** are written by judges (called "justices" on the U.S. Supreme Court and state supreme courts) who agree with the result of the case but who believe that the result should be supported by one or more different reasons than those put forward by the majority of judges. **Dissenting opinions** are written by judges who disagree with the decision and believe that the losing side should really have won the case.

Briefing a Case

When law students and lawyers read judicial opinions, they prepare a one-page "brief," which is a set of notes that helps them to boil down the case into understandable terms. For all of the cases presented in the chapters of this book, you may wish to create a case brief to assist you in understanding what the judges are saying in their judicial opinions. Box 1-6 contains a sample case brief based on *Rummel v. Estelle* (1980). Note how a series of numbers follows the case name in the case excerpt in Box 1-5 and on the case brief. This is called the *citation* to the case. Every case has one or more citations. These

BOX 1-5 *Rummel v. Estelle,* 445 U.S. 263 (1980)

JUSTICE REHNQUIST delivered the opinion of the Court [joined by CHIEF JUSTICE BURGER, JUSTICE BLACKMUN, JUSTICE STEWART, and JUSTICE WHITE].

Petitioner William James Rummel is presently serving a life sentence imposed by the State of Texas in 1973 under its [repeat offender or] "recidivist statute" . . . which provided that "[w]hoever shall have been three times convicted of a felony less than capital shall on such third conviction be imprisoned for life in the penitentiary."

. . . [Rummel is] arguing that life imprisonment is "grossly disproportionate" to the three felonies that formed the predicate for his sentence and that therefore the sentence violated the ban on cruel and unusual punishments of the Eighth and Fourteenth Amendments. . . .

In 1964 the State of Texas charged Rummel with fraudulent use of a credit card to obtain $80 worth of goods or services. Because the amount in question was greater than $50, the charged offense was a felony. . . . Rummel eventually pleaded guilty to the charge and was sentenced to three years' confinement in a state penitentiary.

In 1969 the State of Texas charged Rummel with passing a forged check in the amount of $28.36. . . . Rummel pleaded guilty to this offense and was sentenced to four years' imprisonment.

In 1973 Rummel was charged with obtaining $120.75 by false pretenses. . . . The prosecution chose, however, to proceed against Rummel under Texas recidivist statute, and cited in the indictment his 1964 and 1969 convictions as requiring the imposition of a life sentence if Rummel were convicted of the charge. A jury convicted Rummel of felony theft and also found true the allegation that he had been convicted of two prior felonies. As a result, on April 26, 1973, the trial court imposed upon Rummel the life sentence mandated by [the recidivist statute].

This Court has on occasion stated that the Eighth Amendment prohibits the imposition of a sentence that is grossly disproportionate to the severity of the crime. . . . In recent years this proposition has appeared most frequently in opinions dealing with the death penalty. . . . Rummel cites these . . . opinions dealing with capital punishment as compelling the conclusion that his sentence is disproportionate to his offenses. . . .

. . . [However,] [b]ecause a sentence of death differs in kind from any sentence of imprisonment, no matter how long, our decisions applying the prohibition on cruel and unusual punishments to capital cases are of limited assistance in deciding the constitutionality of the punishment meted out to Rummel.

Outside the context of capital punishment, successful challenges to the proportionality of particular sentences have been exceedingly rare. . . .

Undaunted by earlier cases [in which the Supreme Court rejected Eighth Amendment claims for severe prison sentences], Rummel attempts to ground his proportionality attack on an alleged "nationwide" trend away from mandatory life sentences and toward "lighter, discretionary sentences." . . . According to Rummel, "[n]o jurisdiction in the United States or the Free World punishes habitual offenders as harshly as Texas." . . . In support of this proposition, Rummel offers detailed charts and tables documenting the history of recidivist statutes in the United States since 1776. . . .

Rummel's charts and tables do appear to indicate that he might have received more lenient treatment in almost any State other than Texas, West Virginia, or Washington. The distinctions, however, are subtle rather than gross. A number of States impose a mandatory life sentence upon conviction of four felonies rather than three. Other States require one or more of the felonies to be "violent" to support a life sentence. Still other States leave the imposition of a life sentence after three felonies within the discretion of a judge or jury. It is one thing for a court to compare those States that impose capital punishment for a specific offense with those States that do not. . . . It is quite another thing for a court to attempt to evaluate the position of any particular recidivist scheme within Rummel's complex matrix.

Nor do Rummel's extensive charts even begin to reflect the complexity of the comparison he asks this Court to make. Texas, we are told, has a relatively liberal policy of granting "good time" credits to its prisoners, a policy that historically has allowed a prisoner serving a life sentence to become eligible for parole in as little as 12 years. . . . We agree with Rummel that his inability to enforce any "right" to parole precludes us from treating his life sentence as if it were equivalent to a sentence of 12 years. Nevertheless, because parole is "an established variation on imprisonment of convicted criminals," *Morrissey v. Brewer,* 408 U.S. 471 . . . (1972), a proper assessment of Texas' treatment of Rummel could hardly ignore the possibility that he will not actually be imprisoned for the rest of his life. If nothing else, the possibility of parole, however slim, serves to distinguish Rummel from a person sentenced under a recidivist statute like Mississippi's, which provides for a sentence of life without parole upon conviction of three felonies including at least one violent felony. . . .

. . . Like the line dividing felony theft from petty larceny, the point at which a recidivist will be deemed to have demonstrated the necessary propensities and the amount of time that the recidivist will be isolated from society are matters largely within the discretion of the punishing jurisdiction.

We therefore hold that the mandatory life sentence imposed upon this petitioner does not constitute cruel and unusual punishment under the Eighth and Fourteenth Amendments. The judgment of the Court of Appeals is *Affirmed.*

JUSTICE STEWART, concurring.

I am moved to repeat the substance of what I had to say on another occasion about the recidivist legislation of Texas:

> *"If the Constitution gave me a roving commission to impose upon the criminal courts of Texas my own notions of enlightened policy, I would not join the Court's opinion. For it is clear to me that the recidivist procedures adopted in recent years by many other States . . . are far superior to those utilized [here]. But the question for decision is not whether we applaud or even whether we personally approve the procedures followed in [this case]. The question is whether those procedures fall below the minimum level the [Constitution] will tolerate. Upon that question I am constrained to join the opinion and judgment of the Court."* Spencer v. Texas, *385 U.S. 554* . . .

JUSTICE POWELL, with whom JUSTICE BRENNAN, JUSTICE MARSHALL, and JUSTICE STEVENS join, dissenting.

This Court today affirms the Fifth Circuit's decision. I dissent because I believe that (i) the penalty for a noncapital offense may be unconstitutionally disproportionate, (ii) the possibility of parole should not be considered in assessing the nature of the punishment, (iii) a mandatory life sentence is grossly disproportionate as applied to petitioner, and (iv) the conclusion that this petitioner has suffered a violation of his Eighth Amendment rights is compatible with principles of judicial restraint and federalism. . . .

The scope of the Cruel and Unusual Punishments Clause extends not only to barbarous methods of punishment, but also to punishments that are grossly disproportionate. Disproportionality analysis measures the relationship between the nature and number of offenses committed and the severity of the punishment

(*continued*)

inflicted upon the offender. The inquiry focuses on whether a person deserves such punishment, not simply whether the punishment would serve a utilitarian goal. A statute that levied a mandatory life sentence for overtime parking might well deter vehicular lawlessness, but it would offend our felt sense of justice. The Court concedes today that the principle of disproportionality plays a role in the review of sentences imposing the death penalty, but suggests that the principle may be less applicable when a noncapital sentence is challenged. Such a limitation finds no support in the history of Eighth Amendment jurisprudence. . . .

Examination of the objective factors traditionally employed by the Court to assess the proportionality of a sentence demonstrates that petitioner suffers a cruel and unusual punishment. . . . A comparison of petitioner to other criminal[s] sentenced in Texas shows that he has been punished for three property-related offenses with a harsher sentence than that given to first-time or two-time offenders convicted of far more serious offenses. The Texas system assumes that all three-time offenders deserve the same punishment whether they commit three murders or cash three fraudulent checks.

The petitioner has committed criminal acts for which he may be punished. He has been given a sentence that is not inherently barbarous. But the relationship between the criminal acts and the sentence is grossly disproportionate. For having defrauded others of about $230 [the total amount illegally taken in the three separate crimes], the State of Texas has deprived petitioner of his freedom for the rest of his life. The State has not attempted to justify the sentence as necessary either to deter other persons or to isolate a potentially violent individual. Nor has petitioner's status as a habitual offender been shown to justify a mandatory life sentence. . . .

We are construing a living Constitution. The sentence imposed upon the petitioner would be viewed as grossly unjust by virtually every layman and lawyer. In my view, objective criteria clearly establish that a mandatory life sentence for defrauding persons of about $230 crosses any rationally drawn line separating punishment that lawfully may be imposed from that which is proscribed by the Eighth Amendment. I would reverse the decision of the Court of Appeals.

---

numbers tell you where to find the case in a law library. The first number is the *volume* in which the case is contained. Case law reporters in a law library are each numbered with a volume number on the spine of the book so that you can easily see the desired book on the library shelf. The set of letters in the middle indicates which case law reporter contains the case. In essence, these letters serve as abbreviations for the name of the set of books in which the case can be found. The letters "U.S." in the *Rummel v. Estelle* citation stand for "U.S. Supreme Court Reports." The third number in the citation is the page number where the case begins within the appropriate volume. Finally, the citation contains the year in which the decision was issued.

Regulations

Government agencies create legal rules called *regulations*. Legislatures enact statutes to create and direct government policies and programs. However, legislatures cannot always write all of the detailed rules that will be needed in

| **BOX 1-6** | **CASE BRIEF: *Rummel v. Estelle*, 445 U.S. 263 (1980)** |

Vote: 5 (majority) v. 4 (dissenters)

Author of Majority Opinion: Justice Rehnquist

Facts: Rummel was convicted of fraudulent use of a credit card for $80 in 1964, passing a forged check for $28.36 in 1969, and obtaining $120.75 by false pretenses in 1973. Under Texas law, conviction of three felonies can lead to an automatic life sentence under the repeat offender statute. Rummel was sentenced to life in prison upon conviction of the third felony in 1973.

Issue: Was the life sentence imposed on Rummel for fraudulently obtaining a total of $230 in three separate felonies over a nine-year period so disproportionate to his crimes as to violate the Eighth Amendment's ban on cruel and unusual punishments?

Holding: No. The life sentence imposed on Rummel for fraudulently obtaining a total of $230 in three separate felonies over a nine-year period was not so disproportionate to his crimes as to violate the Eighth Amendment's ban on cruel and unusual punishments.

Reasoning: Very few claims of disproportionate punishment under the Eighth Amendment have been recognized except for death penalty cases. Imprisonment cases are very different from death penalty cases. Rummel's comparisons of the harshness of the Texas repeat offender statute with laws in other states is unpersuasive. Rummel's comparison does not include adequate consideration of the fact that he could be eligible for parole in as little as twelve years and therefore will not necessarily actually spend his life in prison as punishment for these crimes. States have significant authority to define for themselves the proper punishments for crimes committed within their borders.

Concurring Opinion: Justice Stewart: I personally disagree with the Texas law, but I am not authorized to decide cases on that basis. I can only decide if the Texas law falls below the Constitution's standards. It does not.

Dissenting Opinion: Justice Powell: Noncapital sentences can be disproportionate. It was improper for the majority opinion to consider the possibility of parole as a reason to approve this sentence. The life sentence is too severe for the crimes committed by Rummel. Any person can see that Rummel's sentence is grossly unjust.

every situation. Thus, they frequently give government agencies the power to develop detailed regulations. For example, a state department of corrections may create detailed rules about when prisoners can have visitors, how corrections officers will initiate punishment procedures against prisoners who violate prison rules, and how corrections administrators will process and maintain records concerning each prisoner. As a form of law that guides the behavior of corrections officials, regulations often are the subject of legal actions filed by prisoners or corrections employees. These legal actions may claim, for example, that the regulations violate constitutional provisions or statutes, or that corrections officials are not properly adhering to the regulations that they are obligated to follow. In the first instance, the legal action is filed to have particular regulations changed or abolished. In the second, the legal action seeks to have the regulations enforced and obeyed by corrections officials. We will see examples of prison regulations in subsequent chapters.

LEGAL ACTIONS AND THE COURTS

The United States has a "dual-court" system, meaning that there are both state courts and federal courts. Both kinds of courts exist in each state. Indeed, separate state and federal courthouses stand next to each other in many large cities. State and federal courts have separate **jurisdictions,** which refers to the kinds of cases that the court is authorized to hear and the geographic area under the court's authority. State courts generally can hear only cases that arise from events and situations within their borders.

Federal courts can handle three kinds of cases. First, they can hear cases concerning federal law, whether from the U.S. Constitution, federal statutes, or federal agency regulations. For example, cases involving the Eighth Amendment's ban on cruel and unusual punishments can be heard by federal courts because they concern a provision of the U.S. Constitution. Second, they can hear cases in which the U.S. government is involved. For example, if a prisoner files a lawsuit against a federal prison, which is a component of the U.S. Bureau of Prisons, the case will be heard in federal court. Many cases concerning corrections involve federal law or the U.S. government and thus are heard in federal courts. Third, federal courts can hear "diversity of citizenship" cases in which a resident from one state sues the resident of another state for an amount exceeding $50,000. But such cases are much less likely to involve prisoners, corrections institutions, or corrections employees.

Trial Courts

Federal trial courts are called **U.S. district courts.** There are ninety-four districts in the United States, with at least one district in each state. The smaller states, like Connecticut, have only one district court. Many districts have multiple courthouses located in different cities, but all of the judges and courthouses within a district are considered part of one administrative unit, called a "court." Connecticut's is called the U.S. District Court for the District of Connecticut, and the district's cases are handled by judges housed in federal courthouses in Hartford, New Haven, and Bridgeport. Larger states often are broken into multiple districts. Ohio, for example, has two districts: the Northern District of Ohio, with courthouses in Toledo, Cleveland, Akron, and Youngstown; and the Southern District of Ohio, with courthouses at Columbus, Dayton, and Cincinnati.

State trial courts often are divided according to a state's counties, although rural counties may be combined into a single court. States have given their trial courts various names. Most commonly, such courts are called superior courts (e.g., in California), circuit courts (e.g., in Michigan), courts of common pleas (e.g., in Ohio), and district courts (e.g., in Texas).

In criminal cases, charges are filed, plea bargains are struck, trials are conducted, and sentences are imposed by trial judges on convicted criminals. In civil cases, lawsuits are filed in trial courts. These lawsuits are ultimately either dismissed for failing to provide sufficient evidence, settled through negotiation between the opposing parties, or decided after a trial. In trial courts, a single judge presides over the courtroom as lawyers do battle, sometimes before a jury and sometimes with the judge as the lone decision maker. It is in trial courts that witnesses testify, lawyers present evidence, and jurors issue verdicts. Many states have two or more levels of trial courts. The top-level trial courts have general jurisdiction and handle felony cases; the lower-level trial courts have limited jurisdiction. In criminal cases, these lower-level courts typically issue search and arrest warrants, set bail for arrested suspects, hold preliminary hearings, and process misdemeanor cases.

Depending on state law, the upper-level, general-jurisdiction trial courts may handle certain legal actions filed by prisoners. In Michigan, for example, if prisoners wish to file actions to force prison officials to follow their own rules, such actions may be filed in the trial court for the county in which a prisoner is incarcerated or in the trial court in the state capital of Lansing.

Appellate Courts

After a case has passed through a trial court, some convicted offenders (or losing parties in civil cases) will file appeals. Appeals are legal actions filed in a higher court that claim an error was made by the police, prosecutor, trial judge, or jury. There are no juries in appellate courts, nor do lawyers present evidence to appellate courts. The lawyers' arguments and the judges' decisions focus on narrow issues concerning alleged mistakes in interpretations of law and legal procedures that occurred in or were uncorrected by the trial court. In appellate courts, judges make decisions as a group. In most appellate courts, groups of three judges listen to lawyers' arguments and issue judicial opinions to decide the cases. In courts of last resort, however, the decisions are made by the full panel of judges. The U.S. Supreme Court has nine justices; most state supreme courts have either five or seven justices.

The federal court system and all but a dozen states have intermediate appellate courts. The federal appellate courts are called **U.S. circuit courts of appeals.** Each circuit covers a specific geographic region. For example, the U.S. Court of Appeals for the Sixth Circuit handles appeals from federal cases arising in Michigan, Ohio, Kentucky, and Tennessee. When a losing party claims that an error occurred in a U.S. district court, an appeal may be filed in the U.S. circuit court of appeals that handles appeals from that district. Federal circuit judges sit in panels of three judges to hear cases. Because a circuit court may have as many as twenty-eight judges, these appellate courts can hear several cases simultaneously by breaking into groups of three. In important cases that generate significant disagreement among the judges of a circuit, the case may be presented a second time with all of the judges hearing the case together, in what is called an *en banc* **hearing.**

The U.S. Supreme Court and state supreme courts nearly always hear cases *en banc*. Because they sit as an entire group, they must hear cases one at a time. These courts of last resort typically have significant **discretionary jurisdiction.**

In other words, they have the power to pick and choose the cases they want to hear, and can turn down nearly all other cases. People who are unhappy with the decision of an intermediate appellate court have no automatic right to have their appeals heard by the U.S. Supreme Court or a state supreme court.

Most cases arrive at the U.S. Supreme Court in the form of a petition for a **writ of certiorari.** This is a special legal action that asks the high court to call up a case from a lower court. In the 1990s, the U.S. Supreme Court received nearly 7000 certiorari petitions each year. Despite this large number of requests, the Court granted full hearings and decisions to fewer than ninety cases each year.

Although it is regarded as the highest court in the land, the U.S. Supreme Court is not empowered to handle all cases. Like other federal courts, it is limited to hearing cases that involve federal law, the U.S. government, or lawsuits between residents of different states seeking more than $50,000. If a case concerns only the interpretation of a state statute or a provision of a state constitution, then the supreme court of that state is the final authority on that issue. Many criminal cases come to the U.S. Supreme Court from state supreme courts rather than from U.S. circuit courts of appeals. This is because state criminal cases frequently raise issues concerning federal constitutional rights—for example, the Sixth Amendment right to counsel or the Fourth Amendment protection against unreasonable searches and seizures.

PRISONERS AND THE LAW

Earlier in this chapter, we noted that there would be risks of inhumane treatment and conditions in prisons if there were no legal rules to guide and control corrections officials. As indicated by the portion of the judicial opinion from *Hutto v. Finney* (see Box 1-2), American history offers many examples of excessively harsh prison conditions. Despite these risks, some people may wonder why prisoners should have any rights. They might also wonder why judges must interfere in the operations of prisons and other corrections programs and why governors, legislators, or directors of departments of corrections can't ensure that proper procedures are followed in prisons.

Prisoners' Rights

Many people believe that convicted criminals should forfeit all of their rights. According to this argument, because they intentionally violated society's rules and caused harm to society, they should not gain society's benefits, such as the protections offered by constitutional rights. This argument is based on a **social contract theory** of rights. That is, people have entered into an agreement with society that they will respect society's rules in exchange for the protections and benefits of living in that society. If they break society's rules and thereby violate the social contract, they forfeit their claim to any benefits. This theory has been advanced by many respected philosophers throughout history, but it is not the basis for the rights provided by the U.S. Constitution.

The Bill of Rights is based on a **natural rights theory** of rights, which holds that everyone should possess certain protections simply by virtue of being human—whether good or bad. For example, the Fourth Amendment states, "The right of the people . . . against unreasonable searches and seizures shall not be violated." It does not state that the right exists only for law-abiding citizens. The amendment is framed this way to protect against excessive government action, even against people who may be committing crimes.

We must remember that the people who wrote the U.S. Constitution were regarded as "criminals" by the British government against which they had revolted. Furthermore, they did not trust government. They wanted to provide protections for everyone, even criminals, because they feared that many different people might be labeled as "criminals" by a government depending on who was in charge of the government. Remember that as recently as a few decades ago, anyone who engaged in gambling was regarded as a "criminal." Now the government actively encourages people to gamble in state-sponsored lotteries, and governments in various states have approved the building of casinos. The authors of the Constitution knew that the definition of who is a "criminal" would change, but they wanted to ensure that rights would always remain available.

With respect to prisoners, the Eighth Amendment makes it very clear that there are limits to what the government can do in punishing someone. The ban on "cruel and unusual punishments" does not specify what the government can or cannot do to convicted offenders. However, it does clearly indicate that the government cannot do whatever it wants. Even the worst criminals are entitled to some level of protection under the U.S. Constitution, the fundamental law of the land. The U.S. Supreme Court has ruled that each prisoner retains constitutional "rights that are not inconsistent with his [or her] status as a prisoner or with the legitimate penological objectives of the corrections system."[3] This does not mean that convicted offenders enjoy exactly the same rights and protections as law-abiding citizens. In interpreting prisoners' rights, judges have emphasized the broader goal of maintaining safety and security in prisons and corrections programs, which can override and limit the extent of prisoners' actual rights. Thus, prisoners' rights are less extensive than those of law-abiding citizens so that corrections officials can fulfill their responsibility to administer orderly, secure institutions.

The Role of Courts

The authors of the U.S. Constitution were most fearful that Congress or the president would undermine civil liberties by wielding too much power. To guard against this, the citizens of the United States are permitted at regular intervals to elect new members of Congress and a new president. By contrast, the authors of the Constitution regarded the judiciary as the "least dangerous branch" of government. In effect, they gave federal judges lifetime jobs by allowing judges to stay in office "during good behavior." They also protected federal judges against political pressure from Congress and the president—those responsible for the government's budget—by prohibiting judges' salaries from being reduced.

Federal judges are responsible for interpreting and protecting the Constitution. Their power of judicial review permits them to examine whether the other branches of government, legislative (Congress) and executive (the president and federal agencies), have violated the Constitution in any way. If the other branches take actions or create statutes and regulations that clash with the Constitution, the courts can invalidate those actions by declaring them to be unconstitutional. Because federal judges cannot be removed from office (unless they commit a crime or ethical violation and are impeached by Congress), they are positioned to make decisions about the Constitution according to their best judgments. They are not supposed to be exposed to the same pressures from political parties, interest groups, and the voters that influence Congress and the president. Federal judges can use their job security and independence to ensure that individuals' rights are respected by the government.

Legislators and other elected officials may feel pressured by voters to make sure that unpopular individuals and groups have no rights. Such pressures have encouraged racial discrimination and other unfair treatment of racial, religious, and other minorities throughout American history. By contrast, federal judges are positioned to protect the rights of even the most hated individuals, including prisoners. As a result, prisoners and corrections employees bring many legal actions to federal courts when they seek to challenge policies and actions in corrections institutions and programs.

Some cases are heard in state courts if they concern state statutes or state constitutional provisions. Some state judges have made controversial decisions upholding prisoners' rights. However, many of the most famous cases concerning corrections have been made by federal judges. This may stem, in part, from the fact that most state judges have less job security and independence than federal judges. Judges in most states are either elected or subject to periodic retention elections in which voters decide whether they will stay in office. Thus, they do not enjoy the same protections against political pressures as those provided to federal judges by the U.S. Constitution.

Prisoners' Rights in American History

For most of American history, federal judges interpreted the Bill of Rights narrowly. For example, although the First Amendment protects freedom of speech, judges did not regard that freedom as including the right to criticize the U.S. system of government or to advocate alternative systems, such as socialism or communism. It was not until the 1960s that very unpopular people, such as communists, were granted freedom-of-speech protections in decisions by federal judges.

In addition to their narrow interpretations of the Constitution, federal judges refused to apply the Bill of Rights to actions by state and local officials. Until the mid-twentieth century, federal judges regarded the Bill of Rights as only protecting individuals against actions by Congress and the president. They believed that state constitutions provided protections for people against actions by state and local officials. Thus, the Eighth Amendment prohibition on cruel and unusual punishments was not applied to punishments imposed by state governments. This meant that the Eighth Amendment had very little influence over criminal justice because the vast majority of criminal cases are handled by state courts and corrections systems. Relatively few criminal offenders commit the limited number of federal crimes, such as counterfeiting and smuggling (although this has changed in recent years with the increase in federal drug law coverage and enforcement). Similarly, the other parts of the Bill of Rights had little impact on criminal justice. For example, until the 1960s, the Sixth Amendment right to counsel meant that only defendants in federal cases could claim a right to be represented by a defense attorney—unless a state's statutes or constitution provided a comparable right in that state's criminal cases.

Prior to the 1960s, courts were regarded as having a **hands-off policy** with respect to corrections. Judges in some states applied their states' constitutions to correct abuses in jails and prisons.[4] However, most judges would not protect prisoners, because prisoners were not generally regarded as having rights. In addition, judges frequently stated that prison officials, not judges, were the experts on corrections. Therefore, the judges believed that they should stay out of the way and permit corrections officials to handle matters as they saw fit. The nineteenth-century case of *Ruffin v. The Commonwealth of Virginia* (1871), which is excerpted in Box 1-7, presented the most famous characterization of judges' hands-off approach, with the court referring to prisoners as "slaves" of the state who possessed few rights, if any.

In the twentieth century, the U.S. Supreme Court began to apply individual provisions of the Bill of Rights to the states. Beginning with the application of the right to freedom of speech to protect individuals against state and local governments in 1925,[5] the high court gradually extended other individual rights over the next four decades. The Court expanded the application of the Bill of Rights by using the Fourteenth Amendment. Recall that the Fourteenth Amendment specifically limits states' ability to interfere with people's rights: "nor shall any State deprive any person of life, liberty, or property without due process of law." The justices interpreted the vague right to "due process" as meaning that this right contains many of the specific rights in the Bill of Rights, such as the rights to free speech, free press, and free exercise of religion. This process of recognizing specific individual rights within the Fourteenth Amendment is referred to as **incorporation.** The Court incorporated rights from the Bill of Rights into the Due Process Clause of the Fourteenth Amendment.[6]

In 1962, in *Robinson v. California* (1962),[7] the Supreme Court incorporated the Eighth Amendment into the Fourteenth Amendment. From that moment onward, state and local governments were obligated to respect the same ban on "cruel and unusual punishments" that had applied to the federal government since the Bill of Rights was ratified in 1791. In the Robinson case, a California statute made it a crime for a person to be addicted to drugs. After a police officer saw needle marks on Robinson's arm that appeared to be from injecting drugs into his veins, Robinson was convicted of being a drug addict. In its decision, the Supreme Court declared that California and other states

Ruffin v. The Commonwealth of Virginia,
62 Va. 790 (1871) (Court of Appeals of Virginia)

[*Ruffin was an inmate in a Virginia state prison who was convicted of killing a corrections officer. Ruffin claimed that he should have been tried before a jury in the county where the killing occurred rather than before a jury in the state capital as required by state law for trials of inmates.*]

CHRISTIAN, J., delivered the opinion of the court.

. . . A convicted felon, whom the law in its humanity punishes by confinement in the penitentiary instead of with death, is subject while undergoing that punishment, to all the laws which the Legislature in its wisdom may enact for the government of that institution and the control of its inmates. For the time being, dur-

ing his term of service in the penitentiary, he is in a state of penal servitude to the State. He has, as a consequence of his crime, not only forfeited his liberty, but all his personal rights except those which the law in its humanity accords to him. He is for the time being the slave of the State. . . .

The bill of rights is a declaration of general principles to govern a society of freemen, and not of convicted felons and men civilly dead. Such men have some rights it is true, such as the law in its benignity accords to them, but not the rights of free men. They are the slaves of the State undergoing punishment for heinous crimes committed against the laws of the land. . . .

must abide by the Eighth Amendment. The Court invalidated California's statute as unconstitutional because a majority of justices concluded that it was cruel and unusual to impose a criminal punishment on people based on their status as a drug addict. They ruled that it would be permissible to punish someone for possessing, buying, selling, transporting, or smuggling drugs. That is, people could be punished for *doing something* illegal, but not simply for *being something,* such as a drug addict. In supporting its decision, the Court reasoned that it would be possible for someone to be a drug addict without actually doing anything illegal. The Court noted that it would be grossly unfair—as well as cruel and unusual—to punish a patient whose doctor had prescribed too many painkillers and thereby caused the patient to become addicted to drugs or to punish a baby addicted to drugs at birth because of a substance-abusing mother. When the Court incorporated the Eighth Amendment and other rights from the Bill of Rights into the Fourteenth Amendment, it opened the door for prisoners to ask federal judges to examine alleged constitutional violations in state prisons and local jails.

The incorporation of the Eighth Amendment and other rights affecting criminal justice occurred during the **Warren Court era,** which lasted from 1953 to 1969. This era is defined by the period in which Earl Warren, the former governor of California, served as chief justice and led the Supreme Court in making many decisions expanding rights for individuals throughout society. In its most famous decision, in *Brown v. Board of Education* (1954), the Warren

Court stunned the nation by declaring that racial segregation in the public schools, which had long been regarded as an accepted component of American life, violated the Equal Protection Clause of the Fourteenth Amendment.[8] In other decisions, the Warren Court expanded the definitions of freedom of speech, free exercise of religion, and other rights, including the rights to counsel and to protection against unreasonable searches and seizures and against compelled self-incrimination.

Advocates of racial equality achieved success in their arguments before the Warren Court and other federal courts that followed the lead of the Supreme Court. When advocates for other issues saw this success, they decided to pursue the same strategy. Thus, advocates for prisoners' rights, as well as those interested in religious freedom and other issues, began to craft legal arguments to present in courts. They hoped that their arguments would persuade federal judges to interpret the Constitution in new ways that would grant broader protections for prisoners and others. Black Muslim prisoners, in particular, played an important role in initiating early lawsuits on behalf of prisoners' rights because they faced extreme hostility from corrections officials when they sought to exercise their right to religious freedom.[9]

Federal corrections law developed from lawsuits against the Arkansas prison system in the 1960s which claimed that inhuman living conditions and brutal practices violated the Eighth Amendment. The U.S. district court in Arkansas, with the support of federal appellate courts, ordered the state to make changes in its prisons. By the end of the 1970s, federal judges had imposed changes on the operation of prisons and jails in nearly every state. As shown in the case of *Talley v. Stephens,* excerpted in Box 1-8, many prisoners in these early cases risked harsh treatment from prison authorities in retaliation for seeking court decisions to recognize prisoners' rights. In the 1980s and 1990s, lawsuits continued to be filed that challenged conditions and practices in prisons. In many cases, however, the worst abuses of prior decades had already been addressed, and judges stopped expanding the number and nature of prisoners' rights. In the remaining chapters of this book, we will examine many individual cases that have defined the rights of prisoners, as well as statutes and cases that affect corrections employees.

SUMMARY

- The law guides and controls the actions of corrections officials.

- Because prisoners are completely dependent on corrections officials for their food, health, and security, there are serious risks of abusive treatment if corrections officials are not guided by legal rules.

- The law has grown in importance for corrections because of dramatic increases in corrections populations and personnel.

- The law governing corrections has several forms, including constitutions, statutes enacted by legislatures, case law

BOX 1-8

Talley v. Stephens, 247 F. Supp. 683 (1965) (U.S. District Court for the Eastern District of Arkansas)

[*Prisoners filed a legal action claiming that the use of whipping and corporal punishments violated the Eighth Amendment's prohibition on cruel and unusual punishments.*]

HENLEY, Chief Judge:

. . . The Court regrets to say that the record discloses that reprisals have been visited upon [inmate] Talley [the prisoner who filed this legal action] on account of his recourse to this Court and on account of his testimony in support of his claims.

Process [i.e., the legal papers providing notification that a lawsuit has been filed] in this case was served on [prison officials] on August 6 of the current year. On the evening of that day after work in the [prison farm] fields had been concluded and after the [prisoners] had been confined to their barracks, Pike [a murderer convicted of killing a prison warden] . . . and two other [inmate trusty guards, who along with Pike were issued guns and other weapons by prison officials and given responsibility for supervising and punishing other prisoners] . . . entered the barracks where Talley was confined and assaulted him and certain other prisoners who had been complaining [to the courts]

about conditions in the Penitentiary and who refer to themselves as "writ writers" [i.e., the term applied to prisoners who educate themselves about law in order to file legal cases without the assistance of an attorney].

The evidence also shows that for some days after August 6 the writ writers, including Talley, were put into special squads and were worked under the immediate supervision of a shotgun guard; on one occasion that guard discharged his weapon deliberately into the ground behind one of the working men and in such close proximity to him that a buckshot pellet penetrated the man's cotton sack. . . .

More serious in the Court's eyes is the treatment which Talley received on the day following his [courtroom] testimony in this case. It is admitted that on the morning of October 14 Talley and other members of his [farm labor] squad were put to work picking cotton, and that after the work proceeded about 30 minutes Warden Harmon called Talley out of the long line and administered to him nine blows with the strap [a leather strap five feet in length, four inches wide, and about one-fourth inch thick, attached to a wooden handle or shaft about six inches long]. . . .

---

from judges' opinions, and regulations produced by government agencies.

- Judicial opinions present judges' reasoning for an audience of lawyers and judges.

- The dual-court system is composed of state and federal courts, both of which have trial and appellate courts.

- Prisoners' constitutional rights are based on natural rights theory as reflected in the U.S. Constitution, not on a social contract approach.

- Because they have secure jobs, federal judges are positioned to interpret the Constitution and review the actions of other governmental branches without being influenced by political pressure from voters, political parties, and interest groups.

- Most courts took a "hands-off" approach to prisoners' rights claims prior to the 1960s.

- During the twentieth century, the U.S. Supreme Court gradually expanded its interpretations of the Bill of Rights and incorporated those rights into the Fourteenth Amendment to protect individuals against actions by state and local governments.

- The decisions of the U.S. Supreme Court during the Warren Court era (1953–1969) encouraged prisoners' rights advocates to bring cases into the federal courts and led to many judicial decisions that improved conditions and practices in prisons and jails throughout the nation.

Key Terms

case law
case precedent
common law
concurring opinion
constitution
constitutional rights
court of last resort
discretionary jurisdiction
dissenting opinion

en banc hearing
facts
hands-off policy
holding
incorporation
issue
judicial opinion
judicial review
jurisdiction

natural rights theory
reasoning
social contract theory
statutes
U.S. district court
U.S. circuit court of appeals
Warren Court era
writ of certiorari

Additional Readings

Call, Jack E. 1995. "The Supreme Court and Prisoners' Rights." *Federal Probation* 59 (March): 36–46.

Hensley, Thomas R., Christopher E. Smith, and Joyce A. Baugh. 1997. *The Changing Supreme Court: Constitutional Rights and Liberties.* St. Paul, MN: West.

Jacobs, James B. 1977. *Stateville: The Penitentiary in Mass Society.* Chicago: University of Chicago Press.

Smith, Christopher E. 1997. *Courts, Politics, and the Judicial Process,* 2nd ed. Chicago: Nelson-Hall.

Washington, Jerome. 1994. *Iron House: Stories from the Yard.* New York: Vintage Books/Random House.

Notes

1. Kathleen Maguire and Ann L. Pastore, eds., *Sourcebook of Criminal Justice Statistics— 1996* (Washington, DC: U.S. Department of Justice, Bureau of Justice Statistics, 1997), p. 513.

2. Ibid., p. 502.

3. Pell v. Procunier, 417 U.S. 817 (1974).

4. Donald H. Wallace, "The Eighth Amendment and Prison Deprivations: Historical Revisions," *Criminal Law Bulletin* 30 (1994): 3–29.

5. Gitlow v. New York, 268 U.S. 652 (1925).

6. In *Duncan v. Louisiana,* 391 U.S. 145 (1968), the Court noted the rights that had been incorporated and applied to the states through the Due Process Clause of the Fourteenth Amendment. In the Court's words, by 1968, "that clause now protects the right to compensation for property taken by the State; the rights to speech, press, and religion covered by the First Amendment; the Fourth Amendment rights to be free from unreasonable

searches and seizures and to have excluded from criminal trials any evidence illegally seized; the right guaranteed by the Fifth Amendment to be free of compelled self-incrimination; and the Sixth Amendment rights to counsel, to speedy and public trial, to confrontation of opposing witnesses, and to compulsory process for obtaining witnesses."

7. Robinson v. California, 370 U.S. 660 (1962).

8. Brown v. Board of Education, 347 U.S. 483 (1954).

9. Christopher E. Smith, "Black Muslims and the Development of Prisoners' Rights," *Journal of Black Studies* 24 (1993): 131–146.

CHAPTER TWO

Prisoners' Legal Cases

On January 8, 1962, the Clerk's Office at the U.S. Supreme Court received a large envelope from Clarence Earl Gideon, an inmate in a Florida state prison. Inside the envelope were lined pages with the "Correspondence Regulations" of the Florida prison system printed at the top of each page. On the pages, Gideon had carefully printed the legal claim that he hoped the Supreme Court justices would decide in his favor. Gideon was serving a five-year sentence for breaking into a pool hall and stealing some change and a few bottles of beer and wine. He claimed that the Florida trial court had violated his Sixth Amendment right to counsel by forcing him to act as his own attorney during his trial. He wanted the U.S. Supreme Court to erase his conviction and order a new trial—with a defense attorney provided for him. Gideon was a fifty-one-year-old man who had spent much of his life in prison. His formal education ended when he ran away from home at age fourteen. He was first locked up for burglary at age sixteen, and he spent time in jails and prisons for six additional offenses in the years prior to filing his petition in the Supreme Court. Despite his lack of education and the fact that he drafted his petition without a lawyer's help, the Supreme Court eventually decided the case in Gideon's favor.[1]

The case that began with an uneducated prisoner's hand-written petition to the Supreme Court produced the famous decision in *Gideon v. Wainwright* (1963).[2] The *Gideon* decision established that poor criminal defendants have a constitutional right to receive free representation by a defense attorney when they face the possibility of six months or more in prison on state criminal charges.

Does Gideon's case prove that American courts are receptive to claims from even the poorest, lowliest citizen? Does it prove that American courts stand ready to consider carefully the claims of society's most hated individuals, convicted criminals? Does it prove that justice will always prevail? No. Gideon was very lucky.

Gideon's case arrived at the Supreme Court at a time when several justices were interested in framing new rules about providing legal counsel for poor defendants. Previously, other prisoners who had presented the same claim as Gideon's had been turned away without a hearing. But after the Court received Gideon's petition, the justices appointed one of the most famous and powerful lawyers in the country to argue Gideon's case before the high court. Gideon's attorney, Abe Fortas, had several lawyers from his prominent Washington, DC, law firm help him prepare Gideon's case. By contrast, the state of Florida was represented by one young attorney who had never before presented a case to the Supreme Court. In this mismatch of legal resources and talent, Gideon had a clear advantage. The fame and influence of Gideon's attorney became even more obvious just two years later when Fortas was appointed by President Lyndon Johnson as an associate justice of the U.S. Supreme Court.

Gideon's case shows that it is *possible* for a prisoner to file a case and win a victory in an appellate court. But Gideon's case is hardly typical. Like Gideon, most prisoners must prepare and file their own legal actions. Unlike Gideon, however, most of them do not receive a court-appointed attorney when they file actions in state supreme courts or pursue postconviction claims in federal courts. Not surprisingly, the legal papers filed by these prisoners—typically uneducated amateurs who lack formal legal training—rarely result in favorable court decisions. As you will see in this chapter, it is difficult for prisoners to initiate successful cases. Part of the problem for prisoners is that many of them do not have a valid legal claim. However, another part of the problem, even for prisoners with a genuine legal issue, is the serious difficulty facing anyone who seeks to initiate court proceedings without the help of a lawyer.

TYPES OF PRISONER CASES

Inmates in prisons and jails are removed from society, but not from society's laws. For example, divorces and child custody disputes can move forward even though one spouse is behind bars. We will not focus on these "regular" kinds of legal cases, such as divorce and child custody, that affect people throughout society. Instead, we will focus on the types of legal actions that apply primarily to people in the corrections system. Convicted offenders and pretrial detainees throughout the country present three primary types of legal actions to courts: appeals, habeas corpus petitions, and civil rights lawsuits. These types of cases are central to corrections law as it affects prisoners. Other types of actions, discussed in Box 2-7, vary according to the state or federal jurisdiction in which a prisoner is under corrections supervision. And in later chapters, we will discuss types of cases that affect corrections employees.

Appeals

After people are convicted of crimes, they may challenge their conviction by filing an appeal. The appeal will go to the intermediate appellate court in the particular state or federal court system in which the trial court is located. An appeal of a U.S. district court decision in Indiana, for example, will go to the U.S. Court of Appeals for the Seventh Circuit in Chicago, the appellate court that handles federal appeals from Indiana, Illinois, and Wisconsin. An appeal from a state trial court goes to the intermediate appellate court for that state. In the thirteen states without intermediate appellate courts, the state supreme court must handle all appeals.

Appeals must claim that the trial court made an error in applying the law or in following legal procedures. The appeals court does not examine evidence; it does not decide whether the defendant was really guilty; and it does not state whether it agrees with the sentence imposed by the trial judge. Instead, the appeals court considers whether the defendant has correctly identified some error serious enough to warrant a new trial. For example, did the trial judge improperly admit evidence against the defendant that should have been excluded? Did the trial judge give improper instructions to the jury? Did the trial judge fail to notice a constitutional right that was violated by the police in searching or questioning the defendant?

Normally, an appeal cannot be filed about an issue unless the defendant's attorney objected to the trial judge's action at the time it occurred. For example, if an appeal is to be based on a claim that a trial judge admitted improper evidence into court, the defense attorney must have said, "**Objection**, your Honor," and asked that the evidence be excluded at the time the trial judge decided to permit its presentation. If the defense attorney does not explicitly object to something that happens during the trial, then the defendant loses the opportunity subsequently to complain about it to an appeals court. Obviously, if a defense attorney does a poor job of representing a defendant at trial, the attorney's performance will hamper future efforts to have an appeals court examine possible errors.

Defendants who are convicted after a trial usually have the best chance to claim that the trial judge made an error. Many decisions are made during the course of trials: how the jury may be selected, what questions potential jurors may be asking, what evidence may be presented in court, and so on. It is easy for judges to make mistakes when dealing with so many complicated situations and complex issues. Of course, not all mistakes automatically ensure that the defendant will get a new trial. Mistakes considered too minor to affect the outcome of a case or to invalidate a trial are known as **harmless errors.**

According to decisions by the U.S. Supreme Court, criminal defendants who are too poor to hire their own attorneys are entitled to have the government provide attorneys for them if they are facing the possibility of a jail or prison sentence (*Gideon v. Wainwright*, 1963; *Argersinger v. Hamlin*, 1972).[3] The Court also has extended this right to counsel to the first appeal of right, which is an initial appeal in a state with laws that obligate intermediate appellate courts to accept and review criminal cases (*Douglas v. California*, 1963).[4] However, in ***Ross v. Moffitt* (1974),**[5] the Court ruled that defendants have no constitutional right to counsel after the first appeal. Second and subsequent appeals typically go to courts that exercise discretion in determining which cases to accept for decision. In other words, poor defendants receive free representation when they appeal to a state's intermediate appellate court. But if they wish to pursue the case in a state supreme court or file an action to move the case from a state to a federal court, the U.S. Constitution does not guarantee legal representation. Some states may provide attorneys beyond the first level of appeal, but the Constitution does not require them to do so.

Because convicted offenders have no right to free counsel beyond the first appeal, those who wish to pursue additional appeals frequently must prepare their own legal arguments and papers. Typically, this means they must try to educate themselves about the law in prison law libraries so they can represent themselves in the appeals process. People who represent themselves in court without the assistance of an attorney are called *pro se* **litigators.** Individuals who appeal normally are required to file **appellate briefs,** which are detailed written arguments that discuss relevant statutes and judicial decisions. It requires significant knowledge of law and considerable legal research skill to write an effective legal brief. In addition, appeals usually must be filed under strict time limits. Many prisoners lose their opportunities to appeal simply because they are unfamiliar with the detailed procedures to follow and the courts do not always make exceptions for them. Few convicted offenders can educate themselves well enough to undertake the appeal preparation tasks that are usually handled by lawyers.

Most convicted offenders have little chance of filing a successful appeal. This is because most defendants are convicted in the plea bargaining process instead of at trial. When they enter their guilty plea, they voluntarily admit their guilt, as well as giving up their right to a trial. In doing so, they sacrifice all the opportunities that trials create for claiming that errors occurred. For example, of the 773,000 people convicted of state felonies in 1994, 89 percent were convicted upon entering a guilty plea; only 11 percent of convictions were the result of trials.[6] People who enter guilty pleas may appeal by claiming that the prosecutor applied improper pressure during the plea bargaining process or that their own attorneys lied to them about the meaning of the plea. However, such claims are rarely successful.

Some of these convicted offenders will attempt to appeal anyway. Such appeals may be regarded by the courts as needlessly taking time away from other matters. In Michigan, for example, voters approved a referendum in 1994 to block appeals from offenders who entered guilty pleas unless those offenders get a court's permission to file an appeal. The underlying idea of such a reform is that people who voluntarily admit their guilt and voluntarily give up their right to a trial should not be permitted subsequently to change their minds about their guilt unless they can show some extraordinary reason.

Habeas Corpus

Even if convicted offenders are unsuccessful in their attempts to appeal, they can still challenge their convictions by filing **habeas corpus petitions.** Because appeals usually must be filed under strict time limits, habeas corpus also provides the opportunity for prisoners to challenge their convictions if they discover new information about improper actions by police, prosecutors, or judges after the deadline for appeals has passed. Habeas corpus is the traditional legal process for people in government custody to challenge the legality of their detention. Although it is used most often by prisoners, it can also be used by other people in government custody, such as patients in mental hospitals.

Habeas corpus was a traditional legal action in England that was brought to America by English colonists and enshrined in the U.S. Constitution. Unlike most constitutional rights for individuals, which were added to the Constitution beginning in 1791 with the Bill of Rights, habeas corpus is spelled out in the original body of the Constitution, which was ratified in 1788. Obviously, the framers of the Constitution believed that citizens must have a method to challenge government actions that deprive them of their liberty. Thus, if individuals believe that they were improperly arrested or otherwise held by the government, habeas corpus permits them to ask a court to examine the legality of their detention. Article I, Section 9 of the Constitution emphasizes this point by stating, "The privilege of the Writ of Habeas Corpus shall not be suspended, unless when in Cases of Rebellion or Invasion the public Safety may require it." In other words, habeas corpus is so important that it should always be available unless the country is under invasion or in the middle of a civil war that prevents the courts from operating.

For prisoners and other convicted offenders, habeas corpus provides a mechanism to claim that one (or more) of their rights was violated in the course of the investigation and prosecution of the case. Unlike appeals, habeas corpus does not provide an opportunity to raise claims about every kind of procedural error or misapplication of the law that may have occurred. Rather, habeas corpus focuses on violations of constitutional rights, such as the Sixth Amendment right to counsel and the Fifth Amendment protection against compelled self-incrimination. Because habeas corpus is premised on a claim of wrongful confinement, prisoners also use habeas corpus to protest an improper loss of "good-time" credits (i.e., time taken off of a sentence for good behavior). Through a habeas corpus petition, prisoners can assert that the restoration of good-time credits would move them beyond their release date and entitle them to immediate freedom.[7] However, rather than restoration of good-time credits, most habeas corpus petitions seek review of alleged rights violations contributing to a criminal conviction.

Many states have their own habeas corpus procedures to provide prisoners and other detainees with an opportunity to raise appropriate claims in state courts. Federal law permits offenders convicted of federal crimes to file habeas corpus petitions in federal courts. The federal habeas corpus process is controversial because it permits federal judges to second-guess decisions made by state judges. State judges resent this intrusion on their authority. Under laws enacted by Congress, persons convicted of *state* crimes can use the *federal* habeas corpus process to move their cases from state to federal court. However, they can only use this process after they have already failed to win their cases on appeal at all available levels of their state's appellate courts. Furthermore, they can only use this process if they are claiming that a *federal* constitutional right was violated during the investigation and prosecution of their case. All federal constitutional rights are not equally available for review by federal judges in the habeas corpus process. For example, the U.S. Supreme Court has declared that claimed violations of the Fourth Amendment right against unreasonable searches and seizures cannot be examined in the federal habeas corpus process if they were already fully considered by a state appellate court (*Stone v. Powell*, 1976).[8] Although there have been efforts to further restrict the list of rights available for habeas corpus review, most other rights of criminal defendants may be raised in federal court.

Under the Supreme Court's interpretations of the U.S. Constitution, convicted offenders have no right to counsel for habeas corpus. Thus, prisoners must prepare their own petitions if they cannot afford to hire an attorney. Under statutes and court rules, prisoners seeking to set aside a death sentence are entitled to representation. However, offenders convicted of noncapital offenses receive appointed attorneys only if their habeas corpus petitions survive initial dismissal and they need assistance in gathering evidence or handling an evidentiary hearing. A judge may appoint an attorney to represent a prisoner if the judge believes that a particular habeas corpus case is especially complicated or highly likely to be meritorious. However, this rarely happens, except in death penalty cases in which the habeas corpus process may be the final opportunity before the execution to ensure that a conviction was properly obtained. Box 2-1 shows some of the instructions contained on special habeas corpus forms made available to prisoners in many institutions. How easy would it be for you to follow these instructions? How easy would it be for a prisoner with limited education or literacy skills to do so?

Federal habeas corpus actions are especially controversial for several reasons. First, critics believe that it is a waste of the federal courts' time to review cases that have already been reviewed in state appeals courts. Moreover, because only about 1 percent of habeas corpus petitions are successful, these critics believe that state courts generally should be the ultimate decision makers

BOX 2-1 | **Petition Under 28 U.S.C. [Section] 2254 for Writ of Habeas Corpus by a Person in State Custody**

(If petitioner is attacking a judgment which imposed a sentence to be served in the future, petitioner must fill in the name of the state where the judgment was entered. If petitioner has a sentence to be served in the future under a federal judgment which he wishes to attack, he should file a motion under 28 U.S.C. [section] 2255, in the federal court which entered the judgment.)

PETITION FOR WRIT OF HABEAS CORPUS BY A PERSON IN STATE CUSTODY

Instructions—Read Carefully

(1) This petition must be legibly handwritten or typewritten, and signed by the petitioner under penalty of perjury. Any false statement of a material fact may serve as the basis for prosecution and conviction for perjury. All questions must be answered concisely in the proper space on the form.

(2) Additional pages are not permitted except with respect to the facts which you rely upon to support your grounds for relief. No citation of authorities need be furnished. If briefs or arguments are submitted, they should be submitted in the form of a separate memorandum.

(3) Upon receipt of a fee of $5 your petition will be filed if it is in proper order.

(4) If you do not have the necessary funds for transcripts, counsel, appeal, and other costs connected with a motion of this type, you may request permission to proceed *in forma pauperis,* in which event you must execute form AO 240 or any other form required by the court, setting forth information establishing your inability to pay the costs. If you wish to proceed *in forma pauperis,* you must have an authorized officer at the penal institution complete

the certificate as to the amount of money and securities on deposit to your credit in any account in the institution. If your personal account exceeds [an amount determined by the court] you must pay the filing fee as required by the rules of the district court.

(5) Only judgments entered by one court may be challenged in a single motion. If you seek to challenge judgments entered by different courts either in the same state or in different states, you must file separate petitions as to each court.

(6) Your attention is directed to the fact that you must include all grounds for relief and all facts supporting such grounds for relief in the petition you file seeking relief from any judgment of conviction.

(7) When the petition is fully completed, the original and at least two copies must be mailed to the Clerk of the United States District Court whose address is _____.

(8) Petitions which do not conform to these instructions will be returned with a notation as to the deficiency.

. . .

(12) State *concisely* every ground on which you claim that you are being held unlawfully. Summarize *briefly* the *facts* supporting each ground. If necessary, you may attach pages stating additional grounds and *facts* supporting same.

CAUTION: *In order to proceed in the federal court, you must ordinarily first exhaust your available state court remedies as to each ground on which you request action by the federal court. If you fail to set forth all grounds in this petition, you may be barred from presenting additional grounds at a later date.*

For your information, the following is a list of the most frequently raised grounds for relief in

(continued)

habeas corpus proceedings. Each statement preceded by a letter constitutes a separate ground for possible relief. You may raise any grounds which you may have other than those listed if you have exhausted your state court remedies with respect to them. However, *you should raise in this petition all available grounds* (relating to this conviction) on which you base your allegations that you are being held in custody unlawfully.

Do not check any of these listed grounds. If you select one or more of these grounds for relief, you must allege facts. The petition will be returned to you if you merely check (a) through (j) or any one of these grounds.

(a) Conviction obtained by plea of guilty which was unlawfully induced or not made voluntarily with understanding of the nature of the charge and the consequences of the plea.

(b) Conviction obtained by use of coerced confession.

(c) Conviction obtained by use of evidence gained pursuant to an unconstitutional search and seizure.

(d) Conviction obtained by use of evidence obtained pursuant to an unlawful arrest.

(e) Conviction obtained by a violation of the privilege against self-incrimination.

(f) Conviction obtained by the unconstitutional failure of the prosecution to disclose to the defendant evidence favorable to the defendant.

(g) Conviction obtained by a violation of the protection against double jeopardy.

(h) Conviction obtained by action of a grand or petit jury which was unconstitutionally selected and impaneled.

(i) Denial of effective assistance of counsel.

(j) Denial of right of appeal.

to avoid needlessly taking up the time of federal judges. Second, habeas corpus raises issues of **federalism**. Federalism is the underlying concept in the American system of government whereby states are granted the authority to control many aspects of their own affairs. Because habeas corpus involves federal judges second-guessing decisions made by state trial and appellate judges, many critics believe that this process undermines the ability of states and their courts to run their own criminal justice systems. Third, habeas corpus petitions often are filed years after a conviction has taken place. When such late petitions are filed, witnesses may have died, prosecutors' memories may have faded, and records may have disappeared or been placed in long-term storage. Thus, it may be unreasonably difficult for state officials to reconstruct all of the events and decisions that the prisoner now claims were improper. Fourth, prosecutors and state judges complain that the habeas corpus process prevents convictions from becoming finalized by permitting prisoners to keep denying their own guilt. If they can challenge their convictions for years after the end of the trial, critics complain, they avoid facing up to their responsibility for violating society's laws.

During the 1980s and 1990s, several Supreme Court justices agreed with these criticisms of habeas corpus. Under the leadership of Chief Justice William Rehnquist, the Court issued several decisions that limited opportunities for prisoners to file habeas corpus petitions. For example, the Court declared that convicted offenders can only raise claims based on violations of rights that were clearly recognized at the time of their convictions. They cannot benefit from new judicial rulings on rights, even if those new rulings indicate that the police or prosecutors did something wrong in a prior case (*Teague v. Lane,* 1989).[9] For example, police in South Carolina questioned Horace Butler concerning an unsolved murder while he was being held in jail on assault charges. Even though he was represented by an attorney on the assault charges, the attorney was not present for the questioning about the murder. After statements made during the questioning led to a murder conviction, Butler claimed that his right to counsel was violated during the questioning. The Supreme Court subsequently decided in a separate case that people in jail are entitled to have their attorneys present, even during questioning on unrelated charges.[10] Thus, even though the police violated a constitutional rule during their questioning of Butler, it did not count as a violation of his rights for habeas corpus purposes because the rule about the right to counsel during questioning was not clearly in existence at the time Butler was questioned (*Butler v. McKellar,* 1989).[11]

The Supreme Court, in *McCleskey v. Zant* (1991),[12] also limited habeas corpus petitions by declaring that prisoners normally must place all constitutional claims in a single petition. They can no longer file new petitions if they identify other ways in which their rights may have been violated during an investigation and trial. In addition, in *Coleman v. Thompson,* (1991),[13] the Court ruled that habeas corpus petitioners forfeit their opportunity to raise claims in federal court if they or their attorneys violated any state procedures during the appeals process. Thus, when a death row inmate's lawyer mistakenly filed an appeal three days late in a Virginia appellate court, the prisoner automatically lost both his appeal and his opportunity subsequently to have a federal judge review his case in the habeas corpus process. These decisions, as well as others by the U.S. Supreme Court, have made it more difficult for convicted offenders to have their cases heard in federal courts.

In 1996, Congress acted to further limit habeas corpus proceedings. The federal **Antiterrorism and Effective Death Penalty Act,**[14] which was signed into law by President Clinton in April 1996, reinforced the limit on the number of habeas corpus petitions that can be filed and limited the ability of federal judges to second-guess certain determinations made earlier in each case by state judges. Box 2-2 provides selected provisions of this law. How will these provisions affect convicted offenders' ability to obtain federal court review of alleged constitutional rights violations in their convictions?

Note that the statute places stringent restrictions on habeas corpus petitioners who seek to file a second petition. A second petition can be based on a new constitutional right made retroactive by the Supreme Court—something the high court rarely does. It can also be based on new facts that were not previously discoverable if those facts indicate not merely a rights violation, but a violation that would have made the court find the defendant not guilty. Moreover, before a second petition can be filed, it must be approved by a three-judge panel of a U.S. circuit court of appeals. The statute also imposes a strict one-year deadline for filing and a presumption of correctness for state court findings that will be difficult to overcome when most cases reach federal court.

BOX 2-2 **Antiterrorism and Effective Death Penalty Act**

18 U.S.C. SECTION 2244

Limits on Second or Successive Applications

(b) (1) A claim presented in a second or successive habeas corpus application under section 2254 that was presented in a prior application shall be dismissed.

(2) A claim presented in a second or successive habeas corpus application under section 2254 that was not presented in a prior application shall be dismissed unless—

(A) the applicant shows that the claim relies on a new rule of constitutional law, made retroactive to cases on collateral review by the Supreme Court, that was previously unavailable; or

(B) (i) the factual predicate for the claim could not have been discovered previously through the exercise of due diligence; and

(ii) the facts underlying the claim, if proven and viewed in light of the evidence as a whole, would be sufficient to establish by clear and convincing evidence that, but for constitutional error, no reasonable factfinder would have found the applicant guilty of the underlying offense.

(3) (A) Before a second or successive application permitted by this section is filed in the district court, the applicant shall move in the appropriate court of appeals for an order authorizing the district court to consider the application.

(B) A motion in the court of appeals for an order authorizing the district court to consider a second or successive application shall be determined by a three-judge panel of the court of appeals.

. . .

(d)(1) A 1-year period of limitation shall apply to an application for a writ of habeas corpus by a person in custody pursuant to the judgment of a State court. . . .

28 U.S.C. SECTION 2254

(b) (1) An application for a writ of habeas corpus on behalf of a person in custody pursuant to the judgment of a State court shall not be granted unless it appears that—

(A) The applicant has exhausted the remedies available in the courts of the State; or

(B) (i) there is an absence of available State corrective process; or

(ii) circumstances exist that render such process ineffective to protect the rights of the applicant.

The new procedural rules established by the Supreme Court and Congress have made it increasingly difficult for prisoners to initiate habeas corpus proceedings. Many habeas corpus petitions are dismissed immediately upon arrival in a federal court because the prisoner has failed to follow one of the many procedural requirements. Because they have no right to counsel, prisoners must try to figure out the procedural rules for themselves. In addition, even if a prisoner manages to obey the necessary procedures, uneducated prisoners usually have a difficult time accurately identifying and effectively presenting the kinds of federal constitutional rights claims that can be raised in habeas corpus petitions. Recall that unlike appeals, which can raise all kinds of allegations about errors that occurred during a trial, habeas corpus petitions must focus on claimed violations of federal constitutional rights. As Box 2-3 discusses, the restrictions on habeas corpus petitions can lead to some surprising consequences.

(2) An application for a writ of habeas corpus may be denied on the merits, notwithstanding the failure of the applicant to exhaust the remedies available in the courts of the State.

(3) A State shall not be deemed to have waived the exhaustion requirement or be estopped from reliance upon the requirement unless the State, through counsel, expressly waives the requirement. . . .

(d) An application for a writ of habeas corpus on behalf of a person in custody pursuant to the judgment of a State court shall not be granted with respect to any claim that was adjudicated on the merits in State court proceedings unless the adjudication of the claim—

(1) resulted in a decision that was contrary to, or involved an unreasonable application of, clearly established Federal law, as determined by the Supreme Court of the United States; or

(2) resulted in a decision that was based on an unreasonable determination of the facts in light of the evidence presented in the State court proceeding;

(e) (1) In a proceeding instituted by an application for a writ of habeas corpus by a person in custody pursuant to the judgment of a State court, a determination of a factual issue made by a State court shall be presumed to be correct. The applicant shall have the burden of rebutting the presumption of correctness by clear and convincing evidence.

(2) If the applicant has failed to develop the factual basis of a claim in State court proceedings, the court shall not hold an evidentiary hearing on the claim unless the applicant shows that—

(A) The claim relies on—

(i) a new rule of constitutional law, made retroactive to cases on collateral review by the Supreme Court, that was previously unavailable; or

(ii) a factual predicate that could not have been previously discovered through the exercise of due diligence; and

(B) The facts underlying the claim would be sufficient to establish by clear and convincing evidence that but for the constitutional error, no reasonable factfinder would have found the applicant guilty of the underlying offense. . . .

(i) The ineffectiveness or incompetence of counsel during Federal or State collateral postconviction proceedings shall not be a ground for relief in a proceeding arising under section 2254.

Civil Rights Lawsuits

Prisoners file many more civil rights lawsuits than habeas corpus petitions. For example, in 1995, only 14,972 habeas corpus petitions were filed by prisoners in federal district courts, as opposed to 41,679 civil rights lawsuits.[16] Civil rights lawsuits provide the mechanism for prisoners to claim that their federal constitutional rights and applicable federal statutory rights have been violated by corrections officials. These lawsuits do not seek to gain the prisoners' freedom. Rather, they seek to have corrections officials change policies and procedures, and they frequently seek to obtain financial compensation for the claimed rights violations. In short, these are not criminal cases, but are civil lawsuits against corrections officials.

Most of the chapters of this book will focus on the various rights under the Bill of Rights that prisoners seek to protect through section 1983 lawsuits.

BOX 2-3   Habeas Corpus and Wrongful Convictions

In the hit movie *The Fugitive,* Harrison Ford plays Dr. Richard Kimble, who is convicted of murdering his wife. He escapes on his way to prison and, while eluding the U.S. marshals who are chasing him, tracks down the men who actually were responsible for his wife's death. In a 1993 article in *The National Law Journal,* attorney Philip Figa points out that according to the U.S. Supreme Court's recent changes in procedures for habeas corpus, Kimble would have had no basis for having his conviction overturned through habeas corpus procedures. Kimble had received a fair trial in which the jury believed that the substantial circumstantial evidence pointed to his guilt. Kimble could have claimed that he was wrongly convicted, but under habeas corpus, he would have had to show that he had a constitutional right violated.

The discovery of new evidence does not automatically entitle a convicted person to a new trial. As Justice Antonin Scalia wrote in a case concerning a death row inmate who sought a new trial after witnesses asserted that the inmate's brother actually had committed the murder: "There is no basis in text, tradition, or even in contemporary practice (if that were enough), for finding in the Constitution a right to demand judicial consideration of newly discovered evidence of innocence brought forward after conviction."[15] Some justices argue that sentencing an innocent person to death would violate the constitutional right against cruel and unusual punishments in the Eighth Amendment. Others, like Scalia, believe that the Constitution guarantees only a fair trial, and not a correct result from that trial. They believe that erroneous convictions should be handled by governors through their power to pardon offenders rather than through the courts in the habeas corpus process. Critics counter that governors are too concerned about political backlash to use the pardon power when the evidence supporting conviction is obviously deficient yet the defendant has no ironclad alibi or clear-cut evidence of innocence.

Source: Adapted from Clarence Page, "In Real Life, 'Fugitive' Would Have Been Toast," (*Chicago Tribune* syndication), *Akron Beacon Journal,* 14 September 1993, p. A9; Christopher E. Smith, "The Constitution and Criminal Punishment: The Emerging Visions of Justices Scalia and Thomas," *Drake Law Review* 43 (1995): 593–613.

Nearly all federal civil rights lawsuits by prisoners are filed under Title 42 of the U.S. Code, section 1983, which is a statute enacted by Congress. These legal actions are commonly referred to as **section 1983** lawsuits. The U.S. Supreme Court declared, in ***Cooper v. Pate*** (1964),[17] that this statute could be used by prisoners to file lawsuits against corrections officials. Box 2-4 gives the wording of the statute.

Two key elements in determining whether a section 1983 lawsuit can be filed in federal court concern whether the targets of the suit are (1) "person[s]" who (2) acted "under color of state law" in violating a constitutional right or other legal protection.

Neither states nor state officials acting in their official capacities are regarded as "person[s]" who can be sued under section 1983. Officials must be sued in an individual capacity, meaning that the lawsuit is directed at and seeks compensation from them personally, rather than treating them as representatives of an agency for liability purposes. In many circumstances, an agency will

---

BOX 2-4   ## Civil Rights Act, 42 U.S.C. [Section] 1983

Every person who, under color of any statute, ordinance, regulation, custom, or usage, of any State or Territory or the District of Columbia, subjects, or causes to be subjected, any citizen of the United States or other person within the jurisdiction thereof to the deprivation of any rights, privileges, or immunities secured by the Constitution and laws, shall be liable to the party injured in an action at law, suit in equity, or other proper proceeding for redress.

---

in fact provide attorneys—often from the state attorney general's office or county attorney's office—and pay any damages for employees found liable in section 1983 lawsuits. This does not mean, however, that the individual named in the lawsuit is merely a representative of the agency for purposes of establishing liability. In other words, for example, a prisoner may not name the governor as the defendant in a lawsuit simply because the governor is someone who represents the state government. There must be a specific basis for bringing a legal action against a particular individual.

There is one context in which compensation can be sought from governments responsible for local jails—by suing a corrections official for actions taken in an official capacity. In such lawsuits, the corrections institution's policies or customs must have contributed to the rights violation in order for the prisoner to win. This doctrine stems from the U.S. Supreme Court's decision in *City of Canton v. Harris* (1989) that a municipality could be held liable for failing to train its officers properly.[18] For example, sheriffs have been held liable as the chief policy-making officials for a county when the county's policies, such as a failure to train officers properly, led to a rights violation.

Although section 1983 actions are limited to "persons" under the statute's wording, the U.S. Supreme Court's interpretation of the statute has expanded the range of litigation targets. In particular, lawsuits may be filed against municipalities and counties. The Court declared in *Monell v. Department of Social Services* (1978) that "[o]ur analysis of the legislative history of the Civil Rights Act of 1871 compels the conclusion that Congress did intend municipalities and other local government units to be included among those persons to whom section 1983 applies."[19] The conclusion that an organizational entity can be a "person" under the law was not new or unique when applied to section 1983. Business corporations, for example, have long been treated as legal "persons" for various purposes under the law.

While municipalities and other local government units may be subject to section 1983 lawsuits, the same is not true of states and state government agencies. The Eleventh Amendment to the U.S. Constitution bars federal courts from hearing lawsuits against states by individuals. The Eleventh Amendment states:

The Judicial power of the United States shall not be construed to extend to any suit in law or equity, commenced or prosecuted against one of the United States by citizens of another State, or by Citizens or Subjects of any Foreign State.

Lawsuits may be filed against states when a statute specifically grants permission for certain types of legal actions. A state may have, for example, a state tort claims statute that permits lawsuits by individuals injured in traffic accidents caused by state employees on official business or property damage and injuries caused by the actions of state officials in other contexts.

Because the Eleventh Amendment bars only federal courts from hearing lawsuits against states, some litigants sought to file section 1983 claims in state courts. The section 1983 action was filed in conjunction with related claims under state law, such as alleged violations of rights under a state constitution, in order to ask a state court to hear both state and federal claims arising out of the same incident or circumstances. Lower court decisions initially contradicted each other on the question of whether states could be treated as "person[s]" under section 1983 for lawsuits filed in state court. The U.S. Supreme Court clarified the law by declaring that states and state agencies are not "person[s]" and may not be sued under section 1983, even in cases heard in state courts (*Will v. Michigan Department of State Police,* 1989).[20]

Under federal law, a defendant being sued can remove a case from state court and force the litigation into federal court in "any civil action brought in a State court of which the district courts of the United States have original jurisdiction" (28 U.S.C. section 1441(a)). If the case contains claims that are barred by the Eleventh Amendment, such as an effort to sue the state or state corrections personnel in their "official" capacity, the federal court will dismiss these claims but may still hear any remaining claims that concern actions by defendants in their "personal" capacity (*Wisconsin Department of Corrections v. Schacht,* 1998).[21]

What about lawsuits against federal officials by people under supervision in the federal corrections system? Obviously, section 1983 applies to actions by state, territorial, or District of Columbia officials. However, the U.S. Supreme Court ruled that individuals may seek damages for violations of their constitutional rights by federal officials (*Bivens v. Six Unknown Named Agents of the Federal Bureau of Narcotics,* 1971).[22] These so-called Bivens actions against federal officials mirror section 1983 actions against state officials. The same legal rules and doctrines generally apply to both kinds of actions. Unlike local agencies, however, the federal government itself may not be sued because of the traditional doctrine of government immunity, which bars lawsuits against the government unless a specific law is enacted granting permission to sue. For example, the Federal Tort Claims Act provides the basis for citizens to seek compensation for injuries caused by federal officials, such as injuries sustained in a car accident involving a U.S. Postal Service vehicle.

The second requirement of section 1983 lawsuits requires that the individual acted "under the color of state law" to cause a violation of a constitutional right. It should be noted that even people who work in corrections under a contract with the state (e.g., some doctors and dentists), rather than as state employees, may be regarded as acting "under the color of state law." Section 1983 cannot be used to file a lawsuit simply because someone alleges that a corrections system employee or contractor (e.g., a doctor or dentist) violated someone's constitutional rights. The rights violation generally must occur in the course of the official's actions at work, actions asserting authority under corrections laws and policies, actions using government equipment, or actions carrying out corrections practices and programs. Thus, a corrections officer who punches a probationer in the middle of the street during an argument about a traffic accident would not be subject to a lawsuit alleging excessive use of force as a violation of the Eighth Amendment's prohibition on cruel and unusual punishments. However, if that corrections officer punches an inmate inside a prison to punish the inmate for talking back, then a section 1983 lawsuit might very well be filed.

As you can imagine from this description of "person[s]" whom prisoners may sue, section 1983 lawsuits can be very complicated. Because there is no right to counsel for civil rights lawsuits, prisoners must figure out for themselves what constitutional rights can be claimed under such lawsuits, which "person[s]" can be sued under the statute, and what procedures to take to initiate the litigation. These are difficult tasks for people who lack legal training. And they are especially difficult for the many prisoners who are mentally retarded, illiterate, mentally ill, or not fully fluent in the English language.

The other key elements of section 1983 lawsuits are *causation* and a *constitutional rights violation,* that is, the "injury" claimed by litigant. Both of these elements must be proved. In some cases, it is difficult for a prisoner to prove that he or she actually suffered an "injury" that constitutes a rights violation. For example, if a prison practice improperly prevents prisoners from consulting with their attorneys, litigants would have to prove that the practice actually stopped them from communicating with an attorney in order to show that they were personally "injured" by a constitutional rights violation. In other cases, causation may be difficult to prove, especially when the prisoner must demonstrate the responsibility of a particular corrections official rather than the state itself.

Despite the uphill battle many prisoners face in preparing and proving civil rights lawsuits, such legal actions are important for corrections. These lawsuits provide one primary means for an outside "watchdog"—namely, the courts—to monitor the legality of practices and conditions within prisons—institutions that are closed off, in many respects, from the outside world. Box 2-5 contains some of the instructions for prisoners' civil rights lawsuits on forms made available by a court in one state. How do these instructions differ from those for the habeas corpus petition in Box 2-1?

A civil rights lawsuit may raise many kinds of issues related to the rights listed in the Bill of Rights and the Fourteenth Amendment (see Chapter 1). For example, if prisoners believe that they were denied the opportunity to freely practice their religion, a civil rights lawsuit would provide a means to ask a federal judge to examine whether the prison interfered with inmates' First

Form to Be Used by a Prisoner Filing a Complaint Under the Civil Rights Act, 42 U.S.C. [Section] 1983

. . . This packet contains four copies of a complaint form. To start an action you must file an original and one copy of your complaint for each defendant you name and one copy for the court. For example, if you name two defendants you must file the original and three copies of the complaint. You should keep an additional copy of the complaint for your own records. *All copies of the complaint must be identical to the original.*

The clerk will not file your complaint unless it conforms to these instructions and to these forms.

Your complaint must be legibly handwritten or typewritten. You, the plaintiff, must sign and declare under penalty of perjury that the facts are correct. If you need additional space to answer a question, you must use the reverse side of the form or an additional blank page.

Your complaint can be brought in this court only if one or more of the named defendants is located within this district. Further, you must file a separate complaint for each claim that you have unless they are all related to the same incident or issue.

You are required to furnish, so that the United States marshal can complete service, the *correct name and address of each person you have named as a defendant.* A PLAINTIFF IS REQUIRED TO GIVE INFORMATION TO THE UNITED STATES MARSHAL TO ENABLE THE MARSHAL TO COMPLETE SERVICE OF THE COMPLAINT UPON ALL PERSONS AS DEFENDANTS.

In order for this complaint to be filed, it must be accompanied by a filing fee of $150.00. In addition, the United States marshal will require you to pay the cost of serving the complaint on each of the defendants.

If you are unable to pay the filing fee and service costs for this action, you may petition the court to proceed in forma pauperis by completing and signing the attached declarations. . . . If you wish to proceed in forma pauperis you must have an authorized officer at the penal institution complete the certificate as to the amount of money and securities on deposit to your credit in any account in the institution. If your prison account exceeds [an amount determined by the court], you must pay the filing fee and service costs.

You will note that you are required to give facts. THIS COMPLAINT SHOULD NOT CONTAIN ANY LEGAL ARGUMENTS OR CITATIONS.

When these forms are completed, mail the original and the copies to the Clerk of the United States District Court _____ .

Amendment right to freedom of religion. Similarly, concerns about whether conditions within a corrections institution violated the Eighth Amendment prohibition on cruel and unusual punishments could be raised through a section 1983 lawsuit. Because most prisoners lack knowledge of law, they also raise other issues in civil rights lawsuits, such as complaints about the quality of the food or regulations on watching television. When these other kinds of complaints do not concern constitutional rights, the federal courts have no power to examine them in a civil rights lawsuit.

Government officials complain that prisoners flood the courts with civil rights lawsuits. Even though most of these actions have no legitimate basis, attorneys for a state or county still must spend time preparing counterarguments. Officials also complain that federal judges use prisoners' civil rights lawsuits as an excuse to improperly interfere with or take over the administration of prisons and jails. As with habeas corpus, there are concerns that prisoners' lawsuits undermine the principles of federalism when *federal* judges become too involved in running *state* corrections institutions. Corrections officials are concerned as well that they could be forced to pay money, and potentially large sums of money, to an inmate who wins a civil rights case against them.

Congress addressed some of these concerns in 1996 by enacting the **Prison Litigation Reform Act** (PLRA).[23] The new law limits federal judges' authority to impose orders on corrections institutions concerning how they should handle their affairs.[24] The law also makes it more difficult for prisoners to file lawsuits without paying the usual court fees. Previously, prisoners could have court fees waived by filing an *in forma pauperis* **petition,** which asserted that they were too poor to pay the fees. Now inmates must make a partial payment if they have money in their accounts at the prison, and they must make further payments amounting to 20 percent of the monthly income credited to their accounts. The new law is intended to ensure that prisoners are sufficiently serious about their claims to actually spend their own money in pursuing the claim. Previously, there were concerns that some inmates filed unsubstantiated claims simply to annoy corrections officials. In the months following passage of the PLRA, the number of prisoners' civil rights cases filed in the federal courts dropped. Ultimately, there was a 9 percent overall decrease in prisoners' civil rights cases for 1996 compared to the previous year.[25] It is still too early to know the long-term impact of the PLRA. (The PLRA will be discussed in greater detail in Chapter 8.)

Other Federal Civil Rights Statutes

Although section 1983 provides the primary vehicle for prisoners' civil rights lawsuits, whenever Congress enacts a civil rights statute there will be questions about whether it applies to prisoners. Unless Congress places language in the statute explicitly to exclude prisoners from coverage, incarcerated individuals may seek to use available laws to gain access to privileges, protections, or other benefits bestowed on law-abiding citizens by the statute. In 1998, the Supreme Court addressed the issue of whether prisoners were protected by the Americans with Disabilities Act of 1990 (ADA). The ADA was enacted by Congress and signed into law by President George Bush because of the lawmakers' belief that people afflicted with disabilities needed protection against discrimination or exclusion from participation in government programs and services. Box 2-6 contains the Supreme Court's opinion in *Pennsylvania Department of Corrections v. Yeskey.* Does this decision indicate that the Supreme Court is creating new rights for prisoners? Does it suggest that the justices are sympathetic to prisoners' rights? What is likely to happen as a result of this decision? How might Congress respond to this decision?

Actions filed under the ADA seek access and reasonable accommodation for disabled people to enable them to take advantage of services and programs.

BOX 2-6

Pennsylvania Department of Corrections v. Yeskey, 118 S.Ct. 1952 (1998)

JUSTICE SCALIA delivered the opinion of the unanimous Court.

The question before us is whether Title II of the Americans with Disabilities Act of 1990 (ADA), . . . 42 U.S.C. [section] 12131 et seq., which prohibits a "public entity" from discriminating against a "qualified individual with a disability" on account of that individual's disability, . . . covers inmates in state prisons. Respondent Ronald Yeskey was such an inmate, sentenced in May 1994 to serve 18 to 36 months in a Pennsylvania correctional facility. The sentencing court recommended that he be placed in Pennsylvania's Motivational Boot Camp for first-time offenders, the successful completion of which would have led to his release on parole in just six months. . . . Because of his medical history of hypertension, however, he was refused admission. He filed this suit against petitioners, the Commonwealth of Pennsylvania's Department of Corrections and several department officials, alleging that his exclusion from the Boot Camp violated the ADA. The District Court dismissed for failure to state a claim . . . holding the ADA inapplica-

ble to inmates in state prison; the Third Circuit [U.S. Court of Appeals] reversed. . . .

Petitioners argue that state prisoners are not covered by the ADA for the same reason we held in *Gregory v. Ashcroft*, 501 U.S. 452 (1991), that state judges were not covered by the Age Discrimination in Employment Act of 1967. *Gregory* relied on the canon of construction that absent an "unmistakably clear" expression of intent to "alter the usual constitutional balance between the States and the Federal Government," we will interpret a statute to preserve rather than destroy the States' "substantial sovereign powers." . . . It may well be that exercising ultimate control over the management of state prisons, like establishing the qualifications of state government officials, is a traditional and essential State function subject to the plain-statement rule of *Gregory*. "One of the primary functions of government," we have said, "is the preservation of societal order through enforcement of the criminal law, and the maintenance of penal institutions is an essential part of that task." *Procunier v. Martinez* . . . (1974). . . . "It is difficult to imag-

Notice that in this case, the Supreme Court was not interpreting the Constitution, but was merely interpreting the words of the statute. Because the case focused on statutory interpretation and because legislatures ultimately can control the meaning of the statutes they enact, it will be possible for Congress to enact an amendment to the ADA to exclude prisoners from coverage. Undoubtedly, some members of Congress will respond to the Supreme Court's decision by proposing such changes in the ADA, but it remains to be seen whether those changes will be enacted by Congress. It seems fairly certain that unless Congress revises the ADA, some prisoners will seize upon the Supreme Court's decision to consider ways in which the ADA might enable them to gain greater access to services and programs in prison.

State laws provide additional opportunities for legal actions by prisoners, although the number and nature of these opportunities vary from state to state. As you read about the legal actions described in Box 2-7, try to think of situations in which prisoners might succeed in pursuing each of these actions.

ine an activity in which a State has a stronger interest," *Preiser v. Rodriguez,* . . . (1973).

Assuming, without deciding, that the plainstatement rule does govern application of the ADA to the administration of state prisons, we think the requirement of the rule is amply met: the statute's language unmistakably includes state prisons and prisoners within its coverage. The situation here is not comparable to that in *Gregory.* There, although the [Age Discrimination in Employment Act] plainly covered state employees, it contained an exception for "appointee[s] on the policymaking level" which made it impossible for us to "conclude that the statute plainly cover[ed] appointed state judges." . . . Here the ADA plainly covers state institutions without any exception that could cast the coverage of prisons into doubt. . . . State prisons fall squarely within the statutory definition of "public entity," which includes "any department, agency, special purpose district, or other instrumentality of a State or States or local government." . . .

Petitioners contend that the phrase "benefits of the services, programs, or activities of a public entity," . . . creates an ambiguity, because state prisons do not provide prisoners with "benefits" of "programs, services, or activities" as those terms are ordinarily understood. We disagree. Modern prisons provide inmates with many recreational "activities," medical "services," and educational and vocational "programs," all of which at least theoretically "benefit" the prisoners (and any of which disabled prisoners could be "excluded from participation in"). . . . Indeed, the [state] statute establishing the Motivational Boot Camp at issue in this very case refers to it as a "program." . . . The text of the ADA provides no basis for distinguishing these programs, services, and activities from those provided by public entities that are not prisons.

We also disagree with petitioners' contention that the term "qualified individual with a disability" is ambiguous insofar as concerns its application to state prisoners. The statute defines the term to include anyone with a disability. . . .

Because the plain text of Title II of the ADA unambiguously extends to state prison inmates, the judgment of the Court of Appeals is affirmed.

ALTERNATIVES TO LITIGATION

The Problems of Litigation

The litigation process is difficult for prisoners. Because they have no right to counsel in habeas corpus and civil rights cases, they must struggle to identify and present effectively their complaints about rights violations. As the high dismissal rates for both kinds of cases clearly indicate, few prisoners are capable of representing themselves effectively in court. Thus, even legitimate complaints may never be recognized and remedied by the courts. Genuine issues about rights violations may be overlooked either because the prisoners cannot identify and present claims effectively or because prisoners in general have lost credibility in the eyes of decision makers as a result of the large numbers of meritless claims. In addition, there may be other kinds of legitimate grievances that do

Other Legal Actions by Convicted Offenders

Depending on the jurisdiction in which the offender is under correctional supervision, other kinds of legal actions may be filed in state or federal courts.

TORTS

Tort law provides remedies under civil law for harms suffered by a person or entity because of the actions of another person or entity. Tort lawsuits may be filed to recover damages for personal injuries, slanderous statements that harm someone's reputation, or property damage. Some torts are based on *intentional actions,* such as a personal injury lawsuit against a person who punches someone else in the nose. Other torts are based on *negligence,* as when someone causes harm by failing to take due care in his or her behavior. For example, a person who fails to have his or her car's squeaky, malfunctioning brakes checked by a mechanic may not intend to hurt anyone. However, if the faulty brakes result in a car accident, the failure may constitute negligence. That is, when the failure to take due care is the proximate or immediate cause of an injury, the person may be found liable based on negligence. In the corrections context, a prisoner may seek to use a state tort action to bring a medical mal-practice claim alleging that a prison doctor was negligent in treating an illness or injury and thereby caused additional harm to the inmate. Such actions may also claim that prison officials negligently damaged or lost property that was owned by a prisoner.

Negligent actions by corrections officials cannot be a basis for liability under section 1983. In *Daniels v. Williams* (1986),[26] the Supreme Court found no rights violation when a prisoner claimed an injury was caused by a jail official's negligence in leaving a pillow on a staircase, which caused the prisoner to fall. Negligence by corrections officials may be actionable under tort lawsuits for personal injuries or property damage.

CRIMINAL CHARGES

Prisoners may seek to file criminal charges against corrections officials for assaulting them, stealing their property, or otherwise violating state criminal laws in victimizing inmates. Prisoners cannot control whether such legal actions move forward because typically the state police, local sheriff, or prosecutor will have to investigate the allegations and decide whether enough evidence exists to pursue formal criminal charges against the corrections personnel.

not concern constitutional rights. If legal actions are the prisoner's only option, then there may be no way to present these grievances to corrections officials.

Litigation presents other problems. It is an expensive process that absorbs the time of government lawyers, corrections officials, and court employees. Government officials and many judges are especially concerned that too much time and effort is spent on these cases that are rarely successful. Furthermore, because prisons often are located in rural areas, there are additional costs for prison officials who must take time off from work to travel many miles to attend pretrial hearings, settlement conferences, and trials. There are also significant expenses involved in transporting and guarding prisoners who must be brought to court for these same proceedings. At least one federal court has sought to reduce these burdens of litigation by sending a U.S. magistrate judge into a prison for one afternoon each week to hold hearings and conferences,

STATE HABEAS CORPUS

States may have their own habeas corpus procedures permitting convicted offenders to claim that their state constitutional rights were violated in the course of the investigative and judicial proceedings resulting in incarceration.

WRIT OF MANDAMUS

Mandamus is a traditional action by which a person seeks to have a judge order an official to take a particular action. Prisoners may file for a writ of mandamus if they want a judge to order corrections officials to follow the rules spelled out in the institution's policies and procedures. Out of the nearly 56,000 prisoners' petitions of all types (habeas corpus, civil rights, and so on) terminated by federal district courts in 1995, fewer than 1000 were mandamus petitions.[27] They were dismissed at a higher rate than all other cases.

DECLARATORY JUDGMENT

State courts often possess the authority to issue declaratory judgments. In the prison context, a prisoner may ask the court, "Do I have a particular right in this situation?" In response, the court will issue a decision stating whether a right exists under those circumstances.

APPEAL OF PAROLE DECISIONS

Prisoners may seek to challenge decisions by parole boards or other paroling authorities that decline to approve early release. Courts rarely question the discretionary decisions of parole authorities. There is no right to parole for courts to enforce. Instead, courts look to see whether the parole process followed applicable statutes or rules. Improper procedures likely will require a new hearing, rather than result in release of the offender.

ADMINISTRATIVE APPEALS

Many jurisdictions have processes for prisoners to use in challenging administrative disciplinary actions taken against them by corrections officials. For example, prisoners who are punished for rules violations after a disciplinary hearing typically must appeal within the corrections department before seeking to have a state judge review the case. The scope of judicial review normally is quite limited. The judge is only looking to see if the hearing board or hearing officer abused its discretion in finding that the prisoner violated institutional rules. The judge does not make an independent judgment about the prisoner's infraction and punishment.

thereby avoiding the disruption and expense of transporting corrections officials and prisoners to the federal courthouse.[28]

There are additional concerns that some prisoners misuse the litigation process simply to hassle corrections officials and judges.[29] The U.S. Supreme Court and other federal courts have barred several prisoners from filing any additional civil rights lawsuits without specific permission from a judge to do so. Typically, these prisoners have brought dozens of unsuccessful cases against corrections officials. Since the enactment of the Prison Litigation Reform Act of 1996, the new requirements concerning partial payment of court fees have created a new challenge for prisoners who previously could file cases for free. Although the intent of the act was to deter frivolous lawsuits, prisoners now may be reluctant to present legitimate claims because they do not want to deplete their limited financial resources when the results of litigation are so uncertain. Of course, free citizens often face the same dilemma when considering the expensive prospect of litigation if they have a dispute with a business, the government, or other individuals.

Grievances Outside of Court

Many prisons and corrections departments have grievance procedures that prisoners may use if they have complaints about corrections policies or actions by staff. These procedures often require an investigation and response by a corrections personnel supervisor followed by an opportunity to appeal to the warden or the state department of corrections. Some prisons have experimented with using inmates as mediators or decision makers in the grievance process. However, corrections officials generally do not want any prisoners in a position to make judgments about staff members. Such circumstances would undercut the authority of corrections officers, reduce staff morale, and possibly encourage certain kinds of misbehavior or disobedience. Typically, even if inmates are represented on a grievance committee, the primary decision-making power remains with the corrections institution, which maintains a majority of committee seats. Committee members may include an assistant warden, a prison counselor, or others not directly identified with the officers in the cellblocks against whom many grievances are likely to be filed.

Prison grievance procedures have their shortcomings. For one thing prisons are not required to have grievance procedures. Therefore state corrections departments and county jails may have freedom to decide if and how grievances will be handled unless legislative bodies (e.g., the state legislature or county council) enact statutes concerning grievances. More importantly, prison and jail grievance procedures often lack credibility in the eyes of inmates. Prisoners frequently do not believe that an institution's employees actually will respond to complaints against that institution. In the past, many prisoners did not bother with available grievance procedures, but simply filed section 1983 actions in federal courts. However, the Prison Litigation Reform Act imposed a new requirement in 1996. Now prisoners cannot file any actions concerning prison conditions under section 1983 or other federal laws until they have exhausted the available administrative remedies.[30]

Congress has encouraged prisons to develop grievance procedures. Under the **Civil Rights of Institutionalized Persons Act** (CRIPA), the U.S. attorney general and federal courts can certify grievance procedures as meeting certain requirements. These requirements include an advisory role for employees and inmates in the development of the grievance procedures, time limits for the institution to respond in writing to grievances, priority processing procedures for emergency grievances concerning risks of physical injury, safeguards to avoid reprisals against someone filing a grievance, and an independent review of grievances by someone not under the direct control of the institution.[31] If a state applied for and gained certification of its grievance procedures, then a judge could require prisoners to use the grievance procedures before they are permitted to file section 1983 civil rights lawsuits. And the Prison Litigation Reform Act of 1996 requires that prisoners exhaust available administrative remedies, including grievance procedures, even in corrections systems that do not have certification under CRIPA.

Various states have developed their own grievance mechanisms. Michigan, for example, has a state *ombudsman* for complaints concerning corrections. Based on a system used to investigate and solve disputes in Sweden, an ombudsman is an independent, neutral official who investigates complaints and who possesses the power to mediate or make recommendations for change. The Michigan ombudsman works under the state legislature, not the department of corrections. Thus, the grievance mechanism has greater independence and greater credibility in the eyes of prisoners than a prison grievance committee. The ombudsman provides reports and recommendations to the legislature concerning problems discovered in prisons as a result of complaints and investigations.

Although the Michigan ombudsman originally was obligated to respond to prisoners' complaints and inform prisoners about any decisions not to pursue investigations, the law was rewritten in 1995 to reduce inmates' ability to demand responses from the ombudsman. Under the statute's revised wording, the ombudsman now is required to respond to complaints received from *state legislators* concerning events and policies in prisons. This change effectively forces prisoners to persuade a state legislator to initiate a complaint in order to ensure that the ombudsman will respond. Although this change reduces the ombudsman's burden of dealing with complaints from a prison population that grew rapidly during the 1980s and early 1990s, it undoubtedly reduces the ombudsman's usefulness in the eyes of prisoners.

SUMMARY

- The famous case of *Gideon v. Wainwright* (1963) provides an example of a prisoner preparing and filing his own case, just as nearly all contemporary prisoner litigants must do for habeas corpus petitions, civil rights lawsuits, and appeals beyond the initial appeal of right—the three types of cases most commonly initiated by convicted offenders.

- Appeals involve the claim that specific errors in law and procedure occurred during the trial or plea bargain that produced the conviction.

- After all appeals have been unsuccessful, offenders may file habeas corpus petitions asserting that their constitutional rights were violated during the process leading to conviction. Habeas corpus cases enable state prisoners to have their convictions reviewed by federal judges.

- Prisoners can sue corrections officials for violating their constitutional rights by filing civil rights lawsuits under section 1983 of Title 42 in the United States Code.

- Litigation of civil rights claims is expensive in terms of money, time, and burdens placed on both courts and corrections personnel. Alternative mechanisms, such as the CRIPA procedures and corrections ombudsman, help to resolve prisoners' complaints. However, many prisoners continue to file lawsuits, in part because of concerns about the availability and credibility of alternative procedures.

Key Terms

Antiterrorism and Effective
Death Penalty Act
appellate brief
Coleman v. Thompson (1991)
Cooper v. Pate (1964)
Civil Rights of Institutionalized
Persons Act (CRIPA)

federalism
habeas corpus petition
harmless error
in forma pauperis petition
McCleskey v. Zant (1991)
objection

Prison Litigation Reform Act
of 1996
pro se litigators
Ross v. Moffitt (1974)
section 1983

Additional Readings

Howard, J. Woodford. 1981. *Courts of Appeals in the Federal Judicial System.* Princeton, NJ: Princeton University Press.
Lewis, Anthony. 1964. *Gideon's Trumpet.* New York: Vintage Books/Random House.

Yackle, Larry W. 1994. *Reclaiming the Federal Courts.* Cambridge, MA: Harvard University Press.

Notes

1. Anthony Lewis, *Gideon's Trumpet* (New York: Vintage Books/Random House, 1964), pp. 3–10, 57–78.
2. Gideon v. Wainwright, 372 U.S. 335 (1963).
3. Argersinger v. Hamlin, 407 U.S. 25 (1972).
4. Douglas v. California, 372 U.S. 353 (1963).
5. Ross v. Moffitt, 417 U.S. 600 (1974).
6. Kathleen Maguire and Ann L. Pastore, eds., *Sourcebook of Criminal Justice Statistics—1996* (Washington, DC: U.S. Department of Justice, Bureau of Justice Statistics, 1997), p. 471.
7. Preiser v. Rodriguez, 411 U.S. 475 (1973).
8. Stone v. Powell, 428 U.S. 465 (1976).
9. Teague v. Lane, 489 U.S. 288 (1989).
10. Arizona v. Roberson, 486 U.S. 675 (1988).
11. Butler v. McKellar, 494 U.S. 407 (1990).
12. McCleskey v. Zant, 499 U.S. 467 (1991).
13. Coleman v. Thompson, 501 U.S. 722 (1991).
14. Antiterrorism and Effective Death Penalty Act of 1996, Pub. L. No. 104-132, 110 Stat. 1217 (1996).
15. Herrera v. Collins, 113 S.Ct. at 874-875 (1993).
16. Maguire and Pastore, *Sourcebook* p. 517.
17. Cooper v. Pate, 378 U.S. 546 (1964).
18. City of Canton v. Harris, 489 U.S. 378 (1989).
19. Monell v. Department of Social Services, 436 U.S. 658 (1978).
20. Will v. Michigan Department of State Police, 491 U.S. 58 (1989).
21. Wisconsin Department of Corrections v. Schacht, 118 S.Ct. 2047 (1998).
22. Bivens v. Six Unknown Named Agents of the Federal Bureau of Narcotics, 403 U.S. 388 (1971).
23. Prison Litigation Reform Act, Pub. L. No. 104-134, section 801, 110 Stat. 1321 (1996).
24. 42 U.S.C. 3626.
25. "Long-Term Effect of Prisoner Litigation Reform Act Not Yet Clear," *The Third Branch* 29 (July 1997): 1, 5–6.
26. Daniels v. Williams, 474 U.S. 327 (1986).
27. John Scalia, *Prisoner Petitions in the Federal Courts, 1980–1996* (Washington, DC: U.S. Department of Justice, Bureau of Justice Statistics, October 1997), p. 6.

28. Christopher E. Smith, "United States Magistrates and the Processing of Prisoner Litigation," *Federal Probation* 52 (December 1988): 16–17.

29. Jeffrey H. Maahs and Rolando V. del Carmen, "Curtailing Frivolous Section 1983 Inmate Litigation: Laws, Practices, and Proposals," *Federal Probation* 59 (December 1995): 53–61.

30. 42 U.S.C. 1997e(a).

31. Michael Mushlin, *Rights of Prisoners*, Vol. 1, 2nd ed. (Colorado Springs, CO: Shepard's/McGraw-Hill, 1993), p. 344, n. 72.

CHAPTER THREE

Decision Making in Prisoners' Cases

Imagine you are a U.S. district judge. You are kept busy with a never-ending flow of cases, and you have important responsibilities at various stages of each case. Some responsibilities, such as meeting with lawyers in pretrial conferences to schedule each stage of the case, may not take much time. But other responsibilities, such as presiding over jury selection and trials in criminal cases, may take days or even weeks. As U.S. district judge, you are the only individual authorized to preside over trials in felony cases. Moreover, because of the legal rules about speedy trials, criminal cases cannot be unduly delayed while the judge handles other matters. Each trial has its own personality and drama, and many judges consider presiding over trials to be the most interesting and important component of their jobs. Furthermore, criminal trials leap to the front of the line ahead of other kinds of cases when the clock begins ticking down on defendants' speedy trial rights.

On top of these responsibilities, you face a steady flow of petitions from prisoners. Habeas corpus petitions and civil rights lawsuits by prisoners are not criminal proceedings and thus have no speedy-trial requirement. Moreover, these petitions and lawsuits are almost always defective in some fatal way that requires early dismissal, so they absorb time but seldom lead to any important or interesting results. If you enjoy presiding over trials and you are the only official in the courthouse authorized to oversee a long list of waiting trials, what can you do with these other cases? Can you treat all cases equally? Do you have the time and interest to devote the same attention to each and every case, whether it is a prisoner's petition or criminal trial? As you imagine the context in which U.S. district judges work, you can easily see why prisoners' cases often are delegated to other court personnel.

Because many federal courts receive a steady flow of new filings from prisoners, many have developed standardized procedures for handling such cases. Judges argue that because courts have limited time, money, and personnel, they need to find ways to make decisions efficiently. By contrast, critics raise concerns that prisoners' cases are a low priority for the federal courts. As a result, there is a risk that some courts may pay less attention to such cases and dismiss these cases too readily. In this chapter, we examine the prisoner litigation process, focusing first on decision making by the courts and then on an actual prisoner's case.

THE DECISION-MAKING PROCESS

Prisoner Litigation in the Federal Courts

Prisoners' habeas corpus petitions and civil rights lawsuits are filed in U.S. district courts. The initial filing in any civil lawsuit, including a prisoner's civil rights lawsuit, is called a **complaint.** District judges, however, do not make the actual decisions in many of these cases. These cases are delegated to others within the court who make recommendations to the judge about how each case should be decided.

In some courts, the cases go directly to *pro se* law clerks, typically young attorneys, often fresh out of law school, who gain experience working for the federal court. *Pro se* law clerks have one primary responsibility: They read and analyze petitions and complaints from people who are representing themselves in court.[1] Most of these filings come from prisoners, although other people represent themselves when they are too poor to hire an attorney (e.g., people filing claims for Social Security disability benefits or initiating civil rights lawsuits against government officials). The *pro se* clerk evaluates whether the petition or complaint meets all of the court's procedural requirements, whether the instructions on court forms were followed, and whether the filing raises a potentially valid issue about a federal constitutional right. In most cases, the clerk will conclude that the filing is missing one or more of these elements and thus will write a memo to the judge recommending dismissal. Normally, the judge will issue an order dismissing the case based on the recommendation of the *pro se* law clerk.

In district courts that do not have *pro se* law clerks, prisoners' cases typically either are handled by the judge's law clerk or are delegated to a U.S. magistrate judge. These law clerks are recent law school graduates who spend one or two years after graduation working as assistants to federal judges. Unlike the *pro se* clerks, the law clerks conduct legal research on all kinds of cases. They evaluate prisoners' petitions and complaints while also carrying out various other assignments for the judge. They make recommendations to the judge—usually for dismissal—and the judge issues an order.

U.S. magistrate judges hold a judicial office that was created in 1968 to provide more professional assistance for U.S. district judges. U.S. magistrate judges are lawyers who have at least five years of legal experience and who are appointed by district judges to serve for renewable eight-year terms (four-year terms for part-time magistrate judges). Under federal law, they possess the authority to handle virtually anything handled by a district judge except for felony criminal trials. For civil trials and some other hearings that can directly result in disposal of a case, the litigants must agree to have a magistrate judge preside over the case. For matters that result in a recommendation to a district judge, the judge can assign these tasks to magistrate judges whether the litigants want the case delegated or not. In many courts, magistrate judges become the experts on prisoner cases, Social Security cases, and any other matters that become "routine" by arriving in large numbers and raising the same kinds of issues over and over again.[2]

Magistrate judges also have law clerks working solely for them, to whom they may delegate prisoner petitions. These law clerks may further delegate cases to law students working as part-time interns. In some circumstances, inexperienced law students may be the only ones to read the actual petitions and complaints. Typically, the law student writes a memo recommending dismissal and passes it on to the magistrate judge's law clerk. The law clerk approves the memo and sends it along to the magistrate judge. The magistrate judge submits an official report and recommendation based on the memo to the district judge. As the memo and the report and recommendation move up the chain of command, there is a risk that it will receive a "rubber stamp" approval at each level if the magistrate judge and district judge do not carefully supervise and monitor the inexperienced law clerks and law students who work for them.

An additional concern about prisoners' cases involves the care and attention applied to determine whether a valid constitutional question is being raised. Because most prisoners must file petitions and lawsuits on their own, they are often very ineffective in identifying and presenting their claims. Federal courts are supposed to take extra care in examining filings from *pro se* litigants to make sure that a valid claim is not obscured by the amateurish legal presentation. However, observations of the decision-making process in some courthouses have raised questions about the mindset that law clerks and others bring to their analysis of prisoners' cases. Instead of beginning with the question "Is there a valid claim somewhere in this filing?" some law clerks begin by asking, "How can I dismiss this case?"[3] This is the result not of a conspiracy against prisoners and their cases, but of law clerks' experience that most prisoner filings do not fulfill necessary requirements. Therefore, they develop the attitude that such cases should be disposed of as quickly as possible so that more interesting and important work on other cases may be undertaken. This attitude and approach may have no impact on the majority of cases that are destined for dismissal because of clear deficiencies. However, in a borderline case where a genuine issue may be hidden in the prisoner's awkward wording, the orientation toward quick dismissals may mean that the issue is overlooked.

It is also possible that beginning law clerks will give prisoners the benefit of the doubt for fear of mistakenly rejecting a valid claim. After a while, however, the law clerks will gain a better sense of what constitutes a legitimate claim and, perhaps just as importantly, their supervising judges' interest in and attention to prisoners' petitions. Law clerks may begin their careers by leaning in favor of permitting prisoners' petitions to move on to the next stage of the process. Eventually, however, their actions likely will be shaped strongly by the guidance and example provided by supervising judicial officers, as well as by caseload pressures, which often place prisoners' repetitive petitions at the lower end of the court's priority list in a resource-scarce environment in which all cases cannot receive the same careful attention.

There is a risk that busy officials in federal courthouses will have even less time to devote to prisoners' petitions in the future because the number of such petitions is expected to rise steadily in conjunction with increases in prison populations. A forecasting study by the National Center for State Courts did three different projections for prison growth and its effect on prisoner litigation. The study predicted increases of 93 to 98 percent in the number of habeas corpus petitions filed in the federal district courts by the year 2007, and increases of 56 to 108 percent in section 1983 lawsuits.[4] However, there is no reason to expect that the size or resources of the federal judiciary will grow at the same pace to handle this increase in prisoners' petitions.

Most habeas corpus petitions and section 1983 complaints are dismissed quickly because they do not fulfill the necessary requirements for moving forward. They usually have failed to follow some procedural rule or failed to properly raise a federal constitutional issue. When an indigent prisoner files a petition, extra care may be taken to ensure that groundless claims do not move forward in the litigation process in order to spare U.S. marshals the time and expense involved in delivering court papers (called "service of process") to all parties on behalf of the penniless prisoner. Litigants who can afford to pay court costs are required to pay for service of process, but litigation by indigent prisoners imposes these and other costs upon the court system.

Petitions and complaints that survive initial examination at the district court are delivered to (or, in legal terms, "served upon") the government officials being challenged. The government response is called the **answer**. This is usually filed by lawyers in the state attorney general's office, city or county attorney's office, or private law firms hired to represent local governments. Additional dismissals often occur when law clerks or magistrate judges have the opportunity to see the government's response, which often points out errors or deficiencies in the prisoners' claims.

Habeas corpus petitions that survive initial dismissal move to a hearing stage. At the hearing, the prisoner—who now may be represented by a court-appointed attorney—typically will square off against a lawyer from the state attorney general's office. Local prosecutors usually do not have the time or resources to handle legal proceedings beyond the initial appeal. Thus, attorneys for the state frequently take over. Depending on the issues involved, some habeas corpus hearings resemble a second trial, albeit without a jury, as the original trial is reconstructed to see if a constitutional rights violation, such as ineffective assistance of counsel, occurred. Ultimately, the decision about whether to grant the writ of habeas corpus—in effect, an order that the detention is improper—is made by judges. Generally, a prisoner who succeeds in a habeas corpus case is entitled to a new trial, unless the prosecution decides not to prosecute the case again.

Civil rights lawsuits that survive early dismissal enter the same kinds of court processes as other civil lawsuits. The two sides engage in **discovery,** the process through which they gather evidence from each other. Each side may ask to take **depositions** from the opposing party and from key witnesses. Depositions are sworn testimony given outside of court in response to questioning by both side's lawyers and recorded by a court reporter. Such testimony helps each side develop its case and may be used to check the consistency of testimony later presented by the same people at any hearings or trials. Each side may ask the other side to respond to **interrogatories,** which are requests for written responses to questions. In addition, each side may request that the other side provide copies of relevant documents. In prisoner cases, it is most often the prisoner who requests documents from corrections officials rather than the other way around.

The district judge usually will order each side to meet with the judge or with a magistrate judge to discuss the schedule for discovery, hearings, and trial. In addition, they may be required to meet in pretrial conferences to discuss settlement possibilities. Many federal judges and magistrate judges work hard to encourage opponents in civil lawsuits to reach voluntary, negotiated agreements. Sometimes, corrections officials will resolve cases to change questionable policies and practices or to pay a sum of money to the prisoner for the harm caused by a rights violation. However, unlike in other civil cases, there is often great reluctance to settle prisoners' cases, in particular because of a fear that settlements will simply encourage other prisoners to dream up reasons to file civil rights lawsuits. Many federal courts have rules that require civil cases to pass through alternative dispute resolution (ADR) procedures, such as mediation or arbitration, before they are permitted to go to trial. In such proceedings, outside attorneys are selected to listen to each side's case and then to suggest approaches to settlement or to provide advisory opinions about how the case is likely to turn out if it goes to trial. Ultimately, some cases will move all the way through the civil litigation process to reach the trial stage, in which a jury will make findings about whether corrections officials are liable for committing rights violations.

A Picture of Habeas Corpus Cases

A study published by the National Center for State Courts in 1995 provides a picture of habeas corpus cases—the issues presented and the results in the courts.[5] The study was conducted by examining habeas corpus petitions in eighteen federal district courts that together handle about half of the petitions in the nation.

Most prisoners who file habeas corpus petitions were convicted of violent crimes and given severe sentences. For example, 23 percent of habeas corpus petitioners have been convicted of murder while less than 11 percent of all prisoners have been convicted of that offense.[6] Most habeas corpus petitions are from prisoners serving long sentences because of the long time period required to enter the habeas corpus process. Remember that prisoners must first take their cases through the entire appeals process before they can file a habeas corpus petition. Because the appeals process can move slowly, nearly five years typically elapses between the date of a conviction and the date when a habeas corpus petition is filed. Thus, prisoners serving short sentences may be released or approaching their release date before they would even be eligible to file a habeas petition.[7]

In creating new rules to change habeas corpus procedures, the Supreme Court and Congress focused on their desire to speed up death penalty cases. In fact, however, death penalty cases account for only 1 percent of habeas corpus petitions. This raises questions about whether the Supreme Court justices and members of Congress understand the actual operation of the habeas corpus process.

Table 3-1 lists the types of issues raised in habeas corpus petitions. As the table shows, prisoners were most dissatisfied with the performance of their defense attorneys. Such claims are based on an assertion that an attorney's performance was so poor as to effectively prevent the defendant from receiving the benefit of the Sixth Amendment right to counsel. These claims may come from prisoners who were dissatisfied with their attorneys' performances, but were unable to identify specific rights that were violated during their trials or plea negotiations. Thus, general unhappiness with the court process, the attorney, or the fact of incarceration may result in claims about the attorney's ineffectiveness. Ninety-three percent of habeas petitioners prepare their own petitions and, again, many are not skilled in identifying and presenting appropriate constitutional claims.

Alternatively, the alleged problems of ineffective assistance of counsel may stem from the uneven quality of defense representation in courts throughout the country. Some counties have experienced, dedicated, full-time public defenders to defend criminal defendants. Other counties appoint private attorneys on a case-by-case basis to handle such cases, even though these attorneys may be very inexperienced and have little interest in criminal law. Despite the recognized problems in the representation of poor criminal defendants, it is very difficult to prove a claim of ineffective assistance of counsel under the Supreme Court's established rules for such cases.[8]

TABLE 3-1	Types of Issues Raised in Habeas Corpus Petitions, 1992
Ineffective assistance of counsel	25%
Trial court errors	15
14th Amendment	14
5th Amendment	12
6th Amendment	7
8th Amendment	7
Prosecutorial misconduct	6
4th Amendment	5
Other	9

Source: Roger A. Hanson and Henry W. K. Daley, *Federal Habeas Corpus Review: Challenging State Court Convictions* (Washington, DC: U.S. Department of Justice, Bureau of Justice Statistics, 1995), p. 14.

The study found that 63 percent of the petitions were dismissed by the courts without an examination of the petitioners' claims. This usually means that the prisoner violated a procedural rule, such as filing the petition before completing the entire appeals process. Another 35 percent were dismissed after the courts examined the prisoners' claims and found that no rights violation existed to justify a new trial. Some of these dismissals also were based on procedural problems discovered in the examination of the issues raised. A mere 1 percent of petitions were granted by the court, which presumably set the stage for a new trial or for dismissal of charges by the prosecutor. Another 1 percent of petitions were remanded, or sent back, to the state courts for reconsideration of some issue. Table 3-2 shows the reasons for the dismissal of habeas corpus issues.

When federal district courts received the habeas corpus petitions, there were wide variations in the length of time it took to render a decision. The median case processing time was about six months. Ten percent of the cases were decided in less than one month, but another 10 percent took more than two years.[9]

A Picture of Prisoners' Section 1983 Civil Rights Lawsuits

The National Center for State Courts also produced a study of prisoners' civil rights lawsuits in 1995. The study examined cases in nine states that accounted for nearly half of all civil rights lawsuits filed by prisoners. Most of the lawsuits

TABLE 3-2   **Reasons for Dismissal of Habeas Corpus Petitions, 1992**

Failure to exhaust state remedies (e.g., complete the entire state appeals process)	57%
Procedural default (e.g., forfeit claim for violating a state procedural rule)	12
Failure to meet court deadlines or court rules	7
Failure to present recognizable constitutional issues	6
Government's motion to dismiss granted	5
Prisoner no longer in custody	3
Improperly filed more than one petition	3
Other	5

Source: Roger A. Hanson and Henry W. K. Daley, *Federal Habeas Corpus Review: Challenging State Court Convictions* (Washington, DC: U.S. Department of Justice, Bureau of Justice Statistics, 1995), p. 17.

were filed by state prison inmates (62 percent) and jail inmates (36 percent), with only a small percentage filed by individuals on parole or other forms of correctional release (2 percent). The lawsuits were filed most often against corrections officers (26 percent) or wardens and jail administrators (22 percent). Corrections medical staff also were regularly named as defendants (9 percent).[10] Table 3-3 shows the frequency of various kinds of claims raised in prisoners' civil rights lawsuits.

Physical security issues and medical treatment issues, which were the two most frequent claims, are considered part of convicted offenders' Eighth Amendment right to be free from cruel and unusual punishments. Incarcerated offenders' claims concerning physical conditions and living conditions also involve issues of cruel and unusual punishment. By contrast, unconvicted pretrial detainees in jails who are awaiting trials, dismissal of charges, or plea negotiations are not covered by the Eighth Amendment because they are not yet being "punished." Instead, their constitutional protections are based on their right to due process under the Fourteenth Amendment for state and local detainees and under the Fifth Amendment for federal detainees. Issues based on other specific rights were raised less frequently, although prisoners regularly presented claims concerning the right to due process, especially in disciplinary matters. The percentage of section 1983 complaints that mistakenly presented habeas corpus challenges to a conviction were the predictable result of many prisoners' limited understanding of legal matters when they try to prepare cases for themselves.[11]

Only 3 percent of prisoners' civil rights lawsuits reached the stage of pretrial hearings on evidence and only 2 percent ultimately resulted in a trial ver-

TABLE 3-3	Issues in Section 1983 Lawsuits, 1992

Physical security (e.g., attacked by other prisoners or by corrections officers)	21%
Medical treatment	17
Due process (e.g., transfered to disciplinary cell without proper procedures)	13
Challenges to conviction (e.g., prisoners mistakenly raised habeas corpus issues in section 1983 action)	12
Physical conditions in prison	9
Access to courts, lawyers, and communication with others	7
Living conditions (e.g., denied access to recreation)	4
Religious expression	4
Assault by arresting officer	3
Other	11

Source: Roger A. Hanson and Henry W. K. Daley, *Challenging the Conditions of Prisons and Jails* (Washington, DC: U.S. Department of Justice, Bureau of Justice Statistics, 1995), p. 17.

dict. Prisoners won less than half of the cases that went to trial. Seventy-four percent were dismissed by the court based on the prisoner's complaint. Another 20 percent were dismissed after the government responded to the complaint and requested dismissal. A small percentage (4 percent) were dismissed with the agreement of the prisoner, perhaps in cases where settlement negotiations resolved the case.[12]

The average processing time for various types of claims ranged from sixteen months for challenges to physical conditions to two years for assault claims against an arresting officer. Table 3-4 gives the reasons for court dismissals of prisoners' civil rights lawsuits. As the table shows, most dismissals were based on prisoners' failure to follow court rules and inability to present proper constitutional issues. This is not surprising given that, as noted previously, 96 percent of prisoners who file civil rights actions prepare and present their own cases.[13]

In picturing the nature of prisoner litigation, bear in mind that decision making in prisoners' cases may not happen very quickly. Prisoners often wait many months before eventually being notified that their case has been dismissed. In 1995, the average habeas corpus petition took nearly ten months (297 days) from filing to termination and the average case processing time for civil rights cases was nine months (276 days), although half of the cases were terminated in five months (161 days).[14]

Now that you have considered what kinds of issues are raised in prisoners' cases and how the cases are decided by the courts, let us examine an actual case.

TABLE 3-4 — Reasons for Dismissal of Section 1983 Lawsuits, 1992

Prisoner failed to follow court rules in filing case	38%
No evidence exists of constitutional rights violation	19
Issue is frivolous (e.g., has no arguable basis for the claim in law or fact)	19
Issue presented is not covered by section 1983 (e.g., mistakenly raises habeas corpus issues about the basis for the conviction)	7
Defendant is a judge or prosecutor and therefore is protected by law against lawsuits	4
Defendant does not work for the state	3
Other	9

Source: Roger A. Hanson and Henry W. K. Daley, *Challenging the Conditions of Prisons and Jails* (Washington, DC: U.S. Department of Justice, Bureau of Justice Statistics, 1995), p. 20.

CORRECTIONS LAW IN ACTION

Prisoners face challenges in identifying complaints that will be accepted by a court. Because they may lack other avenues for pursuing complaints, prisoners often translate all of their grievances, large or small, into legal actions. Without the assistance of lawyers, however, they may be unable to recognize what kinds of claims involve genuine legal issues. And when the claims are presented, court officials may struggle in attempting to determine whether the claims involve valid legal issues. Thus, even if prisoners' complaints actually raise genuine issues, the issues may be presented so ineffectively that courts will dismiss these cases. As you read the complaint in Box 3-1, which was actually filed by a prisoner, consider the following questions: Is the prisoner raising issues concerning actual constitutional rights? If so, is the prisoner presenting these issues effectively enough to persuade a busy judge and his or her staff that judicial action is needed? If the prisoner has not presented proper legal issues, is he presenting legitimate grievances that would justifiably upset anyone who had these experiences? Thus, is the basic problem simply that the prisoner has no avenue other than the courts for presenting his grievances? Could these same complaints be presented more effectively by a lawyer? If you were this prisoner, would you do anything differently to increase your chances of winning the case?

In the federal courts, prisoners' cases often are assigned to U.S. magistrate judges who make recommendations to their supervising U.S. district judges.

| **B O X   3 - 1** | **Actual Prisoner's Claim in a Civil Rights Lawsuit** |

[The actual claim was handwritten. The following excerpt contains the exact words of the complaint, except that the names, dates, and places have been replaced with fictitious substitutes.]

IV. STATEMENT OF CLAIM

STATE HERE, AS BRIEFLY AS POSSIBLE, THE FACTS OF YOUR CASE. DESCRIBE HOW EACH DEFENDANT IS INVOLVED. INCLUDE ALSO, THE NAMES OF OTHER PERSONS INVOLVED, DATES, AND PLACES. DO NOT GIVE ANY LEGAL ARGUMENTS OR CITE ANY CASES OR STATUTES. IF YOU INTEND TO ALLEGE A NUMBER OF RELATED CLAIMS, NUMBER AND SET FORTH EACH CLAIM IN A SEPARATE PARAGRAPH. USE AS MUCH SPACE AS YOU NEED. ATTACH EXTRA SHEETS IF NECESSARY.

I was confined on or about March 14, 1996 at the Johnson County Jail. During the intake process I was asked about my medical history, which I stated that since childhood I suffer from Asthma and chronic eczema. Additionally, I have severe allergic reactions to eggs and foods containing eggs; detergent and lipid based soaps and allergic reactions to wool and cotton. These conditions medically have been previously documented throughout my life as well as during previous years confined here at the Johnson County Jail.

I submitted a myriad of kites [written notes] to Nurse Francis about continual problems I was having in the above areas. Nurse Francis usually responded within 24–48 hours. He did provide me with some medication until I ran out of money and I began to have great difficulty getting mediation after my inmate [account] ran into deficit. I became very frustrated and had to have my wife, Mrs. Susan Green provide me with medical supplies for asthma and cremes for rash. Mrs. Green suffers from chronic sickle cell anemia and her illness suffered greatly. The problems began when I entered the county [jail] on March 14, 1996, and these problems escalated throughout May

and June 1996. My rash got so bad all over my body that I am scarred and itchy all the time. My wife's condition worsened and I lost earned good time because I became so stressed out and I had to take pain medication for my rashes and also for another medical condition every single day. My body is so scarred and my family life was adversely affected because of the Johnson County Jail's medical practices.

This pattern of making it difficult for me continued during the period commencing March 14, 1996 through the present date of 18 July 1996.

As to myself, Daniel Green I see so many black and brown spots on my arms and my legs, these marks weren't on my body before I came to jail. I also have marks on my stomach. Additionally because I was in severe itchy pain constantly I felt depressed and very angry.

My beloved wife, Susan Green had to travel over an hour from our residence in Akron, Ohio. My wife (Susan) has to have blood transfusions, frequent doctor appointments and often becomes weak because of her condition. However, Johnson County Jail, under the administration of Sheriff Abraham Hutchinson by omission of his responsibility allowed the medical department of the jail to delay and at times deny appropriate medical treatment for my condition. Their behavior (Johnson County Jail, Nurse Francis, and Sheriff Hutchinson) also indirectly caused my wife's condition to aggravate and caused much stress to my wife and family's life.

Mr. Francis seemed to be unconcerned about my medical condition when my account balance became low, often remarking about the high cost(s) of medicines and the like. I wrote grievances, and lost my good time because I was so upset, my skin severely scarred, and I also worried constantly about my wife who drove long distances to provide me with medical supplies that the Johnson County Jail denied or simply delayed.

(continued)

Finally, as to my (Daniel Green's) allergies: I am allergic to eggs and foods containing eggs or egg bi-products. From the period beginning March 14, 1996, it took almost two (2) months for the medical department and the jail to approve a "special" diet. Although I attempted to avoid foods which I was allergic to, i.e., cookies, puddings, etc., I often encountered foods that caused swelling around my eyes and severe rashes. Finally, a staff member upon seeing me states, "oh, you really are allergic to somethings." I also was still issued wool and cotton sheets and blankets and itches and skin rashes continued.

Also at end of June I was requested a tooth to be pulled. The medical department finally approved it and a van pulled up and a dentist filled my tooth. I asked him if he was going to x-ray my mouth and he said it wasn't necessary. So without x-rays he filled my tooth and when he was filling it I went through great pain. The tooth continued to hurt as of this writing (7/18/96) and every four hours I have to have some kind of pain medication. Often my request(s) are ignored. I have notified the medical department (Mr. Francis) who is nurse, he responds to my requests, at the average of 48 hours. This is a summary of our claims of medical abuse, cruel and unusual punishment, and Johnson County Jail, et al grossly and adversely and unnecessarily aggravating both (Susan/Daniel's) medical conditions.

V. RELIEF

STATE BRIEFLY, EXACTLY WHAT YOU WANT THE COURT TO DO FOR YOU. MAKE NO LEGAL ARGUMENTS. CITE NO CASES OR STATUTES.

I, Daniel Green and Susan Green bring this action for several purposes and relief. We want to insure that other inmates and their families won't suffer the same unnecessary cruelty and inhumane treatment. The unprofessionalism which the Johnson County Jail and its medical department was capricious, mean spirited, and arbitrary. I, Daniel Green will have to receive treatment for my severely scarred body and I want to be able to afford that treatment and I really need and want counselling because this treatment has left me and my wife hostile feelings toward Johnson County Jail and white people in general. I also want my wife to be able to be treated for the stress she's suffered because the defendants' attitudes and behavior also caused great suffering to her. We ask the Honorable Court to award financial resources in the amount of $250,000 for medical costs and $250,000 for pain and suffering. The total relief we are seeking $500,000.00 (FIVE HUNDRED THOUSAND DOLLARS.) Thank you.

7/18/96   [signed] Daniel Green
7/20/96   [signed] Susan Green

The U.S. district judge seldom reads such cases, but rather relies on the magistrate judges' report and recommendations in making a decision. Read the actual report and recommendation for this case presented in Box 3-2. Do not worry if you don't understand all of the cases and issues being discussed. You will learn about the details of prisoners' rights, including the right to medical treatment, in later chapters. The purpose of this material is to give you a realistic idea of how cases are actually decided. As you read, consider the following questions: Did the magistrate judge accurately describe Green's claims? Did the magistrate judge give adequate consideration to the prisoner's complaint? If you were the magistrate judge, would you have made a different decision? What is a "frivolous" lawsuit?

Note the consequences of the prisoner's legal claim. Not only was the claim rejected by the magistrate judge for failing to present a valid constitutional

| BOX 3-2 | **Actual Report and Recommendation of the U.S. Magistrate Judge** |

[The names, places, dates, court, and case number have been replaced with fictitious substitutes.]

UNITED STATES DISTRICT COURT
EASTERN DISTRICT OF OHIO
SOUTHERN DIVISION

DANIEL GREEN,
SUSAN GREEN,
     Plaintiffs,

v.   Hon. C. Stewart August

JOHNSON COUNTY JAIL,   Case No. 2: 96 CV 171
JOHNSON COUNTY JAIL MEDICAL
DEPARTMENT, ABRAHAM HUTCHINSON,
and EDGAR FRANCIS,
     Defendants.

MAGISTRATE JUDGE'S REPORT AND RECOMMENDATION

Plaintiffs, Daniel and Susan Green, filed *pro se* this action under 42 U.S.C. [section] 1983 on July 27, 1996. They allege that defendants violated their federal constitutional rights in the provision of bedding, food, and prescription medicines to Daniel Green while he is incarcerated at the Johnson County Jail. 28 U.S.C. [section] 1915A permits the dismissal of an *in forma pauperis* complaint if the Court finds that the action is frivolous or otherwise fails to state a claim upon which relief can be granted. I respectfully recommend that the complaint in this action should be dismissed for failure to state a claim upon which relief can be granted.

Plaintiff Daniel Green is an inmate presently incarcerated in the Johnson County Jail. Also named as a plaintiff is Susan Green, Daniel Green's wife. Named as defendants are the Johnson County Jail/Johnson County Jail Medical Department; Abraham Hutchinson, Sheriff of Johnson County; and Edgar Francis, a nurse at the Johnson County Jail. Daniel Green alleges he was confined at the Johnson County Jail on or around March 14, 1996. He alleges that during the intake process, he related that he suffers from asthma and chronic eczema,

and that he experiences severe allergic reactions to detergents and lipid-based soaps, wool and cotton, and eggs and food containing eggs. He alleges that Francis provided him with medications until he ran out of money. Plaintiff Daniel Green alleges that after he ran out of money, his wife had to provide him with medical supplies. He alleges that his rash got so bad that he itches all the time and he has sustained scarring. Plaintiff Daniel Green alleges that his wife suffers from chronic sickle cell anemia and that her illness has suffered greatly as the result of having to travel to the Johnson County Jail to deliver his medications.

Daniel Green also alleges that it took almost two months for the Medical Department at the Jail to provide him with a special diet. He also alleges that he was issued wool and cotton sheets and blankets which caused his skin to itch and develop rashes. Plaintiff Daniel Green also alleges that at the end of June, he requested that a tooth be pulled. He alleges that instead of pulling the tooth, a dentist filled the tooth without taking x-rays. Plaintiff alleges that the Johnson County Jail and its Medical Department is capricious, mean-spirited, and arbitrary. For relief, plaintiffs request $500,000 in damages.

(continued)

Plaintiffs' complaint should be dismissed for failure to state a claim upon which relief can be granted for various reasons. First, the Johnson County Jail owed no constitutional obligation to Susan Green in the provision of medical services to her husband. Because the government has incarcerated prisoners, the government has the affirmative obligation to provide the constitutionally minimum amount of medication treatment. *Estelle v. Gamble,* 429 U.S. 97, 104-05 (1976). Such a conclusion is predicated upon the very fact that once incarcerated, prisoners have been deprived of the freedom to seek medical treatment on their own. Accordingly, the prisoner and the state government have a special relationship, which mandates that the government has the affirmative obligation to provide the constitutionally required minimum amount of treatment. However, Susan Green has not been incarcerated by Johnson County. Hence, she does not stand in a special relationship vis-a-vis defendants in which defendants owed any duty to provide her with any kind of medical attention. See *DeShaney v. Winnebago Co. Dept. of Soc. Serv's.,* 489 U.S. 189, 200 (1989); *Hiser v. City of Bowling Green,* 42 F.3d 382, 384 (6th Cir. 1994), *cert. denied,* 115 S. Ct. 1984 (1995). Because defendants did not stand in any relationship with Susan Green, I respectfully recommend that her complaint fails to state a claim upon which relief can be granted, and should be dismissed in total.

I also recommend that plaintiffs fail to state a claim upon which relief can be granted against Sheriff Hutchinson and Johnson County Jail. Plaintiffs do not allege any actions on the part of Hutchinson which somehow caused the alleged constitutional violations. It is a well established principle of [section] 1983 jurisprudence that liability will not be premised upon a *respondeat superior* [i.e., let the master answer for the servant's actions] theory of liability. *Rizzo v. Goode,* 423 U.S. 362, 375-76 (1976). The mere fact that Hutchinson occupies a position of authority, or that he may have been aware of illegal conduct by subordinates after the fact does not justify the imposition of

[section] 1983 liability. *Poe v. Haydon,* 853 F.2d 418, 429 (6th Cir.), *cert. denied,* 488 U.S. 1007 (1989); *Weaver v. Toombs,* 756 F. Supp. 335, 337 (W.D. Mich. 1989), *aff'd,* 915 F.2d 1574 (6th Cir. 1990). Plaintiffs have not alleged any type of affirmative link between the alleged constitutional violations and any actions by Hutchinson which could have caused that violation. *Rizzo v. Goode,* 423 U.S. at 371. Accordingly, I respectfully recommend that plaintiffs are attempting to hold Hutchinson liable pursuant to [section] 1983 solely on the basis of the position which Hutchinson occupies. I likewise recommend that plaintiffs' claim, asserted against Johnson County Jail, fails to state a claim upon which relief can be granted. A local governmental entity cannot be held liable solely because it employs a tortfeasor [i.e., a wrongdoer who commits a civil harm, such as injuring someone or violating someone's rights]. *Monell v. Department of Social Serv's.,* 436 U.S. 658, 691 (1978); *Johnson v. Hardin County,* 908 F.2d 1280, 1285 (6th Cir. 1990). Instead, a county or municipality can be held liable under [section] 1983 only when it *caused* the alleged constitutional violation either from an unconstitutional policy or custom, or the unconstitutional acts were taken by a "policy maker" whose acts or edicts may fairly be said to represent official policy. *City of St. Louis v. Praprotnik,* 485 U.S. 112 (1988); *Pembaur v. Cincinnati,* 475 U.S. 469 (1986); *Leach v. Shelby Co. Sheriff,* 891 F.2d 1241, 1244 (6th Cir. 1989), *cert. denied,* 495 U.S. 932 (1990). Plaintiffs have not pled that Johnson County should be held liable on the basis of an unconstitutional custom or policy, or that any of the individually named defendants are policy makers whose acts or edicts can be said to represent official County policy. Plaintiffs are held to a higher pleading standard in order to proceed upon a claim such as is asserted in this case. Plaintiffs must allege sufficient facts to establish the probable existence of the policy of which they claim. *Bartalone v. County of Berrien,* 643 F. Supp. 574, 579 (W.D. Mich. 1986); see also, *Simmons v. Chemung County Dept. of Social Serv's.,* 770 F.Supp. 795, 802

(W.D. N.Y.), *aff'd*, 948 F.2d 1276 (2d Cir. 1991); *Taylor v. Castenada,* 740 F.Supp. 542, 546 (N.D. Ill. 1990). In light of the absence of any type of specificity in plaintiffs' allegations, I respectfully recommend that plaintiffs have failed to state a claim upon which relief can be granted against either Johnson County Jail or Sheriff Abraham Hutchinson.

I further recommend that plaintiff Daniel Green's claim, premised upon failure to provide medical treatment, fails to state a claim upon which relief can be granted. He clearly alleges that Francis provided him with medications. Indeed, plaintiff's Inmate Trust Account transaction sheet, attached to his complaint, indicates that from March 15 through July 17, 1996, plaintiff was able to withdraw from his prison account thirteen times in order to pay for prescriptions or office visits. It appears that plaintiff's primary complaint is premised upon the fact that occasionally his wife had to bring him prescription medications. Every Eighth Amendment cruel and unusual punishment claim involves an objective and a subjective component. *Hudson v. McMillian,* 503 U.S. 1, 8 (1992). The objective component of a cruel and unusual punishment claim involving medical treatment is established by showing that the medical need is serious. *Id.* at 9; *Estelle v. Gamble,* 429 U.S. at 103-04. Plaintiff has failed to specify what specific medical need he has that would rise to the level of a serious medical need to which defendants could be indifferent. Even if he had so specified a serious medical need, I would respectfully recommend that plaintiff is not proceeding on a claim upon which relief could be granted. It is clear that he has been provided treatment, and that his dispute is over the adequacy of that treatment. He has received numerous office visits for his medical problems. He has been provided with numerous medications, as evidenced from the withdrawals from his prison trust account. The mere fact that plaintiff had to pay for some of the prescription medications does not state an Eighth Amendment cause of action. *Johnson v. Department of Pub. Safety & Corr. Serv's.,* 885 F.Supp. 817, 820 (D. Md. 1995); *Martin v. DeBruyn,* 880 F.Supp. 610, 615 (N.D. Ind. 1995). "The Eighth

Amendment guarantees only that states will not ignore an inmate's serious medical needs; it does not guarantee free medical care." *Martin v. DeBruyn,*880 F.Supp. at 615. Plaintiff Daniel Green requested treatment for his tooth, and the tooth was filled instead of pulled. "Where a prisoner has received some medical attention and the dispute is over the adequacy of the treatment, federal courts are generally reluctant to second-guess medical judgments and to constitutionalize claims which sound in state tort law." *Westlake v. Lucas,* 537 F.2d 857, 860-61, n.5 (6th Cir. 1976). I respectfully recommend that plaintiff Daniel Green has received medical treatment, and his dispute is over the adequacy of that treatment and the fact that his wife brought some of his prescriptions to him. This does not state an Eighth Amendment cause of action.

Finally, plaintiff complains of the food he received and the sheets and blankets he was provided at the jail. He alleges that because of his severe allergies, he should not have been provided some of his food or the sheets and blankets. Under the Eighth Amendment to the United States Constitution, the Johnson County Jail had the obligation to provide plaintiff Daniel Green with a diet sufficient to keep him in good health. *Cunningham v. Jones,* 667 F.2d 565, 566 (6th Cir. 1982). Plaintiff does not make any allegation that the food he was provided, absent items to which he was allergic, failed to provide him with adequate nourishment in a constitutional sense. Likewise, there is no indication that if plaintiff did not use the cotton or woolen bedding that he was subjected to a condition of confinement which deprived him of "the minimal civilized measure of life's necessities" thereby rising to the level of the objective component necessary to proceed on a cruel and unusual punishment cause of action. *Wilson v. Seiter,* 501 U.S. 294, 298 (1991). Indeed, routine discomfort in a prison is "part of the penalty that criminal offenders pay for their offenses against society." *Rhodes v. Chapman,* 452 U.S. 337, 347 (1981). In light of the foregoing, I respectfully recommend that plaintiffs' attempt to proceed against the Johnson

(continued)

County Jail, Sheriff Abraham Hutchinson, and Edgar Francis on a claim for which the law does not provide a remedy. I respectfully recommend that plaintiffs' complaint be dismissed pursuant to 28 U.S.C. [section] 1915A.

Finally, it should be noted that Congress has recently amended 28 U.S.C. [section] 1915. Under the Prison Litigation Reform Act, Pub. L. No. 104-134, 110 Stat. 1321 [section] 804, a prisoner will be barred from filing suit if, during his period of incarceration, he has filed a total of three or more suits that have been dismissed on the grounds that they were frivolous, malicious, or failed to state a claim upon which relief could be granted. There is one exception to this statute. An inmate will still be allowed to file suit if he is under imminent danger of serious physical injury. *Id.* In the instant case,

assuming this Report and Recommendation is adopted, plaintiff Daniel Green will have filed a frivolous lawsuit. As a result, if he files two more suits that are adjudged to be frivolous, malicious, or fail to state a claim upon which relief can be granted, plaintiff Daniel Green will be unable to initiate any further litigation, absent a finding that he is under imminent danger of serious physical injury.

OBJECTIONS to this Report and Recommendation must be filed with the Clerk of Court within ten (10) days of the date of service of this notice. 28 U.S.C. [section] 636(b)(1)(C). Failure to file objections within the specified time waives the right to appeal the District Court's order. *Thomas v. Arn,* 474 U.S. 140 (1985); *United States v. Walters,* 638 F.2d 947 (6th Cir. 1981).

Respectfully submitted,

DATED: August 15, 1996

[signed]   Mary J. Graham
HON. MARY J. GRAHAM
UNITED STATES MAGISTRATE JUDGE

issue, but the plaintiff also used up one of his three opportunities to file prisoners' rights lawsuits *in forma pauperis.* As noted by the U.S. magistrate judge, the Prison Litigation Reform Act does not permit additional filings *in forma pauperis* if three or more prior filings were dismissed as "frivolous, malicious, or fails to state a claim upon which relief can be granted."[15] After three such dismissals, a prisoner would have to pay the costs of any future litigation unless the prisoner claimed to be "under imminent danger of serious physical injury."[16] In addition, the procedures used for reports and recommendations give the prisoner only ten days to file objections to the magistrate judge's conclusion. If the prisoner does not file objections within that brief time span and the district judge ultimately accepts the magistrate judge's recommendations, then the case is dismissed. The failure to file objections effectively bars the plaintiff from pursuing the case further in the court of appeals. Box 3-3 provides the district judge's actual order in the case.

As you can see, the district judge's order is short and to the point. There is no indication that the judge had to do anything more than read and endorse the U.S. magistrate judge's report and recommendation. The U.S. district judge is the official decision maker whose order officially terminates this case. However, the research into and analysis of the prisoner's claim clearly was under-

| BOX 3-3 | **Actual District Court Order** |

[The names, places, dates, court, and case number have been replaced with fictitious substitutes.]

UNITED STATES DISTRICT COURT
EASTERN DISTRICT OF OHIO
SOUTHERN DIVISION

DANIEL GREEN,
SUSAN GREEN,
     Plaintiffs,

v.   Hon. C. Stewart August

JOHNSON COUNTY JAIL,   Case No. 2: 96 CV 171
JOHNSON COUNTY JAIL MEDICAL
DEPARTMENT, ABRAHAM HUTCHINSON,
and EDGAR FRANCIS,
     Defendants.

**ORDER APPROVING MAGISTRATE'S
REPORT AND RECOMMENDATION AND
DISMISSING PLAINTIFF'S COMPLAINT**

The Court has reviewed the Report and Recommendation filed by the United States Magistrate in this action. The Report and Recommendation was duly served on the parties. No objections have been filed. The Court finds the Report and Recommendation to be well-reasoned and in accord with applicable law.

DATED: September 15, 1996

Therefore, IT IS HEREBY ORDERED that the Report and Recommendation of the Magistrate Judge is ADOPTED as the opinion of the Court, pursuant to 28 U.S.C. [section] 636(b)(1) and E.D. Ohio L.R. 13(b).

IT IS FURTHER ORDERED, in accordance with the Report and Recommendation, that plaintiffs' complaint is hereby DISMISSED.

[signed]   C. Stewart August

          C. STEWART AUGUST
          UNITED STATES DISTRICT JUDGE

taken by the U.S. magistrate judge—or perhaps even the magistrate judge's law clerk. The process of delegating responsibilities to subordinates within the federal district court saves the judiciary's resources and frees the district judge to handle other responsibilities, such as presiding over trials. Delegation of responsibilities in such cases always presents risks if the district judge does not take sufficient care in reviewing the magistrate judge's work or the magistrate judge does not adequately supervise his or her law clerks. If the district judge merely rubber-stamps the subordinate's recommendations, then the judiciary has ceased to fulfill its responsibilities for providing considered judgments by official judicial officers.

SUMMARY

- Prisoners' cases filed in the federal courts often are delegated to U.S. magistrate judges, law clerks, and even law student interns who make recommendations to district judges about case disposition. In most cases, these recommendations result in dismissal for failure to state a proper claim or failure to follow required procedures.

- The claim most commonly raised in habeas corpus petitions is ineffective assistance of counsel, a very difficult issue to prove. Because of time lags in the appellate process, most habeas corpus petitions are filed by inmates serving long sentences. Nearly two-thirds of habeas corpus petitions are dismissed at the initial evaluation for violating court procedures. Only 1 percent of habeas claims are ultimately successful.

- Physical security and medical treatment claims are raised more frequently than other claims in section 1983 lawsuits. More than 90 percent of such lawsuits are dismissed in their early stages. Only 2 percent result in jury verdicts, and fewer than half of these verdicts favor the prisoners.

- As indicated by the actual case (with names changed) of *Green v. Johnson County Jail*, prisoners often have difficulty effectively identifying and raising proper issues that will survive immediate dismissal by the federal court.

Key Terms

answer	depositions	interrogatories
complaint	discovery	U.S. magistrate judge

Additional Readings

Smith, Christopher E. 1990. *United States Magistrates in the Federal Courts*. New York: Praeger.

Notes

1. Donald H. Ziegler and Michele G. Herman, "The Invisible Litigant: An Inside View of Pro Se Actions in the Federal Courts," *New York University Law Review* 47 (1972): 159–257.

2. Carroll Seron, *The Roles of Magistrates: Nine Case Studies* (Washington, DC: Federal Judicial Center, 1985).

3. Christopher E. Smith, "U.S. Magistrates and the Processing of Prisoner Litigation," *Federal Probation* 52 (December 1988): 13–18.

4. Fred Cheesman II, Roger A. Hanson, and Brian J. Ostrom of the National Center for State Courts, "To Augur Well: Future Prison Population and Prisoner Litigation," research paper presented at the Federal Judicial Center, Washington, DC, 20 May 1998, pp. 18–19.

5. Roger A. Hanson and Henry W. K. Daley, *Federal Habeas Corpus Review: Challenging State Court Criminal Convictions* (Washington, DC: U.S. Bureau of Justice Statistics, 1995).

6. Kathleen Maguire and Ann L. Pastore, eds., *Sourcebook of Criminal Justice Statistics—1993*. (Washington, DC: U.S. Department of Justice, Bureau of Justice Statistics, 1994), p. 612.

7. Hanson and Daley, *Federal Habeas Corpus Review,* pp. 11–12.

8. Strickland v. Washington, 466 U.S. 668 (1984); Lockhart v. Fretwell, 506 U.S. 364 (1993).

9. Hanson and Daley, *Federal Habeas Corpus Reveiw,* p. 19.

10. Roger A. Hanson and Henry W. K. Daley, *Challenging the Conditions of Prisons and Jails: A Report on Section 1983 Litigation* (Washington, DC: U.S. Bureau of Justice Statistics, 1995), p. 16.

11. Ibid., p. 18.

12. Ibid., p. 19.

13. Ibid., p. 22.

14. John Scalia, *Prisoner Petitions in the Federal Courts, 1980–1996* (Washington, DC: U.S. Department of Justice, Bureau of Justice Statistics, October 1997), p. 7.

15. 28 U.S.C. 1915(g).

16. Ibid.

CHAPTER FOUR

Access to the Courts and Communication Rights

Imagine you are a corrections officer. You are walking through a corridor, and as you pass two prisoners whispering to each other, you hear the words "escape plan." You keep walking but wait at the end of the corridor until one of the prisoners passes by.

"Hey, what were you guys talking about down there?" you ask.

"We weren't talking about anything," he replies.

You give the prisoner a stern look. "Davidson, you and I both know that you aren't going to get that job you want in the prison furniture factory if you get into any trouble."

"I haven't done anything wrong."

"I heard you talking about an escape."

He looks surprised. "Oh, that. That has nothing to do with me. He was just telling me about a rumor that this guy named Van Allen in Cell Block C has been getting stuff he's not supposed to in the mail from his lawyer."

"You mean 'stuff' like escape plans."

He shrugs his shoulders. "Whatever. Like I said, it's just a rumor."

You go to the mail room and arrive just as Van Allen appears to get his mail. You pick up an envelope addressed to him from a lawyer. "Is there anything improper in this letter, Van Allen?"

The prisoner responds angrily. "Hey, that's mine. It's from my lawyer, and you have no business touching it!"

What do you do? Should you open the envelope to see what's inside? Do you have the authority to open the envelope? Can you seize the envelope and seek the warden's permission to open it?

As this example demonstrates, there are many situations in which a prison's strong interest in maintaining safety and security may clash with a prisoner's desire to communicate with the outside world. Do prisoners have protected rights related to their contacts with the outside world? In this chapter, we examine how the law defines the extent of prisoners' rights to maintain outside contacts.

ACCESS TO THE COURTS

If corrections officials had complete power over every aspect of prisoners' lives, they could easily keep prisoners from having any contacts with the outside world. They could keep prisoners locked in their cells all day and prevent them from making or receiving telephone calls and from sending or receiving mail. However, the use of absolute power would present serious problems. Most importantly, if prisoners were being tortured, starved, or otherwise abused, they would have no way to inform the outside world. Such complete control in the closed environment of the prison would prevent judges from protecting any constitutional rights that prisoners are supposed to enjoy, and prisoners would not be able to file civil rights lawsuits. Prisoners need protected **access to the courts** to ensure that corrections officials follow the law.

Access to Legal Communications

Prisoner–attorney communication poses a ticklish problem for corrections officials. Legal communications are essential to the lawsuits that prisoners file against corrections officials. If these officials could hinder prisoners' communications with attorneys and courts, they could reduce their own burden of responding to legal claims, including claims that have no merit. Corrections officials have a legitimate interest in making sure that prisoners' communications with the outside are not a source of **contraband** (e.g., drugs) or other dangerous items (e.g., escape plans) that can arrive in letters and packages. However, these officials may also have an improper self-interest in interfering with prisoners' legal cases, especially those raising claims about violations of constitutional rights within the prison. Thus, in creating rules for legal communications, judges must be careful not to permit corrections officials to stop legal communications by claiming that they are protecting safety and security when they are really interfering with needed communication related to access to the courts.

The basic rule concerning mail between prisoners and their attorneys was outlined by the U.S. Supreme Court in **Wolff v. McDonnell (1974).**[1] In *Wolff*, a prisoner challenged a number of regulations in a Nebraska prison, including one that permitted corrections officials to open and inspect mail in the presence of prisoners. However, the Court ruled in favor of the prison. Although officials are not permitted to read mail from attorneys, they can open the mail and pour the contents on the table in front of the prisoner to ensure that contraband is not contained in envelopes and packages. Justice Byron White wrote:

> *As to the ability to open the mail in the presence of inmates, this could in no way constitute censorship, since the mail would not be read. Neither could it chill such communications, since the inmate's presence insures that prison official will not read the mail.*[2]

The prison's rule attempted to strike a balance between maintaining the prison's security interests and protecting prisoners' interest in confidential communications with their attorneys. Other corrections systems have introduced similar rules in order to achieve this balance of interests approved by the Supreme Court.

Lower courts interpreting the Supreme Court's *Wolff* decision generally have concluded that inmates' letters to their attorneys are protected against inspection and censorship,[3] unless there is probable cause to believe the envelope's contents threaten institutional security or inmate safety.[4] Because concerns about contraband do not apply to outgoing mail, prisoners can place sealed envelopes addressed to lawyers into the prison mail system.[5] By contrast, ordinary outgoing mail does not receive the same level of protection, because of concerns that such mail may be used to plan escapes or criminal activities. Presumably, such risks do not exist to the same extent with respect to mail sent to lawyers. Moreover, unlike in the past, mail to lawyers receives confidentiality protections.[6] Prior to court decisions in the 1970s protecting correspondence sent to lawyers, prison officials regularly opened and censored mail sent from prisoners to their attorneys.[7]

Court decisions also protect in-person communications between prisoners and their attorneys. Prisoners are entitled to receive visits from their lawyers,[8] as well as to meet with paralegals and law students who are working for these lawyers (*Procunier v. Martinez*, 1974).[9] Corrections officials may observe the prisoner and the lawyer during the visit, but they must do so under conditions that do not violate the confidentiality of lawyer–client communications. That is, corrections officers cannot stand within earshot of a prisoner and lawyer who are discussing legal matters.[10]

Like other visitors, lawyers are subject to certain regulations when meeting with their clients in prison. For example, they may be required to pass through a metal detector or to undergo a limited search to make sure that they are not bringing drugs, weapons, or other contraband into the prison. However, prison officials normally cannot force lawyers (or other visitors) to undergo a strip search, unless there are definite grounds for suspicion that they are attempting to smuggle drugs or weapons into the prison. By contrast, prisoners may be subjected to strip searches after they meet with attorneys.[11]

Another aspect of legal communications concerns prisoners' letters, petitions, and complaints sent to courts. If these documents could be intercepted or censored by prison officials, prisoners' opportunities to pursue appeals, habeas corpus petitions, and civil rights lawsuits would be limited or eliminated. One of the U.S. Supreme Court's earliest decisions concerning prisoner's rights involved this issue. In *Ex parte Hull* (1941), the Court examined a Michigan prison regulation that required "all legal documents, briefs, petitions, motions, habeas corpus proceedings, and appeals . . . to be submitted to the institutional welfare office and . . . the legal investigator to the Parole Board." Parole board investigators forwarded the documents to the court if they believed they were properly written, but they sent them back to prisoners if they believed the documents did not comply with court regulations. In effect, state officials had the power to determine which communications from prisoners would actually be sent to the courthouse.

The Supreme Court rejected the Michigan regulation. As Justice Frank Murphy, a former governor of Michigan wrote:

> *The regulation is invalid. The considerations that prompted its formulation are not without merit, but the state and its officers may not abridge or impair petitioner's right to apply to a federal court for a writ of habeas corpus. Whether a petition for a writ of habeas corpus addressed to a federal court is properly drawn and what allegations it must contain are questions for that court alone to determine.*[12]

And subsequent decisions by many courts reaffirm the importance of protecting inmates' communications with courts. Such communications are central to a prisoner's right of access to the courts—a right that has been described by one expert as "the most basic of the rights possessed by inmates; certainly it is the foundation for every other right an inmate has. . . . Without access, inmates have no way of vindicating their rights through judicial action."[13]

Such statements highlight an interesting question: Where in the Constitution do we find any mention of the "right of access to the courts"? If you check the Bill of Rights (see Box 1-3), you will see no such right specified. However, it is not unusual for the Supreme Court to recognize constitutional rights that are not clearly stated in the Constitution. Usually, specific fundamental rights are identified as components of the right to "due process" in the Fifth and Fourteenth Amendments, even if the Constitution does not mention them. The concept of prisoners' right of access to the courts fits logically within the idea of a right to due process. Thus, there is a strong consensus among both liberal and conservative jurists about the existence of this right of access. The same cannot be said about other due process-based rights identified by the Supreme Court throughout history, such as the right to choice in abortion and the right to decline medical treatment.[14]

Access to Legal Resources

As discussed in Chapter 2, prisoners do not have a constitutional right to counsel for habeas corpus petitions, civil rights lawsuits, or appeals beyond the first appeal of right. In most of these cases, prisoners must conduct their own legal research and prepare their own legal petitions, complaints, and appellate briefs. If prisoners did not have legal resources to help them prepare their cases, then their right of access to the courts would be meaningless. That is, a protected right to mail letters to the court would mean little if there was no possibility of preparing the legal papers necessary to initiate a case concerning constitutional rights and other legal matters.

The U.S. Supreme Court's initial major decision on prisoners' right to legal resources came in *Johnson v. Avery* (1969), which is excerpted in Box 4-1. The case concerned whether a **"jailhouse lawyer"**—a prisoner self-educated in law and possessing skills in preparing legal filings—could provide legal assistance for other prisoners. As you read the case, try to identify precisely what right or rights are possessed by prisoners according to the Court's opinion.

BOX 4-1   *Johnson v. Avery,* **393 U.S. 483 (1969)**

JUSTICE FORTAS delivered the opinion of the Court.

Petitioner is serving a life sentence in the Tennessee State Penitentiary. In February 1965 he was transferred to the maximum security building in the prison for violation of a prison regulation which provides:

> *No inmate will advise, assist, or otherwise contract to aid another, either with or without a fee, to prepare Writs or other legal matters. . . . Inmates are forbidden to set themselves up as practitioners for the purpose of promoting a business of writing Writs.*

. . . Only when he promised to refrain from assistance to other inmates was he restored to regular prison conditions and privileges. . . .

. . . The [U.S.] Court of Appeals for the Sixth Circuit . . . conclud[ed] that the [prison's] regulation did not unlawfully conflict with the federal right of habeas corpus. According to the Sixth Circuit, the interest of the State in pre-

serving prison discipline and in limiting the practice of law to licensed attorneys justified whatever burden the regulation might place on access to federal habeas corpus. . . .

Since the basic purpose of the writ [of habeas corpus] is to enable those unlawfully incarcerated to obtain their freedom, it is fundamental that access of prisoners to the courts for the purpose of presenting their complaints may not be denied or obstructed. For example, the Court has held that a State may not validly make the writ available only to prisoners who could pay a $4 filing fee. . . . And it has insisted that, for the indigent as well as for the affluent prisoner, post-conviction proceedings must be more than a formality. For instance, the State is obligated to furnish prisoners not otherwise able to obtain it, with a transcript or equivalent recordation of prior habeas corpus hearings for use in further proceedings. . . .

Tennessee urges, however that the contested regulation in this case is justified as part of the

(continued)

State's disciplinary administration of the prisons. There is no doubt that discipline and administration of state detention facilities are state functions. They are subject to federal authority only where paramount federal constitutional and statutory rights supervene. It is clear, however, that in instances where state regulations applicable to inmates of prison facilities conflict with such rights, the regulations may be invalidated. . . .

There can be no doubt that Tennessee could not constitutionally adopt and enforce a rule forbidding illiterate or poorly educated prisoners to file habeas corpus petitions. Here Tennessee has adopted a rule which, in the absence of any other source of assistance for such prisoners, effectively does just that. The District Court concluded that "for all practical purposes, if such prisoners cannot have the assistance of a 'jail-house lawyer,' their possibly valid constitutional claims will never be heard in any court." . . . The record supports this conclusion.

Jails and penitentiaries include among their inmates a high percentage of persons who are totally or functionally illiterate, whose educational attainments are slight, and whose intelligence is limited. This appears to be equally true of Tennessee's prison facilities. . . .

Tennessee does not provide an available alternative to the assistance provided by other inmates. The warden of the prison in which petitioner was confined stated that the prison provided free notarization of prisoners' petitions. That obviously only meets a formal requirement. . . .

. . . By contrast, in several States [prisoners are assisted by public defenders, law students, or volunteer lawyers]. We express no judgment concerning these plans, but their existence indicates that techniques are available to provide alternatives if the State elects to prohibit mutual assistance among inmates.

Even in the absence of such alternatives, the State may impose reasonable restrictions and restraints upon the acknowledged propensity of prisoners to abuse both the giving and the seeking of assistance in the preparation of applications for relief: for example, by limitations on the time and location of such activities, and the imposition of punishment for the giving or receipt of consideration in connection with such activities. . . . But unless and until the State provides some reasonable alternative to assist inmates in the preparation of petitions for postconviction relief, it may not validly enforce a regulation such as that here in issue, barring inmates from furnishing assistance to other prisoners. . . .

As indicated by the Court's opinion, prisoners are entitled to obtain legal assistance from other prisoners unless the prison provides an alternative form of legal resources that will enable inmates to prepare necessary legal documents. Note that the Court also stated that prison officials can impose reasonable regulations on the activities of jailhouse lawyers. As in other cases concerning prisoners' rights, the Court sought to strike a balance between prisoners' constitutional rights and the prison's need for order and security.

Several years later, the Supreme Court returned to the issue of prisoners' right to legal resources as a component of the right of access to the courts. Many prison officials did not want jailhouse lawyers to gain power and influence by making other prisoners indebted to them because they had provided legal assistance. Thus, questions emerged about what alternative forms of legal resources fulfilled constitutional requirements. In *Bounds v. Smith* (1977), which is excerpted in Box 4-2, the Court addressed the issue of law libraries

| BOX 4-2 | *Bounds v. Smith*, 430 U.S. 817 (1977) |

JUSTICE MARSHALL delivered the opinion of the Court.

The issue in this case is whether States must protect the right of prisoners to access to the courts by providing them with law libraries or alternative sources of legal knowledge. In *Younger v. Gilmore* [1971] . . . , we held **per curiam** that such services are constitutionally mandated. Petitioners, officials of the State of North Carolina, ask us to overrule that recent case, but for reasons explained below, we decline the invitation and reaffirm our previous decision. . . .

[North Carolina] contend[s], however, that [its] constitutional duty merely obliges States to allow inmate "writ writers" [also known as "jailhouse lawyers"] to function. They argue that under *Johnson v. Avery* as long as inmate communications on legal problems are not restricted, there is no further obligation to expend state funds to implement affirmatively the right of access. This argument misreads the cases. . . .

Moreover, our decisions have consistently required States to shoulder affirmative obligations to assure all prisoners meaningful access to the courts. It is indisputable that indigent inmates must be provided at state expense with paper and pen to draft legal documents, with notarial services to authenticate them, and with stamps to mail them. States must forgo collection of docket fees otherwise payable to the treasury and expend funds for transcripts. . . . This is not to say that economic factors may not be considered, for example, in choosing the methods used to provide meaningful access. But the cost of protecting a constitutional right cannot justify its total denial. Thus, neither the availability of jailhouse lawyers nor the necessity for affirmative state action is dispositive of [the prisoners'] claims [in this case]. The inquiry is rather whether law libraries or other forms of legal assistance are needed to give prisoners a reasonably adequate opportunity to present claimed violations of fundamental constitutional rights to the courts. . . .

We reject the State's claim that inmates are "ill-equipped to use" "the tools of the trade of the legal profession," making libraries useless in assuring meaningful access. . . . [T]his Court's experience indicates that *pro se* petitioners are capable of using lawbooks to file cases raising claims that are serious and legitimate even if ultimately unsuccessful. . . .

We hold, therefore, that the fundamental constitutional right of access to the courts requires prison authorities to assist inmates in the preparation and filing of meaningful legal papers by providing prisoners with adequate law libraries or adequate legal assistance from persons trained in the law. . . .

It should be noted that while adequate law libraries are one constitutionally acceptable method to assure meaningful access to the courts, our decision here, as in *[Younger v.] Gilmore* [1971], does not foreclose alternative means to achieve that goal. Nearly half of the States and the District of Columbia provide some degree of professional or quasi-professional legal assistance to prisoners. . . . Such programs take many imaginative forms and may have a number of advantages over libraries alone. Among the alternatives are the training of inmates as paralegal assistants to work under lawyers' supervision, the use of paraprofessionals and law students, either as volunteers or in formal clinical programs, the organization of volunteer attorneys through bar associations or other groups, the hiring of lawyers on a part-time consultant basis, and the use of full-time staff attorneys, working either in new prison legal assistance organizations or as part of public defender or legal services offices. Legal services plans not only result in more efficient and skillful handling of prisoner cases, but also avoid the disciplinary problems

(continued)

associated with writ writers. . . . Independent legal advisors can mediate or resolve administratively many prisoner complaints that would otherwise burden the courts, and can convince inmates that other grievances against the prison or the legal system are ill-founded, thereby facilitating rehabilitation by assuring the inmate that he has not been treated unfairly. . . . Nevertheless, a legal access program need not include any particular element we have discussed, and we encourage local experimentation. Any plan, however, must be evaluated as a whole to ascertain its compliance with constitutional standards. . . .

provided for prisoners inside correctional institutions. According to the Supreme Court, what exactly are states required to do to ensure that prisoners have access to the courts?

As indicated by the *Bounds* decision, prisons are responsible for providing the necessary resources for prisoners to pursue legal actions. Not only must prisons provide reasonable supplies of pencils, papers, and stamps for indigent prisoners to file legal papers,[15] they also must provide law libraries or an equivalent form of legal assistance, such as attorneys or paralegals to advise inmates. Many prisons decided to provide law libraries. This decision produced additional cases concerning the exact kinds of books that need to be in the library and the accessibility of library materials, especially for prisoners being held in isolation for disciplinary or safety reasons (often called "administrative segregation"). As you read the hypothetical problem posed in Box 4-3, consider whether law libraries actually can fulfill the legal needs of all inmates.

For nearly two decades after the *Bounds* decision, various federal judges faced the very questions presented in Box 4-3. Are libraries really enough to fulfill constitutional needs, or was the Supreme Court mistaken in reaching that conclusion? Some judges focused on the underlying right of access rather than *Bounds'* endorsement of law libraries in ordering prisons to create additional programs to serve the special needs of prisoners who cannot make use of law libraries. States in turn objected to these additional requirements. In 1996, the U.S. Supreme Court reexamined the issue in **Lewis v. Casey.** As you read the case, which is excerpted in Box 4-4, ask yourself how much power district judges have to decide how prisons should design legal assistance programs.

The Supreme Court's decision in *Lewis v. Casey* is regarded as a warning to federal judges. Because the Court ruled that individual prisoners must demonstrate how they were harmed by the legal resources offered, district judges cannot easily make a broad examination of flaws in law libraries and legal assistance programs. And even if flaws are identified, judges cannot order remedies unless someone can prove that he or she was harmed by those flaws. The Court decision even indicates that corrections officials and not judges, should take the lead in deciding how to solve problems that are discovered. That is, judges are supposed to let corrections officials run things as much as possible.

In light of *Lewis v. Casey,* how will illiterate or mentally ill prisoners demonstrate that they have been harmed by inadequate legal resources? If a pris-

| BOX 4-3 | **Prison Law Libraries** |

Imagine that you are a federal district judge considering a case in which prisoners claim that a prison's law library does not adequately support the right of access to the courts. A lawyer from a prisoners' rights organization presents evidence showing that 50 percent of the prisoners in the institution read at or below the sixth-grade level. The lawyer also presents evidence showing that many prisoners suffer from mental illnesses that affect their ability to understand things going on around them. In addition, nearly 20 percent of the prisoners speak Spanish as their primary language, and some of these prisoners speak almost no English at all. The lawyer concludes his presentation with a quotation from a federal judge in another state who wrote:

In this court's view, access to the fullest law library anywhere is a useless and meaningless gesture in terms of the great mass of prisoners. . . . To expect untrained laymen to work with entirely unfamiliar books, whose content they cannot understand, may be worthy of Lewis Carroll['s Alice's Adventures in Wonderland], but hardly satisfies the substance of constitutional duty.

Access to full law libraries makes about as much sense as furnishing medical services through books like: "Brain Surgery Self-Taught," or "How to Remove Your Own Appendix," along with scalpels, drills, hemostats, sponges, and sutures.[16]

In response, the assistant attorney general representing the prison argues that the Supreme Court's decision in *Bounds v. Smith* asserts that law libraries satisfy the state's responsibility to the prisoners. The state has provided a law library, she says, so they do not need to take additional actions.

Should you order the state to take additional actions to fulfill the needs of prisoners who cannot realistically make use of law libraries? Should you focus on whether all prisoners have effective access to the courts, or should you merely follow the language in *Bounds,* which indicates that law libraries alone are enough? What if the Supreme Court was mistaken in thinking that law libraries alone could fulfill the right of access to the courts? What would you decide to do?

oner can use legal materials well enough to file a section 1983 lawsuit claiming that the prison library is inadequate, why wouldn't the court respond, "The library must not be so bad for your purposes if you were able to file a lawsuit asking us to examine the prison's legal resources." But if prisoners really are unable to use the law library, how will they be able to file the necessary section 1983 action to ask the court to examine the library's quality? It remains to be seen how effectively prisoners who can demonstrate that they are harmed by inadequate legal resources will be able to bring such problems to a court's attention.

Consider the argument presented by Justice Thomas in his concurring opinion. Thomas asserts that prisoners have no constitutional right to legal resources and assistance. He also would limit the right of access to the courts solely to protection against corrections officials interfering with prisoners' efforts to file legal papers. In addition, Thomas is harshly critical of judges who make decisions that affect corrections policies and programs. If a majority of

BOX 4-4 *Lewis v. Casey*, 116 S.Ct. 2174 (1996)

JUSTICE SCALIA delivered the opinion of the Court.

. . . [Twenty-two prisoners] filed this class action—on behalf of all adult prisoners who are or will be incarcerated by the State of Arizona Department of Corrections [ADOC]. . . . The court identified a variety of shortcomings of the ADOC system, in matters ranging from the training of library staff, to the updating of legal materials, to the availability of photocopying services. In addition to these general findings, the court found that two groups of inmates were particularly affected by the system's inadequacies: "[l]ockdown prisoners" (inmates segregated from the general prison population for disciplinary or security reasons), who "are routinely denied physical access to the law library" and "experience severe interference with their access to the courts," . . . and illiterate or non-English-speaking inmates, who do not receive adequate legal assistance. . . .

. . . [The district court's order] specified in minute detail the times that libraries were to be kept open, the number of hours of library use to which each inmate was entitled (10 per week), the minimal educational requirements for prison librarians (a library science degree, law degree or paralegal degree), [etc.]. . . . [F]or lockdown prisoners [the district court] order[ed] that "ADOC prisoners in all housing areas and custody levels shall be provided regular and comparable visits to the law library," except that such visits "may be postponed on an individual basis because of the prisoner's documented inability to use the law library without creating a threat to safety or security, or a physical condition if determined by medical personnel to prevent library use." . . . With respect to the illiterate and non-English-speaking inmates, the [court order] declared that they were entitled to "direct assistance" from lawyers, paralegals, or "a sufficient number of at least minimally trained prisoner Legal Assistants;" [the court ordered] ADOC [to

take] "particular steps . . . to locate and train bilingual prisoners to be Legal Assistants." . . .

. . . [P]rison law libraries and legal assistance programs are not ends in themselves, but only the means for ensuring "a reasonably adequate opportunity to present claimed violations of fundamental constitutional rights to courts." . . .

Because *Bounds [v. Smith]* did not create an abstract, free-standing right to a law library or legal assistance, an inmate cannot establish relevant actual injury simply by establishing that his prison's law library or legal assistance program is sub-par in some theoretical sense. That would be [the same as a] healthy inmate claiming a constitutional violation because of the inadequacy of the prison [medical services]. Insofar as the right vindicated by *Bounds* is concerned, "meaningful access to the courts is the touchstone," . . . and the inmate therefore must go one step further and demonstrate that the alleged shortcomings in the library or legal assistance program hindered his efforts to pursue a legal claim. He might show, for example, that a complaint he prepared was dismissed for failure to satisfy some technical requirement which, because of deficiencies in the prison's legal assistance facilities, he could not have known. Or that he had suffered arguably actionable harm that he wished to bring before the courts, but was so stymied by inadequacies of the law library that he was unable even to file a complaint.

Although *Bounds* itself made no mention of an actual-injury requirement, it can hardly be thought to have eliminated that constitutional [requirement]. . . .

Here the District Court identified only two instances of actual injury. In describing ADOC's failures with respect to illiterates and non-English-speaking prisoners, it found that "[a]s a result of the inability to receive adequate legal assistance, prisoners who are slow readers have had their cases dismissed with prejudice," and that "[o]ther prisoners have been unable to file legal actions." . . . [T]he court identified only one prisoner in each instance. . . .

[Arizona's] claim appears to be that all inmates, including the illiterate and non-English-speaking, have a right to nothing more than "physical access to excellent libraries, plus help from legal assistants and law clerks." . . . This misreads *Bounds,* which as we have said guarantees no particular methodology but rather the conferral of a capability—the capability of bringing contemplated challenges to sentences or conditions of confinement before the courts. When any inmate, even an illiterate or non-English-speaking inmate, shows that an actionable claim of this nature which he desired to bring has been lost or rejected, or that the presentation of such a claim is currently being prevented, because this capability of filing suit has not been provided, he demonstrates that the State has failed to furnish "adequate law libraries or adequate assistance from persons trained in the law." . . . Of course, we leave it to prison officials to determine how best to ensure that inmates with language problems have a reasonably adequate opportunity to file nonfrivolous legal claims challenging their convictions or conditions of confinement. But it is that capability, rather than the capability of turning pages in a law library, that is the touchstone. . . .

. . . As we have discussed, however, the Constitution does not require that prisoners (literate or illiterate) be able to conduct generalized research, but only that they be able to present their grievances to the courts—a much more limited degree of legal assistance. Apart from the dismissal of [the one identified slow reader's claim and the inability of one non-English speaker to file a claim], there is no finding, and as far as we can discern from the record no evidence, that in Arizona prisons illiterate prisoners cannot obtain the minimal help necessary to file particular claims that they wish to bring before the courts. The constitutional violation has not been shown to be systemwide, and granting a remedy beyond what was necessary to provide

relief to [the two individuals identified as actually suffering harms from inadequate legal resources] was therefore improper.

The District Court here failed to accord adequate deference to the judgment of prison authorities [with respect to decisions about the lockdown prisoners]. . . .

Second, the [order] imposed by the District Court was inordinately—indeed, wildly—intrusive. . . .

Finally, the [court order] was developed through a process that failed to give adequate consideration to the views of state prison authorities. . . .

JUSTICE THOMAS concurring.

. . . It is a bedrock principle of judicial restraint that a right be lodged firmly in the text or tradition of a specific constitutional provision before we will recognize it as fundamental. Strict adherence to this approach is essential if we are to fulfill our constitutionally assigned role of giving full effect to the mandate of the Framers without infusing the constitutional fabric with our own political views.

. . . *Bounds [v. Smith]* forged a right with no basis in precedent or constitutional text: a right to have the State "shoulder affirmative obligations" in the form of law libraries or legal assistance to ensure that prisoners can file meaningful lawsuits. . . .

In the end, I agree that the Constitution affords prisoners what can be termed a right of access to the courts. That right, rooted in the Due Process Clause and the principle articulated in *Ex parte Hull,* is a right not to be arbitrarily prevented from lodging a claimed violation of a constitutional right in the federal court. The State, however, is not constitutionally required to finance or otherwise assist the prisoner's efforts, either through law libraries or other legal assistance. Whether to expend state resources to facilitate prisoner lawsuits is a question of policy

(continued)

and one that the Constitution leaves to the discretion of the States.

There is no basis in history or tradition for the proposition that the State's constitutional obligation is any broader. . . .

. . . We have here yet another example of a federal judge attempting to "direc[t] or manag[e] the reconstruction of entire institutions and bureaucracies, with little regard for the inherent limitations of [his] authority." . . .

. . . [The Constitution] cannot be understood to authorize the federal judiciary to take control of core state institutions like prisons, schools, and hospitals, and assume responsibility for making the difficult policy judgments that state officials are both constitutionally entitled and uniquely qualified to make. . . .

the Supreme Court agreed with the details of Thomas's opinion, what limits would exist to prevent corrections officials from running prisons in whatever manner they wish? Keep this question in mind as you learn about other aspects of prisoners' rights in subsequent chapters.

MAIL AND TELEPHONES

Prisoners are not simply convicted criminals. They are also husbands and wives, fathers and mothers, sons and daughters, sisters and brothers, and friends to people in the outside world. As a result, they are eager to maintain contact with outsiders. Traditionally, experts on corrections have regarded communication with the outside world as an important part of an offender's rehabilitation. Isolating inmates completely behind prison walls is not likely to further the goal of converting them into law-abiding citizens. Although fewer contemporary corrections officials focus on rehabilitation as a primary goal, there is still broad recognition that most prisoners will eventually gain release, either through parole or the completion of sentences. And when they reenter mainstream society, their chances of finding jobs and avoiding additional criminal behavior will be greater if they have contacts maintained in the community. However, communication with the outside world also can cause problems. Visitors and mail are primary methods for bringing illegal items, especially drugs, into a prison. In addition, prisoners may use letters and telephones to plan escapes, harass people outside the prison, and even carry out significant criminal activities, such as fraud schemes. Thus, prison officials have good reason to monitor and regulate some aspects of inmates' communications.

Nonlegal Correspondence

Prior to the 1970s, prison officials controlled inmates' communications with the outside world. Many institutions had regulations permitting officials not merely to read but also to censor incoming and outgoing mail. Corrections officers read letters written by prisoners and crossed out any criticisms of the prison or any statements, such as political opinions, that they did not like. In

1974, the Supreme Court examined California's prison mail censorship regulations in ***Procunier v. Martinez;*** the case is excerpted in Box 4-5. Which constitutional right provided the basis for the Court's decision?

Note that the *Procunier* decision focused on First Amendment free expression rights of a prisoner's *outside correspondent.* But it did not clarify exactly what First Amendment rights are possessed by prisoners. The decision seemed to apply a **strict scrutiny test** to prison regulations concerning censorship of mail. In constitutional law, strict scrutiny standards require the government to prove that its rules are necessary to uphold some important governmental goal. In this case, the Court looked for "substantial governmental interests," although true strict scrutiny analysis usually speaks of "compelling governmental interests." The Court also implied that prisons may use only the least restrictive policy necessary for protecting the "substantial" governmental interest in security and order. If courts place the burden on government to provide

---

BOX 4-5   ***Procunier v. Martinez,* 416 U.S. 396 (1974)**

JUSTICE POWELL delivered the opinion of the Court.

. . . Under these regulations, correspondence between inmates of California penal institutions and persons other than licensed attorneys and holders of public office was censored for nonconformity to certain standards. . . .

. . . In determining the proper standard of review for prison restrictions on inmate correspondence, we have no occasion to consider the extent to which an individual's right to free speech survives incarceration, for a narrower basis of decision is at hand. In the case of direct personal correspondence between inmates and those who have a particularized interest in communicating with them, mail censorship implicates more than the right of prisoners.

. . . The wife of a prison inmate who is not permitted to read all that her husband wanted to say to her has suffered an abridgment of her interest in communicating with him as plain as that which results from censorship of her letter to him. In either event, censorship of prisoner mail works a consequential restriction on the First and Fourteenth Amendment rights of those who are not prisoners. . . .

Applying the teachings of our prior decisions to the instant context, we hold that censorship of prisoner mail is justified if the following criteria are met. First, the regulation or practice in question must further an important or substantial governmental interest unrelated to the suppression of expression. Prison officials may not censor inmate correspondence simply to eliminate unflattering or unwelcome opinions or factually inaccurate statements. Rather, they must show that a regulation authorizing mail censorship furthers one or more of the substantial governmental interests of security, order, and rehabilitation. Second, the limitation on First Amendment freedoms must be no greater than is necessary or essential to the protection of the particular governmental interest involved. Thus a restriction on inmate correspondence that furthers an important or substantial interest of penal administration will nevertheless be invalid if its sweep is unnecessarily broad. This does not mean, of course, that prison administrators may be required to show with certainty that adverse consequences would flow from the failure to censor a particular letter. Some latitude

(continued)

in anticipating the probable consequences of allowing certain speech in a prison environment is essential to the proper discharge of an administrator's duty. But any regulation or practice that restricts inmate correspondence must be generally necessary to protect one or more of the legitimate governmental interests identified above. . . .

We also agree with the District Court that the decision to censor or withhold delivery of a particular letter must be accompanied by minimum procedural safeguards. The interest of the prisoners and their correspondents in uncensored communication by letter, grounded as it is in the First Amendment, is plainly a "liberty" interest within the meaning of the Fourteenth Amendment even though qualified of necessity by the governmental invasion. As such, it is protected from arbitrary governmental invasion. The District Court required that an inmate be notified of the rejection of a letter written by or addressed to him, that the author of that letter be given a reasonable opportunity to protest that decision, and that complaints be referred to a prison official other than the person who originally disapproved the correspondence. These requirements do not appear to be unduly burdensome, nor do appellants so contend. . . .

persuasive justifications for a regulation that collides with a right, they clearly indicate that the right is very important. By contrast, if the individual bears the burden of persuading the court that a law is improper, then the court less frequently provides protection for the asserted right. Although the Court treated First Amendment rights as important in *Procunier,* note that prison officials are not barred from censoring mail. The Court recognized that in some situations, the prison's need for order and security might require censorship.

In *Turner v. Safley* (1987), the Supreme Court examined prisoners' right to send and receive mail when an outsider's First Amendment rights are not involved. Missouri's regulations prohibited correspondence between prisoners in different corrections institutions. In approving the prison regulations, the Court clearly did not apply strict scrutiny to rules affecting prisoners' correspondence with each other. Instead of forcing the government to justify its regulations as supporting a compelling governmental interest, Justice Sandra Day O'Connor's majority opinion applied a four-part test that examined only whether the regulations are reasonably related to legitimate governmental interests. This kind of test is often referred to as a **rational basis test** (or the *reasonableness test*) in constitutional law. The Court merely asks whether the regulation is a rational or reasonable way to advance a governmental interest. The governmental interests in *Turner* were the prison's concerns about security and escape planning that could be affected by private communications between prisoners. O'Connor's four-part test, which is presented in Box 4-6, has been used by the Supreme Court in evaluating whether other kinds of constitutional rights have been violated by prison regulations. How would you summarize the essential meaning of each component of the test?

After *Procunier v. Martinez* and *Turner v. Safley,* it was clear that the Supreme Court provided different levels of protection to correspondence with outsiders and correspondence between prisoners. While the Court denied any intention to apply strict scrutiny analysis to prisoners' rights, it left intact the

BOX 4-6	***Turner v. Safley*, 482 U.S. 78 (1987)**
	A Four-Part Test for Rights Violations in Prisons

. . . First, there must be a "valid, rational connection" between the prison regulation and the legitimate governmental interest put forward to justify it. Thus, a regulation cannot be sustained where the logical connection between the regulation and the asserted goal is so remote as to render the policy arbitrary or irrational. Moreover, the governmental objective must be a legitimate and neutral one. We have found it important to inquire whether prison regulations restricting inmates' First Amendment rights operated in a neutral fashion, without regard to the content of the expression.

A second factor relevant in determining the reasonableness of a prison restriction . . . is whether there are alternative means of exercising the right that remain open to prison inmates. Where "other avenues" remain available for the exercise of the asserted right, courts should be particularly conscious of the "measure of judicial deference owed to corrections officials . . . in gauging the validity of the regulation."

A third consideration is the impact accommodation of the asserted constitutional right will have on guards and other inmates, and on the allocation of prison resources generally. In the necessarily closed environment of the correctional institution, few changes will have no ramifications on the liberty of others or on the use of the prison's limited resources for preserving institutional order. When accommodation of an asserted right will have a significant "ripple effect" on fellow inmates or on prison staff, courts should be particularly deferential to the informed discretion of corrections officials.

Finally, the absence of ready alternatives is evidence of the reasonableness of a prison regulation. By the same token, the existence of obvious, easy alternatives may be evidence that the regulation is not reasonable, but is an "exaggerated response" to prison concerns. This is not a "least restrictive alternative" test: prison officials do not have to set up and then shoot down every conceivable alternative method of accommodating the claimant's constitutional complaint. But if an inmate claimant can point to an alternative that fully accommodates the prisoner's rights at *de minimis* [very minor] cost to valid penological interests, a court may consider that as evidence that the regulation does not satisfy the reasonable relationship standard. . . .

greater protection afforded by *Procunier v. Martinez* to outgoing mail only.[17] For regulations affecting outgoing mail, judges may look more closely at the connection between the prison's asserted interest and the policy chosen to monitor prisoners' correspondence. By contrast, the Court was deferential to prison regulations affecting inmate-to-inmate correspondence. In such circumstances, the Court only looked for a reasonable relationship between the regulation and a legitimate institutional interest. These standards were clarified in ***Thornburgh v. Abbott* (1989)**, which concerned regulations in federal prisons permitting officials to determine which outside publications prisoners may receive and in which the Court applied the *Turner* reasonableness/rational basis test.

In the *Thornburgh* case excerpt in Box 4-7, note how the Supreme Court clarified its intention to apply the reasonableness test rather than strict scrutiny in prisoners' rights cases. The justices explicitly sought to remove the impression created by their opinion in *Procunier v. Martinez* that the government

BOX 4-7   *Thornburgh v. Abbott*, 490 U.S. 401 (1989)

JUSTICE BLACKMUN delivered the opinion of the Court.

Regulations promulgated by the Federal Bureau of Prisons broadly permit federal prisoners to receive publications from the "outside," but authorize prison officials to reject incoming publications found to be detrimental to institutional security. For 15 years, respondents, a class of inmates and certain publishers, have claimed that these regulations violate their First Amendment rights under the standard of review enunciated in *Procunier v. Martinez.* . . .

We now hold that the District Court correctly anticipated the proper inquiry in this case is whether the regulations are "reasonably related to legitimate penological interests," *Turner v. Safley* [1987] . . . , and we conclude that under this standard the regulations are facially valid. . . .

. . . [The regulations] permit an inmate to subscribe to, or to receive, a publication without prior approval, but authorize the warden to reject a publication in certain circumstances. The warden may reject it "only if it is determined detrimental to the security, good order, or discipline of the institution or it might facilitate criminal activity." . . . The warden, however, may not reject a publication "solely because its content is religious, philosophical, political, social, or sexual, or because its content is unpopular or repugnant." . . . The warden is prohibited from establishing an excluded list of publications: each issue of a subscription publication is to be reviewed separately. . . .

The regulations provide procedural safeguards for both the recipient and the sender. The warden may designate staff to screen and, where appropriate, to approve incoming publications, but only the warden may reject a publication. . . . The warden must advise the inmate promptly in writing of the reasons for the rejection, . . . and must provide the publisher or sender with a copy of the rejection letter. . . . The notice must refer to "the specific article(s) or material(s) considered objectionable." . . . The publisher or sender may obtain an independent review of the warden's rejection decision by a timely writing to the Regional Director of the [U.S. Bureau of Prisons]. . . .

In particular, we have been sensitive to the delicate balance that prison administrators must strike between the order and security of the internal prison environment and the legitimate demands of those on the "outside" who seek to enter that environment, in person or through the written word. . . . [P]rison officials may well conclude that certain proposed interactions [between prisoners and outsiders through written and other forms of communication], though seemingly innocuous to laymen, have potentially significant implications for the order and security of the prison. Acknowledging the expertise of these officials and that the judiciary is "ill equipped" to deal with the difficult and delicate problems of prison management, this Court has afforded considerable deference to the determinations of prison administrators who, in the interest of security, regulate the relations between prisoners and the outside world.

In this case, there is no question that publishers who wish to communicate with those who, through subscription, willingly seek their point of view have a legitimate First Amendment interest in access to prisoners. The question here, as it has been in our previous First Amendment cases in this area, is what standard of review this Court should apply to prison regulations limiting that access. . . .

The Court's decision to apply a reasonableness standard in [the cases that came after *Procunier v. Martinez*] rather than *Martinez'* less deferential approach stemmed from its concern that language in *Martinez* might be too readily understood as establishing a standard of "strict" or "heightened" scrutiny, and that such a strict standard simply was not appropriate for consideration of regulations that are centrally concerned with the maintenance of order and security within prisons. See *Turner v. Safley*. . . . Specifically, the Court declined to apply the *Martinez* standard in "prisoners' rights" cases because, as was noted in *Turner*, *Martinez* could be (and had been) read to require a strict "least restrictive alternative" analysis, without sufficient sensitivity to the need for discretion in meeting legitimate prison needs. . . .

We do not believe that *Martinez* should, or need, be read as subjecting the decisions of prison officials to a strict "least restrictive means" test. As noted, *Martinez* required no more than that a challenged regulation be "generally necessary" to a legitimate governmental interest. . . . Certainly, *Martinez* required a close fit between the challenged regulation and the interest it purported to serve. But a careful reading of *Martinez* suggests that our rejection of the regulation at issue resulted not from a least restrictive means requirement, but from our recognition that the regulated activity centrally at issue in that case— outgoing personal correspondence from prisoners—did not, by its very nature, pose a serious threat to prison order and security. . . .

. . . [W]e acknowledge today that the logic of our analyses in *Martinez* and *Turner* requires that *Martinez* be limited to regulations concerning outgoing correspondence. As we have observed, outgoing correspondence was the central focus of our opinion in *Martinez*. The implications of outgoing correspondence for prison security are of a categorically lesser magnitude than the implications of incoming materials. Any attempt to justify a similar categorical distinction between incoming correspondence from prisoners (to which we applied the reasonableness standard in *Turner*) and incoming correspondence from nonprisoners would likely prove futile, and we do not invite it. To the extent that *Martinez* itself suggests such a distinction, we today overrule that case; the Court accomplished much of this step when it decided *Turner*. . . .

[*Note: In the remaining portion of the majority opinion, the Court applied the four-part test*

from Turner v. Safley *to reach the conclusion that the prison regulations are valid.*]

JUSTICE STEVENS, with whom JUSTICES BRENNAN and MARSHALL join, concurring in part and dissenting in part.

. . . Focusing not on the rights of prisoners, but on the "inextricably meshed" rights of nonprisoners "who have a particularized interest in communicating with them," [Justice Powell] wrote [in *Procunier v. Martinez*] that an "undemanding standard of review" could not be squared with the fact "that the First Amendment liberties of free citizens are implicated in censorship of prisoner mail." . . . Thus he chose an "intermediate" means of evaluating speech restrictions, . . . allowing censorship if it "further[ed] an important or substantial governmental interest unrelated to the suppression of expression," and "the limitation of First Amendment freedoms [was] no greater than [was] necessary or essential." . . .

This peculiar bifurcation of the constitutional standard governing communications between inmates and outsiders [established today in the majority opinion] is unjustified. The decision in *Martinez* was based on a distinction between prisoners' constitutional rights and the protection the First Amendment affords those who are not prisoners—not between non-prisoners who are senders and those who are receivers. . . .

In lieu of *Martinez*'s rationale, which properly takes into consideration the effects that prison regulations have on the First Amendment rights of non-prisoners, the Court applies a manipulable "reasonableness" standard to a set of regulations that too easily may be interpreted to authorize arbitrary rejections of literature addressed to inmates. . . .

The feeble protection provided by a "reasonableness" standard applied within the framework of these [prison] regulations [concerning receipt of publications] is apparent in this record. . . .

bore the burden of justifying its regulations with substantial reasons and using only the least restrictive means to advance its objectives.

The U.S. Supreme Court provides guidance to the lower courts through its interpretations of the Constitution. However, the Supreme Court cannot issue decisions about all of the possible situations that may arise. Thus, for rights concerning mail and other issues, other courts, especially U.S. courts of appeals and state appellate courts, develop the law affecting prisoners' rights. With respect to rights regarding correspondence, the decisions in *Procunier, Turner,* and *Thornburgh* represent the primary guidance from the high court.

Because the Supreme Court has never decided whether prison officials can read an inmate's mail—even though it has ruled on issues related to censorship—lower courts have disagreed about whether mail can be read. Some courts have ruled that corrections officials can routinely read inmates' mail, while others have ruled that they cannot do so without good cause.[18] Some courts permit temporary suspension of mail privileges (except for correspondence to lawyers and courts) when an inmate is in segregation for disciplinary reasons.[19] Box 4-8 gives the actual mail policy in one high-security prison. Does the policy adhere to the legal procedures as discussed in this section's cases?

Telephone Contacts

Courts generally recognize prisoners' right to use the telephone to talk to family and friends.[20] Typically, prisons and jails permit inmates to place *collect* phone calls, but not to receive incoming calls. Many convicted offenders have generated significant financial problems for their families with too-frequent collect calls. Corrections officials are permitted to regulate telephone calls, and there may be more restrictive regulations for inmates outside of the general population, such as those in administrative segregation.[21] Some institutions have arrangements with telephone companies so that inmates' calls are automatically cut off after a standard time period, such as fifteen minutes or a half-hour. Prisons may regulate the number of nonemergency calls that inmates make each week. There may be other restrictions, in accordance with the *Turner* principles, if they bear a reasonable relationship to an institution's interests in security and order.[22]

Many prisons routinely monitor or tape prisoners' telephone conversations, and prisoners generally are made aware of such practices. Courts recognize that corrections officials need to prevent prisoners from using the telephone to plan escapes, commit crimes, or harass outsiders.[23] However, judges forbid use of taped conversations between prisoners and their attorneys unless court orders have authorized such use—for example, when there is probable cause to suspect that an attorney is assisting with an escape plan.[24]

Although telephone access for convicted offenders can be closely regulated and monitored, pretrial detainees in jails have immediate communication needs related to their right of access to the courts. Thus, although jails may have reasonable regulations that prevent detainees from having phone access on demand, pretrial detainees cannot be barred from communicating in order to obtain legal representation and make arrangements for bail.

B O X 4 - 8	**Actual Prisoner Mail Policy**

Correspondence is permitted as long as institutional rules and postal regulations are not violated. Any correspondence that contravenes law or postal regulations, contains statements or objects that are obscene, threatening or untruthful in nature, or is addressed to any party who expressly objects to receiving mail from any prisoner(s), constitutes a violation of institutional regulations.

Any person(s) offering volunteer services at this facility wishing to send information to a prisoner shall route it to the group's institution coordinator (i.e., religious material to the religious coordinator, Alcoholics Anonymous/Narcotics Anonymous material to the program coordinator). *NO DIRECT CORRESPONDENCE MAY TAKE PLACE BETWEEN PRISONERS AND THOSE OFFERING VOLUNTEER SERVICES AT THIS FACILITY.*

The institution reserves the right to intercept, open, and deny transmittal of mail (other than privileged correspondence to courts and public officials) when there are reasonable grounds to believe it violates institutional mail rules. You are granted access to the Governor's Office, [state] Civil Rights Commission, all state and federal courts, attorneys, all administrative offices of the Department of Corrections, and the Attorney General in the form of sealed and uncensored letters.

If you are in general population, you are permitted to send uncensored letters to any person. Unlimited incoming and outgoing first-class correspondence is authorized. General population prisoners may purchase stamps or stamped envelopes from the Prison Store. Prisoners in administrative segregation may have certain mail subject to inspection. You must pay for special handling of mail (i.e., registered, certified, overweight, special delivery, foreign, and air mail).

You must notify the Mail Office by kite [i.e., written note] of attorney(s) designated as your attorney of record. Mail from previously designated attorneys should be clearly marked "Attorney Special Handling" to facilitate identification and sorting for special handling. The mail must be mailed in an official envelope with the full return address to ensure proper handling. It should be understood that the special handling may result in some delay in mail service.

NOTE: Enclosures are restricted to unmounted non-Polaroid photographs and money in the form of postal money orders, express money orders, or cashiers check. CASH WILL NOT BE ACCEPTED. Stamps will not be accepted.

All incoming mail, including packages, must have your full name and number, and will be opened and checked for contraband. Every effort will be made to process incoming and outgoing mail as quickly as possible.

When you send mail out—your name and number MUST appear above the address.

CONTACT WITH VISITORS

Contact with family and friends on prison visits long has been regarded as beneficial for rehabilitation and for prisoner morale. By keeping in close contact with their social networks, offenders may have an easier transition back into society upon release (unless those networks are comprised entirely of individuals who encourage or facilitate the offender's lawbreaking behavior). Visits are important to prisoners, so corrections officials sometimes use their importance to pressure inmates to obey institutional rules. It's no coincidence that many prisons are in rural areas that are distant from the primary population centers. For example, Washington state's maximum-security prison at Walla Walla is hundreds of miles from the population centers of Seattle and Tacoma where many prisoners' families live. Similarly, Michigan's corrections institutions in its Upper Peninsula are far from the major cities of southern Michigan. Officials may threaten inmates with transfers to these distant locations in order to gain cooperative behavior. Many prisoners worry about the possibility of such transfers primarily because it would make it difficult, if not impossible, for family and friends to visit.

Visitors and Rights

The U.S. Supreme Court has never interpreted the Constitution as guaranteeing a right of prisoners to have visitors. Thus, prison officials have significant authority to regulate visits and even bar specific visitors unless, as in New York, a state court has identified a right to visits within the state constitution.[25] One exception is that many courts have intervened if prisons permit visitors but impose flat rules against visits by prisoners' children or spouses.[26]

In *Kentucky v. Thompson* (1989), the U.S. Supreme Court raised the possibility that a state's prison regulations could create "a protected liberty interest" (i.e., right) for prisoners if the regulation forbade corrections officials from making certain decisions or taking certain actions.[27] Kentucky's regulations stated that "it is the policy [of the prison] to respect the right of inmates to have visits." However, the Court ultimately concluded that a right to have visits was not actually created by these regulations, because they did not mandate visits and they explicitly stated that "administrative staff reserves the right to allow or disallow visits." Although the possibility was raised that a state might create a protected right to visits through the wording of its regulations, the Court changed its approach and cast doubt on the possibility in a 1995 decision. In *Sandin v. Conner* (1995), a case concerning disciplinary procedures, the Court stated that the protected rights created by state prison regulations "will be generally limited to freedom of restraint," such as an improper transfer to a mental hospital or the involuntary administration of certain drugs to treat mental illnesses.[28] Such actions affect prisoners' personal liberty in fundamental ways. The Court implied that a denial of opportunities to see visitors would not create the same kind of hardship.

A few states permit conjugal visits, meaning occasional overnight visits by an inmate's spouse in the privacy of a mobile home or apartment within the prison. Such visits are more common in some European countries than in the United States. Although some states permit such visits, prisoners have no right to demand that they are entitled to them.[29]

Prison officials can regulate the time, place, manner, duration, and frequency of visits. Although some courts in the 1970s indicated that prisoners who pose no security risk have a right to "contact visits," the U.S. Supreme Court later indicated that nothing in the Constitution requires that type of visit

(*Block v. Rutherford,* 1984).[30] Unless a state constitution requires that prisoners be permitted to have physical contact with visitors, corrections officials can make visitors speak with prisoners from opposite sides of a glass partition or other barrier.

As indicated by the Michigan statute highlighted in Box 1-4, visitors are subject to being searched to ensure that they are not bringing contraband into the prison. Box 4-9 contains the actual visiting regulations provided to inmates in a high-security prison.

BOX 4-9 **Actual Prison Visitation Rules**

[*These rules are in place at the Michigan Reformatory at Ionia, Level IV (high-security) Institution for Males and apply especially to those ages seventeen to twenty-four serving long sentences.*]

. . . A visitor shall not be placed on a prisoner's visitor list unless the prisoner has requested placement of that person on his visitor list . . . and the visitor has completed [the required state form] and has been approved. Prisoners who have an approved visitors list may add or delete names of immediate family members from their list at any time. However, a prisoner shall be allowed to add or delete names of non-immediate family members no more frequently than once every six months. . . .

VISITING SCHEDULE

Visiting hours for prisoners in Level IV general population and administrative segregation are between the hours of 2:30 p.m. and 8:30 p.m. Tuesday through Sunday. Visiting hours for prisoners in protective segregation are between the hours of 5:30 p.m. and 8:30 p.m. Monday evening and 10:00 a.m. to 12 noon, Wednesday, Saturday, and Sunday.

1. You are allowed five (5) visits per month, two (2) of which may take place on a weekend. Administrative Segregation prisoners are allowed four (4) visits per

month. Visits not used during the month may not be carried over to any subsequent month. . . .

2. Visitors 18 years of age and older *must* have a valid driver's license, Secretary of State identification card or passport which shows the visitor's picture, date of birth, and signature in order to visit. Visitors under the age of 18 *must* be the child, stepchild, or grandchild of the prisoner and be accompanied by a parent or legal guardian or be an emancipated minor. A birth certificate or certificate of adoption *shall* be required. Other minor children must be accompanied by a parent or legal guardian who must present the child's birth certificate or certificate of adoption for the child.

3. Qualified clergy and attorneys and their representatives on official business with proper identification (a card or document identifying him/her as an attorney or clergy) will be allowed unlimited visiting during business hours (Monday through Friday, 8:00 a.m. to 4:30 p.m., except holidays), and scheduled visiting hours. Failure to provide proper identification will result in a visit charged to the prisoner and access during scheduled visiting hours only. If staff have doubts regarding proper

(*continued*)

identification of clergy, they should be forwarded to the religious coordinator (Chaplain) for clarification.

4. Visitors may leave money at the Cashier's Office to be placed in the prisoner's account Monday through Friday, 8:00 a.m. to 12:00 noon and 12:30 to 4:00 p.m. (except state holidays). Money may be in the form of cash, money order, or cashier's check.

5. Visitors (male or female) wearing questionable attire (dresses shorter than knee length, tops that reveal cleavage or are cut to permit access to the breasts, see-through clothing or that which conforms closely to body contours, halter tops, hot pants or short shorts), may be required to wear a smock during the visit, or they will not be allowed to visit. Documentation will be listed on visiting card. If the smock is removed during the visit, the visit will be terminated. The Shift Commander will be consulted if other clothing items appear questionable. After the first visit in a smock, further visits will not be permitted.

. . .

7. You are allowed to kiss and embrace your visitor(s), one time each, upon greeting, departing and when a picture is being taken. You may hold hands during the visit or place an arm around the shoulder of one another, except with "no-contact" visits. Except as just noted, physical contact

during the visit will not be allowed, and will result in termination of the visit, a possible misconduct report, and/or visitor restriction.

. . .

15. Prisoners in segregation units other than the protection unit shall be in bellychains during visits.

16. Administrative Segregation prisoners will be limited to non-contact visiting status . . . but are not restricted to immediate family. Prisoners may also be placed on non-contact visiting status as the result of visitor restriction. This can result from misconduct related to visiting or repeated termination of visits due to inappropriate behavior. . . .

. . .

19. Prisoners may not wear coats, outer sweater (i.e., other than over an undershirt), jackets, personal [as opposed to state-issued] shoes, shorts, watches, hooded sweatshirts, or garments with elastic or drawstring waist. Prisoners must keep their shirts buttoned up. Prisoners must have their I.D. card when reporting for a visit.

. . .

23. Visits will be terminated if visiting rules are violated. If permanent or temporary (90 day) restriction is pursued, there will be a hearing conducted by the Hearings Division.

Note that the prison's regulations permit "qualified clergy . . . on official business with proper identification" to have unlimited visiting during business hours and scheduled visiting hours. Just as contact with attorneys is connected to a particular set of constitutional rights (e.g., right to counsel and contact with the courts), contact with clergy is connected to First Amendment religious freedom rights. Moreover, American corrections has a long tradition of linking religion with rehabilitation. As we will see in Chapter 5 concerning prisoners' right to religious freedom, judicial decisions recognize corrections officials' paramount interests in safety and security when questions of religious rights arise. Thus, prisons are permitted to have reasonable regulations about prisoners' access to religious leaders, and clergy may be subjected to searches to ensure that they are not smuggling contraband. Note that the Michigan

Department of Corrections regulations concerning searches of visitors, which are excerpted in Box 4-10, include attorneys and clergy but may exclude state officials and others escorted by the warden. Pay particular attention to the department's instructions to personnel about arresting or detaining visitors. The wording of the policy directive seeks to avoid any excessive assertion of force or arrest power that might lead to a civil rights lawsuit by a visitor.

BOX 4-10   **Actual Policy on Searching Visitors**

[*These policy and practice instructions are given to corrections personnel in the Michigan Department of Corrections.*]

N. Visitors to correctional facilities must be searched to prevent the introduction of contraband. Anyone who refuses to be searched will be prohibited from visiting on that occasion. However, in no case shall a visitor who refuses to submit to a search be forced to do so unless a search warrant has been obtained.

O. Attorneys and members of the clergy are to be treated the same as other visitors and are thus subject to search, as described in this policy. However, elected State officials, prosecutors, judges and anyone who is personally escorted by the warden shall not be subject to search except on specific orders of the warden or his/her designee.

P. Use of Screening Devices; Frisk and Clothed Body Searches

  1. There are three types of searches which may be required of visitors, both those who visit individual prisoners and those who are part of a group which is visiting the facility;

    a. Where screening devices are available, all visitors shall be required to walk through the screening device or submit to the use of a handheld device.

    b. A frisk search shall be routinely conducted for all visitors. If possible,

frisk searches should be conducted by an employee of the same sex as the person being searched. If a baby is brought in as a visitor, the adult who is accompanying the child shall be required to partially remove the baby's diaper to allow the employee conducting the search to visually inspect to ensure that contraband is not being concealed. Baby bottles, extra diapers, etc. shall also be thoroughly searched.

    c. A clothed body search will be required if there is a reasonable suspicion that the visitor is concealing contraband. Such searches shall be conducted by an employee of the same sex as the person being searched.

Q. Strip Search

  1. A visitor shall not be forced to submit to a strip search unless a search warrant has been obtained.

. . .

S. Search of Vehicles

  1. Employees shall not search the vehicle of a visitor. If it is suspected that there is contraband in a vehicle, the matter shall be referred to the appropriate police agency.

  2. If a vehicle is discovered in an area of the facility grounds which has been posted

(*continued*)

against trespassing, the vehicle and its occupants may be detained while police are summoned. However, only reasonable non-deadly force shall be employed unless the person detained attempts to use deadly force.

. . .

V. A visitor or employee found to be in possession of an alcoholic beverage, a poisonous substance, a controlled substance, a prescription drug, unless permission is given by the Warden or his/her designee, or a weapon should be detained if possible, using whatever non-deadly force is necessary, awaiting the arrival of the appropriate police agency.

. . .

X. Although Department employees are not law enforcement officials, they do have authority to make arrests of private citizens under the following conditions:

1. For a felony committed in their presence;

2. When the arrestee is known to have committed a felony, though not in the employee's presence; and,

3. When requested by a police official to assist the officer in making an arrest.

. . .

Contact with News Media

Prisoner requests to speak to reporters raise issues concerning inmates' right to freedom of expression. Even more important, perhaps, are issues concerning freedom of the press, especially if a reporter seeks to speak with a specific prisoner. The news media are important "watchdogs" who make sure that government officials obey the law. As demonstrated by the Watergate scandal in the early 1970s, which led to the resignation of President Richard Nixon, if the news media do not investigate improper activities within government, the public may never learn what is really going on. Because prisons are secure, closed institutions, there are always potential risks that abuses occurring within the walls, whether beatings of inmates or embezzlement of funds by administrators, will not be easily discovered. Thus, the news media potentially play an important role in monitoring corrections, just as they monitor other institutions and actors in the government. As you read the hypothetical situation in Box 4-11, think about how you would resolve the case.

The U.S. Supreme Court addressed these kinds of issues in two cases—*Pell v. Procunier* (1974) and *Saxbe v. Washington Post* (1974).[31] *Pell* examined a state's regulations denying news media requests for specific prisoner interviews, and *Saxbe* concerned similar federal regulations. The Court ultimately concluded that

> *newsmen have no constitutional right of access to prisons or their inmates beyond that afforded the general public. The First and Fourteenth Amendments bar government from interfering in any way with a free press. The Constitution does not, however, require government to accord the press special access to information not shared by members of the public generally.*[32]

| BOX 4-11 | **Prisoners and the Press** |

Imagine you are a federal judge faced with the following case. The relative of a prisoner provides a news reporter with information about beatings and torture occurring inside a maximum-security institution. The relative expresses concern that her cousin may be killed by corrections officers as they try to eliminate witnesses to their illegal actions. Prison officials decline to grant the news reporter permission to visit the inmate. The newspaper and television stations file a lawsuit seeking a court order requiring prison officials to permit them to interview the prisoner in question. They argue that the public's right to learn about its government and to have freedom of the press under the First Amendment are being violated by the prison's refusal to permit the interview. The prison claims that the prisoner in question is a dangerous security risk who is in an isolation cell for disciplinary reasons. The prison denies the allegations about abuses and charges that many inmates will make wild claims about abuses in order to try to get interviewed on television. Thus, officials will not agree to permit the news reporters to interview the prisoner as requested.

Are the freedom-of-the-press issues involved here more important than the prison's fears about security? Is there a way to permit the interview to occur without threatening order and security in the institution? Should prisoners ever be permitted to talk to news reporters? What would you decide?

In its reasoning, the Court emphasized that the prison's interest in security and order could be maintained without depriving the news media of information. For example, prisoners who wish to supply information to reporters can write letters to those reporters. In addition, corrections officials permitted reporters to tour prisons and to speak to prisoners whom they encountered while touring. Thus, reporters could serve their freedom-of-the-press function by gathering information and reporting it to the public. The officials objected to giving reporters the power to demand to speak to specific inmates, and the Supreme Court supported the officials' authority to control access to the prisons. The same reasoning was applied to reject a claim by television reporters that they should have access to a county jail.[33] Despite reporters' claims of freedom of the press, the high court views news media representatives as having no greater right of access to prisons than those possessed by other citizens.

SUMMARY

- Prisoners' right of access to the courts is the key right upon which judicial protection of all other rights rests.

- Corrections officials cannot interfere with communications between prisoners and their attorneys. Officials can open legal mail in front of prisoners to check the envelopes for contraband. However, they generally cannot read the mail or listen to conversations between inmates and attorneys.

- Corrections officials must permit jail-house lawyers to assist other prisoners in preparing cases if no other form of legal assistance is provided.

- Corrections officials must supply reasonable quantities of paper, writing supplies, and stamps for indigent prisoners' legal mail. They also must supply a law library or legal assistance to enable inmates to prepare legal filings.

- Prisoners can claim that their right of access to the courts was violated by inadequate prison law libraries only if they can show that their cases were harmed (i.e., they suffered a specific injury) as a result of the inadequacies. This judicial decision effectively limits federal judges' power to identify and broadly remedy deficiencies in law libraries and legal assistance programs.

- Censorship of communications between an outsider and a prisoner may violate the outsider's First Amendment rights to free expression. With respect to rules affecting prisoners' outgoing correspondence, judges may look closely at the connection between the government's interest (e.g., safety and security) and regulations implemented to protect that interest.

- Correspondence between inmates can be censored or banned. Officials need only show that such actions reasonably contribute to a legitimate institutional goal, such as safety or security.

- The Supreme Court developed a four-part test to apply to inmate-to-inmate correspondence and subsequently applied the same test to prison regulations affecting other asserted rights. The test includes consideration of (1) the reasonable and rational connection between the regulation and legitimate institutional goals, (2) the availability of alternative means to exercise the right that conflicts with the regulation, (3) the impact that accommodation of the asserted right will have on the prison and staff, and (4) the absence of an easily applied alternative regulation to achieve the same purpose. The test encourages deference to the judgment of correctional administrators.

- There is no general constitutional right to prison visits, unless it is a right based on state constitutional law. By contrast, visits between attorneys and their clients in prison are protected as part of the right to counsel and the right of access to the courts.

- News reporters possess no greater rights than other citizens for demanding interviews with specific inmates or opportunities to visit specific parts of a prison or jail.

Key Terms

access to the courts
Bounds v. Smith (1977)
contraband
Ex parte Hull (1941)
jailhouse lawyers

Johnson v. Avery (1969)
Lewis v. Casey (1996)
per curiam
Procunier v. Martinez (1974)
rational basis test

strict scrutiny test
Thornburgh v. Abbott (1989)
Turner v. Safley (1987)

Additional Readings

Eisenberg, Howard. 1993. "Rethinking Prisoner Civil Rights Cases and the Provision of Counsel." *Southern Illinois University Law Journal* 17: 417–490.

Hinckley, Steven. 1987. "Bounds and Beyond: A Need to Reevaluate the Right of Prisoners'

Access to the Courts." *University of Richmond Law Review* 22: 19–49.

Myers, John. 1985. "The Writ-Writers: Jailhouse Lawyers' Right of Meaningful Access to the Courts." *Akron Law Review* 18: 649–665.

Notes

1. Wolff v. McDonnell, 418 U.S. 539 (1974).

2. Wolff v. McDonnell, 418 U.S. 539, 577 (1974).

3. Adams v. Carlson, 488 F.2d 619 (7th Cir. 1973); Burton v. Kuchel, 865 F.Supp. 456 (N.D. Ill. 1994).

4. Wright v. McMann, 460 F.2d 126 (2d Cir. 1972); Commonwealth v. Boyd, 580 A.2d 393 (Pa. Sup. Ct. 1990).

5. Washington v. James, 782 F.2d 1134 (2d Cir. 1986).

6. Ibid.

7. Michael Mushlin, *Rights of Prisoners,* Vol. 2, 2nd ed. (Colorado Springs, CO: Shepard's/McGraw-Hill, 1993), p. 49.

8. Dreher v. Sielaff, 636 F.2d 1141 (7th Cir. 1980).

9. Procunier v. Martinez, 416 U.S. 346 (1974).

10. Mushlin, *Rights of Prisoners,* p. 50; Wright v. State, 250 Ga. 570 (Ga. S.Ct. 1983)

11. Mushlin, *Rights of Prisoners,* p. 51; Henry v. Perrin, 609 F.2d 1010 (1st Cir. 1979).

12. Ex parte Hull, 312 U.S. 546 (1941).

13. Mushlin, *Rights of Prisoners,* pp. 3–4.

14. Roe v. Wade, 410 U.S. 113 (1973) (abortion); Cruzan v. Missouri, 467 U.S. 261 (1990) (decline medical treatment).

15. Wade v. Kane, 448 F.Supp. 678 (E.D. Pa. 1978).

16. Falzerano v. Collier, 535 F.Supp. 800, 803 (D. N.J. 1982).

17. Thornburgh v. Abbott, 490 U.S. 401 (1989).

18. Mushlin, *Rights of Prisoners,* p. 127.

19. Ibid., p. 137.

20. Ibid., p. 142; Johnson v. Galli, 596 F.Supp. 135 (D. Nev. 1984).

21. Mushlin, *Rights of Prisoners,* p. 144.

22. Ibid., p. 145.

23. United States v. Horr, 963 F.2d 1124 (8th Cir. 1992); United States v. Amen, 831 F.2d 373 (2d Cir. 1987).

24. Mushlin, *Rights of Prisoners,* p. 53; Tucker v. Randall, 948 F.2d 388 (7th Cir. 1991).

25. Cooper v. Morin, 399 N.E.2d 1188 (1979).

26. Mushlin, *Rights of Prisoners,* p. 110.

27. Kentucky v. Thompson, 490 U.S. 454 (1989).

28. Sandin v. Connor, 515 U.S. 472 (1995).

29. Hernandez v. Coughlin, 18 F.3d 133 (2d Cir. 1994).

30. Block v. Rutherford, 468 U.S. 576 (1984).

31. Pell v. Procunier, 417 U.S. 817 (1974); Saxbe v. Washington Post, 417 U.S. 843 (1974).

32. Pell v. Procunier, 417 U.S. 817, 824 (1974).

33. Houchins v. KQED, 438 U.S. 1 (1978).

CHAPTER FIVE

Prisoners' Personal Rights

I magine you are the warden at a maximum-security prison, and some prisoners ask to meet with you about a religious service they wish to hold. You meet with seven prisoners who are active in a Christian organization within the prison. They are all model prisoners who do not violate prison rules.

"We need to hold an Easter prayer service, but we can't hold it on Easter Sunday," says the leader of the group.

"Why not?" you ask.

"Our Bible study group has been reading some books by famous religion professors. One book told us the actual date of Easter. So in order to be true to our religious beliefs, we need to hold our service on the actual date rather than the particular Sunday that has been selected to serve as Easter."

"What day is that?"

"The Wednesday before the calendar's Easter Sunday."

"But you can't do it then because the theater club is already scheduled to put on this year's play in the chapel that night. The governor and the director of the state department of corrections are coming to see it."

The prisoners' group leader frowns. "We have to do it then. God commands it."

"Maybe you could hold the service in the cafeteria. Oh, wait. The reception after the theater performance is going to be in the cafeteria."

"We need the chapel. We're going to have communion. We already asked Reverend Browning to handle it."

You think about it for a minute. "Sorry. I don't see how you're going to be able to have a church service on that day.

"What about our right to freedom of religion. Isn't that more important than some play?"

You begin to assert your authority in a strong voice. "Hey, you can have your service on Easter Sunday like you're supposed to. These guys have rehearsed the play for a couple months, and it took a long time to persuade the governor to come to see how well this prison is being run."

The prisoners have a look of determination. Their leader says quietly, "We had hoped it would not be necessary. But we'll file a civil rights action if we have to. We believe that the courts will protect our First Amendment right to freedom of religion if you won't obey the Constitution."

Is the prisoner correct? Must the prison give priority to religious ceremonies over other scheduled events at the institution? If you accommodate this group of prisoners, will other prisoners make new demands based on claimed religious beliefs? If a court ultimately rules against you, will the prisoners win money in the lawsuit?

Look back at the Bill of Rights, which is given in Box 1-3. It contains many rights for individuals that most Americans take for granted, including rights to freedom of religion, freedom of speech, and freedom from unreasonable searches and seizures. To what extent do convicted offenders continue to enjoy these rights while under the supervision and control of corrections institutions and programs? The answers to such questions are not always clear. In this chapter, we will examine how courts have interpreted some of these personal rights of convicted offenders.

FREEDOM OF RELIGION

The First Amendment specifies two rights affecting religion. The **Establishment Clause** bars "an establishment of religion." Although it is widely agreed that these words prevent the government from adopting an official national religion, there is disagreement about what else the clause might mean. Court decisions have used the clause to prevent the government from forcing people to engage in certain religious activities. For example, the U.S. Supreme Court's ban on mandatory prayers sponsored by public schools is based on the Establishment Clause. The clause also has been interpreted to prevent government funding for most religious programs. In the prison context, the Establishment Clause would prevent prison officials from forcing inmates to worship or to attend particular church services. However, the clause would not prevent a prison from hiring a chaplain or providing facilities for religious meetings.

BOX 5-1 **Actual Religious Program Schedule at a High-Security Prison**

Tuesday	6:30 p.m. to 8:00 p.m.	Bible Study
Thursday	6:30 p.m. to 8:00 p.m.	Bible Study
Friday	1:00 p.m. to 2:00 p.m.	American Muslim Mission
	2:30 p.m. to 3:30 p.m.	Melanic Islamic Faith
	6:00 p.m. to 7:00 p.m.	Nation of Islam
	7:30 p.m. to 8:30 p.m.	Moorish Science Temple
Sunday	8:30 a.m. to 9:30 a.m.	Protestant Services
	1:00 p.m. to 2:00 p.m.	Catholic Services

Your I.D. card must be stamped with your chosen designation to attend services.

The most difficult problems concern the **Free Exercise Clause.** The First Amendment prohibits governments from making laws "prohibiting the free exercise" of religion. This limitation on government interference with religious practices extends beyond the enactment of laws and also includes the policies and practices of government agencies. Because prisons must place a priority on maintaining order and security, inmates' religious practices may pose problems, particularly because many different religions are represented in the typical American prison. Box 5-1 gives the actual religious program schedule at one prison. Does it interfere with prisoners' freedom of religion to require them to choose a single religion for designation on their I.D. cards? What if a prisoner wants to worship with prisoners from a different religion?

Free Exercise Issues

When prisoners raise religious claims in the courts, judges face the difficult task of evaluating the sincerity of their beliefs *and* determining whether those beliefs are part of a religion or are merely a personal philosophy. For example, the emergence of Islamic religious practices among African-American prisoners in the 1950s and 1960s was met by resistance from corrections administrators. Many wardens viewed the Black Muslims as representatives of a rebellious political movement masquerading as a religion. Muslims thus were denied opportunities to hold religious services, gain access to religious literature and ministers, and observe customs such as growing beards and avoiding pork in their diets. In denying Muslims the opportunity to adhere to their religious beliefs, wardens not only were affecting their free exercise rights under the First Amendment but also were raising questions about Muslims' **equal protection** rights under the Fourteenth Amendment. Christian inmates were permitted to hold services, read Christian literature, and meet with their clergy. Thus, Muslims were being treated differently than prisoners from another religion. The Equal Protection Clause eventually was applied to other religions following legal action, such as that by a Buddhist prisoner who successfully challenged restrictions on his religious practices that were not applied to other prisoners' religions (*Cruz v. Beto*, 1972).[1]

Muslim prisoners likewise filed numerous lawsuits attempting to gain recognition for their religious practices. Their efforts to use the legal system to protect constitutional rights ultimately provided benefits to many prisoners outside of their religious group.[2] Beginning with cases in the early 1960s (e.g., *Fulwood v. Clemmer*, 1962), Muslims gradually gained recognition for their religion and opportunities to exercise the practices of their religion.[3]

A few religions actually have been initiated and fostered within prison walls. Some of these efforts reflected the fact that prisoners viewed the right to free exercise of religion as an opportunity to gain extra privileges, such as special meals. Courts have refused to recognize some of these religions, such as the "Church of the New Song" started by inmates who sought to have the prison pay them as chaplains,[4] but other inmate-created religions have been recognized as legitimate.[5]

Many kinds of religious issues arise as free exercise cases. For example, Muslim and Jewish prisoners need to follow particular religious restrictions with respect to the foods they eat. Inmates have asserted rights to pork-free diets and to kosher meals. Some court decisions have accommodated these religious needs by ruling that prison officials would not be burdened by these special meals.[6] Other court decisions have rejected religion-based claims for special meals, either because the inmate did not demonstrate that a special diet was essential to the religion[7] or because the special diet and cooking procedures would result in prohibitive administrative costs.[8]

Native American prisoners have raised many issues with respect to their religious beliefs and practices. There have been unsuccessful efforts to gain a right of access to "sweat lodges," as well as mixed results in fighting prison rules banning headbands and religious artifacts.[9] In the latter cases, some courts have accepted arguments that contraband can be hidden in long hair despite the importance of hair for some Native American religions.[10] Related issues have arisen concerning other religions, such as Rastafarians' "dread locks" hairstyles and Jewish inmates' yarmulkes.[11]

Such cases must be analyzed in light of the Supreme Court's controlling precedent for free exercise of religion, established in **O'Lone v. Estate of Shabazz** (1987). Following the Supreme Court's reasoning, "courts are generally disinclined to upset prison grooming codes in the post-Shabazz era."[12] As you read the Court's opinion in Box 5-2, consider how it affects prisoners' religious freedom claims. Which religious practices are protected by courts under the approach used in the case? Does the analysis in this case remind you of any other cases you have seen in prior chapters of this book?

The Supreme Court was deeply divided in its decision in *O'Lone:* Five justices supported the prison regulations, while the other four justices feared that

| BOX 5-2 | *O'Lone v. Estate of Shabazz,* 482 U.S. 342 (1987) |

CHIEF JUSTICE REHNQUIST delivered the opinion of the Court.

This case requires us to consider once again the standard of review for prison regulations claimed to inhibit the exercise of constitutional rights. Respondents, members of the Islamic faith, were prisoners in New Jersey's Leesburg State Prison. They challenged policies adopted by prison officials which resulted in their inability to attend Jumu'ah, a weekly Muslim congregation service regularly held in the main prison building and in a separate facility known as "the Farm." Jumu'ah is commanded by the Koran [the sacred religious text of Islam] and must be held every Friday after the sun reaches its zenith and before Asr, or afternoon prayer. . . . There is no question that respondents' sincerely held beliefs compelled attendance at Jumu'ah. We hold that the prison regulations here challenged did not violate respondents' rights under the Free Exercise Clause of the First Amendment. . . .

. . . In the initial stages of outside work details for gang minimum prisoners [a security classification level for some prisoners], officials apparently allowed some Muslim inmates to work inside the main building on Fridays so that they could attend Jumu'ah. This alternative was eventually eliminated in March 1984, in light of the directive of Standard 853 [a new prison regulation] that all gang minimum inmates work outside the main building.

Significant problems arose with those inmates assigned to outside work details. Some avoided reporting for their assignments, while others found reasons for returning to the main building during the course of the workday (including their desire to attend religious services). Evidence showed that the return of prisoners during the day resulted in security risks and administrative burdens that prison officials found unacceptable. Because details of inmates were supervised by only one guard, the whole detail was forced to return to the main gate when one prisoner decided to return to the facility. The gate was the site of all incoming foot and vehicle traffic during the day, and prison officials viewed it as a high security risk area.

In response to these burdens, Leesburg officials took steps to ensure that those assigned to outside details remained there for the whole day. . . . These changes proved insufficient, however, and prison officials began to study alternatives. After consulting with the director of social services, the director of professional services and the prison's imam [Muslim clergyman] and chaplain, prison officials in March 1984 issued a policy memorandum which prohibited inmates assigned to outside work details from returning to the prison during the day except in the case of emergency.

The prohibition on returns prevented Muslims assigned to outside work details from attending Jumu'ah. Respondents filed suit under 42 U.S.C. [section] 1983. . . .

Several general principles guide our consideration of the issues presented here. First, "convicted prisoners do not forfeit all constitutional protections by reason of their conviction and confinement in prison." . . . Inmates clearly retain protections afforded by the First Amendment. . . . Second, "lawful incarceration brings about the necessary withdrawal or limitation of many privileges and rights, a retraction justified by the considerations underlying our penal system." . . . The limitations on the exercise of constitutional rights arise both from the fact of incarceration and from valid penological objectives—including deterrence of crime, rehabilitation of prisoners, and institutional security. . . .

To ensure that courts afford appropriate deference to prison officials, we have determined that prison regulations alleged to infringe constitutional rights are judged under a "reasonableness" test less restrictive than that ordinarily applied to alleged infringements of fundamental constitutional rights [for citizens in society] . . .

(continued)

Turning to consideration of the policies challenged in this case, we think the findings of the District Court establish clearly that prison officials have acted in a reasonable manner. *Turner v. Safley* drew upon our previous decisions to identify several factors relevant to this reasonableness determination. First, a regulation must have a logical connection to legitimate governmental interests invoked to justify it. . . . The policies at issue here clearly meet that standard. The requirement that full minimum and gang minimum prisoners work outside the main facility was justified by concerns for institutional order and security. . . .

The subsequent policy prohibiting returns to the institution during the day also passes muster under this standard. Prison officials testified that the returns from outside work details generated congestion and delays at the main gate, a high risk area in any event. . . .

Our decision in *Turner* also found it relevant that "alternative means of exercising the right . . . remain open to inmates." . . . There are, of course, no alternative means of attending Jumu'ah; respondents' religious beliefs insist that it occur at a particular time. But the very stringent requirements as to the time at which Jumu'ah may be held may make it extraordinarily difficult for prison officials to assure that every Muslim prisoner is able to attend that service. While we in no way minimize the central importance of Jumu'ah to respondents, we are unwilling to hold that prison officials are required by the Constitution to sacrifice legitimate penological objectives to that end. . . . The record establishes that respondents are not deprived of all forms of religious exercise, but instead are free to observe a number of their religious obligations. . . .

Finally, the case for the validity of these regulations is strengthened by examination of the impact that accommodation of respondents' asserted right should have on other inmates, on prison personnel, and on allocation of prison resources. . . . [E]ach of the respondents' suggested accommodations would, in the judgment of prison officials, have adverse effects on the institution. Inside work details for gang minimum inmates would be inconsistent with the legitimate concerns underlying Standard 853. . . . [E]xtra supervision necessary to establish weekend details for Muslim prisoners "would be a drain on scarce human resources." . . . Prison officials also determined that the alternatives would also threaten prison security by allowing "affinity groups" in the prison to flourish . . . and other inmates . . . [would] perceive favoritism. . . . These difficulties also make clear that there are no "obvious, easy alternatives to the policy adopted by [the prison]. . . .

JUSTICE BRENNAN, with whom JUSTICE MARSHALL, JUSTICE BLACKMUN, and JUSTICE STEVENS join, dissenting.

The religious ceremony that these respondents seek to attend is not presumptively dangerous, and the prison has completely foreclosed respondents' participation in it. I therefore would require prison officials to demonstrate that the restrictions they have imposed are necessary to further an important government interest, and that these restrictions are no greater than necessary to achieve prison objectives. . . .

Jumu'ah therefore cannot be regarded as one of several essentially fungible [replaceable with each other] religious practices. The ability to engage in other religious activities cannot obscure the fact that the denial at issue in this case is absolute: respondents are completely foreclosed from participating in the core ceremony that reflects their membership in a particular religious community. If a Catholic prisoner were prevented from attending Mass on Sunday, few would regard that deprivation as anything but absolute, even if the prisoner were afforded other opportunities to pray, to discuss the Catholic faith with others, and even to avoid eating meat on Friday if that were a preference. Prison officials in this case therefore cannot show that "other avenues remain available for the exercise of the asserted right."

. . . In this case, [prison officials] have not established the reasonableness of their policy, because they have provided only bare assertions that the proposals for accommodation offered by [the prisoners' attorneys] are infeasible. . . .

That Muslim inmates are able to participate in Jumu'ah throughout the entire federal prison system suggests that the practice is, under normal circumstances, compatible with the demands of prison administration. Indeed, the Leesburg State Prison permitted participation in this ceremony for five years, and experienced no threats to security or safety as a result. . . .

. . . As the record now stands, prison officials have declared that a security risk is created by a grouping of Muslim inmates in the least dangerous security classification, but not by a grouping of maximum security inmates who are concentrated in work detail inside the main building, and who are the only Muslims assured of participating in Jumu'ah. Surely,

prison officials should be required to provide at least some substantiation for this facially implausible contention. . . .

. . . If the Court's standard of review is to represent anything more than reflexive deference to prison officials, any finding of reasonableness must rest on firmer ground than the record now presents.

Incarceration by its nature denies a prisoner participation in the larger human community. To deny the opportunity to affirm membership in a spiritual community, however, may extinguish an inmate's last source of hope for dignity and redemption. Such a denial requires more justification [by prison officials] than mere assertion that any other course of action is infeasible. . . .

the prisoners' religious rights were being denied without good reason. What are the differences in approaches presented by the majority opinion and the dissenting opinion? What kinds of constitutional rights for prisoners can survive the majority's analysis, as found in *Turner v. Safley* (See Box 4-6)? Is Justice Brennan correct in implying that the majority's approach is simply a way to let corrections officials do what they want without adequately protecting rights?

Free exercise issues extend to regulations governing actual religious services in prison. Box 5-3 gives the rules found in one prison. Do these rules seem too stringent as applied to religious ceremonies?

Look at rule 8, in particular. What kinds of judgments are prison officials forced to make in determining whether a religious practice is proper? Do these judgments create the risk that prison officials will limit activities that prisoners consider to be essential to their religious practices? Are prison officials legally permitted to make such decisions?

Developments After *O'Lone v. Estate of Shabazz*

In 1990, the U.S. Supreme Court decided an important case that involved free exercise of religion outside of the corrections context but that had implications for prisoners' free exercise rights. In *Employment Division of Oregon v. Smith* (1990), the Court considered the case of a Native American drug rehabilitation counselor in Oregon who had lost his job and been denied unemployment compensation as a result of using peyote in a religious ceremony.[13] Peyote is a natural hallucinogenic drug that has been used for centuries in Native Americans' religious practices. Although the drug is illegal, many states permit its use

BOX 5-3

Actual Rules for Prison Religious Services

XIII. CHAPEL RULES

Kite [send a written note] to the Chaplain if you wish to attend services. Prisoners may ordinarily attend services for only one religion at a time.

1. All emergency evacuation guidelines will be posted and strictly enforced and observed by prisoners and staff.

2. All volunteers and visitors must follow directions of staff during emergency evacuations and fire drills.

3. Smoking is not permitted inside any part of the Chapel.

4. Chapel bathrooms may not be occupied by more than one prisoner at a time.

5. All Chapel doors shall be secured when the Chapel area is not occupied.

6. Prisoners may not serve as guards or ushers anywhere. There will be no standing, except when asked to stand during prayer.

7. Prisoners on the podium leading the services may stand for that purpose only.

8. Close order drilling, marching, or giving commands is not permitted. Chants are limited to religious themes appropriate to the service.

9. At the end of the religious service, prisoner religious aides will ensure that the members are instructed to leave the Chapel area one row at a time and immediately exit the building. This will ensure a quick and orderly exit from the Chapel area.

10. Individuals (prisoners) may be restricted from attending services for violation of these rules.

The purpose of these rules is to ensure that all religious services are safe and orderly for prisoners and staff alike.

---

by Native Americans in religious ceremonies. However, the state of Oregon does not permit its use at all. The Court decided that Oregon did not violate the counselor's right to freely exercise his religion by denying him unemployment compensation because of his peyote use. In an opinion written by Justice Antonin Scalia, the Court surprised many lawyers and scholars by declaring that people must obey general laws, even if they hinder free exercise of religion, as long as those laws are not aimed at stopping a religious practice.[14] Oregon's law was interpreted as a general law intended to prevent the use of an illegal drug.

Many members of Congress reacted harshly to the Supreme Court's decision in *Employment Division of Oregon v. Smith*. They passed a new federal law intended to restore protections for religious exercise that were diminished by the Court's decision. The **Religious Freedom Restoration Act of 1993** was intended to force the government to provide compelling justifications for insisting that any law or policy was more important than people's religious practices. In other words, Congress wanted the courts to apply the strict scrutiny test (see Chapter 4) rather than the reasonableness/rational basis test to cases concerning free exercise of religion. Box 5-4 contains a portion of the text of the Religious Freedom Restoration Act. How would you apply this statute to decide the issue raised in *O'Lone v. Estate of Shabazz?*

B O X   5 - 4   **Religious Freedom Restoration Act, 42 U.S.C. [Sections] 2000bb-1**

Free exercise of religion protected

(a) In general. Government shall not substantially burden a person's exercise of religion, even if the burden results from a rule of general applicability, except as provided in subsection (b).

(b) Exception. Government may substantially burden a person's exercise of religion only if

it demonstrates that application of the burden to the person—

(1) is in furtherance of a compelling governmental interest; and

(2) is the least restrictive means of furthering that compelling governmental interest.

Congress debated whether to exclude prisoners from the protections specified in the Religious Freedom Restoration Act. Ultimately, the law did not exclude prisoners from coverage. Although Congress does not usually act to protect the rights of prisoners, the idea of religious freedom is strongly supported by both liberals and conservatives. Thus, even prisoners could benefit in some circumstances from this strongly held view.

Consider the hypothetical problems presented in Box 5-5. What if you were a judge attempting to apply the Religious Freedom Restoration Act? Would the cases be decided differently if you simply applied *O'Lone v. Shabazz*?

The future of free-exercise-of-religion cases in the courts—including cases from outside of the prison context—is uncertain. In 1997, the U.S. Supreme Court declared that the Religious Freedom Restoration Act was unconstitutional (*City of Boerne v. Flores,* 1997).[15] According to the Court, Congress lacked the authority to enact such legislation. Clearly, however, most of the justices also believed that state legislatures possessed the authority to enact such laws to cover their own states. Therefore, legislators in many states began proposing legislation parallel to the Religious Freedom Restoration Act in order to achieve the same purposes in individual states. State legislators are much less likely to include prisoners in such protection because otherwise state officials would be subject to lawsuits and liability for violations. Congress, by contrast, may have felt less compelled to exclude coverage for prisoners because state governments—which control most corrections institutions—would bear the primary burden of compliance. Thus, for example, a bill in the Michigan legislature modeled on the Religious Freedom Restoration Act received approval from a key committee in the state's House of Representatives just weeks after the U.S. Supreme Court struck down the federal law. However, the Michigan proposal specifically excluded prisoners from religious freedom protection after vigorous lobbying by the Michigan Department of Corrections, which claimed that prisoners file too many lawsuits about religious freedom and that the number of such lawsuits had skyrocketed in the aftermath of the federal Religious Freedom Restoration Act.[16]

BOX 5-5   **Freedom of Religion**

Imagine that you are a federal judge considering the following cases.

CASE 1

A Native American prisoner claims that it is central to his religious beliefs that he be permitted to keep his hair long and wear it in braids. In a previous case, a court had enforced the prison's short-hair requirement, even against Native American prisoners, because the prison claimed that drugs, weapons, or other contraband could be hidden in long hair. Now this prisoner wants the issue reconsidered in light of the Religious Freedom Restoration Act (see Box 5-4). His lawyer presents evidence showing that no contraband has been found in any Native American prisoner's long hair in the ten years since the short-hair regulation was enacted.

CASE 2

A jail inmate objects to being forced to attend religious services against his will because of the jail's policy that either all four men in a cell must attend together or none may attend. The local sheriff claims that the policy seeks to prevent possible suicide by a single prisoner being left alone in a cell while his cellmates attend religious services. The sheriff also claims that there are not enough jail personnel to keep watch over prisoners at the services and in the cells if some prisoners stay behind. The inmate has contacted the ACLU, which is pursuing his claim against the jail as a violation of his First Amendment right to religious freedom.

How would you decide these cases? What factors would you consider? Is there any additional information that you want to know?

It remains to be seen which states, if any, will include prisoners in new legislation protecting free exercise of religion. As this political process unfolds in the coming years, ask yourself: Are prisoners entitled to the same legal protections as other Americans for exercising their religious beliefs and practices? If they are excluded from coverage in new laws, do prisoners have adequate protection from the courts to prevent undue interference with sincere religious practices behind prison walls?

ASSOCIATION RIGHTS

Chapter 4 discussed several aspects of prisoners' rights to have contact with others, including correspondence, telephone calls, and visits. Prisoners may claim that they are entitled to maintain other kinds of contacts and relationships. For example, as part of religious freedom rights, some court decisions recognize the right of prisoners to have contact with clergy from their faith (i.e., ministers, priests, rabbis, etc.),[17] although they cannot necessarily choose a particular minister.[18] Many prisoners also have gained opportunities to hold worship services with other inmates who share their religious beliefs.[19] Such rights may not apply equally, however, to prisoners who are on death row or in isolation cells for disciplinary reasons.[20]

Prisoners' Unions

In addition to the religious examples, other types of prisoner relationships may raise legal issues. As you read the case, which is excerpted in Box 5-6, are you surprised at the kind of association presented to the courts as a prisoners' rights case? How much authority does this decision give to corrections administrators who wish to control how prisoners associate with one another?

This case raised interesting questions and revealed a major division within the Supreme Court. What was the nature of Justice Thurgood Marshall's disagreement with the majority decision? Was Marshall correct in concluding that the majority's approach to deciding prisoners' rights cases would effectively eliminate all rights except the right of access to the courts? Regardless of how you answer these questions, it is clear that the Supreme Court currently does not view prisoners' unions as a form of association that can gain protection under the Constitution.

BOX 5-6   *Jones v. North Carolina Prisoners' Labor Union,*
433 U.S. 119 (1977)

JUSTICE REHNQUIST delivered the opinion of the Court.

. . . [A]n organization self-[named] as a Prisoners' Labor Union, was incorporated in late 1974, with a stated goal of "the promotion of charitable labor union purposes" and the formation of a "prisoners' labor union at every prison and jail in North Carolina to seek through collective bargaining . . . to improve . . . conditions. . . ." . . . By early 1975, the Union had attracted some 2,000 inmate "members" in 40 different prison units throughout North Carolina. The State of North Carolina, unhappy with these developments, set out to prevent inmates from forming or operating a "union." While the State tolerated individual "membership," or belief, in the Union, it sought to prohibit inmate solicitation of other inmates, meetings between members of the Union, and bulk mailing concerning the Union from outside sources. Pursuant to a regulation [imposed] by the Department of Correction on March 26, 1975, such solicitation and group activity were [banned].

. . . The Union claimed [in its civil rights lawsuit] that its rights, and the rights of its members, to engage in protected free speech, association, and assembly activities were infringed by the no-solicitation and no-meeting rules. It also alleged a deprivation of equal protection of the laws in that the Jaycees and Alcoholics Anonymous were permitted to have meetings and other organizational rights, such as the distribution of bulk mailing material, that the Union was being denied. . . .

The District Court, we believe, got off on the wrong foot in this case by not giving appropriate deference to the decisions of prison administrators and appropriate recognition to the peculiar and restrictive circumstances of penal confinement. . . . The fact of confinement and the needs of the penal institution impose limitations on constitutional rights, including those derived from the First Amendment, which are implicit in incarceration. . . .

Perhaps the most obvious of the First Amendment rights that are necessarily curtailed

(continued)

by confinement are those associational rights that the First Amendment protects outside of prison walls. . . .

State correctional officials uniformly testified that the concept of a prisoners' labor union was itself fraught with potential dangers, whether or not such a union intended illegally, to press for collective-bargaining recognition. . . .

. . . [Prison officials] permitted membership [in the Union] because of the reasonable assumption that each individual prisoner could believe what he chose to believe, and that outside individuals should be able to communicate ideas and beliefs to individual inmates. . . . [Because] a prisoner apparently may become a member [of the Union] simply by considering himself a member[, the prisons' decision to permit membership but ban meetings] simply reflects the concept that thought control, by means of prohibiting beliefs, would not only be undesirable but impossible.

. . . It is clearly not irrational to conclude that individuals may believe what they want, but that concerted group activity, or solicitation therefor, would pose additional and unwarranted problems and frictions in the operation of the State's penal institutions. The ban on inmate solicitation and group meetings, therefore, was rationally related to the reasonable, indeed to the central, objectives of prison administration. . . .

. . . The case of a prisoners' union, where the focus is on the presentation of grievances to, and encouragement of adversary relations with, institution officials surely would rank high on anyone's list of potential trouble spots. If the [prison officials'] views as to the possible detrimental effects of the organizational activities of the Union are reasonable, as we conclude they are, then the regulations are drafted no more broadly than they need to be to meet the perceived threat—which stems directly from group meetings and group organizational activities of the Union. . . .

. . . [Prison officials] need only demonstrate a rational basis for their distinctions between organizational groups [in order to defeat an equal protection claim]. . . .

. . . Prison administrators may surely conclude that the Jaycees and Alcoholics Anonymous differ in fundamental respects from the appellee Union, a group with no past to speak of, and with the avowed intent to pursue an adversary relationship with prison officials. . . .

. . . It is precisely in matters such as this, the decision as to which of many groups should be allowed to operate within the prison walls, where, confronted with claims based on the Equal Protection Clause, the courts should allow the prison administrators the full latitude of discretion, unless it can be firmly stated that the two groups are so similar that discretion has been abused. That is surely not the case here. There is nothing in the Constitution which requires prison officials to treat all inmate groups alike where differentiation is necessary to avoid an imminent threat of institutional disruption or violence. . . .

JUSTICE MARSHALL, with whom JUSTICE BRENNAN joins, dissenting.

In testing restrictions on the exercise of [the] right [to have Union activities] the Court asks only whether the restrictions are "rationally related to the . . . objectives of prison administration," . . . and whether the reasons offered in defense of the restrictions have been "conclusively shown to be wrong." . . .

The approach I advocate is precisely the one this Court has followed in other cases involving the rights of prisoners. In *Johnson v. Avery,* 393 U.S. 483 (1969), for example, the Court expressly acknowledged the rationality of the rule at issue which prohibited inmate writ writers from aiding fellow prisoners in preparing legal papers. . . . We nevertheless concluded that the rule was unconstitutional because of its impact on prisoners' right of access to the courts. In *Lee v. Washington,* 390 U.S. 333 (1968), we did not even inquire whether segregating prisoners by race was rational, although it could be argued that integration in a southern prison would lead to disorder among inmates; we held that in any event segregation was prohibited by the Fourteenth Amendment. And in

Bounds v. Smith [1977] . . . ; *Wolff v. McDonnell* [1974] . . . ; and *Cruz v. Beto* [1972] . . . , we followed the approach in *Lee*. . . .

Once it is established that traditional First Amendment principles are applicable in prisoners' rights cases, the dispute here is easily resolved. The three-judge court not only found that there was "not one scintilla of evidence to suggest that the Union had been utilized to disrupt the operation of the penal institutions," . . . as the Court['s majority opinion] acknowledges, . . . it also found no evidence "that the inmates intend to operate [the Union] to hamper and interfere with the proper interests of government," . . . or that the Union posed a "present danger to security and order, . . ." In

the face of these findings, it cannot be argued that the restrictions on the Union are "imperatively [justified]. . . .

If the mode of analysis adopted in today's [majority] decision were to be generally followed, prisoners eventually would be stripped of all constitutional rights, and would retain only those privileges that prison officials, in their "informed discretion," deigned to recognize. The sole constitutional constraint on prison officials would be a requirement that they act rationally. Ironically, prisoners would be left with a right of access to the courts, see *Bounds v. Smith* [1977] . . . ; *Johnson v. Avery* [1969] . . . , but no substantive rights to assert once they got there. . . .

Marriage and Family

Although the Supreme Court did not accept the claim that prisoners should be able to form an active union, other forms of association have a stronger historical and social basis—even for convicted offenders. In particular, intimate associations within families traditionally are regarded as an important component of any individual's life. These forms of association, especially marriage, may be regulated by the government (e.g., the requirement of obtaining a marriage license). However, Americans do not want too much interference by government into their decisions about private matters, such as marriage. In light of the approach taken by the Supreme Court in the union case, how would a court decide the hypothetical issue raised in Box 5-7?

The Constitution does not mention any right to get married, nor does it explicitly address other personal, family issues. Nevertheless, the Supreme Court historically has recognized that people are entitled to protections for certain private decisions. For example, court decisions have protected people's right to make various personal choices—for example, concerning their children's education and lives,[21] concerning marriage to someone from a different race,[22] and concerning abortion.[23] Some of these court decisions have been based on freedom of religion or equal protection, but others have been based on personal rights identified as part of a larger right to privacy. Privacy is not mentioned in the Constitution. But courts have followed the lead of the U.S. Supreme Court in recognizing the existence of a constitutional right to privacy by implication, and they have applied this right in many contexts since the 1960s.

Even if marriage is part of the right to privacy or is otherwise treated as a protected private decision under the Constitution, that does not mean that prisoners enjoy that same right. The nature of prisoners' rights often differs from

Prison Marriages

Imagine you are warden of a state prison. You agree to meet with an inmate who has complained bitterly that the prison is preventing him from getting married. The prisoner is the twenty-one-year-old son of very wealthy parents. He has served two years of a ten-year sentence for vehicular homicide. While under the influence of alcohol and cocaine, he lost control of his sports car at high speed and killed a small child walking down the sidewalk.

"What seems to be the problem, Anderson?" you ask.

"The assistant warden says I can't get married. I just wanted to give you a chance to clear this up before my Dad's lawyer hauls you and a bunch of other people around here into court for violating my rights," comes the defiant response.

"Whom do you plan to marry?"

"It's a girl from the Philippines who has been my pen pal for a couple of months. My parents are bringing her over here next week."

"Doesn't this violate some kind of immigration laws or something?"

"Don't worry about that, Warden. My parents have it all taken care of, and I'm planning to get married in the visiting room a week from Saturday."

"Look, you can't just automatically decide when you're going to get married. There could be some kind of illegal activity going on. We're going to have to check this out and think about it."

Anderson reacts angrily: "You better get your lawyers ready!"

Should the prisoner have a constitutional right to get married while in prison? What power should prison officials have over an inmate's marriage decision? Does the Supreme Court's approach to prisoners' rights cases give you any clues about whether a warden can stop a prisoner's planned wedding?

the rights possessed by people in free society. Thus, courts have been asked to consider how much freedom prisoners should have to make decisions about marriage. Traditionally, prison officials had complete control over such decisions. However, the U.S. Supreme Court has reconsidered this issue in recent decades, as the concept of prisoners' rights developed.

The most important case concerning prison marriage was *Turner v. Safley* (1987), the same case we examined in Chapter 4 concerning correspondence between inmates. Cases often raise more than one issue. This case challenged a prison regulation on marriage, as well as a regulation on correspondence. As you read the judicial decision, excerpted in Box 5-8, ask yourself whether prisoners have a right to marry and, if so, how limited or unlimited that right should be.

The opinion by Justice John Paul Stevens repeats a theme we have seen in dissenting opinions by other justices. That is, the justices disagree with one another about the level of protection to provide for various rights of prisoners. Although the majority invalidated the Missouri marriage regulation under the reasonableness test, the prison officials easily could have won the case. According to Stevens, the prison official simply needed to claim that a particular

BOX 5-8	*Turner v. Safley*, 482 U.S. 78 (1987)

JUSTICE O'CONNOR delivered the opinion of the Court.

. . . The challenged marriage regulation which was promulgated while this litigation was pending, permits an inmate to marry only with the permission of the superintendent of the prison, and provides that such approval should be given only "when there are compelling reasons to do so." The term "compelling" is not defined, but prison officials testified at trial that generally only a pregnancy or the birth of an illegitimate child would be considered a compelling reason. . . .

In support of the marriage regulation, [prison officials] first suggest that the rule does not deprive prisoners of a constitutionally protected right. They concede that the decision to marry is a fundamental right under . . . *Loving v. Virginia* [1967], but they imply that a different rule should obtain . . . "[in] a prison forum." . . .

We disagree. . . . It is settled that a prison inmate "retains those rights that are not inconsistent with his status as a prisoner or with the legitimate penological objectives of the corrections system." The right to marry, like many other rights, is subject to substantial restrictions as a result of incarceration. . . .

. . . [But] we conclude that . . . a constitutionally protected marital relationship [exists] in the prison context. . . .

. . . [E]ven under the reasonable relationship test, the marriage regulation does not withstand scrutiny.

[Prison officials] have identified both security and rehabilitation concerns in support of the marriage prohibition. The security concern emphasized by [prison officials] is that "love triangles" might lead to violent confrontations between inmates. With respect to rehabilitation, prison officials testified that female prisoners often were subject to abuse at home or were overly dependent on male figures, and that this dependence or abuse was connected to the crimes they had committed. The [prison] superintendent . . . testified that in his view, these women prisoners needed to concentrate on developing skills of self-reliance and that the prohibition on marriage furthered this rehabilitative goal. . . .

We conclude on this record, the Missouri prison regulation, as written, is not reasonably related to these penological interests. . . . There are obvious, easy alternatives to the Missouri regulation that accommodate the right to marry while [placing a minimal] burden on the pursuit of security objectives. . . . [For example,] marriage by inmates in federal prison [is] generally permitted, but not if [the] warden finds that it presents a threat to the security or order of the institution, or to public safety. . . . [The prison officials] have pointed to nothing in the record suggesting that the marriage regulation was viewed as preventing ["love triangles"]. . . .

Nor, on this record, is the marriage restriction reasonably related to the articulated rehabilitation goal. First, in requiring refusal of permission absent a finding of a compelling reason to allow the marriage, the rule sweeps much more broadly than can be explained by petitioners' penological objectives. Missouri prison officials testified that generally they had experienced no problem with the marriage of male inmates, and the District Court found that such marriages had routinely been allowed as a matter of practice at Missouri correctional institutions prior to adoption of the rule. The proffered justification thus does not explain the adoption of a rule banning marriages by these inmates. Nor does it account for the prohibition on inmate marriages to civilians. . . . The rehabilitation concern appears from the record to have been centered almost exclusively on female inmates marrying other inmates or ex-felons; it does not account for the ban on inmate-civilian marriages. . . .

It is undisputed that Missouri prison officials may regulate the time and circumstances under

(continued)

which the marriage ceremony itself takes place. On this record, however, the almost complete ban on the decision to marry is not reasonably related to legitimate penological objectives. We conclude, therefore, that the Missouri regulation is facially invalid. . . .

JUSTICE STEVENS, with whom JUSTICE BRENNAN, JUSTICE MARSHALL, and JUSTICE BLACKMUN join, concurring in part and dissenting in part.

. . . [I]f the standard [applied by the majority] can be satisfied by nothing more than a "logical connection" between the regulation and any legitimate penological concern perceived by a cautious warden, it is virtually meaningless. Application of the standard would seem to permit disregard for inmates' constitutional rights whenever the imagination of the warden produces a plausible security concern and a deferential trial court is able to discern a logical connection between that concern and the challenged regulation. . . .

marriage raised security issues in order to block the marriage. By contrast, Stevens and the justices who joined him would have required prison officials to clearly demonstrate the harm of a particular marriage. They would not have accepted mere fears about security, which might pass muster under the reasonableness test, as a sufficiently compelling justification to block a prisoner's right to marry.

Some critics question whether both parts of the *Turner v. Safley* decision make sense. Recall that the Court upheld the regulations banning prisoners' correspondence with one another (see Chapter 4) but rejected the marriage ban. Thus, in effect, a female inmate could marry a male inmate because marriage is an important fundamental right that supersedes the state's overly broad regulation. Yet, after marrying the other inmate, the husband and wife could not even write to each other—despite the fact that communication between spouses easily could be viewed as an important aspect of marriage, and therefore as a protected right.[24]

Imprisonment has other negative effects on marriages and families. A few states have laws that make imprisonment a ground for the free spouse to gain a divorce, simply based on the fact that other spouse is locked up. Very few states would permit an inmate's children to be put up for adoption without the inmate's permission. However, some scholars believe that courts put such great weight on the parent's imprisonment as a reason for finding the inmate an "unfit parent" that incarceration has the practical impact of threatening a convicted offender's parental rights.[25] Imprisoned mothers of newborn babies, who either entered prison pregnant and gave birth while in custody or who gave birth just prior to being locked up, have no constitutional right to raise their children.[26] Some states have statutes or prison rules providing imprisoned mothers with opportunities to spend time with their babies, but most do not. Despite the importance of bonding between mothers and infants, the law does not place this need above the punishment and security goals of prisons.[27]

SEARCHES

The Fourth Amendment provides protection against "unreasonable searches and seizures." Obviously, what is "reasonable" in free society may be very different from what is "reasonable" in prisons and other corrections contexts. Prisons need to emphasize safety and security. Both corrections officers and prisoners may be placed at risk if officials cannot check inmates and their cells for weapons and drugs. Thus, not surprisingly, the courts provide relatively little protection for prisoners' privacy and property.

Searches of Cells

In free society, the U.S. Supreme Court often provides protection for people's **reasonable expectations of privacy.** In prison settings, however, the courts tend to regard it as unreasonable for prisoners to expect that their clothing or cells will receive protection against searches. As indicated by the Supreme Court's opinion in one of its leading cases on the subject, *Hudson v. Palmer* (1984), the Fourth Amendment provides little protection for prisoners' cells. As you read the decision, which is excerpted in Box 5-9, think about what protections—if any—prisoners should have against searches of their cells or their possessions.

The Supreme Court's opinion made it quite clear that prisoners have no Fourth Amendment protections against cell searches. As the Court noted, however, this does not necessarily mean that prisoners have no legal protections

---

BOX 5-9   *Hudson v. Palmer,* **468 U.S. 517 (1984)**

CHIEF JUSTICE BURGER delivered the opinion of the Court.

The facts underlying this dispute are relatively simple. Respondent Palmer is an inmate at Bland Correctional Center in Bland, Va., serving sentences for forgery, uttering [passing a forged check], grand larceny, and bank robbery convictions. On September 16, 1981, petitioner Hudson, an officer at the Correctional Center, with a fellow officer, conducted a "shakedown" search of respondent's prison locker and cell for contraband. During the "shakedown," the officers discovered a ripped pillow-case in a trash can near respondent's cell bunk. Charges against Palmer were instituted under prison disciplinary procedures for destroying state property. After a hearing, Palmer was found guilty on the charge [and ordered to pay for the property]. He also had a reprimand placed in his prison record. [Palmer filed a civil rights lawsuit claiming that his Fourth Amendment rights were violated.]

The first question we address is whether respondent has a right of privacy in his prison cell entitling him to the protection of the Fourth Amendment against unreasonable searches. . . .

(continued)

. . . [P]ersons imprisoned for crime enjoy many protections of the Constitution, [but] it is also clear that imprisonment carries with it the circumspection or loss of many significant rights. . . . The curtailment of certain rights is necessary, as a practical matter, to accommodate a myriad of "institutional needs and objectives" of prison facilities, chief among which is internal security. Of course, these restrictions or retractions also serve, incidentally, as reminders that, under our system of justice, deterrence and retribution are factors in addition to correction.

We have not before been called upon to decide the specific question whether the Fourth Amendment applies within a prison cell, but the nature of our inquiry is well defined. We must determine here, as in other Fourth Amendment contexts, if a "justifiable" expectation of privacy is at stake. . . . The applicability of the Fourth Amendment turns on whether "the person invoking its protection can claim a 'justifiable,' a 'reasonable,' or a 'legitimate expectation of privacy' that has been invaded by government action." . . .

Notwithstanding our caution in approaching claims that the Fourth Amendment is inapplicable in a given context, we hold that society is not prepared to recognize as legitimate any subjective expectation of privacy that a prisoner might have in his prison cell and that, accordingly, the Fourth Amendment proscription against unreasonable searches does not apply within the confines of the prison cell. The recognition of privacy rights for prisoners in their individual cells simply cannot be reconciled with the concept of incarceration and the needs and objectives of penal institutions.

Within this volatile "community" [of a prison], prison administrators are to take all necessary steps to ensure the safety of not only the prison staffs and administrative personnel, but also visitors. They are under an obligation to take reasonable measures to guarantee the safety of the inmates themselves. . . . [T]hey must prevent, so far as possible, the flow of illicit weapons into the prison; they must be vigilant to detect escape plots, in which drugs or weapons may be involved, before the scheme materialize. . . .

. . . Virtually the only place inmates can conceal weapons, drugs, and other contraband is in their cells. Unfettered access to these cells by prison officials, thus, is imperative if drugs and contraband are to be ferreted out and sanitary surroundings are to be maintained.

Determining whether an expectation of privacy is "legitimate" or "reasonable" necessarily entails a balancing of interests. The two interests here are the interest of society in the security of its penal institutions and the interest of the prisoner in privacy within his cell. The latter interest, of course, is already limited by the exigencies of the circumstances: A prison "shares none of the attributes of privacy of a home, an automobile, an office, or a hotel room." We strike the balance in favor of institutional security, which we have noted is "central to all other corrections goals." A right to privacy in traditional Fourth Amendment terms is fundamentally incompatible with the close and continual surveillance of inmates and their cells required to ensure institutional security and internal order. We are satisfied that society would insist that the prisoner's expectation of privacy always yield to what must be considered the paramount interest of institutional security. We believe that it is accepted by our society that "[l]oss of freedom of choice and privacy are inherent incidents of confinement."

Our holding that respondent does not have a reasonable expectation of privacy enabling him to invoke the protections of the Fourth Amendment does not mean that he is without a remedy for calculated harassment unrelated to prison needs. Nor does it mean that prison attendants can ride roughshod over inmates' property rights with impunity. The Eighth Amendment always stands as a protection against "cruel and unusual punishments." By the same token, there are adequate state tort and common-law remedies available to [the prisoner] to redress the alleged destruction of his personal property. . . .

against the harmful consequences of some searches, such as those that constitute planned harassment or that destroy inmates' property. In such cases, prisoners must file lawsuits in state courts against corrections officials. But would such lawsuits be effective? If a jury heard a case concerning a prisoner's lawsuit about property damaged in a cell search, might the jury be biased against the inmate or in favor of the corrections officials? What kind of circumstances or damage to property would be required before a prisoner could reasonably expect to win such a lawsuit?

The Supreme Court addressed the issue of prisoners' property rights because inmates had filed lawsuits claiming that their right to due process was violated when officials were responsible for property damage. The due process right was raised because the Fourteenth Amendment states that state officials cannot deprive people of property without due process of law. For example, if the government plans to "condemn" a farm in order to force the farmer to sell the property to the state so that the state can build a highway across that land, the government must hold a hearing—that is, provide due process—before seizing the property and paying "just compensation" for it. Prisoners claimed that they, too, should have a hearing before their property was taken or damaged by officials.

In *Parratt v. Taylor* (1981), a prisoner filed a section 1983 action seeking recovery for a $23.50 hobby kit that was lost due to the alleged negligence of corrections officials.[28] Although many commentators joke about the case because the property had so little value, the issue presented the Supreme Court with the opportunity to provide guidance to lower courts about due process and prisoner property cases. The justices decided that the prisoner could not bring a due process claim to court because the property was not lost due to actions produced by any established state procedures. Indeed, the Court declared that "the deprivation [of property] occurred as a result of the unauthorized failure of agents of the state [i.e., corrections officials] to follow established state procedure." Thus, the property loss did not fit under section 1983's requirement that the rights violation occur under "color of law."

In a portion of *Hudson v. Palmer* not presented in Box 5-9, the Supreme Court held that even if corrections officials intentionally damage inmate property, no due process violation occurs as long as there are state mechanisms by which inmates can seek reimbursement or pursue other remedies after the incident has occurred. There is no requirement that prisoners must receive protection for their property before the damage to the property occurs. The protection exists in the opportunities for seeking recovery after the fact, such as through filing state lawsuits.

State laws do not necessarily provide any greater protection for prisoners and their property. Although state statutes and constitutions may provide legal protections for prisoners, those protections likely will be interpreted and defined by the same concerns for institutional safety and security that federal judges rely on in interpreting the U.S. Constitution. The state court case excerpted in Box 5-10 provides an example by addressing the following question: If state laws and prison regulations permit prisoners to obtain certain

Cain et al. v. Michigan Department of Corrections, 88-6116 (1997)

(Court of Claims, Ingham County Circuit Court)

JUDGE GIDDINGS:

In 1989, the [Michigan] legislature passed the Prisoner Personal Property Statute . . . which superseded the former Department of Corrections administrative rule [from] 1979 . . . and represented a change in philosophy with regard to prisoner personal property regulations. Up to that time, the Department allowed any personal property subject to reasonable regulation grounded upon the public health, security, order, and housekeeping of the facility. . . . [The new statute was intended, in part, to place very strict limits on personal property permitted in cells and to require prisoners to wear prison-issue clothing instead of their own clothes.]

. . . The Department may restrict not only how much property a prisoner can possess, but how much property can be brought into the system. Indeed, the Department may properly prohibit an inmate from bringing any property whatsoever into the prison system. The Department is required to provide only that property necessary to fulfill a prisoner's basic needs without violating federal and state statutes and constitutional proscriptions against cruel and unusual punishment. . . .

. . . The property which [the prisoners] seek to protect was acquired with the Department's blessing, from Department approved vendors, and pursuant to Department rules and policies which specifically authorized its acquisition. . . .

At issue here is whether the Department for administrative reasons may declare such lawfully acquired property contraband and take it from prisoners without a hearing and without compensation. . . .

. . . [T]his Court agrees with [Michigan] that the state-created entitlement of [prisoners] here to acquire property in the future may be properly dissolved by administrative or legislative action without a hearing. The reason is that these legislative and administrative acts are putting an end to an entitlement—that is, the right of prisoners to acquire and possess certain items of property. This entitlement was created earlier by similar and equivalent actions. . . . [The new regulations] d[o] not violate the [prisoners'] procedural due process rights. . . .

[Under the new regulations], a prisoner placed in a higher security prison may be deprived of some of his/her property. Where a prisoner is placed in a higher security classifica-

items of property—and the prison even sells the property to the inmates—can the state later change the rules and force the inmates to send the property outside of the prison?

Searches of Persons

Although the Supreme Court did not provide any Fourth Amendment protections for prisoners' cells, search and seizure issues also arise with respect to searches of prisoners' bodies. As you read the hypothetical case presented in Box 5-11, consider how you might apply the Fourth Amendment to body searches.

There are several levels of searches of prisoners' bodies. The least intrusive searches employ technology, such as metal detectors. Such devices advance the

tion following conviction of a major misconduct, the misconduct hearing presumably satisfies constitutional requirements and his property may be taken. The same is true where there has been a reclassification done with a proper hearing. On the other hand, to the extent that a prisoner is placed involuntarily in a higher level prison without a hearing, the resultant taking of lawfully acquired property may violate procedural due process. Thus, the propriety of Department procedures in this regard can only be judged according to each situation and, therefore, must be determined in the classification portion of the case. . . .

. . . There is nothing arbitrary about the Department and the legislature reducing the amount of property available to inmates. The processing of such property creates, as we have seen, logistical problems for the Department. Moreover, this Court agrees that particular items, not to mention the sheer volume of them, may create health and safety and security concerns. This is true despite the fact that individually some items are not dangerous. The state has expansive police power, and surely it is within

the scope of that broad authority to control and, if necessary, to reduce the amount of property—including non-dangerous property—available to inmates. No violation of substantive due process has been or can be shown.

To construe th[e prior] authorization to possess items of personal property in such a way as to require compensation upon the termination of that right would create an encumbrance not authorized by Michigan law. It would mean that in administering the Department and in deciding whether to allow certain items on the premises, by engaging in certain practices and adopting administrative rules, the Department could effect limits on its own authority to carry out its statutory duties. . . . Whatever [property] rights are created [by the prior regulations], they are subject to change at the will of the Department. In short, while a "taking" of possessory rights may have occurred, that "taking" is not compensable under the Michigan Constitution. . . .

institution's important interest in confiscating weapons and other contraband while imposing a minimal intrusion on prisoners. Thus, it is highly unlikely that a prisoner could ever successfully claim that such searches violate Fourth Amendment rights. And improvements in technology are giving corrections officials increased capacity to search for contraband. For example, Maryland's prisons employ a device called an "Ionscan 400," which looks like a hand-held vacuum cleaner but can detect tiny traces of drugs on a person. The device supposedly is more effective than a drug-sniffing dog and also has been used to catch prison visitors and corrections officers who have been in contact with illegal narcotics.[29]

The next level of intrusiveness is the **pat-down search,** in which the corrections officer moves his or her hands down the prisoner's body on the outside of the clothing. Such a search is designed to detect weapons, drugs, or other

BOX 5-11 **Body Searches**

Imagine you are a federal district judge considering the following section 1983 claim. A female prisoner states that she was returning from the visiting room where she had seen her mother and teenage daughter. The visiting room always has three corrections officers present, and there are strict rules limiting physical contact to brief hugs and handshakes. When returning to her cell, the prisoner was prepared for the usual partial strip search. But instead of having merely to remove her shirt and pants so that the pockets could be searched, she was subjected to a full strip search and body cavity inspection. In her complaint, she asserts that she was outraged and humiliated at the close, visual, flashlight-illuminated inspection of every inch of her naked body. She further claims that the search was unjustified and that it violated her Fourth Amendment rights because she has a reasonable expectation of privacy in her body, and especially the private parts of her body.

Were her Fourth Amendment rights violated? How would you balance her privacy interests, if any, against the institution's need to control weapons and contraband?

contraband that causes lumps under a prisoners' clothing. There are two basic kinds of pat-down searches, each with a different degree of intrusiveness. A "frisk search" involves the officer quickly running his or her hands around the outside of the prisoner's body to detect any obvious contraband. A slower, more thorough "clothed body search" involves, in the words of Michigan Department of Corrections' policies, "a thorough manual and visual inspection of all body surfaces, hair, clothing. . . . includes inspection of the mouth, ears, and nasal cavity. Removal of clothing is not required except outerwear, e.g., jacket or coat, and shoes and socks to allow inspection of the shoes and soles of the feet." Courts uphold the pat-down practice as long as it is done in a professional manner.[30] It cannot be done in a manner intended to injure or harass the prisoner.

The next level of search is the **strip search,** which involves the visual inspection of nude prisoners, including visual inspection of body cavities. A few courts have held that such searches cannot be conducted without specific suspicions that a prisoner has hidden contraband on his or her body. Most courts, however, have followed the U.S. Supreme Court's lead on this issue. The Court recognizes the need for such searches but states that such searches cannot be used simply to humiliate or abuse prisoners. Thus, the Court determines whether such searches were conducted in reasonable circumstances by balancing the need for the search against the invasion of privacy rights involved.[31] This means that such searches may be more justified for prisoners returning from contact visits with outsiders than for those who were escorted by corrections officers to a one-on-one meeting with the warden, guarded while there, and then escorted back to the cellblock.[32]

Because there is always the possibility of prisoners carrying contraband from their cells to another location or picking up contraband while outside of their cells at virtually any other location, corrections officials have succeeded in gaining approval for visual inspections in a variety of situations. One scholar has summarized the state of law by concluding:

> *There is no question about the fact that the current view of an overwhelming majority of courts is that visual strip searches of prisoners, for virtually any reason or for no reason at all, do not violate the Fourth Amendment and may be conducted almost at will, even where logic defies an answer and where courts go to great lengths to see a legitimate penological concern or purpose, where there is, in fact, none.*[33]

Fundamentally, courts seem to accept the concerns about the dangers of weapons and drugs in prison. As a result, judges are reluctant to second-guess corrections' officials efforts to find dangerous contraband.

Bell v. Wolfish (1979), a case concerning pretrial detainees in a federal jail, involved a challenge to **body cavity searches.** In the jail, unconvicted inmates—who are presumed to be innocent until proven guilty—were subject to such inspections and searches, just as were the convicted offenders in this and other institutions. Box 5-12 excerpts the Supreme Court decision about body cavity searches. As you read the case excerpt, ask yourself: Do unconvicted detainees receive any greater constitutional protection than convicted offenders while incarcerated?

The Supreme Court concluded that unconvicted pretrial detainees may be subjected to body cavity searches after contact visits without any probable cause to believe that they are hiding contraband. Notice that the Court reached this conclusion even though it conceded that guards conduct some searches in an abusive manner. Did the Court do anything to protect against abusive searches in this humiliating context? Did it adequately weigh the inmates' interests against those of the institution? The majority of justices seem to have strong concerns about maintaining institutional security and order, and unconvicted detainees apparently enjoy no more rights than do convicted offenders.

For comparison, read Justice Thurgood Marshall's dissenting opinion concerning body cavity searches in Box 5-13. In light of the facts presented by Marshall, do you agree with the majority's conclusion that body cavity searches are necessary for institutional security?

Are the jail's security justifications sufficiently strong in light of the facts supplied by Marshall? It would seem to be extremely difficult for an inmate who was wearing a one-piece jumpsuit and being constantly observed by guards while in a glass-enclosed room to hide contraband in a body cavity. Marshall would accept body cavity searches of prisoners who are observed disrobing or acting suspicious. Such actions would constitute probable cause to justify searching a particular prisoner. However, Marshall is opposed to the blanket authority to conduct body cavity searches of all inmates, even when there is no basis to suspect wrongdoing.

For their part, corrections officials tell stories about ingenious efforts by inmates to obtain and hide contraband even while being watched by corrections officials. Corrections officials thus argue that strip searches may be necessary for safety and security reasons even when there is little concrete

BOX 5-12   *Bell v. Wolfish*, 441 U.S. 520 (1979)

JUSTICE REHNQUIST delivered the opinion of the Court.

Inmates at all [federal] Bureau of Prisons facilities, including the MCC, are required to expose their body cavities for visual inspection as part of a strip search conducted after every contact visit with a person from outside the institution. Corrections officials testified that visual cavity searches were necessary not only to discover but also to deter the smuggling of weapons, drugs, and other contraband into the institution. The District Court upheld the strip search procedure but prohibited the body-cavity searches absent probable cause to believe that the inmate is concealing contraband. . . . Because [jail officials] proved only one instance in the MCC's short history where contraband was found during a body-cavity search, the Court of Appeals affirmed [the District Court's ban on body cavity searches]. . . . In its view, the "gross violation of personal privacy inherent in such a search cannot be out-weighed by the government's security interest in maintaining a practice of so little actual utility." . . .

Admittedly, this practice instinctively gives us the most pause. However, assuming for present purposes that inmates, both convicted prisoners and pretrial detainees, retain some Fourth Amendment rights upon commitment to a corrections facility, . . . we nonetheless conclude that these searches do not violate that Amendment. The Fourth Amendment prohibits only unreasonable searches . . . and under the circumstances, we do not believe that these searches are unreasonable.

The test of reasonableness under the Fourth Amendment is not capable of precise definition or mechanical application. In each case it requires a balancing of the need for the particular search against the invasion of personal rights that the search entails. Courts must consider the scope of the particular intrusion, the manner in which it is conducted, the justification for initiating it, and the place in which it is conducted. . . . A detention facility is a unique place fraught with serious security dangers. Smuggling of money, drugs, weapons, and other contraband is all too common an occurrence. And inmate attempts to secrete these items into the facility by concealing them in body cavities are documented in th[e records presented for this case]. . . . That there has been only one instance when an MCC inmate was discovered attempting to smuggle contraband into the institution on his person may be more a testament to the effectiveness of this search technique as a deterrent than to any lack of interest on the part of the inmates to secrete and import such items when the opportunity arises.

We do not underestimate the degree to which these searches may invade the personal privacy. Nor do we doubt, as the District Court noted, that on occasion a security guard may conduct the search in an abusive fashion. . . . Such abuse cannot be condoned. The searches must be conducted in a reasonable manner. . . . But we deal here with the question whether visual body-cavity inspections as contemplated by the MCC rules can *ever* be conducted on less than probable cause. Balancing the significant and legitimate security interests of the institution against the privacy interests of the inmates, we conclude that they can [conduct the searches]. . . .

evidence that a given prisoner has obtained and hidden contraband on his or her body.

Is Marshall correct in charging that the majority of justices seem willing to accept any practice or condition as long as jail officials claim it relates to security, despite the fact that the degrading practices are applied to unconvicted

BOX 5-13	***Bell v. Wolfish*, 441 U.S. 520 (1979)**

JUSTICE MARSHALL dissenting.

In my view, the body-cavity searches of MCC inmates represent one of the most grievous offenses against personal dignity and common decency. After every contact visit with someone from outside the facility, including defense attorneys, an inmate must remove all of his or her clothing, bend over, spread the buttocks, and display the anal cavity for inspection by a correctional officer. Women inmates must assume a suitable posture for vaginal inspection, while men must raise their genitals. And, as the [majority] neglects to note, because of time pressures [during the search process], this humiliating spectacle is frequently conducted in the presence of other inmates.

The District Court found that the stripping was "unpleasant, embarrassing, and humiliating." . . . A psychiatrist testified that the practice placed inmates in the most degrading position possible, . . . a conclusion amply corroborated by the testimony of the inmates themselves. . . . There was evidence, moreover, that these searches engendered among detainees fears of sexual assault, . . . were the occasion for actual threats of physical abuse by guards, and caused some inmates to forgo personal visits.

Not surprisingly, the Government asserts a security justification for such inspections. These searches are necessary, it argues, to prevent inmates from smuggling contraband into the facility. In crediting this justification despite the contrary findings of the two courts below, the Court overlooks the critical facts. As respondents point out, inmates are required to wear one-piece jumpsuits with zippers in the front. To insert an object into the vaginal or anal cavity, an inmate would have to remove the jumpsuit, at least from the upper torso. . . . Since contact visits occur in a glass-enclosed room and are continuously monitored by corrections officers, . . . such a feat would seem extraordinarily difficult. There was medical testimony, moreover, that inserting an object into the rectum is painful and "would require time and opportunity which is not available in the visiting areas, . . . and that visual inspection would probably not detect an object once inserted. . . . Additionally, before entering the visiting room, visitors and their packages are searched thoroughly by a metal detector, fluoroscope, and by hand. . . . Corrections officers may require that visitors leave packages or handbags with guards until the visit is over. . . . Only by blinding itself to the facts presented on this record can the Court accept the Government's security rationale. . . .

That the Court [majority] can uphold these indiscriminate searches highlights the bankruptcy of its basic analysis. Under the test adopted today, the rights of detainees apparently extend only so far as detention officials decide that cost and security will permit. Such unthinking deference to administrative convenience cannot be justified where the interests at stake are those of presumptively innocent individuals, many of whose only proven offense is the inability to afford bail.

I dissent.

detainees who may simply be too poor to afford bail? Marshall's dissent helps to illustrate how the Supreme Court weighs inmates' asserted rights—whether they are unconvicted pretrial detainees or convicted offenders—against corrections officials' interests in security and order. In light of the acceptance of body cavity searches in *Bell v. Wolfish*, it is difficult to think of situations in which the Court might rule that an inmate's right outweighs the concern for institutional security.

The next level of search involves physical examinations of the inside of a prisoner's body. This may involve such things as a finger probe of a prisoner's bodily openings, an x-ray of an inmate's stomach to see if contraband (e.g., a balloon filled with drugs) was swallowed, or the forced administration of a laxative under such circumstances. With the finger probe search, often referred to as a **digital examination** (e.g., digital rectal exam), there must be reasonable suspicion based on the factual circumstances to justify such a humiliating, body-invasive procedure. For example, if an officer observes an inmate receiving an unidentifiable small item from a visitor and sneaking quickly into the restroom, an intrusive search may be justified if no items were found in an initial pat-down search and visual inspection. X-rays of prisoners' digestive tracts also have been justified by such reasonable suspicions.[34] Courts generally have not required that digital exams be conducted by medical personnel. However, there is an expectation that they will be conducted through sanitary procedures (i.e., the use of latex gloves) and in a manner not intended to inflict pain or injure the inmate.[35]

The issue of visual and body cavity searches has been further complicated by the employment of men and women as corrections officers. Many lawsuits have sought to stop opposite-sex officers from viewing or searching inmates' bodies. Some male Muslim inmates, for example, assert a violation of their religious principles if they are subjected to a physical search by female corrections officers. Some courts have ruled that the prisoners' constitutional rights were violated. However, other courts have declared that banning officers from conducting certain searches in turn constitutes a violation of employment discrimination laws. In effect, male or female officers may have their rights violated if they are prevented from carrying out the same job responsibilities, including searches of opposite-sex prisoners, as those conducted by all other officers.[36]

An additional kind of intrusive search conducted with increasing frequency is scientific testing of the body and bodily fluids. For example, random urinalysis testing of prisoners has been approved, as long as the selection process was truly random and not a form of harassment.[37] Mandatory blood tests for HIV and AIDS have been upheld, as well. However, prisoners have won lawsuits concerning privacy rights against corrections officials when those officials revealed, either intentionally or accidentally, the results of AIDS tests to nonmedical personnel and other prisoners.[38]

In general, courts strike their balance in favor of the prisons' interests in security and safety when examining search and seizure issues. Only the most intrusive physical searches must be justified by reasonable suspicions that the prisoner has hidden contraband inside his or her body. Corrections departments need to be cognizant of the rules developed by courts in developing training and procedures for their personnel to follow in conducting searches. If a department's policies and practices do not follow the guidance of judicial decisions, there is an increased chance of successful prisoner civil rights lawsuits against corrections personnel.

As you read the Michigan Department of Corrections' policy on searches of prisoners in Box 5-14, consider whether these instructions provide adequate

| BOX 5-14 | **Actual Policy on Searches of Prisoners** |

A. For purposes of this policy directive, the following definitions shall apply:

...

4. Reasonable Suspicion: Suspicion based on a specific fact or facts, and rational inferences drawn from those facts, based upon the knowledge and experience of Corrections staff. Examples of information on which a reasonable suspicion may be based include but are not limited to, the following:

 a. A tip which is from an identified source who is reasonably reliable and credible;

 b. An anonymous tip which is corroborated by some other evidence;

 c. Discovery of a suspicious item during a frisk search;

 d. Observance of unusual behavior such as appearing to conceal an item in clothing.

...

G. Frisk, Clothed Body, and Cell/Room Searches

1. As part of their responsibility to maintain security, order and discipline in a correctional facility, Department employees have authority to conduct frisk and clothed body searches of prisoners at any time. Institutional staff shall determine whether a frisk or clothed body search is more appropriate in each situation, depending on the circumstances necessitating the search.

2. During a frisk or clothed body search, a prisoner may be required to remove all items from his/her pockets. If the prisoner refuses to do so, or there is a reasonable suspicion that a weapon or drugs are present, the staff member may remove the items. These searches need not be conducted by a staff member of the same sex as the prisoner being searched.

3. Each non-housing unit custodial officer who has direct prisoner contact shall conduct frisk or clothed body searches of a minimum of five randomly selected prisoners per shift. Both housing unit and non-housing unit staff may be required to conduct additional searches, at the discretion of the individual wardens. Such searches shall be recorded in the appropriate logbook, including the name and number of the prisoner being searched, the date and time of the search, and the name and clock number of the employee.

4. If a prisoner flees when an employee notifies him/her of a search, the employee shall make every effort to identify the prisoner and charge him/her with the appropriate misconduct violations. However, an employee ordinarily should not pursue a fleeing prisoner under circumstances which might endanger the employee or arouse other prisoners. A prisoner may be forced to submit to a search, subject to the guidelines [on] "Use of Force [by Corrections Personnel]."

5. A prisoner's possessions, living area and work area are subject to search at any time, with or without suspicion that contraband is present. However, no search shall be conducted for the purpose of harassing or humiliating a prisoner.

6. Staff members conducting a search in a prisoner's living or work area shall use reasonable care in conducting the search to protect and safeguard the prisoner's property and shall attempt to leave searched areas in a similar condition to what they were prior to the search. The search need not be conducted in the prisoner's presence.

7. Each housing unit officer shall conduct searches of a minimum of three randomly selected cells/rooms/living areas per shift,

(continued)

except the 10 p.m. to 6 a.m. shift. Additional searches may be required, at the discretion of the individual wardens. Such searches shall be recorded in the appropriate log book. Recorded information shall include the date and time of the search and the name(s) of the employee(s) conducting the search.

8. Dogs trained to detect controlled substances may also be used at any time to assist in the search of prisoners, their possessions, their living areas, and any other areas of an institution.

H. Strip Search

1. A prisoner may be subjected to a strip search whenever it is determined by staff that such a search is necessary. If the prisoner resists, s/he may be forced to submit, subject to the guidelines [on "Use of Force by Corrections Personnel"]. All prisoners except those in Level I facilities shall be subject to a strip search after each contact visit and that search shall include a visual inspection of the entrance to the rectal cavity. Female prisoners shall also be subject to a visual inspection of the entrance of the vagina.

2. A strip search shall be performed by and only in the presence of employees of the same sex as the person being searched, except (1) in an emergency; (2) when a staff member who is of the opposite sex is specifically assigned to transport a prisoner to a destination outside the prison facility; or (3) if the staff member is a supervisory employee whose presence is required by policy. In such cases, a strip search may be conducted by or in the presence of employees of the opposite sex.

3. Whenever a strip search is conducted by or in the presence of an employee of the opposite sex due to an emergency, a full written report of that search shall be submitted to the warden within 24 hours.

4. Strip searches shall be conducted in a place which prevents the search from

being observed by those not assisting in that search, unless an emergency requires that it be conducted immediately and there is no opportunity to move to a sheltered area.

I. Body Cavity Search

1. A prisoner may be forced to submit to a body cavity search if all the following conditions are met:
   a. Prior to the search, written authorization must be obtained from the Warden or, in his/her absence, the acting warden, who may authorize such a search only when there is reasonable suspicion that the prisoner is attempting to carry contraband within a body cavity.
   b. The search must be conducted by a licensed physician or a physician's assistant, licensed practical nurse, or registered nurse acting with the approval of a licensed physician.
   c. Medical personnel who perform a body cavity search need not be of the same sex as the prisoner being searched. However, all other persons who are present during the search shall be of the same sex as the prisoner, and there shall always be at least one staff member present who is the same sex as the prisoner being searched.
   d. The search shall be conducted in a place which prevents it from being observed by a person not conducting or necessary to assist with the search.
   e. A written report of the search shall be completed as soon as possible on Form CAJ-289, Strip Search/Body Cavity Search Report. The original of that report shall be sent to the warden and a copy must be given to the prisoner, subject to deletions permitted by the Freedom of Information Act.
   f. If it is determined to be appropriate by the warden or acting warden, a prisoner suspected of concealing contraband in his/her rectal cavity may be

isolated as described below in Section J rather than being subjected to a body cavity search.

J. Isolation of Prisoners to Retrieve Contraband

1. Whenever a prisoner is suspected of swallowing an item of contraband, or concealing contraband in his/her rectal cavity, s/he may be held in isolation, at the request of the warden or, in his/her absence, the acting warden, after consultation with appropriate licensed Health Care staff. The prisoner may be held in isolation for a reasonable period of time, as determined in consultation with appropriate medical staff, to determine whether the contraband is excreted.

guidance to corrections personnel about when and how to search prisoners. Under this policy, do prisoners have any ability to protect their privacy against searches being undertaken—other than an after-the-fact lawsuit to challenge the legality of a search that was already undertaken? What is the purpose of each individual policy directive? What consideration is given to the possibility that a search might be undertaken by an officer of the opposite sex than the prisoner? Do the procedures provide adequate safeguards for the privacy interests of prisoners?

SUMMARY

- Free exercise of religion poses the most difficult problems concerning prisoners' religious freedom. Other important issues involve the establishment of religion and equal protection.

- The emergence of new religious traditions among prisoners, some legitimate and some invented, has forced the courts to determine which practices and beliefs deserve legal protection.

- Free exercise cases may concern a range of issues including access to religious literature and services, special diets, and hair length.

- The U.S. Supreme Court's decision in *O'Lone v. Estate of Shabazz* set a standard that required courts to defer to corrections officials in many respects when examining free exercise cases.

- The future of free exercise issues in prisons is uncertain because in 1997 the U.S. Supreme Court invalidated the federal Religious Freedom Restoration Act. Many states are considering their own legislation, but it is unclear which states, if any, will include prisoners in their statutory protections for religious freedom.

- Prisoners have failed to gain constitutional protection for the right to operate a union.

- Prisoners have succeeded in getting some restrictive rules limiting choices about marriage overturned. However, imprisonment may hurt prisoners' legal protections with respect to divorce and parental rights.

- The U.S. Supreme Court applies a balancing test in Fourth Amendment search cases to weigh the safety and security interests of the prison against the privacy interests of the prisoner.

- There is no Fourth Amendment protection against searches of cells, although there might be some legal remedies for damage to inmates' property as a result of such searches.

- Only the most intrusive searches of prisoners' bodies require specific justification by corrections officials. Pat-down searches and visual inspections of inmates' nude bodies usually gain court approval when challenged.

Key Terms

body cavity search
digital examination
equal protection
Establishment Clause

Free Exercise Clause
Hudson v. Palmer (1984)
O'Lone v. Estate of Shabazz (1987)

pat-down search
reasonable expectation of privacy
strip search

Additional Readings

Gardner, Martin. 1985. "*Hudson v. Palmer*—'Bright Lines' but Dark Directions for Prisoner Privacy Rights." *Journal of Criminal Law and Criminology* 76: 75–115.

Rigoli, Lisa Martin. 1990. "Power Exercised in the Shadows: *O'Lone v. Shabazz* as a Signal of the Court's Return to Interpretivism in Institutional Reform Litigation." *New England Journal on Criminal and Civil Confinement* 16: 141–170.

Schanabel, Mary. 1993. "The Religious Restoration Act: A Prison's Dilemma." *Willamette Law Review* 29: 323–341.

Notes

1. Cruz v. Beto, 405 U.S. 319 (1972).

2. Christopher E. Smith, "Black Muslims and the Development of Prisoners' Rights," *Journal of Black Studies* 24 (1993): 131–146.

3. Fulwood v. Clemmer, 206 F.Supp. 370 (D.C. Cir. 1962).

4. Theriault v. Silber, 391 F.Supp. 578 (W.D. Tex. 1975).

5. Remmers v. Brewer, 494 F.2d 1277 (8th Cir. 1974); Abdool-Rashaad v. Seiter, 690 F.Supp. 598 (S.D. Ohio 1987).

6. Kahane v. Carlson, 527 F.2d 492 (2d Cir. 1975).

7. Johnson v. Moore, 926 F.2d 571 (2d Cir. 1991).

8. Kahey v. Jones, 836 F.2d 948 (5th Cir. 1988).

9. Hamilton v. Schriro, 74 F.3d 1545 (8th Cir. 1996); Standing Deer v. Carlson, 831 F.2d 1525 (9th Cir. 1987); Hall v. Bellmon, 935 F.2d 1106 (10th Cir. 1991).

10. Iron Eyes v. Henry, 907 F.2d 810 (8th Cir. 1990).

11. Benjamin v. Coughlin, 905 F.2d 571 (2d Cir. 1990); Young v. Lane, 922 F.2d 370 (7th Cir. 1991).

12. Michael Mushlin, *Rights of Prisoners,* Vol. 1, 2nd ed. (Colorado Springs, CO: Shepard's/McGraw-Hill, 1993), p. 289.

13. Employment Division of Oregon v. Smith, 494 U.S. 872 (1990).

14. David A. Schultz and Christopher E. Smith, *The Jurisprudential Vision of Justice Antonin Scalia* (Lanham, MD: Rowman & Littlefield, 1996), pp. 110–112.

15. City of Boerne v. Flores, 117 S.Ct. 2157 (1997).

16. Greta Guest, "House Panel Approves Bill to Shield Religious Freedom," *Lansing State Journal,* 3 July 1997, p. B3.

17. Sapanajin v. Gunter, 857 F.2d 463 (8th Cir. 1988).

18. Reimers v. Oregon, 846 F.2d 561 (9th Cir. 1988).

19. Knuckles v. Prasse, 435 F.2d 1255 (3rd Cir. 1970); Termunde v. Cooke, 684 F.Supp. 255 (D. Utah 1988).

20. Peterkin v. Jeffes, 661 F.Supp. 895 (E.D. Pa. 1987).

21. Wisconsin v. Yoder, 406 U.S. 205 (1972).

22. Loving v. Virginia, 388 U.S. 1 (1967).

23. Roe v. Wade, 410 U.S. 113 (1973).

24. Lynn S. Branham and Sheldon Krantz, *The Law of Sentencing, Corrections, and Prisoners' Rights,* 5th ed. (St. Paul, MN: West, 1997), p. 313 n. 15.

25. Michael Mushlin, *Rights of Prisoners,* Vol. 2, 2nd ed. (Colorado Springs, CO: Shepard's/McGraw-Hill, 1993), pp. 161–167.

26. Southerland v. Thigpen, 748 F.2d 713 (5th Cir. 1986).

27. Mushlin, *Rights of Prisoners,* Vol. 2, pp. 174–176.

28. Parratt v. Taylor, 451 U.S. 527 (1981).

29. Ivan Penn, "Vacuum to Keep Prisons Drug-Free," *Lansing State Journal* (from *Baltimore Sun* wire service), 20 October 1997, p. A7.

30. Mushlin, *Rights of Prisoners,* Vol. 1, p. 380; Bagley v. Watson, 579 F.Supp. 1099 (D. Or. 1983).

31. Mushlin, *Rights of Prisoners,* Vol. 1, pp. 380–383; Covino v. Patrissi, 967 F.2d 73 (2d Cir. 1992).

32. Arruda v. Fair, 710 F.2d 886 (1st Cir. 1983).

33. Mushlin, *Rights of Prisoners,* Vol. 1, pp. 384–385.

34. United States v. Oakley, 731 F.Supp. 1363 (S.D. Ind. 1990).

35. Mushlin, *Rights of Prisoners,* Vol. 1, p. 387; Vaughn v. Ricketts, 663 F.Supp. 401 (D. Ariz. 1987).

36. Katherine Bennett, "Constitutional Issues in Cross-Gender Searches and Visual Observation of Nude Inmates by Opposite-Sex Officers: A Battle Between and Within the Sexes," *Prison Journal* 75 (1995): 90–112.

37. Mushlin, *Rights of Prisoners,* Vol. 1, pp. 391–392; Storms v. Coughlin, 600 F.Supp. 1214 (S.D. N.Y. 1984); Jensen v. Lick, 589 F.Supp. 35 (D. N.D. 1984).

38. Mushlin, *Rights of Prisoners,* Vol. 1, p. 390; Dunn v. White, 880 F.2d 1188 (10th Cir. 1989).

CHAPTER SIX

Discipline and Due Process

Imagine you are the warden of a maximum-security prison. A new governor has just been elected on a law-and-order platform. During the campaign, he vowed to abolish parole, ban televisions and weight lifting for prisoners, and make prison life as harsh as possible immediately upon taking office. A few days after taking office, the governor arrives at the prison accompanied by newspaper reporters and demands a tour. You cooperate by personally escorting the governor and the reporters around the prison.

As you walk along one tier of cells, a prisoner shouts, "Hey, that's the jerk who just became governor!"

Voices yell from various cells: "You SOB!" "You don't know anything!" "Go back where you came from!"

Suddenly, a liquid substance is thrown out of a cell and sprays all over the governor. "What was that?" a startled reporter asks as the governor's state police bodyguards leap between the cell and governor. Moments later, everyone realizes that the prisoner threw a cup of urine on the governor.

The governor, his face purple with rage, glares at the laughing culprit as prisoners throughout the cellblock whistle and hoot. Pointing his finger at the prisoner, the governor turns to you and yells, "I want him! Open that cell. I'm not taking any crap from some convict."

"No. We shouldn't do that, Governor," you say, trying to calm the irate politician. "Don't worry, we'll handle this situation."

As the reporters quickly scribble on their notepads, the governor announces, "That man is going to get solitary confinement and bread and water for a year, or you are not going to be a warden much longer."

How do you respond? Can you follow the governor's orders? What will you do to the prisoner?

DISCIPLINE AND RULES IN PRISONS

Discipline is an important issue in prisons. The safety of inmates and staff depends on maintaining order, and so there are many rules and regulations. Yet it can be very difficult to apply rules and regulations to people who have proved that they will break rules. Prisoners may lack self-control and maturity. They may be filled with rage at society, at the prison, at other people, and at themselves. They may look for ways to strike back against the world by causing trouble for prison officials. And many of them have little to lose. When prisoners misbehave and receive punishment, their lives are not much different from their everyday life in prison—and perhaps not much harsher than the life on the streets from which many of them came. If inmates are serving long sentences, it is difficult to give them a reason to cooperate.

How can a prison inform inmates about their rights and responsibilities? There are so many rules in such a controlled environment that it may be difficult for prisoners to learn all of the rules quickly. This may be especially true of prisoners who have literacy or language difficulties that hinder them from reading the rules listed in a prison guidebook. To understand the nature of rules imposed on prisoners—the rules that, if broken, will be the source of disciplinary proceedings—let's examine some rules in an actual prison.

At the Michigan Reformatory in Ionia, a high-security prison for male offenders serving long sentences, new prisoners are required to attend an orientation session and are given a guidebook of prison rules. Prisoners also are told that they may read the state Department of Corrections' Operating Procedures in the prison library. The Operating Procedures provide the statewide rules concerning disciplinary hearings, health care, visiting rules, religious services, grievance procedures, and other relevant matters. After the orientation session, prisoners are required to sign a statement acknowledging that they were provided with information about each aspect of the prison's rules. The statement is placed in the prisoner's file, presumably so inmates cannot later claim that they were never informed about a particular rule.

The prison guidebook informs prisoners about the various staff members who are responsible for counseling and other functions. The guidebook also warns prisoners up front about the penalties for unacceptable behavior. As you read this general warning notice in Box 6-1, consider whether it sounds threat-

| BOX 6-1 | **Actual Prison Regulations Governing "Unacceptable Behavior"** |

I.E. *Unacceptable Behavior:* It is your responsibility to follow the rules of this facility. Gambling, borrowing, and homosexual behavior are not allowed. If found guilty of a minor misconduct one of the following sanctions will be imposed: (1) toplock [i.e., confined to own cell], (2) loss of privileges, (3) extra duty, (4) counsel and reprimand, and (5) restitution of values less than $10.00. If found guilty of a major misconduct, one of the following sanctions will be imposed: (1) detention [i.e., segregated from general population], (2) toplock, (3) loss of privileges, (4) extra duty, and (5) restitution of values more than $10.00. In addition, a guilty finding of major misconducts may result in (1) classification to a higher level of security, including Administrative Segregation; or (2) loss of accumulated good time earned for the month in which the misconduct "was incurred." Any escape attempts from this facility will result in an increase in your custody level and a referral will be made to the State Police for prosecution.

ening enough to prevent inmates, especially those serving long sentences, from misbehaving.

Although the number of potential punishments available to corrections officials are limited, prisoners do risk losing what little freedom and few privileges they possess. Indeed, multiple major offenses can lead to **disciplinary segregation** or a transfer to a more restrictive institution. In addition, prisoners risk the loss of recently earned **good time,** or time taken off a sentence by virtue of good behavior. In effect, repeated misbehavior will keep prisoners in prison longer, through missed opportunities either for good-time reductions or for early release on parole.

The prison's guidebook specifies rules for each area of the prison: individual cells, dayrooms, indoor recreation area, yard, school, hobby/craft center, barbershop, chapel, dining room, and visiting room. Many of the same rules apply to each area, with special rules also applying depending on the kind of activities occurring. Recall that lists of rules for a prison visiting room and for a prison chapel were presented in Chapters 4 and 5, respectively. Box 6-2 provides examples of rules that apply to prisoners in their cells. What do you think is each rule's purpose? What would be an appropriate punishment for a violation of each rule?

As indicated by the examples in Box 6-3, additional issues arise when prisoners are together in a larger area of the prison. As you examine the yard rules for prisoners in protective custody, again consider the purpose of each rule. What would be an appropriate punishment for violations?

Corrections officers play an important role in rule enforcement. They must make judgments about when rules have been broken, and they may use their **discretion** to overlook some rule violations. Prisoners also may attempt to persuade officers to use discretion in their favor by claiming that something about their situation makes an apparent rule violation actually a misunderstanding.

VII. HOUSING UNIT RULES

...

2. You shall make your bed in a neat manner Monday through Friday, affording a clear view underneath the bed, with the cover blanket tucked. Beds shall be made by 8:00 a.m. and remain so until 3:30 p.m. The second blanket will be folded when out of your cell. Your bed will be made anytime you are out of your cell.

...

5. Nothing is allowed on your walls or ceiling except the Bulletin Board, cell card and mirror which are to remain in the authorized place. Painting or defacing of walls or furnishings will result in misconduct. Your cell card (name and number) MUST be on the wall directly over the mirror.

6. You may not drape sheets, blankets, towels, clothing or anything else across the cell or attach, tie, or hang items on or under the bars.

...

12. You may do personal laundry in your cell between the hours of 4:00 p.m. and 8:00 a.m., Monday through Friday, and any time on weekends and holidays. There will be no laundering of clothes in the showers. Clotheslines are not permitted at any time. Wet clothing may be hung from the sink on a hanger until dry between 4:00 p.m. and 8:00 a.m. One damp/wet washcloth and towel may be hung from the sink until dry.

13. Your radio, TV and/or tape player must be stored on the desk/shelf when not in use. Your radio, tape player or TV is not to be left on when you are out of your cell. Authorized earphones must be used in conjunction with TV's, radios, and tape players at *all* times. Only one length of cable for your TV is allowed.

...

22. Stopping, standing, or loitering will not be permitted anywhere in the living units.

23. When released, you shall proceed directly from your cell to the gate. On your return, you shall go directly to your cell. Any other movement in the unit requires Staff authorization.

24. Loud talking, shouting, laughing, or other noise deemed to be disruptive is not permitted in the housing unit.

25. Loaning, borrowing, trading, selling, or buying of personal property is prohibited. Violation of this rule will result in a misconduct report; and MAY result in the loss of the property.

...

Officers also may use their discretion to target particular prisoners for punishment, especially if they are not committed to using their power in a professional manner or to applying rules equally. Disciplinary actions in prisons are not initiated until a corrections official decides that a prisoner should be punished for violating a rule. Whenever discretion is an important element of rule enforcement, some degree of unequal treatment likely will result. Either different corrections officers will apply rules in a slightly different manner, or the same corrections officer will apply rules differently when dealing with two prisoners who have engaged in similar behavior. The involvement of human beings in decision making prevents any institution from applying all rules equally and consistently in all situations.

BOX 6-3	**Actual Protection Yard Rules**

. . .

2. No "horseplaying" is allowed; there is to be no body punching, grabbing or pushing of any kind.

3. You must stay inside the yellow line painted around the perimeter of the yard. Entering the area between the yellow line and the fence or building without staff permission may be considered as out of place, attempted escape, or escape.

4. Nothing is to be passed through the fence to people in the segregation yard modules or who lock on I-Block outside. No talking/yelling at prisoners in segregation exercise modules or to I-Block prisoners.

5. No tackle football or contact games.

6. No throwing snowballs, stones, or other objects, except softballs and/or basketballs.

7. No meetings in the yard . . . or Recreation Center. Any congregation of more than six (6) prisoners will be considered a meeting.

8. No team activities, unless approved and supervised by the Recreation Department.

. . .

11. Choose the yard or the . . . Recreation Center; you are there for the entire period. No going back and forth.

12. Absolutely no gambling or gambling paraphernalia is allowed. Only four (4) prisoners allowed at the yard tables at a time.

. . .

14. The only personal property allowed on the yard is table games (chess sets, cards, checkers). Appliances are not allowed!

15. Anyone who breaks or damages a [basketball] backboard or rim will be financially responsible for replacement, including labor and costs.

16. ANY VIOLATION OF THESE RULES MAY RESULT IN A MISCONDUCT REPORT AND MAY RESULT IN RESTRICTION FROM THE YARD OR [RECREATION CENTER] (IF VIOLATION OCCURRED THERE).

DISCIPLINARY PROCEEDINGS

Corrections officials historically ordered immediate punishment for prisoners who disobeyed rules. If the officials were unprofessional or unfair, there were risks that punishments would be excessively harsh or improperly applied. In recent decades, most top corrections officials have been educated professionals, people who studied corrections-related subjects in college. These professionals are more likely to make sure that written regulations exist to guide decisions by corrections officers, including decisions about discipline and punishment. In addition, courts have monitored corrections practices more closely to ensure that prisoners' constitutional rights are not violated. Of particular interest in discipline cases is the right to due process. As you will recall from Chapter 1, according to the Fourteenth Amendment, states shall not deprive people of life, liberty, or property without due process of law. In this context, due process usually means that certain procedures must be followed to ensure that punishments are imposed fairly and appropriately. Fair procedures provide a mechanism to prevent corrections officials from using their discretion to punish inmates improperly.

State-Created Liberty Interests

As the courts became more receptive to prisoners' civil rights lawsuits, individual inmates filed cases claiming that prisons used unfair procedures—procedures that violated the right to due process—in imposing punishments for violating prison rules. The key U.S. Supreme Court case to address this issue was *Wolff v. McDonnell* (1974). As you read the excerpted *Wolff* decision in Box 6-4, look carefully at what the Supreme Court said about the right to due process. Are there specific procedures required in all prison discipline cases? Do some procedures apply only to certain kinds of cases? How does the Court determine if a right to due process exists?

Notice in *Wolff* that the Court did not assert that the Due Process Clause requires that hearings be held in every prison disciplinary case. Rather, the Court stated that the right to due process—and therefore a right to certain procedural steps—existed because the state had given the prisoners an entitlement to good-time credits. This is known as a **state-created liberty interest.** In other words, the right to due process exists because of state regulations that give something valuable to prisoners, and therefore the prisoners are entitled to fair procedures when the state decides to take that valuable thing away for disciplinary reasons. The concept of due process applied in *Wolff* was based on prior decisions concerning the procedural steps that must be followed in revoking parole and probation in order to send released offenders back to prison.[1] These earlier cases will be discussed in Chapter 10.

The *Wolff* case applied specifically to the situation of good-time credits being lost for misbehavior. The protections would also apply to extended confinement in disciplinary segregation. Such a deprivation of liberty would seem to fall directly under the principles of the Due Process Clause. These were not, however, the only circumstances in which the *Wolff* analysis could be applied. Because the Supreme Court issued the decision, other federal courts followed the high court's lead in examining other situations and deciding whether a right to due process—with its specific fair procedures—exists for other infractions and punishments.

The *Wolff* decision did not require a full trial, even when good-time credits could be lost as the form of punishment. Disciplinary proceedings do not follow court rules concerning evidence and standards of proof. Indeed, the Supreme Court has declared that a presentation of "some evidence" satisfies due process in finding that an infraction occurred and sanctions are justified.[2] This is a far cry from the proof beyond a reasonable doubt that is required in criminal cases. The *Wolff* rule required only certain procedures: (1) notice of the charges to the inmate, (2) time to prepare a response at a disciplinary hearing, (3) the opportunity to present evidence and witnesses if prison security will not be threatened as a result, (4) a sufficiently impartial decision-making body, and (5) a written statement of the decision makers' conclusions and reasons for

B O X   6 - 4   *Wolff v. McDonnell,* 418 U.S. 539 (1974)

JUSTICE WHITE delivered the opinion of the Court.

. . . [T]he Nebraska Treatment and Corrections Act provides that the chief executive officer of each penal facility is responsible for the discipline of inmates in a particular institution. The statute provides for a range of possible disciplinary action. "Except in flagrant or serious cases, punishment for misconduct shall consist of deprivation of privileges. In cases of flagrant or serious misconduct, the chief executive officer may order that a person's reduction of term [good-time credit] . . . be forfeited or withheld and also that the person be confined to a disciplinary cell." . . .

[Prison officials] assert that the procedure for disciplining prison inmates for serious misconduct is a matter of policy raising no constitutional issue. If the position implies that prisoners in state institutions are wholly without the protections of the Constitution and the Due Process Clause, it is plainly untenable. . . . [T]hough his rights may be diminished by the needs and exigencies of the institutional environment, a prisoner is not wholly stripped of constitutional protections when he is imprisoned for crime. There is no iron curtain drawn between the Constitution and the prisons of this country. . . .

. . . [T]he fact that prisoners retain rights under the Due Process Clause in no way implies that these rights are not subject to restrictions imposed by the nature of the regime to which they have been lawfully committed. . . . Prison disciplinary proceedings are not part of a criminal prosecution, and the full panoply of rights due to defendants in such proceedings does not apply. . . . In sum, there must be mutual accommodation between institutional needs and objectives and the provisions of the Constitution that are of general application.

We also reject the assertion by the State that whatever may be true of the Due Process Clause in general or of other rights protected by the Clause against state infringement, the interest of prisoners in disciplinary procedures is not included in that "liberty" protected by the Fourteenth Amendment. It is true that the Constitution itself does not guarantee good-time credit for satisfactory behavior while in prison. But here the State itself has not only provided a statutory right to good time but also specifies that it is to be forfeited only for serious misbehavior. Nebraska may have the authority to create, or not, a right to a shortened prison sentence through the accumulation of credits for good behavior, and it is true that the Due Process Clause does not require a hearing "in every conceivable case of government impairment of private interest." . . . But the state having created the right to good time and itself recognizing that its deprivation is a sanction authorized for major misconduct, the prisoner's interest has real substance and is sufficiently embraced within Fourteenth Amendment "liberty" to entitle him to those minimum procedures appropriate under the circumstances and required by the Due Process Clause to insure that the state-created right is not arbitrarily abrogated [violated]. . . .

. . . We think a person's liberty is equally protected, even when the liberty itself is a statutory creation of the State. The touchstone of due process is protection of the individual against arbitrary action of government. . . . Since prisoners in Nebraska can only lose good-time credits if they are guilty of serious misconduct, the determination of whether such behavior has occurred becomes critical, and the minimum requirements of procedural due process appropriate for the circumstances must be observed. . . .

. . . Prison disciplinary proceedings . . . take place in a close, tightly controlled environment peopled by those who have chosen to violate the criminal law and who have been lawfully incarcerated for doing so. . . . [Prisoners] may

(continued)

have little regard for the safety of others or their property or the rules designed to provide an orderly and reasonably safe prison life. . . .

It is against this background that disciplinary proceedings must be structured by prison authorities; and it is against this background that we must make our constitutional judgments, realizing that we are dealing with the maximum security institution as well as those where security considerations are not paramount. The reality is that disciplinary hearings and imposition of disagreeable sanctions necessarily involve confrontations between inmates and authority and between inmates who are being disciplined and those who would charge or furnish evidence against them. Retaliation is much more than a theoretical possibility; and the basic and unavoidable task of providing reasonable personal safety for guards and inmates may be at stake, to say nothing of the impact of disciplinary confrontations and the resulting encapsulation of personal antagonisms on the important aims of the correctional process. . . .

Two of the procedures . . . extended to parolees facing revocation proceedings . . . must be provided to prisoners in the Nebraska Complex if the minimum requirements of procedural due process are to be satisfied. These are advance written notice of the claimed violation and a written statement of the factfinders as to the evidence relied upon and the reasons for the disciplinary action taken. . . .

Part of the function of the notice is to give the charged party a chance to marshal the facts in his defense and to clarify what the charges are, in fact. . . . We hold that written notice of the charges must be given to the disciplinary-action defendant in order to inform him of the charges and to enable him to marshal the facts and prepare a defense. At least a brief period of time after the notice, no less than 24 hours, should be allowed to the inmate to prepare for the appearance before the Adjustment Committee.

We also hold that there must be a "written statement by the factfinders as to the evidence relied on and the reasons" for the disciplinary action. . . . [T]he actions taken at such proceedings may involve review by other bodies. They might furnish the basis of a decision by the Director of Corrections to transfer an inmate to another institution . . . and are certainly likely to be considered by the state parole authorities in making parole decisions. Written records of proceedings will thus protect the inmate against collateral consequences based on a misunderstanding of the nature of the original proceeding. Further, as to the disciplinary action itself, the provision for a written record helps to insure that administrators, faced with possible scrutiny by state officials and the public, and perhaps even the courts, where fundamental constitutional rights have been abridged, will act fairly. Without written records, the inmate will be at a severe disadvantage in propounding his own cause to or defending himself from others. It may be that there will be occasions when personal or institutional safety is so implicated that the statement may properly exclude certain items of evidence, but in that event the statement should indicate the fact of the omission. Otherwise, we perceive no conceivable rehabilitative objective or prospect of prison disruption that can flow from the requirement of these [written] statements.

We are also of the opinion that the inmate facing disciplinary proceedings should be allowed to call witnesses and present documentary evidence in his defense when permitting him to do so will not be unduly hazardous to institutional safety or correctional goals. Ordinarily, the right to present evidence is basic to a fair hearing; but the unrestricted right to call witnesses from the prison population carries obvious potential for disruption and for interference with the swift punishment that in individual cases may be essential to carrying out the correctional program of the institution. . . . [W]e must balance the inmate's interest in avoiding loss of good time against the needs of the prison, and some amount of flexibility and accommodation is required. Prison officials must have the necessary discretion to keep the hearing within reasonable limits and to refuse to call witnesses that may create a risk of reprisal or undermine authority, as well as to limit access to other inmates to collect statements or to compile other documentary evidence. Although we do not prescribe it, it would be useful for the Committee to state its reason for refusing to call a witness, whether it be for irrelevance, lack of necessity, or the hazards presented in individual cases. . . . There is this much play in the joints of the Due Process Clause, and we stop short of imposing a more demanding rule with respect to witnesses and documents.

Confrontation and cross-examination present greater hazards to institutional interests. If confrontation and cross-examination of those furnishing evidence against the inmate were to be allowed as a matter of course, as in criminal trials, there would be considerable potential for havoc inside the prison walls. . . . We think the Constitution should not be read to impose the procedure at the present time and that adequate bases for decision in prison disciplinary cases can be arrived at without cross-examination. . . .

The insertion of counsel into the disciplinary process would inevitably give the proceedings a more adversary cast and tend to reduce their utility as a means to further correctional goals. There would also be delay and very practical problems in providing counsel in sufficient numbers at the time and place where hearings are to be held. At this stage of the development of these procedures we are not prepared to hold

that inmates have a right to either retained or appointed counsel in disciplinary proceedings.

Where an illiterate inmate is involved, however, or where the complexity of the issue makes it unlikely that the inmate will be able to collect and present the evidence necessary for an adequate comprehension of the case, he should be free to seek the aid of a fellow inmate, or if that is forbidden, to have adequate substitute aid in the form of help from the staff or from a sufficiently competent inmate designated by the staff. . . .

Finally, we decline to rule that the Adjustment Committee which conducts the required hearings at the Nebraska Prison Complex and determines whether to revoke good time is not sufficiently impartial to satisfy the Due Process Clause. The Committee is made up of the Associate Warden of Custody as chairman, the Correctional Industries Superintendent, and Reception Center Director. The Chief Corrections Supervisor refers cases to the Committee after investigation and an initial interview with the inmate involved. The Committee is not left at large with unlimited discretion [because regulations require it to consider specific factors in reaching decisions]. . . . We find no warrant [reasons] in the record presented here for concluding that the Adjustment Committee presents such a hazard of arbitrary decisionmaking that it should be held violative of due process of law.

imposing punishment. Illiterate prisoners could have assistance from staff or other prisoners. The Court did not require that a prisoner be given any opportunity to cross-examine witnesses during the hearing or that an attorney be provided to represent the prisoner. The *Wolff* rule provided the basic model for fair procedures in the serious disciplinary cases in which prisoners have due process rights, although these exact procedures are not necessarily required in all circumstances.

After the *Wolff* case, some courts interpreted the Supreme Court's opinion as requiring procedural protections whenever a prisoner suffered a "grievous loss" as a result of decisions by corrections officials. However, in *Meachum v. Fano* (1976), the Supreme Court rejected this interpretation.[3] In *Meachum*, some prisoners were transferred from a medium-security prison to several

JUSTICE WHITE delivered the opinion of the Court.

. . . Relying on *Miranda v. Arizona* [1966] . . . and *Mathis v. United States* [1968], . . . [the appellate court] held that prison inmates are entitled to representation at prison disciplinary hearings where the charges involve conduct punishable as a crime under state law, not because of the services that counsel might render in connection with the disciplinary proceedings themselves, but because statements inmates might make at the hearings would perhaps be used in later state-court prosecutions for the same conduct.

Neither *Miranda* . . . nor *Mathis* has any substantial bearing on the question whether counsel must be provided at [prison disciplinary hearings]. . . . The Court has never held, and we

decline to do so now, that the requirements of those cases must be met to render pretrial statements admissible in other than criminal cases.

We see no reason to alter our conclusion so recently made in *Wolff* that inmates do not "have a right to either retained or appointed counsel in disciplinary hearings." . . . Plainly, therefore, state officials were not in error in failing to advise Palmigiano to the contrary. . . .

Had the State desired Palmigiano's testimony over his Fifth Amendment objection, we can but assume that it would have extended whatever use immunity [i.e., immunity from having the statements used against him in a criminal proceeding]. Had this occurred and had Palmigiano nevertheless refused to answer it, it surely would not have violated the Fifth Amendment to draw whatever inference from his silence that

---

maximum-security prisons after a series of fires were set inside the medium-security prison. The prisoners claimed that their due process rights required that they be given hearings before they could be transferred. The Supreme Court disagreed. Although the transfer to a higher-security institution meant that the prisoners likely would lose a certain amount of freedom, as well as some privileges, this form of loss did not trigger the due process protections required in *Wolff*. According to Justice Byron White's majority opinion:

> *Transfers between institutions, for example, are made for a variety of reasons and often involve no more than informed predictions as to what would best serve institutional security or the safety and welfare of the inmate. Yet under the approach urged here, any transfer, for whatever reason, would require a hearing as long as it could be said that the transfer would place the prisoner in substantially more burdensome conditions than he had been experiencing. We are unwilling to go that far.*

In *Baxter v. Palmigiano* (1976), which is excerpted in Box 6-5, the Supreme Court further explained the rights provided to prisoners by the *Wolff* decision. Notice what the decision says about any protection against self-incrimination in prison disciplinary processes.

The *Palmigiano* decision emphasized that neither attorneys nor a right to remain silent are necessary or required for prison disciplinary hearings. The privilege against compelled self-incrimination that exists for criminal proceed-

the circumstances warranted. Insofar as the privilege [against compelled self-incrimination] is concerned, the situation is little different where the State advises the inmate of his right to silence but also plainly notifies him that his silence will be weighed in the balance.

. . . In criminal cases, where the stakes are higher and the State's sole interest is to convict, [case precedent] prohibits the judge and prosecutor from suggesting to the jury that it may treat the defendant's silence as substantive evidence of guilt. Disciplinary proceedings in state prisons, however, involve the correctional process and important state interests other than conviction for crime. We decline to extend [the privilege against self-incrimination] to this context. . . .

[The Court of Appeals required prison authorities to provide written reasons to inmates denied the opportunity to cross-examine or confront witnesses against them in disciplinary hearings]. This conclusion is inconsistent with *Wolff*. We characterized as "useful," but did not require, written reasons for denying inmates the limited right to call witnesses for their defense. We made no such suggestion with respect to confrontation and cross-examination which, as was there pointed out, stand on different footing because of their inherent danger and the availability of adequate bases of decision without them. . . . Mandating confrontation and cross-examination, except where prison officials can justify their denial on one or more grounds that appeal to judges, effectively preempts the area that *Wolff* left to the sound discretion of prison officials. . . .

ings does not exist for prison disciplinary proceedings. The Court's opinion also reminded lower court judges that the Supreme Court does not want to expand the procedures developed in *Wolff*. None of these cases established any right for prisoners to appeal adverse decisions in the disciplinary hearing process.

In later cases, the Court refused to apply due process rights to transfers undertaken specifically for disciplinary reasons (*Montanye v. Haymes*, 1976),[4] even when the transfer involved sending a prisoner to another state thousands of miles from his home (*Olim v. Wakinekona*, 1983).[5] Although such transfers can impose significant hardships on prisoners, such as the inability to have family visitors, the Court concluded that prisoners have no reason to expect that they will serve their sentences in any particular location. Prisoners also have been unsuccessful in relying on due process rights to claim that they are entitled to expect that parole release will be granted (*Greenholtz v. Nebraska Penal Inmates*, 1979).[6]

Constitution-Based Due Process Rights

The Supreme Court's analysis of due process rights generally focused on whether the state had created a liberty interest that triggered an entitlement to procedural protections. In some circumstances, however, the Court was willing to find a general constitutional requirement of due process, even if the state did not have a regulation that created an entitlement for the prisoner. The Court's decision in **Vitek v. Jones** (1980) represented such a case. As you read the opinion, excerpted in Box 6-6, pay close attention to the circumstances in which the Constitution imposes due process protections for prisoners.

In *Vitek v. Jones*, the Supreme Court approved the following minimum procedures to be followed before a prisoner could be transferred to a mental hospital:

A. *Written notice to the prisoner that a transfer to a mental hospital is being considered;*

B. *A hearing, sufficiently after the notice to permit the prisoner to prepare, at which the disclosure to the prisoner is made of the evidence being relied upon for the transfer and at which an opportunity to be heard in person and to present documentary evidence is given;*

C. *An opportunity at the hearing to present testimony of witnesses by the defense and to confront and cross-examine witnesses called by the state, except upon a finding, not arbitrarily made, of good cause for not permitting such presentation, confrontation, or cross-examination;*

D. *An independent decisionmaker;*

E. *A written statement by the factfinder as to the evidence relied on and the reasons for transferring the inmate;*

F. *Availability of legal counsel, furnished by the state, if the inmate is financially unable to furnish his own; and*

G. *Effective and timely notice of all the foregoing rights.*

In *Vitek*, the Court viewed the involuntary transfer to a mental hospital as automatically constituting an adverse impact that was so severe that the right to due process required a hearing that met specific procedural requirements. Other situations may also trigger due process protections, such as the forced administration of drugs to treat prisoners with mental illnesses. In *Washington v. Harper* (1990), the Court approved the forced administration of such drugs after the treatment decision had passed through several procedural steps, including a hearing and review by medical professionals.[7]

The *Vitek* requirement of providing an attorney at state expense (item F) expanded the due process requirements established by *Wolff*. However, the Court justified this new requirement by the circumstances involved in *Vitek v. Jones* and similar cases that would later arise. The Court noted its position that illiterate and uneducated prisoners are likely to need greater assistance than other prisoners in protecting their rights and presenting their side of the story at a hearing. In reviewing the situation of prisoners who may be mentally ill, the Court declared:

> *A prisoner thought to be suffering from a mental disease or defect requiring involuntary treatment probably has an even greater need for legal assistance, for such a prisoner is more likely to be unable to understand or exercise his rights. In these circumstances, it is appropriate that counsel be provided to indigent prisoners whom the State seeks to treat as mentally ill.*

| BOX 6-6 | *Vitek v. Jones*, 445 U.S. 480 (1980) |

[*Jones was transferred from a prison to a state mental hospital under a statute that said, in part, "if the physician or psychologist (designated by prison officials to examine the prisoner) is of the opinion that the person cannot be given proper treatment in that (prison) facility, the director (of corrections) may arrange for his transfer for examination, study, and treatment to any medical-correctional facility, or to another institution . . . where proper treatment is available." Jones filed a section 1983 action claiming that his due process rights were violated.*]

JUSTICE WHITE delivered the opinion of the Court.

. . . The District Court was also correct in holding that independently of [the liberty interest created by the Nebraska statute under which the transfer occurred], the transfer of a prisoner from a prison to a mental hospital must be accompanied by appropriate procedural protections. The issue is whether after a conviction for robbery, Jones retained a residuum of liberty that would be infringed by a transfer to a mental hospital without complying with minimum requirements of due process.

We have recognized that for the ordinary citizen, commitment to a mental hospital produces "a massive curtailment of liberty" and in consequence "requires due process protection." The loss of liberty produced by an involuntary commitment is more than a loss of freedom from confinement. It is indisputable that commitment to a mental hospital "can engender adverse social consequences to the individual" and that "[w]hether we label this phenomena 'stigma' or choose to call it something else . . . we recognize that it can occur and that it can have a very significant impact on the individual." Also, "[a]mong the historic liberties" protected by the Due Process Clause is the "right to be free from, and to obtain judicial relief for, unjustified intrusions on personal security." Compelled treatment in the form of mandatory behavior modification programs, to which the District Court found Jones was exposed in this case, was a proper factor to be weighed by the District Court. . . .

. . . [I]nvoluntary commitment to a mental hospital is not within the range of conditions of confinement to which a prison sentence subjects an individual. A criminal conviction and sentence of imprisonment extinguish an individual's right to freedom from confinement for the term of his sentence, but they do not authorize the State to classify him as mentally ill and to subject him to involuntary psychiatric treatment without affording him additional due process protections. . . .

The Rise and Fall of State-Created Liberty Interests

In *Hewitt v. Helms* (1983), the Supreme Court expanded opportunities for prisoners to identify state-created liberty interests that would trigger due process protections.[8] The case itself involved the immediate placement of an inmate in segregation after a disturbance without requiring a presegregation hearing in emergency situations. The importance of *Hewitt v. Helms* stemmed from the conclusion that a state creates a liberty interest for prisoners by having mandatory language in its relevant statutes and regulations (although such language did not exist in relevant regulations to benefit the claimant in

Hewitt). When a statute or regulation said that the state "shall" or "will" take a certain action, the mandatory language created an enforceable liberty interest for prisoners. If a state left procedural matters largely under the discretion of corrections officials, no liberty interest would be created to trigger due process rights. However, by mandating that certain procedures be followed, the state was, in effect, obligating itself to uphold procedural standards that protect the due process rights triggered by a state-created liberty interest.

The Supreme Court's analysis had two consequences. First, it encouraged prisoners to examine regulations in order to identify mandatory language to use as the basis for seeking enforcement of protections and privileges. Thus, the phrasing of regulations could create new and potentially unexpected procedural requirements for corrections officials seeking to punish, transfer, or otherwise manage a prisoner. At the same time, the Court's reasoning effectively discouraged prisons from writing careful regulations. Corrections officials suddenly had an incentive to leave many matters under the discretionary control of wardens and others so that no mandatory language would appear that could be used by prisoners to trigger due process protections. This situation creates its own problems because administrators are less able to give guidance to lower-level corrections officers and less able to ensure that they do not make bad decisions. Such was the state of affairs until the Supreme Court's decision in *Sandin v. Conner* (1995). As you read the *Sandin* decision, excerpted in Box 6-7, try to identify how the Supreme Court changed its approach to evaluating state-created liberty interests.

The key language in *Sandin v. Conner* limited the circumstances in which a state-created liberty interest would be recognized. Instead of triggering due process whenever mandatory language appeared in a statute or prison regulation, the Court limited state-created liberty interests to those situations affecting freedom from restraint and imposing special hardships. In the most important language of the Court's opinion, Chief Justice William Rehnquist concluded:

> [W]e recognize that States may under certain circumstances create liberty interests which are protected by the Due Process Clause. . . . But these interests will be generally limited to freedom from restraint which, while not exceeding the sentence in such an unexpected manner as to give rise to protection by the Due Process Clause by its own force . . . nonetheless imposes atypical and significant hardship on the inmate in relation to the ordinary incidents of prison life.

Note how Justice Ginsburg's dissent takes a broader view of the right to due process and emphasizes that the Constitution, rather than state regulations, should be a source of that right. Take note, as well, that *Sandin v. Conner* was a five-to-four decision. If a member of the majority should retire and be replaced by a new appointee, especially a Democratic appointee of President Clinton who might share the views of Clinton's other appointees, Ginsburg and Stephen Breyer, the Court may revisit this issue and change its approach to these cases.

| BOX 6-7 | *Sandin v. Conner,* 115 S.Ct. 2293 (1995) |

CHIEF JUSTICE REHNQUIST delivered the opinion of the Court.

We granted certiorari to reexamine the circumstances under which state prison regulations afford inmates a liberty interest protected by the Due Process Clause. . . .

. . . In August 1987, a prison officer escorted [Conner] from his cell to the module program area. The officer subjected Conner to a strip search, complete with an inspection of the rectal area. Conner retorted with angry and foul language directed at the officer. Eleven days later he received notice that he had been charged with disciplinary infractions. The notice charged Conner with "high misconduct" for using physical interference to impair a correctional function, and "low moderate misconduct" for using abusive or obscene language and for harassing employees.

Conner appeared before an adjustment committee on August 28, 1987. The committee refused Conner's request to present witnesses at the hearing, stating that "[w]itnesses were unavailable due to a move to the medium facility and being short staffed on the modules." . . . At the conclusion of the proceedings, the committee determined that Conner was guilty of the alleged misconduct [and he was given 30 days in disciplinary segregation as punishment]. . . .

[Conner filed a lawsuit alleging, among other things, that the disciplinary proceedings violated his right to due process.] The [U.S.] Court of Appeals . . . concluded that Conner had a liberty interest in remaining free from disciplinary segregation and that there was a disputed question of fact with respect to whether he received all of the process due under this Court's pronouncement in *Wolff v. McDonnell.* . . . The Court of Appeals based its conclusion on a prison regulation that instructs the committee to find guilt when a charge of misconduct is supported by substantial evidence. . . . The Court of Appeals reasoned . . . that the

committee's duty to find guilt was nondiscretionary. From the language of the regulation, it drew a negative inference that the committee may not impose segregation if it does not find substantial evidence of misconduct. . . . It viewed this as a state-created liberty interest, and therefore held that respondent was entitled to call witnesses by virtue of our opinion in *Wolff.* . . . We . . . now reverse.

Our due process analysis begins with *Wolff.* . . . We held [in *Wolff*] that the Due Process Clause itself does not create a liberty interest in credit for good behavior, but that the statutory provision created a liberty interest in a "shortened prison sentence" which resulted from good time credits, credits which were revocable only if the prisoner was guilty of serious misconduct. . . .

. . . In evaluating the claims of inmates [in *Hewitt v. Helms,* 1983] who had been confined to administrative segregation, [the Court] first rejected the inmates' claim of a right to remain in the general population as protected by the Due Process Clause. . . . The Due Process Clause standing alone confers no liberty interest in freedom from state action taken "within the sentence imposed." . . . [The Court] then concluded that the transfer to less amenable quarters for nonpunitive reasons was "ordinarily contemplated by a prison sentence." . . . Examination of the possibility that the State had created a liberty interest by virtue of its prison regulations followed. . . . [T]he Court asked whether the State had gone beyond issuing mere procedural guidelines and had used "language of an unmistakably mandatory character" such that the incursion on liberty would not occur "absent specified predicates." . . . Finding such mandatory directives in the regulations before it, the Court decided that the State had created a protected liberty interest . . . [but] procedures conferred in *Wolff* were unnecessary to safeguard the inmates' interest

(continued)

and, if imposed, would undermine the prison's management objectives. . . .

Hewitt has produced at least two undesirable effects. First, it creates disincentives for States to codify prison management procedures in the interest of uniform treatment. . . . States may avoid creation of "liberty" interests by having scarcely any regulations or by conferring standardless discretion on correctional personnel.

Second, the *Hewitt* approach has led to the involvement of federal courts in the day-to-day management of prisons, often squandering judicial resources with little off-setting benefit to anyone. In so doing, it has run counter to the view expressed in several of our cases that federal courts ought to afford appropriate deference and flexibility to state officials trying to manage a volatile environment. . . .

. . . [W]e believe that the search for a negative implication from mandatory language in prisoner regulations has strayed from the real concerns undergirding the liberty protected by the Due Process Clause. The time has come to return to the due process principles we believe were correctly established and applied in *Wolff* and *Meachum*. Following *Wolff*, we recognize that States may under certain circumstances create liberty interests which are protected by the Due Process Clause. . . . But these interests will be generally limited to freedom from restraint which, while not exceeding the sentence in such an unexpected manner as to give rise to protection by the Due Process Clause by its own force . . . nonetheless imposes atypical and significant hardship on the inmate in relation to the ordinary incidents of prison life. . . .

. . . Admittedly, prisoners do not shed all constitutional rights at the prison gate, . . . but "[l]awful incarceration brings about the necessary withdrawal or limitation of many privileges and rights, a retraction justified by the considerations underlying our penal system." . . . Discipline by prison officials in response to a wide range of misconduct falls within the expected parameters of the sentence imposed by a court of law. . . .

. . . We hold that Conner's discipline in segregated confinement did not present the type of atypical, significant deprivation in which a state might conceivably create a liberty interest. The record shows that, at the time of Conner's punishment, disciplinary segregation, with insignificant exceptions, mirrored those conditions imposed upon inmates in administrative segregation and protective custody. . . .

We hold, therefore, that neither the Hawaii prison regulation in question, nor the Due Process Clause itself, afforded Conner a protected liberty interest that would entitle him to the procedural protections set forth in *Wolff*. The [punishment] to which he was subjected as a result of the misconduct hearing was within the range of confinement to be normally expected for one serving an indeterminate term of 30 years to life. . . .

JUSTICE GINSBURG, with whom JUSTICE STEVENS joins, dissenting.

. . . Unlike the Court, I conclude that Conner had a liberty interest, protected by the Fourteenth Amendment's Due Process Clause, in avoiding the disciplinary confinement he endured. As Justice BREYER details [in a separate dissenting opinion], Conner's prison punishment effected a severe alteration in the conditions of his incarceration. . . . Disciplinary confinement as punishment for "high misconduct" not only deprives prisoners of privileges for protracted periods; unlike administrative segregation and protective custody, disciplinary confinement also stigmatizes them and diminishes parole prospects. Those immediate and lingering consequences should suffice to qualify such confinement as liberty-depriving for purposes of Due Process protection.

I see the Due Process Clause itself, not Hawaii's prison code, as the wellspring of the protection due Conner. Deriving protected liberty interests from mandatory language in local prison codes would make of the fundamental right something more in certain States, something less in others. . . .

Deriving the prisoner's due process right from the code for his prison, moreover, yields this practical anomaly: a State that scarcely attempts to control the behavior of its prison guards may, for that very laxity, escape constitutional accountability; a State that tightly cabins the discretion of its prison workers may, for that attentiveness, become vulnerable to constitutional claims. An incentive for ruleless prison management disserves the State's penological goals and jeopardizes the welfare of prisoners.

To fit the liberty recognized in our fundamental instrument of government, the process due by reason of the Constitution similarly should not depend on the particularities of the local prison's code. Rather, the basic, universal requirements are notice of the acts of misconduct prison officials say the inmate committed, and an opportunity to respond to the charges before a trustworthy decisionmaker. . . .

Consider the hypothetical situation presented in Box 6-8, and decide whether the Supreme Court would recognize a state-created liberty interest in these circumstances.

The Supreme Court's decision in *Sandin* changed the way courts must analyze claims concerning state-created liberty interests. As described by corrections law experts, "Focusing the analysis on the 'nature of the deprivation' rather than on the 'language used' in agency manuals or regulations relieves the courts of having to scrutinize prison manuals and state regulations to determine if the wording is mandatory as to trigger due process protections."[9] No one knows for certain what situations will qualify as "atypical and significant hardships" under *Sandin*. However, it clearly will be much more difficult for inmates to establish the existence of state-created liberty interests that require due process protections.[10] The lower federal courts will be forced to struggle with individual cases filed by prisoners alleging due process violations. It remains to be seen whether these decisions will spur the Supreme Court to clarify its view of the applicable circumstances, if any, in which a state-created liberty interest will be recognized.

SUMMARY

- Prisons must have a variety of rules and regulations in order to maintain security and control.

- Prisons must find ways to inform inmates about the numerous rules, which may differ from one setting to another within the prison, because such rules serve as the basis for disciplinary actions that result in punishments, such as loss of privileges and disciplinary segregation.

- The U.S. Supreme Court applied the concept of state-created liberty interests in *Wolff v. McDonnell* (1974) to establish procedural requirements for disciplinary

BOX 6-8   **State-Created Liberty Interests**

Imagine you are the head of community corrections programs for a state department of corrections. You have authority over convicted offenders who are on electronic tethers, those who live in halfway houses, those who live at home but report daily to a community corrections center, and those who are out on parole. You have the authority to send offenders back to prison if they violate the rules of their community programs.

In one city, many offenders have been showing up late for their required urinalysis tests, which they must take once a week at the community corrections center before they go to work or school. These are offenders who have committed either minor crimes (e.g., shoplifting) or moderately serious crimes (e.g., drug possession). They live at home, hold down regular jobs or go to school, and live relatively normal lives—except for reporting once each week to the community center for a drug test. You call the director of the community center to find out about the situation.

"Why are you having such problems with tardiness?" you ask.

"Well, the word on the streets is that people know the prisons are all full so they think they won't really be sent to prison for a minor rules violation."

You think for a moment. "We cannot let this slide. It will only lead to more misbehavior. I want you to tell all of your people that the next person who shows up late for a drug test is going to be in big, big trouble. You tell them that I said so."

"Okay—but I don't think they will really believe it."

hearings resulting in the withdrawal of good-time credits.

- *Wolff* mandated notice to the prisoner of disciplinary charges, the opportunity to prepare a response, the opportunity to call witnesses and present evidence if such presentations will not disrupt prison security, a hearing before impartial decision makers, and written explanations of conclusions and reasons for imposing punishment. Prisoners have no right to cross-examine witnesses, to be represented by an attorney, or to appeal hearing decisions.

- Due process rights may be recognized in some situations as stemming from constitutional requirements rather than from state-created liberty interests. One example would be an involuntary transfer from a prison to a mental hospital, which requires similar procedural steps as those described in *Wolff,* with the additional requirement of representation by an attorney at the hearing.

- The concept of a state-created liberty interest was expanded in *Hewitt v. Helms* (1983) to include situations when statutes or prison regulations contained mandatory language limiting prison officials' discretion.

- In 1995, in *Sandin v. Conner,* the Supreme Court switched course and limited the recognition of state-created liberty interests to those situations affecting freedom from restraint and imposing atypical and significant hardships on prisoners.

The next week, a young man convicted of multiple shoplifting offenses arrives five minutes late for the drug test. Unlike many other offenders assigned to the center, he has never been late before. He claims that he was late because a slow train blocking a railroad crossing held up traffic for fifteen minutes. In front of all of the other offenders, the local director orders the young man to be held while he telephones you at the state department of corrections.

"What's his sentence?" you ask.

"He has thirteen months to go on an eighteen-month sentence."

"Well, he's spending the next portion of his time in prison. I checked around this morning. The prisons are completely full at the moment, and many of them are under court order not to take additional prisoners. The only place that

I know for sure I can send him is some empty cells in disciplinary segregation at a maximum-security prison. But, hey, if that's what we've got—then that's where he's going. We need to show that we will stand behind what we say."

The local director pauses. "Isn't that going to be a little bit harsh—going from a community center to complete lockdown in isolation twenty-three hours each day?"

"It can't be helped," you respond.

"Isn't this likely to cause some lawsuits about his rights?" you are asked.

"I have the authority to transfer people and that's what I'm doing. Period."

Was the local director correct in worrying about a possible lawsuit? How does the Court's reasoning in *Sandin v. Conner* apply to this situation?

- As a result of the *Sandin* decision, it is clearly more difficult for prisoners to gain recognition of a state-created liberty interest that would trigger due process rights. It remains to be seen how lower courts will apply the Supreme Court's new reasoning.

Key Terms

disciplinary segregation
discretion
good time

Sandin v. Conner (1995)
state-created liberty interest
Vitek v. Jones (1980)

Wolff v. McDonnell (1974)

Additional Readings

Connor, Richard. 1985. "Classifying and Transferring Prisoners Are Inherently Governmental Functions Entitled to Sovereign Immunity." *Stetson Law Review* 14: 761–782.

Lilly, Michael, and James Wright. 1986. "Interstate Inmate Transfers After *Olim v.*

Wakinekona." *New England Journal on Criminal and Civil Confinement* 12: 71–97.

Plachta, Michael. 1993. "Human Rights Aspects of the Prison Transfer in Comparative Perspective." *Louisiana Law Review* 53: 1043–1089.

Notes

1. Morrissey v. Brewer, 408 U.S. 471 (1972); Gagnon v. Scarpelli, 411 U.S. 778 (1973).

2. Superintendent v. Hill, 472 U.S. 445 (1985).

3. Meachum v. Fano, 427 U.S. 215 (1976).

4. Montayne v. Hayes, 427 U.S. 236 (1976).

5. Olim v. Wakinekona, 461 U.S. 238 (1983).

6. Greenholtz v. Nebraska Penal Inmates, 442 U.S. 1 (1979).

7. Washington v. Harper, 494 U.S. 210 (1990).

8. Hewitt v. Helms, 459 U.S. 460 (1983).

9. Rolando V. del Carmen, Katherine Bennett, and Jeffrey D. Dailey, "State-Created Liberty Interest in Prisons: What the Court Giveth, the Court Also Taketh Away," *Prison Journal* 76 (1996): 357.

10. Ibid., p. 370.

The Use of Force

Imagine you are a corrections officer on duty in a prison dining hall. You overhear one of the other officers telling an inmate, "Quit talking so loudly during the meal. You know the rules."

The inmate jumps up, hurls his entire tray of food onto the floor, and hollers, "That does it. I'm not going to take this crap anymore."

As you quickly move toward the table while watching how other prisoners are reacting, the officer yells at the inmate, "You are going to have to clean this mess up *and* I'm writing you up for this."

The inmate gets right in the officer's face and screams, "You can't make me do anything. You've got a uniform and you think you can yell at everyone, but you're nothing and everybody knows it."

The officer screams back, "You better get out of my face right now, mister!"

At that moment, the prisoner spits directly into the officer's face. The officer instantly reacts by punching the prisoner in the face. The prisoner stumbles backwards a few steps and then begins to charge back toward the officer, but three other officers arrive just in time to intercept and restrain him. As he is dragged away, the inmate shouts, "I'm going to get you for this—and I'm going to sue you for a million dollars. You're not going to get away with this. I've got witnesses!"

The officer is shaken by the altercation. He looks at you and says, "I had to do it. You saw him. You saw what he did. He had it coming. You'll back me up, won't you?"

How would you respond? Did the officer act properly in throwing the punch? Did this action violate the prisoner's rights in any way?

THE CONSTITUTION AND OFFICIALS' USE OF FORCE

The Fourth Amendment and the Use of Force

The U.S. Constitution does not mention the use of force. When people believe that government officials have used physical force improperly and wish to claim a rights violation, they must identify a provision of the Constitution that applies to their situation. For example, in *Tennessee v. Garner* (1985), a Memphis police officer shot and killed an unarmed teenager who was running away from the scene of burglary.[1] The U.S. Supreme Court determined that the officers had violated the dead youth's Fourth Amendment right against "unreasonable . . . seizures." That is, by shooting the unarmed, fleeing youth, the officer had used a bullet as an unreasonable way to stop—and thereby "seize"—the teenager.

The Supreme Court also applies the Fourth Amendment to the use of non-deadly, excessive force by police officers. In *Graham v. Connor* (1989), a diabetic man suffering from a low blood sugar level stopped at a convenience store to buy some orange juice.[2] When he entered the store, he saw a long line at the cash register, so he dashed out to find another store. Two police officers saw his abrupt departure, became suspicious, and stopped his car. After the officers got him out of his car, he passed out due to his low blood sugar. When he regained consciousness, the officers not only refused to listen to his explanation about diabetes but also broke his foot and caused other injuries while putting him into the patrol car. As in the case of the shooting, the Supreme Court regarded this as a violation of the Fourth Amendment right to protection against unreasonable seizures.

However, the same Fourth Amendment right does not apply to actions by corrections officers against inmates, because prisoners do not have the same Fourth Amendment rights as people in free society. Prisoners are legitimately in the custody of and under the authority of corrections officials, and the courts have looked to other parts of the Constitution in considering the use of force in corrections settings.

The Use of Force in Corrections

Why did courts apply the Fourth Amendment, and not the Eighth Amendment ban on cruel and unusual punishments to situations in which police officers use excessive force? These situations do not fall under the Eighth Amendment because the people involved are not being *punished*. "Punishment" generally is regarded as government treatment of individuals who have been convicted of crimes. Except for isolation or loss of privileges applied to unconvicted detainees for violating jail rules, people are not supposed to be sanctioned by government officials until it has been legally established that they deserve sanctions. Thus, punishment imposed by a government official against an unconvicted individual would violate that person's right to due process of law. Because police encounters with citizens do not involve punishment, as defined by the courts for Eighth Amendment purposes, the Supreme Court has been forced to look elsewhere—namely, the Fourth Amendment—to find a constitutional provision to apply to excessive use of force by police. The same is true of unconvicted detainees in jail. They are not supposed to be subjected to "punishment" (except for limited circumstances of rule violations) until they are convicted of a crime. The courts evaluate conditions and practices in jails to see if the unconvicted detainees are being "punished" in violation of their due process rights.[3]

By contrast, the Eighth Amendment does apply to the treatment of convicted inmates by corrections officers. Prison inmates have been convicted of crimes and thus are being punished. Actions taken against them by corrections officers—the representatives of the government—constitute punishment and therefore may involve the Eighth Amendment provision on cruel and unusual punishments.

Legal standards applied to issues involving the use of force may change from decade to decade or even from year to year. That is, certain kinds of force used against prisoners in one year may be prohibited by courts a few years later. Unlike other constitutional provisions, such as freedom of speech, which Supreme Court justices often present as having a specific, fixed meaning, the meaning of the Eighth Amendment changes over time. In fact, the Supreme Court has openly declared that the meaning of the Cruel and Unusual Punishments Clause will change as society changes. If society's values change and the public's views about acceptable punishments change, then the Supreme Court will change the rules about which punishments are permissible. These changes can affect the rules regarding use of force.

In *Trop v. Dulles* (1958), the Warren Court declared that the Eighth Amendment must be defined according to "the evolving standards of decency that mark the progress of a maturing society."[4] This notion that the definition of cruel and unusual punishments will change over time remains intact despite the significant changes in the Supreme Court's composition in the four decades since *Trop*. Even most of the conservative justices on the Rehnquist Court accept that the permissibility of punishments, including physical punishments, must be judged in light of contemporary society's ideas and values.

It is worth noting that some cases of excessive use of force do not involve the U.S. Constitution at all. Prisoners' lawsuits under section 1983 regarding the use of force in prisons cite the Eighth Amendment because these inmates must allege a constitutional violation to take this kind of legal action. Pretrial detainees making similar allegations against jail officials may allege a violation of their constitutional right to due process. Other lawsuits, however, could be brought under state **tort law**. Tort law covers personal injury cases and other situations in which someone is injured or suffers property damage. A tort suit permits individuals to seek money from the wrongdoer to pay for the damage. Thus, instead of claiming that excessive use of force violated a constitutional right, the prisoner may be able to request compensation for injuries wrongfully inflicted by corrections officials. For example, if a corrections officer punches a prisoner without proper justification (e.g., self-defense), the inmate may be able to sue for the tort of "battery" (i.e., wrongful touching) and receive money to compensate for any injuries suffered as a result of the punch.

Different states have their own rules regarding tort suits, which determine who can be sued, under what circumstances, and how much money may be recovered. Section 1983 actions under federal law provide an opportunity to sue for constitutional rights violations that is available throughout the entire country. More importantly, while state tort lawsuits may require a showing of personal injury for prisoners to win anything more than nominal damages (i.e., a minimal, symbolic award), section 1983 actions may create more opportunities for recovery because the prisoner may be able to demonstrate that a right was violated even if no lingering physical injury occurred. In addition, section 1983 cases typically go to federal courts, where the judges may be less connected to local politics because they are appointed to office and have job security. By contrast, prisoners may lack confidence in state courts because many state judges must run for reelection regularly. Judges who face political opposition at each election may not want to be known for ruling in favor of convicted criminal offenders. State prisoners also may fear that state judges know about their crimes or had some contact with their criminal case. Thus, prisoners may believe, correctly or not, that the federal courts will provide a more open-minded hearing for their claims against corrections officials.

CORPORAL PUNISHMENT

For most of American history, corrections officials possessed significant discretion about how best to punish prisoners for misbehavior. Because these officials controlled virtually all aspects of prisoners' daily lives, they had many punishment options. For example, prisoners could be locked into solitary confinement cells or in special punishment cells that lacked the facilities available to other prisoners. Prisoners' food could be restricted. Prisoners could be given extra work assignments or denied various privileges. Or prisoners could be subjected to **corporal punishment**—beatings with whips, boards, fists, or other means of inflicting physical pain. As recently as the 1960s, various prison systems employed corporal punishment as an official method of punishment. In other prisons, corporal punishment existed—and may continue to exist—as an "unofficial" and unapproved method of dealing with prisoners. Because it is now regarded as illegal to employ beatings as a means of punishment, contemporary corrections officials who wish to continue such practices in secret would have to

| BOX 7-1 | **Administering Beatings to Prisoners: Does It Still Occur?** |

In 1997, the international human rights organization Amnesty International reported on the case of a young man from Somalia named Mohamed Hassan. He entered the United States illegally and then immediately sought asylum—permission to stay in the country—because his family had been murdered in his country's civil war (he was shot and survived by pretending to be dead) and he feared for his life if he returned home. Hassan spent more than two years in various American jails while waiting for the Immigration and Naturalization Service (INS) to process his appeal. According to Amnesty International, Hassan, who was not convicted of any crime but was locked up with convicted offenders, was victimized by corrections officers.

Shortly after [Attorney] Kolinchak took on the Hassan case, she received an urgent call

from prison. Her client had been beaten up, allegedly by prison guards at the instigation of a criminal inmate. Mohamed remembers being dragged into the room, the guards placing black plastic garbage bags over the windows to block the proceedings from view and then pummeling him.

"I was furious," remarks Kolinchak. "I went to see him in segregation and he was bruised all over his body. He was frightened. It was right before his hearing. If it had been a criminal case I could go into court. I could talk to a judge. But with an INS case there is no clear way to go. I have never felt so powerless as a lawyer."

Source: Based on Ron Lajoie, "795 Days: Refugee Freed from the Labyrinth of the U.S. Asylum System," *Amnesty Action,* Summer 1997, pp. 1, 10–11.

deny that such actions took place or claim that such actions really involved self-defense or a necessary effort to control unruly inmates. Prisoners sometimes complain that officers beat them up to "teach them a lesson" about talking back or filing complaints. However, such alleged beatings usually occur without witnesses present, so that even if true, the prisoner may have difficulty proving what happened. Box 7-1 concerns one such case. As you read the case, ask yourself how such incidents can be prevented. Can the law keep these episodes from occurring?

By the time the federal courts looked closely at corporal punishment and moved toward abolishing the practice, most states had abandoned the use of beatings as means of punishment. Therefore, the primary effect of the federal court action was to pull the remaining states employing beatings into line with the rest of the states that had abolished the practice. When Singapore applied six lashes with a cane to an American teenager convicted of vandalism in 1994, debates emerged in the United States concerning the pros and cons of corporal punishment. Many people probably would have no objection to the beating of unruly prisoners, especially those convicted of violent crimes—because they believe that imprisonment alone does not adequately punish offenders. However, the federal courts' likely would stop a return to beatings as a form of corporal

BOX 7-2

Talley v. Stephens, 247 F. Supp. 683 (U.S. District Court for the Eastern District of Arkansas, 1965)

HENLEY, Chief Judge:

. . . The Court next turns to the most serious complaint of [the prisoners], namely, the infliction of corporal punishment. As administered at the Penitentiary, that punishment consists of blows with a leather strap five feet in length, four inches wide, and about one-fourth inch thick, attached to a wooden handle or shaft about six inches long. Ordinarily, the punishment is inflicted by the Assistant Warden. . . . [T]he inmate to be whipped is required to lie down on the ground fully clothed, and the blows are inflicted on his buttocks. . . .

There are no written rules or regulations prescribing what conduct or misconduct will bring on a whipping or prescribing how many blows will be inflicted for a given act of misconduct. The punishment is administered summarily, and whether an inmate is to be whipped and how much he is to be whipped are matters resting within the sole discretion of the prison employee administering the punishment, subject to the present informal requirement of [prison officials] that the blows administered for a single offense shall not exceed ten. . . .

[Adult male inmates work on the prison farm.] The actual physical labor incident to the farming operations is performed by convicts, known as "rankers," who work ordinarily ten hours a day . . . without pay. The rankers, including [the prisoners who filed this lawsuit], are guarded by other convicts known as "trusty guards," armed with shotguns, pistols, and high powered rifles. These guards are frequently hardened criminals themselves. . . .

No individual convict has set for him in advance a quota of work which he is expected to perform within a given time. A convict is expected to do "the best he can," and if his performance is not satisfactory to his Assistant Warden, he may be whipped. Here again the infliction of punishment is determined upon and administered summarily.

The evidence is sharply conflicting as to how many times [inmate] Talley has been whipped since he came to the Penitentiary about 1961. He says that he has been whipped about 70 times. [Assistant Warden] Harmon says that Talley has been whipped only six or seven times. Talley probably exaggerates; Harmon probably

punishment in prisons, even though the U.S. Supreme Court has never issued its own definitive decision on the use of beatings as punishment in prisons. Few people would expect the Supreme Court to reverse the trends of the past three decades by approving a reactivation of corporal punishment for convicted offenders. Indeed, on the contemporary Supreme Court, one of the two justices most opposed to the recognition of rights for prisoners, Justice Antonin Scalia, has admitted that even he would not approve of a return to whippings and beatings as forms of criminal punishments.[5]

The federal courts banned beatings and other pain-inflicting corporal punishments through a series of decisions focused on Arkansas prisons in the 1960s. As you read *Talley v. Stephens* (1965) in Box 7-2, note the kinds of issues and problems raised by the use of corporal punishment.[6] There is a risk of arbitrary and discriminatory beatings if a low-level official is permitted to simply decide— especially in the heat of anger—that a prisoner needs to be whipped immediately.

minimizes. In the Court's eyes that conflict in testimony is not material.

The evidence also discloses that on two occasions Talley has been assaulted and beaten by James Pike, the [trusty guard] assigned to Talley's [work detail]. Pike, an illiterate, is a convicted murderer serving a sentence for beating to death a warden at the Mississippi County Penal Farm where Pike was formerly confined on a misdemeanor charge. . . .

Still further disclosed by the evidence is the fact that on occasions Talley has been whipped by Harmon on the report of Pike that Talley had done insufficient work. Pike's reports seem to have been acted upon by Harmon automatically and without investigation. . . .

In evaluating [the] contention [that corporal punishment is unconstitutional] it should be said first that in the present context it is beside the point whether the use of such punishment is good or bad penology, or whether its infliction is necessary to control Arkansas convicts or to run the Penitentiary efficiently, or whether the Judge of the Court, as an individual, approves of such punishment. The question is whether the use of

the strap at the Arkansas Penitentiary is a cruel and unusual punishment in the constitutional sense. . . .

. . . It must be recognized, however, that corporal punishment has not been viewed historically as a constitutionally forbidden cruel and unusual punishment, and this Court is not prepared to say that such punishment is per se unconstitutional [i.e., in all circumstances]. . . .

But, the Court's unwillingness to say that the Constitution forbids the imposition of any and all corporal punishment on convicts presupposes that its infliction is surrounded by appropriate safeguards. It must not be excessive; it must be inflicted as dispassionately as possible and by responsible people; and it must be applied in reference to recognizable standards whereby a convict may know what conduct on his part will cause him to be whipped and how much punishment given conduct may produce.

The Court finds that those safeguards do not exist at the Arkansas Penitentiary today, and until they are established the further corporal punishment [of prisoners] must and will be enjoined [i.e., forbidden]. . . .

You may recall from Box 1-9 that Talley, the prisoner who initiated this case, suffered from discriminatory and brutal treatment, including nine lashes with a leather strap, for having the nerve to file a legal action against prison officials. Obviously, there is also a risk of brutality when whippings or beatings are administered. In Arkansas, these problems were compounded by the fact that certain prisoners were selected to supervise other prisoners. These prisoners could decide which inmates under their supervision should be whipped and, in some cases, carried out the whippings themselves. Unfortunately, the prisoners selected to supervise often were the most violent and brutal inmates, because prison officials were concerned only with maintaining order and keeping prison farms running, no matter what miseries were imposed on the prisoners. Note that in the *Talley* case, the prisoner selected to supervise and punish other prisoners was an illiterate convicted murderer serving time for beating to death the warden at a different prison farm.

BOX 7-3

Jackson v. Bishop, 404 F.2d 371 (U.S. Court of Appeals for the Eighth Circuit, 1968)

[*This appeal stemmed from prisoner lawsuits seeking a ban on whipping and the use of homemade electroshock devices in the Arkansas prisons.*]

BLACKMUN, J.:

. . . Although we are advised that a substantial percentage of the Arkansas prison population is black, the three plaintiffs, the prison officials concerned, and the witnesses are all white. No issue of race, as such, is present. . . .

[The evidence showed that the administrative regulations concerning whipping that were created after the *Talley* decision were not always followed.]

. . . [W]e have no difficulty in reaching the conclusion that the use of the strap in the penitentiaries of Arkansas is punishment which, in this last third of the 20th century, runs afoul of the Eighth Amendment; that the strap's use, irrespective of any precautionary conditions which may be imposed, offends contemporary concepts of decency and human dignity and precepts of civilization which we profess to possess;

and that it also violates those standards of good conscience and fundamental fairness enunciated by this court [in previous cases].

Our reasons for this conclusion include the following: (1) We are not convinced that any rule or regulation as to the use of the strap, however seriously or sincerely conceived and drawn, will successfully prevent abuse. The present record discloses misinterpretation even of the newly adopted January 1966 rules. (2) Rules in this area seem often to go unobserved. Despite the January 1966 requirement that no inmate was to inflict punishment on another, the record is replete with instances where this very thing took place. (3) Regulations are easily circumvented. Although it was a long-standing requirement that a whipping was to be administered only when the prisoner was fully clothed, this record discloses instances of whippings upon the bare buttocks, and with consequential injury. (4) Corporal punishment is easily subject to abuse in the hands of the sadistic and the unscrupulous. (5) Where power to punish is granted to persons in lower levels of administra-

The Abolition of Corporal Punishment in Prisons

The *Talley* case did not ban corporal punishment, but it pressured Arkansas to develop standards and procedures for such punishments—standards and procedures that were supposed to prevent arbitrary, discriminatory, and excessively brutal beatings. In *Jackson v. Bishop* (1968), however, the federal court of appeals revisited the Arkansas prison system and found that the standards and procedures did not prevent unacceptable abuses from occurring.[7] As you read *Jackson v. Bishop*, which is excerpted in Box 7-3, think about the problems with corporal punishment that led the Court of Appeals to abolish the practice. Is there any way to use corporal punishment in corrections without encountering these problems?

As indicated by the *Jackson* opinion, the federal court concluded that standards and procedures could not keep abuses from occurring. Officials did not always follow the written procedures, and excessively brutal whippings still took place. In turn, the beatings generated hatred among the prisoners that served to

tive authority, there is an inherent and natural difficulty in enforcing the limitations of that power. (6) There can be no argument that excessive whipping or an inappropriate manner of whipping or too great frequency of whipping or the use of studded or overlong straps all constitute cruel and unusual punishment. But if whipping were to be authorized, how does one, or any court, ascertain the point which would distinguish the permissible from that which is cruel and unusual? (7) Corporal punishment generates hate toward the keepers who punish and toward the system which permits it. It is degrading to the punisher and the punished alike. It frustrates correctional and rehabilitative goals. This record cries out with testimony to this effect from the expert penologists, from the inmates, and from their keepers. (8) Whipping creates other penological problems and makes adjustment to society more difficult. (9) Public opinion is obviously adverse. Counsel concedes that only two states still permit the use of the strap. Thus almost uniformly has it been abolished. It has been expressly outlawed by statute in a number of states. . . . And 48 states,

including Arkansas, have constitutional provisions against cruel and unusual punishment. . . .

We choose to draw no significant distinction between the word "cruel" and the word "unusual" in the Eighth Amendment. . . . We would not wish to place ourselves in the position of condoning punishment which is shown to be only "cruel" but not "unusual" or vice versa. In any event, the testimony of the two expert penologists clearly demonstrates that the use of the strap in this day is unusual and we encounter no difficulty in holding that its use is cruel.

Neither do we wish to draw, in this context, any meaningful distinction between punishment by way of sentence statutorily prescribed and punishment imposed for prison disciplinary purposes. It seems to us that the Eighth Amendment's proscription has application to both. . . .

[*Note: Judge Harry Blackmun, who authored the* Jackson *opinion, later became Justice Harry Blackmun of the U.S. Supreme Court, where he served for more than two decades until his retirement in 1994.*]

hinder any progress toward rehabilitating inmates or preparing them for their return to society. Thus, whippings violated the Eighth Amendment's prohibition on cruel and unusual punishments. Judge Blackmun's reference to public opinion and the public's opposition to corporal punishment reflected the idea that the Cruel and Unusual Punishments Clause must be defined in accordance with contemporary social values, just as the Supreme Court instructed in *Trop v. Dulles* (1958).

Corporal Punishment in Other Contexts

In light of the problems highlighted by Blackmun's opinion in *Jackson*, it is interesting to compare prisons to schools with respect to corporal punishment. Although officials are not allowed to beat inmates, even the most violent and unruly inmates, as a means of punishment, the Supreme Court declared in 1977 that the Constitution does not prohibit the use of corporal punishment—including beatings with large wooden paddles—on schoolchildren. As indicated by

Ingraham v. Wright (1977), the Supreme Court declined to apply any constitutional ban on corporal punishment in schools, even where students suffered injuries as a result of beatings.[8] The Court declared that the Eighth Amendment protection applies only to convicted criminals, and not to students in schools. The majority of justices also rejected claims that the administration of corporal punishment in schools violates the right to due process. Unlike in the *Talley* decision issued by the Arkansas federal district court, the justices did not even seem interested in ensuring that standards and procedures are in place in schools to prevent arbitrary, discriminatory, and brutal beatings. Although many states and individual school districts have banned corporal punishment, the practice continues in many places, notwithstanding strong research evidence of discrimination in administration and of adverse psychological effects on paddled children.[9]

As you read the *Ingraham* case, which is excerpted in Box 7-4, ask yourself if there is any inconsistency in the law when schoolchildren can be struck with wooden paddles at the discretion of a teacher or principal but violent, convicted criminals are protected against such physical punishments no matter how badly they misbehave.

Although the courts have outlawed whippings in prison, other forms of punishments exist that are intended to impose physical discomfort. Some of these punishments are well accepted. For example, many prisons physically separate prisoners from the inmate population and confine them in the small space of a punishment cell (often called disciplinary segregation). And many states run "boot camps" in which youthful offenders must perform rigorous exercises and physically demanding tasks as part of their punishment. This may technically be regarded as corporal punishment because of its physical nature, but we usually associate corporal punishment with methods more specifically intended to cause pain or discomfort. Other new forms of corporal punishment are less well accepted. For example, in 1997, a U.S. magistrate judge ruled that Alabama could not shackle prisoners outdoors to an iron bar as a means of punishment. These prisoners had been chained in awkward positions to a bar in the prison yard for up to nine hours, with no protection against the sun and rain, and sometimes without drinking water or access to a toilet.[10] This modern-day version of the "stocks" used for punishment in colonial America was declared to be a violation of Eighth Amendment protections against cruel and unusual punishments. Although it is often stated that the *Jackson* decision "abolished corporal punishment," it must be remembered that the decision applied only to prisons—not schools—and it did not prevent corrections systems, such as Alabama's in the 1990s, from experimenting with new forms of physical punishment. Moreover, because *Jackson* was a court of appeals decision rather than a U.S. Supreme Court decision, officials who wish to resume corporal punishment may argue that *Jackson* technically only bars corporal punishment within one federal judicial circuit—the Eighth Circuit, which encompasses Arkansas, Iowa, Minnesota, Missouri, Nebraska, South Dakota, and North Dakota. However, there is no indication that the Supreme Court would be persuaded by this argument as a justification for the return of corporal punishment in prisons.

| **BOX 7-4** | ***Ingraham v. Wright,* 430 U.S. 651 (1977)** |

JUSTICE POWELL delivered the opinion of the Court.

This case presents questions concerning the use of corporal punishment in public schools. First, whether the paddling of students as a means of maintaining school discipline constitutes cruel and unusual punishment in violation of the Eighth Amendment; and, second, to the extent that paddling is constitutionally permissible, whether the Due Process Clause of the Fourteenth Amendment requires proof of notice and an opportunity to be heard. . . .

[In the Dade County, Florida, schools,] [t]he authorized punishment consisted of paddling the recalcitrant student on the buttocks with a flat wooden paddle measuring less than two feet long, three to four inches wide, and about one-half inch thick. The normal punishment was limited to one to five "licks" or blows with the paddle and resulted in no apparent physical injury to the student. School authorities viewed corporal punishment as a less drastic means of discipline than suspension or expulsion. Contrary to the procedural requirements of the statute and regulation, teachers often paddled students on their own authority without first consulting the principal [as required by state law and school board regulations].

. . . The evidence, consisting mainly of the testimony of 16 students, suggests that the regime at Drew [Junior High School] was exceptionally harsh. The testimony of Ingraham and Andrews[, the students who filed the lawsuits], in support of their individual claims for damages, is illustrative. Because he was slow to respond to his teacher's instructions, Ingraham was subjected to more than 20 licks with a paddle while being held over a table in the principal's office. The paddling was so severe that he suffered a hematoma [i.e., the consequence of an injury in which a local mass of blood and discoloration exists within tissue at the site of the injury] requiring medical attention and keeping him out of school for several days.

Andrews was paddled several times for minor infractions. On two occasions he was struck on his arms, once depriving him of the full use of his arm for a week. . . .

An examination of the history of the [Eighth] Amendment and decisions of this Court construing the proscription against cruel and unusual punishment confirms that it was designed to protect those convicted of crimes. We adhere to this long-standing limitation and hold that the Eighth Amendment does not apply to the paddling of children as a means of maintaining discipline. . . .

. . . Observing that the Framers of the Eighth Amendment could not have envisioned our present system of public and compulsory education, with its opportunities for noncriminal punishments, [the students' lawyers] contend that extension of the prohibition against cruel punishments is necessary lest we afford greater protection to criminals than to schoolchildren. It would be anomalous, they say, if schoolchildren could be beaten without constitutional redress, while hardened criminals suffering the same beatings at the hands of their jailers might have a valid constitutional claim under the Eighth Amendment. . . . Whatever force this logic may have in other settings, we find it an inadequate basis for wrenching the Eighth Amendment from its historical context and extending it to traditional disciplinary practices in the public schools. . . .

[Unlike the prisoner in the closed, harsh environment of prison,] [t]he schoolchild has little need for the protection of the Eighth Amendment. Though attendance may not always be voluntary, the public school remains an open institution. Except perhaps when very young, the child is not physically restrained from leaving school during school hours; and at the end of the school day, the child is invariably free to return home. Even while at school, the child brings with him the support of family and

(*continued*)

friends and is rarely apart from teachers and other pupils who may witness and protest any instances of mistreatment.

. . . As long as the schools are open to public scrutiny, there is no reason to believe that the common-law constraints [i.e., state battery and personal injury lawsuits against teachers and principals] will not effectively remedy and deter excesses such as those alleged in this case. . . .

[With respect to the alleged right to due process,] [w]ere it not for the common-law privilege permitting teachers to inflict reasonable corporal punishment on children in their care, and the availability of the traditional remedies for abuse, the case requiring advance procedural safeguards would be strong indeed. But here we deal with a punishment—paddling—within that tradition [and common law remedies are adequate to afford due process protection]. . . .

Elimination or curtailment of corporal punishment would be welcomed by many as a societal advance. But when such a policy choice may result from this Court's determination of an asserted right to due process, rather than

from the normal processes of community debate and legislative action, the societal costs cannot be dismissed as insubstantial. . . .

. . . In view of the low incidence of abuse, the openness of our schools, and the common-law safeguards that already exist, the risk of error that may result in violation of a school-child's substantive rights can only be regarded as minimal. . . .

[*Note: This was a five-to-four decision. The four dissenters—Justices White, Brennan, Marshall, and Stevens—argued that paddling in schools does constitute "punishment" for Eighth Amendment purposes and that the Eighth Amendment has been applied to non-criminal punishment situations, such as medical treatment for prisoners and punishment of children who run away from state institutions. They also argued that common law remedies are inadequate, and perhaps nonexistent, in part because no Florida court has ever awarded damages for these kinds of injuries.*]

ACCEPTABLE USE OF FORCE

Although corporal punishment is not permitted in prisons, the use of force is acceptable in many situations. Corrections officers must maintain security, safety, and order while walking among convicted offenders who may be difficult to control. Many offenders have histories of violent action, lack self-control, are consumed by rage, or suffer from psychological problems. Furthermore, there may be few incentives available to encourage good behavior. Some prisoners act as if they have nothing to lose by challenging the authority of officials or by attacking their fellow inmates. The situation is compounded by the fact that corrections officers are *unarmed* inside the walls and significantly outnumbered by the prisoners. Typically, there are several dozen prisoners for every corrections officer in the cellblocks and yard. Under these circumstances, it is not easy to maintain order, and situations arise in which corrections officers feel obliged to use force.

Justifications for the Use of Force

There are several situations in which it is acceptable for corrections officers to use force. As you will see in Box 7-5, the Michigan Department of Corrections' policy on the use of force lists six situations in which nondeadly force may be used and five situations in which deadly force may be used. Broadly speaking, the situations in which the use of force may be permissible include self-defense, defense of others, prevention of crime, maintenance of order and control, and prevention of escapes.

Self-Defense If corrections officers are threatened with physical attack, they can use a reasonable level of force to protect themselves from harm. Under American law, anyone threatened with physical attack can respond with appropriate force in **self-defense,** so corrections officers benefit from the legal protection available to everyone. But this is not a justification for killing or injuring prisoners during a scuffle. The force used in self-defense may only be that which is "reasonably necessary" to fend off the threat; the victim of the attack, including corrections officers, may not use the occasion to inflict additional "punishment" upon the attacker. If corrections officers seek to inflict additional punishment in such circumstances, they risk having their actions regarded as "malicious and sadistic" and thereby subjecting themselves to a section 1983 lawsuit. Obviously, if officers are attacked by prisoners using weapons, a higher level of force and the use of weapons in self-defense may be justified. And if they are threatened or attacked with deadly force, they may be justified in killing the attacker. Certainly, corrections officers must respond to violent situations by using their best judgment in the immediate circumstances. There is a risk, however, that they may be successfully sued or even convicted of a crime if a jury later finds that their use of self-defense was not justified or that they used a level of force that was not appropriate under the circumstances. The "excessive use of force" is a common claim in prisoners' civil rights lawsuits alleging that prison officials violated their Eighth Amendment right to be free from cruel and unusual punishments.

In light of the self-defense justification, reconsider the scenario at the beginning of the chapter. Did the prisoner's action pose a sufficient threat to the officer to justify a punch in the face?

Defense of Other Persons As with self-defense, in the defense of third persons, only reasonably necessary force may be used. In the prison context, this is an important justification because corrections officers are likely to encounter inmates attacking or threatening staff members or, more frequently, one another. Because corrections officers are responsible for maintaining safety and order, they are much more likely than people elsewhere in society to encounter situations in which they must intervene with force to protect someone else from injury or death. Under Michigan's policy, deadly force may be used to prevent the taking of hostages under the defense-of-third-persons justification. A variation on this justification is illustrated by Michigan's authorization of the use of nondeadly force to prevent suicides by prisoners. Although this is not actually the defense of third persons, it represents the defense of someone other than the correction officer.

In its categories for the use of deadly force, Michigan describes particular situations in which such force may be needed for the defense of others. In one situation, deadly force may be used to prevent major damage to state property during a disturbance if corrections officers reasonably believe that the damage may cause death or serious injury. The obvious example of such a situation, which is specifically cited in the policy, is when prisoners try to set a building on fire during a disturbance. Corrections officers also may use deadly force to prevent prisoners from unlocking other prisoners without authorization if they reasonably believe that the unlocking may result in death or serious physical injury to others. When prisoners seize control of cellblocks during riots, certain prisoners may be killed if other prisoners believe they are snitches or otherwise view them with contempt. In the infamous New Mexico prison riot of 1980, for example, twelve inmates in a protective custody wing were murdered in grisly fashion because other prisoners believed that they were snitches.[11] Thus, the Michigan policy empowers corrections officers to use deadly force to prevent such a situation from occurring.

When corrections officers use excessive force, there is always a risk that they will be sued. One corrections officer in California, for example, broke up a fist fight between two prisoners by shooting one prisoner in the arm with an assault rifle. A jury subsequently awarded financial damages to the prisoner because the officer's use of force was judged to constitute assault and battery under state tort law.[12]

Prevention of Crimes by Prisoners   Force may be used to stop a crime from being committed by a prisoner. Michigan's policy specifies that nondeadly force may be used to prevent the commission of a felony by a prisoner. Obviously, using force to stop an assault represents the defense of a third person. Reasonable force also may be used to prevent other kinds of crimes. For example, an officer may physically apprehend and restrain a prisoner caught in the act of stealing something from a prison workshop. If the use of force were not permitted, officers would have little ability to stop prisoners from committing crimes against each other and against the corrections institution.

Maintenance of Order and Control by Upholding Prison Rules   If prisoners refuse to obey prison rules, corrections officers may have to use force to maintain safety and security. For example, if a prisoner refuses an order to leave one area of the prison and return to his or her cell, officers may physically move the prisoner, either to the cell or to a punishment wing. This action may require that the prisoner be handcuffed or otherwise physically controlled, and it likely will require several officers, even if it is a single inmate who refuses to cooperate. If the inmate's resistance amounts to assault against one or more of the officers, then the self-defense (or defense-of-third-persons) justification may permit a higher level of force to be employed.

Some prisons maintain crisis teams of officers, often wearing helmets and protective clothing, who respond when a prisoner or prisoners engage in significant misbehavior. The crisis team may, for example, enter a prisoner's cell, subdue the prisoner, and transport him or her to administrative segregation, psychiatric care facilities, or some other appropriate location. Prisoners sometimes complain that these crisis teams amount to "goon squads" that look for excuses to "rough up" prisoners. However, there is no escaping the fact that corrections officials must develop these or other techniques to address situations in which prisoners' refusal to obey prison rules threatens the order and security within an institution.

Again, if the actions taken in enforcing rules injure prisoners, there is always a risk that the matter will end up in court in a civil rights or tort lawsuit alleging excessive use of force. But judges and juries often are reluctant to find that corrections officials used "unreasonable" force in response to rules violations unless the force employed clearly exceeded that which was reasonably necessary to handle the situation. In one case, a mentally ill California prisoner won a substantial judgment against corrections officers who forced him into a tub of scalding water and held him there for fifteen minutes. The prisoner had smeared himself with his own excrement, and the guards were supposed to clean him off. Instead, he suffered extensive second- and third-degree burns over much of his body, went into shock, and nearly died.[13]

Prevention of Escapes Officers may use force to prevent escapes, which threaten both the well-being of people in society and the safety and order within corrections institutions. Historically, many prisons automatically used deadly force to stop prisoners attempting to escape. This meant that the armed guards observing from watchtowers or patrolling the perimeter of a prison would shoot anyone trying to climb the fence, escape through a tunnel, or otherwise make a break for freedom. Such practices were consistent with the old rule that permitted police officers to shoot fleeing felons. Escape from prison constitutes a felony, so it simply provided a specific situation in which the general rule applied. However, the old rule no longer is automatically valid. For example, many corrections facilities are now minimum-security institutions that may be located within a community. Should someone convicted of a misdemeanor be killed for ignoring an order to stop walking away from a halfway house on a city street?

As indicated by the description of *Tennesee v. Garner* at the beginning of the chapter, law enforcement officials are subject to Fourth Amendment lawsuits if they shoot fleeing felons—unless they have a reasonable belief that the felon is armed and poses an immediate danger (not unlike a self-defense or defense-of-third-persons justification). The standard for liability in Eighth Amendment cases is different, because it requires a showing of excessive force that was malicious and sadistic, and that was applied for the very purpose of causing harm.[14] Thus, although the Eighth Amendment standard gives corrections officials greater leeway for using lethal force against fleeing escapees, corrections officers no longer can freely shoot escapees. The expectation is that shooting to kill will not necessarily be the first reflexive action by corrections officers, but that corrections officials will shout a warning and then fire a warning shot. A major impediment to shooting a prisoner attempting to escape is probably the risk of a lawsuit for inadvertently shooting a bystander outside the prison.

Corrections officials are obligated to try to protect the public from escapees. They must do what they can to prevent prisoners from escaping, or they risk the wrath of (and possibly lawsuits from) members of the public who may be harmed by those escapees. Even if corrections officials are unlikely to lose such lawsuits, they do not want to incur litigation expenses, negative publicity, and attendant pressures from politicians for failing to prevent escapes. Thus, corrections officials have a stronger justification than law enforcement officers for using force to prevent escapes, even if they know that the prisoner attempting to escape is unarmed. Even unarmed convicted offenders may be dangerous to members of the public if they make it out of an institution. If a prisoner ignores an order to "Stop or I'll shoot," then the corrections officers may have few options other than shooting.

Policies on the use of the force on escapees vary from agency to agency. The Federal Bureau of Prisons limits the use of deadly force to prisoners whom a reasonable person would believe to present a danger to society. Some agencies bar the use of lethal force against juvenile escapees. Some agencies require their officers to shoot at escapees. For example, corrections officers in Nebraska and Texas may face disciplinary action if they fail to use deadly force.[15] Although the U.S. Supreme Court clarified the permissible policies for police officers' use of deadly force in the *Garner* decision, future decisions may affect corrections. Read the Michigan Department of Corrections' policy on the use of force, which is excerpted in Box 7-5. How do corrections officers determine the appropriate amount of force to use in a given situation? What are Michigan's regulations on the use of deadly force? Which policies appear designed to prevent potential lawsuits?

BOX 7-5   **Actual Policy on the Use of Force by Corrections Personnel**

A. Employees have the right to protect themselves and a duty to protect prisoners, other staff, and members of the public who are threatened by actions of offenders. Employees are also required to prevent escapes, maintain order and control within the facility, and protect State property. Employees may use all necessary and suitable means to perform these duties, including the use of physical force. Such force may be used to control members of the public who are on Department property, as well as prisoners, parolees and probationers, if the requirements of this policy are met. However, force shall not be used for vindicative or retaliatory purposes. The use of excessive or unreasonable force may lead to criminal prosecution, a civil suit, and disciplinary action against the employee. . . .

AMOUNT OF FORCE

D. Employees are permitted to use as much force as is reasonably necessary to perform their duties and to protect themselves from harm. The amount of force which is reasonable depends upon the circumstances of the particular incident. The controlling factors are:

1. The degree of force threatened or used by the individual, including whether s/he possesses a weapon, such as a knife or any object which could be used to cause physical injury.

2. The employee's reasonable perception of the danger of death or serious physical injury.

3. The alternatives available to control the situation without the use of force.

E. The appropriateness of the type and amount of force used by the employee, e.g., the kind of weapon used, the area of the body struck, etc., will be examined using the preceding factors. Only force which is reasonable in responding to the situation is permissible.

ALTERNATIVES TO USE OF FORCE

F. Employees must always remain alert to the development of dangerous situations and violent confrontations. To avoid such situations, employees must be aware of their surroundings at all times, including, whenever possible, the history of offenders with whom they are in contact, the presence or absence of other staff in the immediate area, the avenues of escape in any setting, and the available means of summoning assistance. Personal safety, and the safety of other staff, offenders, visitors, and members of the public must be a primary concern of employees at all times.

G. If potentially violent confrontations develop, employees must be aware of and use any alternatives to the use of force which do not conflict with their duties and responsibilities. Such alternatives include:

1. The use of verbal and non-verbal de-escalation techniques to defuse a potentially violent situation;

2. Waiting for the offender to "cool down" if this can be safely done, e.g., a prisoner who is disruptive but is confined and is not physically harming himself/herself or others or causing undue disruption of others;

3. Calling additional staff to present a show of force;

4. The use of evasive tactics, followed by retreat and the summoning of assistance.

DEADLY FORCE

H. Deadly force is that degree of force which is likely to result in death or serious physical injury. Such force may be used only as a last resort, when there are no safe and reasonable alternatives to accomplish the objective. Deadly force is to be avoided wherever possible and, when it cannot be avoided, the force used must be the least injurious appropriate for the situation. Knives and firearms are always considered to be instruments of deadly force; however, a blow or hold to the head, neck, throat, or other vulnerable area of the body may also be deadly force.

I. If gunfire is used for warning shots, it shall be directed with the intent to stop the person or persons at whom the gunfire is directed. A verbal warning and a warning shot shall precede gunfire directed at a person, if time and circumstances permit such warnings. A warning shot must be directed in a manner which avoids risk to those not involved in the incident and presents the least possible risk to the prisoner(s) being warned. For example, a warning shot may be aimed into the ground or in another direction where there is clearly no one present. However, at times it may be appropriate to aim warning shots into the ground directly in front of a person or persons who are advancing on a target, or above their heads, if this is the only effective means of stopping them short of shooting to stop.

J. Warning shots shall only be used in a situation which occurs inside the security perimeter of an institution or to prevent an escape or storming of the security perimeter from the outside if the institution is located in an area where a warning shot can be fired safely.

K. Deadly force shall be used only in the following situations:

1. To prevent death or serious physical injury to self, other staff, offenders, or other persons who are threatened;

2. To prevent the taking of hostages;

3. To prevent escape of any prisoner assigned to an institution which is Level II or higher; however, Level II prisoners detailed to Level I assignments shall be treated as Level I prisoners;

(*continued*)

4. To prevent major damage to State property during a disturbance within an institution if it is reasonably believed that the damage may cause death or serious physical injury to any person. For example, if prisoners are attempting to burn a building and there is any possibility that the building is occupied or that the fire may spread to an occupied building, deadly force may be used. In these situations, use of deadly force must be authorized by a shift commander or higher authority.

5. To prevent prisoners from unlocking other prisoners without authorization if it is reasonably believed that the unlocking may result in death or serious physical injury to others. Such a belief may be based upon the words and actions of the prisoners, the security level of the institution, and any other factors deemed relevant by corrections staff. In this instance, the use of deadly force must be authorized by a shift commander or higher authority.

L. The Director shall appoint a shoot review team which shall receive reports regarding any use of gunfire as deadly force, including the use of warning shots, to determine whether the use was appropriate and proper policy and procedures were followed. The shoot review team shall issue a written report to the Director on each such occurrence. An employee who has used deadly force shall not be placed on an assignment which requires the use of firearms until the Director has reviewed the report of the shoot review team and determined that the use of firearms was appropriate.

M. Only those employees who are authorized by Department policy may carry and use firearms in the performance of their duties.

NONDEADLY FORCE

N. Nondeadly force is that degree of force which is *not* likely to cause death or serious physical injury, e.g., use of chemical agents, certain self-defense and prisoner control techniques or strikes to areas of the body unlikely to result in serious physical injury. Reasonable nondeadly force may be used in the following situations:

1. Self-defense;

2. Defense of others;

3. Prevention of suicide;

4. Maintaining order and control in a facility, including prevention of damage to State property;

5. Prevention of escape from any security level;

6. Prevention of a felony by an offender.

RECORDING AND REPORTING

O. If there is an opportunity to plan strategy beforehand in dealing with disruptive or violent prisoners, an audiovisual recording of the incident shall be made, including staff efforts to defuse the situation without the use of force. Such recording shall be retained for at least one year after the date of the incident. If a lawsuit is filed or an investigation is underway involving the incident, the recording shall be retained until the investigation or lawsuit is completed. The Central Office Litigation Coordinator may be contacted to determine if a lawsuit is still pending.

P. Any employee who uses or observes the use of force shall report the incident to his/her supervisor immediately. The employee must also submit a written report which includes a description of the amount and kind of force used, the exact holds used, if blows were delivered, methods of restraint, areas of the body struck and whether weapons were used. The report must also cover the presence of others, including offenders, employees, and others, and describe their participation in the incident. The report shall also include verbal orders given before or during the incident, any conversation, and whether profanity or racial epithets were used by employees, offenders, or others. . . .

Q. Failure of any employee to report accurately and completely any incident where force was used may result in disciplinary action. . . .

Liability for Improper Use of Force

What happens if corrections officers use force inappropriately? What if there are questions about whether a use of force was appropriate? Prisoners are likely to file lawsuits against corrections officials claiming that their rights were violated and that they should receive compensation for injuries. In such circumstances, how will a judge and jury decide if the use of force was within the bounds of the law? Judges and juries—as well as corrections officers themselves—must be guided by the legal standards established by the U.S. Supreme Court (for federal constitutional law) and state appellate courts (for state law).

The leading Supreme Court case establishing standards for liability and, by extension, rules for corrections officers' behavior is ***Whitley v. Albers*** **(1986)**, which is excerpted in Box 7-6. Albers was an inmate living in a cellblock in which other prisoners had taken a corrections officer hostage during a prison disturbance. When corrections officers stormed the cellblock to rescue their colleague, Albers was shot while trying to return to his cell—even though he was not involved in the disturbance and hostage taking that led the officers to storm the cellblock. Albers attempted to sue the officers for the injuries he suffered. A divided Supreme Court rejected his claim that his Eighth Amendment rights were violated when the officer shot him. As you read the case, look carefully for the standard established by the Supreme Court to define liability for corrections officers' inappropriate use of force. What is the rule established by the case?

As you can see, in the context of a prison disturbance, prisoners would have great difficulty proving that any force employed by corrections officials was excessive. The Supreme Court did not focus on whether the prisoner was at fault in the disturbance. Nor did the majority focus on the extent of the prisoner's injuries. Instead, the Court's primary concern was with the *intentions* of the corrections officers in using force against prisoners. To win the lawsuit, the prisoner would have had to show that the force was employed "maliciously and sadistically for the very purpose of causing harm." But it is always difficult to prove what someone else's intentions were, especially in the context of a prison disturbance, where officers must react quickly to uncertain and changing circumstances.

Apparently, the majority of justices were especially concerned about giving corrections officers sufficient flexibility to permit them to make quick judgments in dangerous situations. Thus, the Court's decision protects officers from most risks of liability, even if their decisions turn out to be mistakes or they unintentionally injure innocent prisoners. By contrast, the four dissenters preferred to let civilian juries decide whether the corrections officers' actions were reasonable, even if there was no malicious intent.

In light of the decision in *Whitley v. Albers,* return again to the scenario at the beginning of the chapter. Was the dining hall altercation a disturbance situation in which the *Whitley* rule should apply? Could the officer be found liable under the rule in *Whitley*?

The *Whitley* decision provides guidance about the legal standard to be applied in determining officers' liability for the excessive use of force. However, the decision did not clarify all issues related to the improper use of force. For

JUSTICE O'CONNOR delivered the opinion of the Court.

This case requires us to decide what standard governs a prison inmate's claim that prison officials subjected him to cruel and unusual punishment by shooting him during the course of their attempt to quell a prison riot. . . .

[A corrections officer was taken hostage in a cellblock disturbance in which a prisoner with a homemade knife demanded to speak to the news media. Captain Whitley went back and forth to the cellblock to negotiate with the prisoner holding the officer hostage.]

. . . When [Captain] Whitley returned to cellblock "A," he was taken to see [Officer] Fitts [the hostage being held] in cell 201. Several inmates assured Whitley that they would protect Fitts from harm, but [inmate] Klenk [the armed instigator of the incident] threatened to kill the hostage if an attempt was made to lead an assault [against the cellblock by armed officers]. . . . Meanwhile, [Albers, an inmate who was not involved in the uprising] had left his cell on the upper tier to see if elderly prisoners housed on the lower tier could be moved out of harm's way in the event that tear gas was used. [Albers] testified that he asked Whitley for a key to the row of cells housing the elderly prisoners, and Whitley indicated that he would return with a key. [By contrast,] Whitley denied that he spoke to [Albers] at any time during the disturbance. . . .

[The prison superintendent and assistant superintendent ordered an assault on the cellblock to rescue the hostage.] Whitley gave the final orders to the assault team, which was assembled in the area outside cellblock "A." [Officer] Kennicott and two other officers armed with shotguns were to follow Whitley, who was unarmed, over the barricade the inmates had constructed at the cellblock entrance. A second group of officers, without firearms, would be behind them. Whitley ordered Kennicott to fire a warning shot as he crossed the barricade. He also or-

dered Kennicott to shoot low at any prisoners climbing the stairs toward cell 201, since they could pose a threat to the safety of the hostage or to Whitley himself, who would be climbing the stairs in an attempt to free the hostage.

. . . [When Whitley approached the barricade, Albers,] who was standing at the bottom of the stairway, asked about the key. Whitley replied, "No," clambered over the barricade, yelled "shoot the bastards," and ran toward the stairs after Klenk, who had been standing in an open areaway along with a number of other inmates. Kennicott fired a warning shot into the wall opposite the cellblock entrance as he followed Whitley over the barricade. He then fired a second shot that struck a post near the stairway. Meanwhile, Whitley chased Klenk up the stairs, and shortly thereafter [Albers] started up the stairs. Kennicott fired a third shot that struck [Albers] in the left knee. Another inmate was shot on the stairs and several others on the lower tier were wounded by gunshot. The inmates in cell 201 prevented Klenk from entering, and Whitley subdued Klenk at the cell door, freeing the hostage.

As a result of the incident, [Albers] sustained severe damage to his left leg and mental and emotional distress. [He filed a section 1983 lawsuit alleging a violation of his right against cruel and unusual punishment under the Eighth Amendment.] . . .

Not every governmental action affecting the interests or well-being of a prisoner is subject to Eighth Amendment scrutiny, however. "After incarceration, only the 'unnecessary and wanton infliction of pain' . . . constitutes cruel and unusual punishment forbidden by the Eighth Amendment." . . . To be cruel and unusual punishment, conduct that does not purport to be punishment at all must involve more than ordinary lack of due care for the prisoner's interests or safety. . . . The infliction of pain in the course of a prison security measure, therefore, does not amount to cruel and unusual punishment simply because it may appear in retrospect that the degree of force authorized or applied for security purposes was unreasonable, and hence unnecessary in the strict sense. . . .

Where a prison security measure is undertaken to resolve a disturbance, such as occurred in this case, that indisputably poses significant risks to the safety of inmates and prison staff, we think the question whether the measure taken inflicted unnecessary and wanton pain and suffering ultimately turns on "whether force was applied in a good faith effort to maintain or restore discipline or maliciously and sadistically for the very purpose of causing harm." . . . [I]nferences may be drawn as to whether the use of force could plausibly have been thought necessary, or instead evinced such wantonness with respect to the unjustified infliction of harm as is tantamount to a knowing willingness that it occur. . . .

. . . Accepting that [Albers] could not have sought safety in a cell on the lower tier, the fact remains that had [Albers] thrown himself to the floor he would not have been shot at. Instead, after the warning shot was fired, he attempted to return to his cell by running up the stairs behind Whitley. That is equivocal conduct. While [Albers] had not been actively involved in the riot and indeed had attempted to help matters, there is no indication that Officer Kennicott knew this, nor any claim that he acted vindictively or in retaliation. . . . Under these circumstances, the actual shooting was part and parcel of a good-faith effort to restore prison security. As such, it did not violate [Albers'] Eighth Amendment right to be free from cruel and unusual punishments. . . .

JUSTICE MARSHALL, with whom JUSTICES BRENNAN, BLACKMUN, and STEVENS join, dissenting.

. . . The Court's treatment of the expert testimony is equally insensitive to its obligation to resolve all disputes in favor of [Albers before dismissing Albers' claim prior to trial]. [Albers'] experts testified that the use of deadly force under these circumstances was not justified by any necessity to prevent imminent danger to the officers or the inmates; and that even if deadly force had been justified it would have been unreasonable to unleash such force without a clear warning to allow nonparticipating inmates to return to their cells. . . .

The majority suggests that the existence of more appropriate alternative measures for controlling prison disturbances is irrelevant to the constitutional inquiry, but surely it cannot mean what it appears to say. For if prison officials were to drop a bomb on a cellblock in order to halt a fistfight between two inmates, for example, I feel confident that the Court would have difficulty concluding as a matter of law, that such an action was not sufficiently wanton to present a jury question, even though concededly taken in an effort to restore order in the prison. Thus the question of wantonness in the context of prison disorder, as with other claims of mistreatment under the Eighth Amendment, is a matter of degree. And it is precisely in cases like this one, when shading the facts one way or the other can result in different legal conclusions, that a jury should be permitted to do its job. Properly instructed, a jury would take into account the [prison officials'] legitimate need to protect security, the extent of the danger presented, and the reasonableness of force used, in assessing liability. Moreover, the jury would know that a prisoner's burden [of proof] is a heavy one. Whether [Albers] was able to meet that burden here is a question for the jury. From the Court's usurpation of the jury's function, I dissent. . . .

example, Albers was denied any recovery even though he was seriously injured from being shot in the leg. What if his injury had been less serious? Could someone with a less serious injury win a lawsuit if the injury was caused by an officer's malicious intentions and actions? The Supreme Court addressed these issues in *Hudson v. McMillian* (1992), which is excerpted in Box 7-7. In this case, Hudson was beaten by corrections officers, but he did not sustain serious injuries.

The *Hudson* decision clarified the rule from *Whitley v. Albers* in two important ways. First, *Hudson* indicated that the *Whitley* rule is not limited to situations in which officers are addressing a prison disturbance. The *Whitley* rule applies whenever a prisoner claims that officers used excessive force in violation of the Eighth Amendment's prohibition on cruel and unusual punishments. Second, *Hudson* indicated that prisoners could sue even if they did not suffer serious or lasting injuries. Any physical injury, even a minor injury, can produce a lawsuit if the officers acted maliciously and sadistically for the purpose of causing harm. The key element in evaluating if the force used by a corrections officer was excessive is whether the officer deliberating and unjustifiably intended to harm the prisoner, not the extent of the injury suffered by the prisoner. Based on the *Hudson* decision, has your evaluation of the scenario at the beginning of the chapter changed? Would the officer be liable for violating the prisoner's rights by punching him?

Notice in the dissenting opinion that Justice Clarence Thomas, joined by Justice Antonin Scalia, questioned whether the Eighth Amendment provides any protection at all for prisoners against abusive actions by corrections officers. Thomas noted that the early history of the Eighth Amendment indicated that there was no expectation that prisoners would be protected, and prisoners' cases were routinely rejected by courts. This approach to analyzing the Eighth

---

B O X   7 - 7   *Hudson v. McMillian*, **503 U.S. 1 (1992)**

JUSTICE O'CONNOR delivered the opinion of the Court.

This case requires us to decide whether the use of excessive physical force against a prisoner may constitute cruel and unusual punishment when the inmate does not suffer serious injury. We answer that question in the affirmative.

. . . During the early morning hours of October 30, 1983, [Inmate] Hudson and [Officer] McMillian argued. Assisted by [Officer] Woods,

McMillian then placed Hudson in handcuffs and shackles, took the prisoner out of his cell, and walked him down toward the penitentiary's "administrative lockdown" area. Hudson testified that, on the way there, McMillian punched Hudson in the mouth, eyes, chest, and stomach while Woods held the inmate in place and kicked and punched him from behind. He further testified that [Officer] Mezo, the supervisor on duty, watched the beating but merely told the officers "not to have too much fun." . . .

Hudson suffered minor bruises and swelling of his face, mouth, and lip. The blows also loosened Hudson's teeth and cracked his partial dental plate, rendering it unusable for several months.

Hudson sued the three corrections officers in . . . [a section 1983 lawsuit] alleging a violation of the Eighth Amendment's prohibition on cruel and unusual punishments. . . . [A U.S. magistrate judge] found that McMillian and Woods used force when there was no need to do so and that Mezo expressly condoned their actions. . . . The [U.S.] Magistrate [Judge] awarded Hudson damages of $800. . . .

. . . [W]e hold that whenever prison officials stand accused of using excessive physical force in violation of the Cruel and Unusual Punishments Clause, the core judicial inquiry is that set out in *Whitley [v. Albers]*: whether the force was applied in a good-faith effort to maintain or restore discipline, or maliciously and sadistically to cause harm. . . .

Under the *Whitley* approach, the extent of injury suffered by an inmate is one factor that may suggest "whether the use of force could plausibly have been thought necessary" in a particular situation, "or instead evinced such wantonness with respect to the unjustified infliction of harm as is tantamount to a knowing willingness that it occur." In determining whether the use of force was wanton and unnecessary, it may also be proper to evaluate the need for application of force, the relationship between that need and the amount of force used, the threat "reasonably perceived by responsible officials," and "any efforts made to temper the severity of a forceful response." . . . The absence of serious injury is therefore relevant to the Eighth Amendment inquiry, but does not end it.

[The corrections officers] nonetheless assert that a significant injury requirement . . . is mandated by what we have termed the "objective component" of Eighth Amendment analysis. . . .

. . . [T]he Eighth Amendment's prohibition of cruel and unusual punishments "draw[s] its meaning from the progress of a maturing society," and so admits of few absolute limitations.

The objective component of an Eighth Amendment claim is . . . contextual and responsive to "contemporary standards of decency." . . .

. . . When prison officials maliciously and sadistically use force to cause harm, contemporary standards of decency are always violated. This is true whether or not significant injury is evident. Otherwise, the Eighth Amendment would permit any physical punishment, no matter how diabolic or inhuman, inflicting less than some arbitrary quantity of injury. . . .

This is not to say that every malevolent touch by a prison guard gives rise to a federal cause action [for constitutional violations]. . . . The Eighth Amendment's prohibition of "cruel and unusual" punishment necessarily excludes from constitutional recognition *de minimis* [i.e., minimal] uses of physical force, provided that the force is not of a sort "repugnant to the conscience of mankind."

In this case . . . the blows directed at Hudson, which caused bruises, swelling, loosened teeth, and a cracked dental plate, are not *de minimis*. The extent of Hudson's injuries thus provides no basis for the dismissal of his [section] 1983 claim. . . .

JUSTICE STEVENS, concurring in part and concurring in the judgment.

. . . The Court's opinion explained that the justification for that particularly high standard of proof [in *Whitley v. Albers*, i.e., "maliciously and sadistically for the very purpose of causing harm"] was required by the exigencies present during a serious prison disturbance. . . . Absent such special circumstances, however, the less demanding standard of "unnecessary and wanton infliction of pain" should be applied. . . . In this case, because there was no prison disturbance and "no need to use any force, since the plaintiff was already in restraints," . . . the prison guards' attack upon petitioner resulted in the infliction of unnecessary and wanton pain. . . . Although I think that the Court's reliance on the malicious and sadistic standard is misplaced,

(continued)

I agree with the Court that even this more demanding standard was met here. . . .

JUSTICE BLACKMUN, concurring in the judgment.

. . . I do not read anything in the Court's opinion to limit injury cognizable under the Eighth Amendment to physical injury. It is not hard to imagine inflictions of psychological harm—without corresponding physical harm—that might prove to be cruel and unusual punishment. See, e.g., *Wisniewski v. Kennard,* 901 F.2d 1276, 1277 (5th Cir.) (guard placing a revolver in inmate's mouth and threatening to blow prisoner's head off). . . . The issue was not presented here, because Hudson did not allege that he feared that the beating incident would be repeated or that it had caused him anxiety and depression.

As the Court makes clear, the Eighth Amendment prohibits the unnecessary and wanton infliction of "pain," rather than "injury.". . . "Pain" in its ordinary meaning surely includes a notion of psychological harm. I am unaware of any precedent of this Court to the effect that psychological pain is not cognizable for constitutional purposes. . . .

To be sure, as the Court's opinion initimates . . . de minimis or nonmeasurable pain is not actionable under the Eighth Amendment. But psychological pain can be more than de minimis. Psychological pain often may be clinically diagnosed and quantified through well established methods, as in the ordinary tort context, where damages for pain and suffering are regularly awarded. I have no doubt that to read a "physical pain" or "physical injury" requirement into the Eighth Amendment would be no less pernicious and without foundation than the "significant injury" requirement we reject today.

JUSTICE THOMAS, with whom JUSTICE SCALIA joins, dissenting.

. . . In my view, a use of force that causes only insignificant harm to a prisoner may be immoral, it may be tortious, it may be criminal, and it may even be remediable under other provisions of the Federal Constitution, but it is not "cruel and unusual punishment." In concluding to the contrary, the Court today goes far beyond our precedents. . . .

. . . [Early judges and commentators] simply did not conceive of the Eighth Amendment as protecting inmates from harsh treatment. Thus, historically, the lower courts routinely rejected prisoner grievances by explaining that the courts had no role in regulating prison life. . . . It was not until 1976—185 years after the Eighth Amendment was adopted—that the Court first applied it to a prisoner's complaint about a deprivation suffered in prison. . . .

. . . After today, the "necessity" of a deprivation is apparently the only relevant inquiry beyond the wantonness of official conduct. This approach, in my view, extends the Eighth Amendment beyond all reasonable limits.

Today's expansion of the Cruel and Unusual Punishment Clause beyond all bounds of history and precedent is, I suspect, yet another manifestation of the pervasive view that the Federal Constitution must address all ills in our society. Abusive behavior by prison guards is deplorable conduct that properly evokes outrage and contempt. But that does not mean that it is invariably unconstitutional. The Eighth Amendment is not, and should not be turned into, a National Code of Prison Regulation. To reject the notion that the infliction of concededly "minor" injuries can be considered either "cruel" or "unusual" "punishment" (much less cruel and unusual punishment) is not to say that it amounts to acceptable conduct. Rather, it is to recognize that primary responsibility for preventing and punishing such conduct rests not with the Federal Constitution but with the laws and regulations of the various States. . . .

Because I conclude that, under our precedents, a prisoner seeking to establish that he has been subjected to "cruel and unusual punishment" must always show that he has suffered a serious injury, I would affirm the judgment of the [court of appeals which ruled against the prisoner].

Amendment—by relying on early history—is quite different from the approach in *Trop v. Dulles* (1958), in which the Court ruled that the Eighth Amendment's meaning evolves and changes as society and social values change.

The Use of Force in Contemporary Corrections

As discussed previously, court decisions from the 1960s through the 1990s have shaped the legal rules concerning the use of force against prisoners. A few decades ago, corrections officials commonly used force against prisoners on a daily basis as a means to both control and punish. But many prison systems abandoned the use of force as a means of punishment, and the courts eventually blocked other prison systems from employing whipping and other pain-inflicting methods of corporal punishment. The courts played an important role in abolishing corporal punishment, but the courts did not act alone to change such practices.

In recent decades, the administration of corrections has changed significantly. Some of the changes resulted from court decisions, not only about the use of force but also about conditions of confinement and other aspects of prisoners' rights. In addition, corrections changed because corrections administration became more professionalized. More college-educated people became corrections administrators. More administrators were hired because of their training and experience, and not merely because of political connections. More academic research explored the problems and challenges of corrections, thereby producing new ideas about effective policies and programs. Corrections systems began to take greater care in selecting and training corrections officers to ensure that officials throughout a prison, from bottom to top, acted in a professional manner according to established policies. There is a concern, however, that most training is primarily directed to supervisory corrections personnel, and not to the officers who must interact on a minute-by-minute basis with prisoners who challenge their authority and test their judgment. Corrections institutions also formalized their policies and procedures by producing handbooks for prisoners and training manuals for officers, so that everyone in the institution would know the rules and procedures.

These trends toward the professionalization of corrections management have played a significant role in limiting the use of force in correctional institutions. But have these trends eliminated concerns about excessive use of force and the risk of abusive behavior by corrections officials? The *Hudson* case demonstrates that the risk of abusive behavior continues to exist—and will always exist. Professional management, planning, and training cannot eliminate the human factors that lead to excessive use of force. Corrections officers who patrol the cellblocks face constant pressures on their ability to maintain self-control and make professional decisions. Prisoners challenge officers' authority in subtle ways—by intentionally moving slowly or pretending not to understand when given an order—as well as in obvious and provocative ways. Thus, it is a challenge for officers to keep their anger in check when prisoners curse them, spit on them, or throw urine and feces on them.

The "clientele" confronting corrections has become more difficult in other ways, too. Many prisons have crowded conditions that increase the conflicts inmates have with one another and with corrections officers. This may be especially true when inmates are housed in a dormitory setting, with many dozens of prisoners in a single large room crowded with bunkbeds or mattresses on the floor. In such circumstances, tempers flare, and officers face an impossible task in attempting to monitor behavior. In addition, because many states have been closing mental hospitals, many former mental patients have ended up in prisons after committing crimes. In Michigan, for example, while the number of prisoners increased by 11 percent from 1993 to 1997, the number of former mental patients in prisons increased by 23 percent over the same time period.[16] Therefore, corrections officers in many institutions have been forced to supervise especially difficult inmates who lack self-control and who behave irrationally and even violently. We must remember that we place significant burdens on corrections officers who, while significantly outnumbered among troubled and troublesome individuals, must maintain order and behave professionally while facing numerous situations that test their judgment and emotions.

In addition, the rapid growth in prison populations has created other pressures. As states hire new corrections officers to staff newly constructed prisons, their immediate need for officers may not permit them to be as selective as they would like to be. Crowded prisons put extra pressure on officers—especially the large number of newly hired and inexperienced officers—who must deal with prisoners who are frustrated and angry about crowded living conditions.

In confronting these difficult circumstances and the conflicts produced within this environment, corrections officers may conclude that many prisoners respect only one thing: force or the threat of force. This may, in fact, be true for some prisoners whose life experiences did not imbue them with traditional middle-class values. If true, this poses a particular problem for corrections officers, whose ability to use force is limited by law.

All of these factors help us to understand why excessive use of force is likely to occur. Yet none of these factors can excuse excessive use of force. The Eighth Amendment protects even the worst convicted offender against cruel and unusual punishments. Court decisions have made it clear that the excessive use of force constitutes an Eighth Amendment violation. Moreover, violations can lead to expensive lawsuits that adversely affect both individual officers and entire state prison systems. Thus, corrections officials—and courts—continue to monitor and evaluate the use of force within corrections institutions.

It is difficult to know the extent to which excessive use of force is a problem in contemporary corrections. As we saw in Chapters 2 and 3, prisoners who file complaints in the courts often do not understand exactly which kinds of actions by corrections officials are, in fact, rights violations. Many prisoners claim that they were victims of excessive force. In some instances, the claims may be untrue. In other cases, a prisoner may have been the object of a corrections officer's use of force, but the situation did not meet the *Whitley* standard—force used "maliciously and sadistically for the very purpose of causing harm." Because many prisoners' complaints fit these two categories of unjustified claims, some people may believe that excessive use of force is no longer a problem or is confined to rare, isolated incidents involving "rotten apple" corrections officers. However, the extent of excessive force is not necessarily so limited. In situations with no witnesses and no permanent injuries, charges of excessive use of force will simply be denied by corrections officers, and prisoners will have no way to prove what occurred. Without additional proof, juries and judges are unlikely to accept the word of a convicted criminal over that of a corrections officer. Many prisoners claim that such situations occur frequently in particular institutions, but corrections officials usually deny these allegations. Thus, unfortunately, there is no reliable way to know exactly how frequently excessive force is used.

Box 7-8 describes allegations of excessive force in a 1997 lawsuit concerning an incident at a Georgia prison in 1996. The allegations attracted national

---

BOX 7-8   ## The Use of Force in a Georgia Prison, 1996

In a deposition—which is testimony produced in response to lawyers' questions that is recorded by a court reporter in preparation for a case—Ray McWhorter, a riot squad lieutenant, supported the allegations of prisoners concerning a bloody attack against inmates initiated by a top aide to the state prison commissioner and witnessed by the prison commissioner himself. The incident began when the commissioner's aide dragged a prisoner across the floor by the hair. According to McWhorter, corrections officers interpreted that action as an invitation to slap, beat, and stomp prisoners, including some who were handcuffed on the floor, to get even with the prisoners for past actions. In McWhorter's words:

When [the commissioner's aide] did that [dragging the inmate by the hair], we were all under the impression that it was O.K. to do. If [he] can slam one, then we can slam, too. . . . It was a dadgum shark frenzy in G building. It was a free-for-all. You know how sharks do. They see a . . . spot of blood, and then here come the sharks everywhere from miles around. . . . We have put up with a lot. In the years I have been working, I have been spit at. I have had urine thrown on me. I have been kicked. I have been punched. When you are dealing with that over and over and over and you are trying to restrain

yourself year after year, and all of a sudden they are saying "Get them, boys," well, hell, you go in there and you get them.

In a separate deposition, another corrections officer, Phyllis Tucker, described how a guard slammed a prisoner's face into a concrete wall: "[The prisoner] screamed. Blood went up the wall. Blood went all over the ground, all over the inmate. I heard it. It had a sickening cracking sound." When Tucker was asked by attorneys why she did not report this incident to her superiors at the prison, she replied: "Because the superiors were there."

Reportedly, the state's corrections commissioner, who witnessed the events, applauded the corrections officers at a dinner afterward. According to McWhorter, "Everybody was high-fiving and shaking hands and congratulating each other and patting each other on the back and bragging about how much butt you kicked."

At least seven witnesses, including corrections officers, a prison counselor, and a prison librarian, have described the attacks in deposition testimony.

Sources: Rick Bragg, "Prison Chief Encouraged Brutality, Witnesses Reported," *New York Times,* 1 July 1997, p. A10; Christina Nifong, "Case Gives Georgians Glimpse of Prison Life," *Christian Science Monitor,* 23 September 1997, p. 3; "Hays State Prison: 'It was a Free-for-All,'" editorial, *Atlanta Journal and Constitution,* 10 July 1997, p. A10.

attention because they were not merely complaints by prisoners; several staff members in the prison supported the prisoners' claims in sworn testimony. Although this would appear to be a highly unusual incident, because it includes allegations against the commissioner of the state prison system, could such an incident be attributed to one "rotten apple" in the system abusing his or her authority? If this incident is true, does the involvement of several members of the prison staff indicate that tensions in prisons create the potential for abuse by angry, frustrated staff members? Even if these allegations are found to indicate that Georgia's prisons have special problems, could you imagine events in other prisons that might trigger episodes of excessive force?

SUMMARY

- Excessive use of force by staff against convicted offenders in prisons and jails is a violation of the Eighth Amendment prohibition on cruel and unusual punishments. Excessive use of force against unconvicted pretrial detainees in jails is a violation of the Due Process Clause of the Fourteenth Amendment. By contrast, excessive force by police officers against unconvicted people on the street violates the Fourth Amendment right against unreasonable "seizures."

- Since the 1958 decision in *Trop v. Dulles,* the Supreme Court has interpreted the Eighth Amendment in a flexible manner. That is, the Amendment's meaning changes as society's values change.

- The use of whipping and other pain-inflicting corporal punishments was common throughout American history, but was gradually abandoned by most states over time. The federal courts barred the practice in decisions focused on Arkansas prisons in the 1960s.

- Although judicial interpretations of the Eighth Amendment prohibit whipping prisoners as punishment, the Supreme Court declined to apply the Eighth Amendment to provide similar protection for schoolchildren. Corporal punishment

is permissible in American schools unless abolished by individual states or local school districts.

- Corrections officials are permitted to use force against prisoners in several situations, including self-defense, defense of third persons, upholding of prison rules, prevention of crimes, and prevention of escapes.

- Force used against prisoners must be employed in an appropriate manner to avoid criminal prosecution according to state laws. Corrections officers who use force "maliciously and sadistically for the very purpose of causing harm" are subject to section 1983 actions for violating the Eighth Amendment. Force may include lethal force, especially if necessary to protect people's safety or to prevent escapes.

- It is difficult for prisoners to prove the intentions of corrections officials in seeking to demonstrate that force was used maliciously and sadistically. Prisoners must show that the force was not applied in a good-faith effort to maintain or restore discipline, but instead was wanton and unnecessary.

- Prison officials may be legally liable for excessive use of force even if the force caused only minor injuries.

- Because of the pressures and tensions within prisons, there are always risks that excessive force may be used in some situations. Under the professionalized management of contemporary American prisons, the use of force is guided—but not necessarily controlled in all circumstances—by established policies and improved staff training.

Key Terms

corporal punishment
Hudson v. McMillian (1992)
Ingraham v. Wright (1978)
Jackson v. Bishop (1968)
self-defense

Talley v. Stephens (1965)
tort law
Trop v. Dulles (1958)

Additional Readings

Mohs, Daniel. 1993. "Opening and Closing the Door to Eighth Amendment Excessive Force Claims." *St. Louis University Law Journal* 37: 465–498.

Nelson, Diana. 1993. "The Evolving Standard of Eighth Amendment Application to Use of Excessive Force Against Prison Inmates." *North Carolina Law Review* 71: 1814–1838.

Sanghavi, Bina. 1993. "The Eighth Amendment Gets a Push and Shove." *Loyola University of Chicago Law Journal* 24: 343–373.

Notes

1. Tennessee v. Garner, 471 U.S. 1 (1985).
2. Graham v. Connor. 490 U.S. 386 (1989).
3. Bell v. Wolfish, 441 U.S. 520 (1979).
4. Trop v. Dulles, 356 U.S. 86 (1958).
5. Antonin Scalia, "Originalism: The Lesser Evil," *University of Cincinnati Law Review* 57 (1989): 861–864.
6. Talley v. Stephens, 247 F.Supp. 683 (E.D. Ark. 1965).
7. Jackson v. Bishop, 404 F.2d 371 (8th Cir. 1068).
8. Ingraham v. Wright, 430 U.S. 651 (1977).
9. Christopher E. Smith, "The Use of Research in Local Policy Making: A Case Study of Corporal Punishment in Public Education," *Educational Policy* 10 (1996): 502–517.
10. "'Painful and Tortuous Punishment' Must Be Abolished, Judge Says," *Southern Poverty Law Center Report* 27 (March 1997): 1, 5.
11. Bert Useem and Peter Kimball, *States of Siege: U.S. Prison Riots 1971–1986* (New York: Oxford University Press, 1991), pp. 105–106.
12. Asshker v. Brodeur, Docket No. 96-15135, 9th Cir., U.S. Court of Appeals (18 April 1997).
13. Madrid v. Gomez, 889 F.Supp. 1146 (N.D. Cal. 1995).
14. Whitley v. Albers, 475 U.S. 312 (1986).
15. Jeffrey T. Walker, "Police and Correctional Use of Force: Legal and Policy Standards and Implications," *Crime & Delinquency* 42 (1996): 144–156.
16. Mark Hornbeck, "Mentally Ill Flood Prisons," *Detroit News*, 4 December 1997, pp. A1, A13.

CHAPTER EIGHT

Conditions of Confinement: Prison Reform Litigation

Imagine you are a federal judge presiding over a prisoner's civil rights lawsuit. The prisoner claims that the prison violated his constitutional right to protection against cruel and unusual punishments because there is asbestos in the material covering the heating pipes that run through the tops of cells and hallways. Asbestos is an insulation material that was used for many years. However, it has not been used in new buildings since the 1970s because scientists discovered that people exposed to asbestos products breathe asbestos dust, which causes crippling and even fatal lung ailments. There is no question that the prison, which was built during the 1940s, has asbestos insulation everywhere. And there is no question that breathing asbestos dust can cause serious lung ailments. Should the prisoner be forced to prove that he has already contracted a lung disease from the asbestos? What kind of order would you issue in the case? Are prisoners entitled to receive money to compensate them for a violation of their Eighth Amendment rights? What, if anything, would you order prison officials to do about the insulation? It is very expensive to remove asbestos insulation because the job must be done by experts. Some experts argue that it is better to leave the insulation in place—as long as the air is tested periodically to check asbestos dust levels—rather than stir up new dust in the removal process. As judge, what will you do?

PRISON CONDITIONS AND CONSTITUTIONAL CONFLICTS

This scenario raises the issue of whether the conditions inside a hypothetical prison meet constitutional standards. Such cases can be especially difficult and controversial for judges. In cases concerning other kinds of rights, for example, judges can simply order prison officials to permit mail to be received or religious services to be held. But this is a different situation. In cases involving conditions of confinement, providing a remedy for the problem may cost hundreds of thousands, if not millions, of dollars—dollars that must come out of the state treasury, either by raising taxes or by cutting government spending on schools, roads, or other necessary programs. Should state taxes be raised or the state budget be rearranged simply to improve living conditions for convicted criminals in prisons? Many people get angry at the thought that additional taxes might be levied on law-abiding citizens to benefit prisoners.

On the other hand, there is the issue of "cruel and unusual punishments," a key protection in the Eighth Amendment of the U.S. Constitution. Should prisoners be forced to live in the freezing cold or be denied clean drinking water? Should an inmate serving a two-year sentence for larceny be at risk of contracting a serious illness and even dying because the conditions within the prison are unsafe or unhealthy?

An additional problem concerns the role of judges in telling prison officials what to do. When conditions of confinement are at issue, judges may be tempted to order prison officials to make drastic and expensive changes in the ways in which prisons are designed and operated. Is it appropriate for judges to decide how prisons will operate? Do judges possess enough knowledge about prisons to decide how they should be managed?

In the American system of government, it is the responsibility of **executive branch** officials—such as prison wardens—to run government agencies. Management decisions supposedly are made by elected officials—such as governors and states' attorneys general—who are accountable to the voters, and by the professional administrators whom they hire to handle the day-to-day decisions in government agencies—such as corrections institutions. In cases concerning conditions of confinement, however, **judicial branch** officials—namely, judges— often make management decisions for corrections institutions because they believe those decisions are necessary to protect prisoners' constitutional rights. Critics of judges' decisions in these cases frequently accuse those judges of **judicial activism,** or of actively going beyond the proper power and authority of the judicial branch in order to make decisions that actually belong in the hands of executive branch officials.

The greatest controversies arise when federal judges' orders require expensive changes in prisons. Federal judges are appointed officials with protected tenure in office; that is, they can serve for life as long as they do not commit criminal or ethical violations that lead to impeachment. If their orders requiring more funding to improve prison conditions lead to higher taxes, isn't that "taxation without representation"—the same grievance that originally led American colonists to revolt against England because the voters have no voice in the decision to spend more money on prisons? In essence, cases involving conditions of confinement, more than any other legal issues in corrections law, may produce a clash between the value Americans place on protecting constitutional rights and the value they place on voters' democratic participation in making public policy decisions, especially those concerning government budgets and taxes.

Prison Conditions Cases in the Federal Courts

In the late nineteenth century and early twentieth centuries, there are examples of cases in which *state* courts found city officials liable for unsafe and unhealthy conditions in local jails. However, because of the traditional legal rule that made governments immune from lawsuits, courts throughout the country agreed "unanimously that a county was not liable for injuries a prisoner received by being confined in an unhealthful or unfit prison."[1] Thus, inmates in federal, state, and county corrections institutions had few opportunities to use the courts and the law to challenge conditions of confinement. As noted in Chapter 2, the U.S. Supreme Court's decision in *Cooper v. Pate,* permitting prisoners to file section 1983 lawsuits against state corrections officials, opened the door for federal judges to examine and correct rights violations in prisons.[2]

Federal judges' initial decisions in cases concerning conditions of confinement often focused on prisons in southern states. As indicated by the discussion of whippings applied to prisoners in Arkansas prisons during the 1960s, the practices and policies of prisons in some southern states differed from those of most corrections institutions elsewhere. Arkansas, Texas, and Alabama in particular invested little money in corrections institutions. Instead of hiring staff to oversee operations within institutions, they often relied on selected prisoners to maintain order—even if it meant employing violence. They also relied on prisoners to make corrections institutions as self-supporting as possible, especially by growing food and other agricultural products, such as cotton. Prisoners worked under harsh conditions as field hands under the supervision of other prisoners, who used force to make sure that the inmates picked the crops. Under the threat of violent punishment, prisoners were also forced to work as unpaid laborers for local businesses.

Not surprisingly, when federal judges began scrutinizing conditions within prisons in the 1960s, these states attracted the most attention. The use of prisoners as supervisors created the risk of abuse. The lack of government funding to maintain corrections institutions meant that facilities were in disrepair. The harsh conditions for prisoner–field hands raised questions about the adequacy of food, medical care, sanitation, and housing within corrections institutions.

According to Malcolm Feeley and Edward Rubin, southern prisons operated much like slave plantations with respect to living conditions, work requirements, and violent punishments. Federal judges' discomfort with this symbolic perpetuation of slavery, which often imposed especially harsh treatment on African-American prisoners, led them to require southern prisons to become more like professionally staffed custodial corrections institutions in the rest of the country. Judges in several southern states were so intent on changing the harsh plantation form of imprisonment that they actually recruited lawyers to file lawsuits on behalf of prisoners alleging unconstitutional conditions of confinement.[3]

But the South was hardly alone in having prison conditions challenged or in having judges issue remedial orders; harsh conditions existed in prisons throughout the country. Eventually, federal judges identified constitutional problems associated with prison conditions in nearly every state. However, the conditions within southern prisons provided the starkest examples of problems and, in effect, "got the ball rolling" as federal judges began to examine prison conditions and intervene into state prison systems.

Box 8-1 contains Judge Frank Johnson's famous opinion on conditions of confinement in Alabama's prisons. His decision in **Pugh v. Locke (1976)** is one of the most well-known—and controversial—decisions affecting prisons. Critics of prisoner litigation and judicial activism often point to Judge Johnson's opinion as an example of a judge who improperly grabbed too much power in making management decisions for a state's correctional system. As you read the opinion, ask yourself: Did the conditions described by Judge Johnson justify a finding that the state violated the Eighth Amendment prohibition on cruel and unusual punishments? If you were the judge and you concluded that unconstitutional conditions existed, what orders would you issue to remedy the violations of the Eighth Amendment?

As you can see, Judge Johnson described living conditions that public health officials labeled unfit for human habitation. The prisons had serious problems with overcrowding, as well as a long list of issues involving prisoners' personal hygiene and diet, the mixing together of prisoners who should have been kept apart, an inadequate number of guards, and other matters. Do these conditions really constitute "cruel and unusual punishment"? Should people who violate the law expect to receive nutritious food and live in a safe, healthy atmosphere? These questions continue to be debated. However, because the U.S. Supreme Court had, since *Trop v. Dulles* in 1958, defined the Eighth Amendment according to the evolving standards of decency of contemporary society, you can see why judges like Judge Johnson would find that these living conditions did not meet society's minimum standards. Indeed, Judge Johnson specifically relied on *Trop v. Dulles* as a precedent to support his decision.

Although Judge Johnson's decision has been criticized, it is difficult to see how his finding of a constitutional violation could be incorrect. After all, the State of Alabama *admitted that its prison conditions violated the Eighth Amendment.* Near the beginning of the opinion, Judge Johnson noted that "[t]he trial concluded with the admission by defendants' lead counsel [representing Alabama prison officials], in open court, that the evidence conclusively

| BOX 8-1 | *Pugh v. Locke,* 406 F.Supp 318 (M.D. Ala. 1976) |

[*This opinion also covered three other lawsuits that had been consolidated into a single case.*]

JOHNSON, Chief Judge:

. . . The complaint in *Pugh v. Locke* was originally filed by an inmate . . . alleg[ing] failure of defendants to adequately protect the plaintiff class from violence on the part of other inmates.

The original complaint in *James v. Wallace* . . . on behalf of all inmates incarcerated in state penal institutions, essentially alleges that defendants failed to provide adequate rehabilitation opportunities for inmates, maintain conditions in these institutions which make rehabilitation impossible, and provide opportunities that do exist in an unequal manner—all in violation of plaintiffs' Eighth and Fourteenth Amendment rights.

After extensive pretrial discovery by parties and amici curiae, the cases were heard beginning August 20, 1975, in a trial that lasted seven days. Because many facts were stipulated, the evidence at the trial consisted largely of expert testimony. . . . The trial concluded with the admission by defendants' lead counsel, in open court, that the evidence conclusively established aggravated and existing violations of plaintiffs' Eighth Amendment rights. . . .

The four principal [corrections] institutions are horrendously overcrowded. At the time of trial of these cases the prison population in the four institutions was as follows:

	Maximum No. for Which Designed	No. in Custody
Fountain [Corr. Center]	632	Over 1100
Holman [Prison]	540	Over 750
Draper [Corr. Center]	632	Over 1000
Kilby [Corr. Facility]	503	Over 700

. . . Following the close of evidence in the instant cases, a joint interim order was entered by this

Court . . . enjoining the defendants from accepting any new prisoners, except escapees and parole violators, into these four institutions until the population in each is reduced to design capacity. The purpose of that emergency order was to prevent aggravation of the conditions created by the grave Eighth Amendment violations.

The effects of severe overcrowding are heightened by the dormitory living arrangements which prevail in these institutions. Bunks often are packed together so closely that there is no walking space between them. Sanitation and security are impossible to maintain. There was testimony that the quarantine population at Kilby is so crowded that inmates have to sleep on mattresses spread on floors in hallways and next to urinals. As will be noted, overcrowding is primarily responsible for and exacerbates all of the other ills of Alabama's penal system.

The dilapidation of the physical facilities contributes to extremely unsanitary living conditions. Testimony demonstrated that windows are broken and unscreened, creating a serious problem with mosquitoes and flies. Old and filthy cotton mattresses lead to the spread of contagious diseases and body lice. Nearly all inmates' living quarters are inadequately heated and ventilated. The electrical systems are totally inadequate, exposed wiring poses a constant danger to inmates, and insufficient lighting results in eye strain and fatigue.

In general, Alabama's penal institutions are filthy. There was repeated testimony at trial that they are overrun with roaches, flies, mosquitoes, and other vermin. A public health expert testified that he found roaches in all stages of development—a certain indicator of filthy conditions. This gross infestation is due in part to inadequate maintenance and housekeeping procedures, and in part to the physical structure of the buildings themselves. For example, floors in many shower rooms are so porous that it is impossible to keep them clean. Plumbing facilities are in an exceptional state of disrepair. In one

(continued)

area at Draper, housing well over 200 men, there is one functioning toilet. Many toilets will not flush and are overflowing. Some showers cannot be turned off and continually drip or even pour water. Frequently, there is no hot running water for substantial periods of time. Witnesses repeatedly commented on the overpowering odor emanating from these facilities.

Personal hygiene is an insurmountable problem in these circumstances. The parties stipulated that the state supplies prisoners only with razor blades and soap. It was further stipulated that the state furnished no toothpaste, toothbrushes, shampoo, shaving cream, razors or combs; but that such items are available for those inmates who can afford them. Further, household cleaning supplies rarely are available for inmates to maintain their living areas.

Food service conditions are equally unsanitary. Food is improperly stored in dirty storage units, and is often infested with insects. Mechanical dishwashers are not adequately maintained and therefore do not even approach the minimum temperature required for proper sanitation. Moreover, food service personnel, many of whom are inmates, are often untrained and do not follow proper sanitation procedures in the handling and preparation of food. Inmates are not supplied with reasonable eating and drinking utensils; some inmates drink from used tin cans, and have to wash and save their own utensils from meal to meal. Garbage sits in large open drums throughout the dining halls. As a general rule, the food is unappetizing and unwholesome. Inmates with some source of funds may supplement their diets from the prison canteen, but the large majority must subsist only on what is supplied by the kitchen. One menu is prepared for all inmates who require a special diet, regardless of whether it meets their particular needs.

One expert witness, a United States public health officer, toured facilities at Draper, Fountain, Holman, and Kilby. He testified at trial that he found these facilities wholly unfit for human habitation according to virtually every criterion used by public health inspectors. With very few exceptions, his testimony was that, if such facilities were under his jurisdiction, he

would recommend that they be closed and condemned as an imminent danger to the health of the individuals exposed to them. This Court credits this testimony and makes it a part of these findings.

There is no working classification system in the Alabama penal system, and the degree to which this impedes the attainment of any proper objective of a penal system cannot be overstated. . . . For no valid reason apparent from the evidence, far too many inmates receive maximum security classifications under the present classification system. . . .

Prison officials do not dispute the evidence that most inmates are assigned to various institutions, to particular dormitories, and to work assignments almost entirely on the basis of available space. Consequently, the appreciable percentage of inmates suffering from some mental disorder is unidentified, and the mentally disturbed are dispersed throughout the prison population without receiving treatment. This Court previously found in an Alabama prison system case that approximately 10 percent of the inmate population are psychotic, and that another 60 percent are disturbed enough to require treatment. The evidence in the instant cases clearly reflects that nothing has been done to alleviate this situation. Some of these inmates should, according to the undisputed evidence presented in these cases, be transferred to a facility for the criminally insane, and many others should be treated within the penal system. The evidence further reflects that there are also a number of mentally retarded inmates who need to be, according to any humanitarian concept, identified and placed in an appropriate environment. . . .

Further effects of the failure to classify are manifold. Violent inmates are not isolated from those who are young, passive, or weak. Consequently, the latter inmates are repeatedly victimized by those who are stronger and more aggressive. Testimony shows that robbery, rape, extortion, theft, and assault are everyday occurrences among the general inmate population. Rather than face this constant danger, some inmates voluntarily subject themselves to the inhuman conditions of prison isolation cells.

Emotional and physical disabilities [among inmates] which require special attention pass unnoticed. . . .

The inmate population also contains a number of aged and infirm who are often housed in dormitories in which conditions are particularly hazardous. There are no special programs to meet the needs of these people and they are frequently unprotected from the general population. For example, in Draper such prisoners—some of them confined to wheelchairs, others scarcely able to move without help—are left without supervision in second-floor quarters that are accessible only by stairway, with no means of evacuation in the event of fire or other physical emergency, and utterly helpless in the event of the sort of medical emergency to which the elderly are susceptible. In this idleness, filth, and despair, the condition of these inmates can be expected only to deteriorate further.

. . . Yet even if the inmate population were reduced to design capacity, the system would still be woefully understaffed. Former Commissioner Sullivan testified that the four large institutions alone need, at a minimum, 692 guards, but that they currently employ only 383. Guards rarely enter the cell blocks and dormitories, especially at night when their presence is most needed. The extremely high inmate-to-staff ratio makes personal interaction between the two virtually impossible because staff members must spend all their time attempting to maintain control or to protect themselves.

Another result of understaffing is that some inmates have been allowed to assume positions of authority and control over other inmates, creating opportunities for blackmail, bribery, and extortion. Some prisoners are used as "strikers" to guard other inmates on farm duty and as "cell flunkies" to maintain order and perform tasks for prison staff. They are afforded special privileges, including the freedom to ignore prison regulations and to abuse other inmates. . . .

. . . The guards, drawn largely from the local population [around the rural prison locations], are practically all white and rural in contrast to the predominantly black and urban inmate population they supervise. A number of witnesses testified that staff members address black inmates with racial slurs, further straining already tense relations.

In view of the foregoing, the rampant violence and jungle atmosphere existing throughout Alabama's penal institutions are no surprise. The evidence reflects that most prisoners carry some form of homemade or contraband weapon, which they consider necessary for self-protection. Shakedowns to remove weapons are neither sufficiently thorough nor frequent enough to significantly reduce the number of weapons. There are too few guards to prevent outbreaks of violence, or even to stop those which occur. . . .

One 20-year-old inmate, after relating that he has been told by medical experts that he has the mind of a five year old, testified that he was raped by a group of inmates on the first night he spent in an Alabama prison. On the second night he was almost strangled by two other inmates who decided instead that they could use him to make a profit, selling his body to other inmates. . . .

Inmates are denied any meaningful opportunity to participate in vocational, educational, or work activities. . . .

The flow of money through Alabama prisons is for all practical purposes uncontrolled. . . . Money can also buy drugs, alcohol, changes in institutional records, special privileges, sex, and housekeeping favors. Interest collected on loans made by inmates with money is exorbitant, and may be collected in a ruthless manner. Gambling, smuggling, and extortion are several of the abuses fueled by the failure of prison officials to control the possession of currency inside the institution. . . .

There is no organized recreation program for Alabama's prisons. . . . Almost no provision is made for inmates to participate in hobbies. . . .

. . . The indescribable conditions in the isolation cells required immediate action to protect inmates from any further torture by confinement in these cells. As many as six inmates were packed in four foot by eight foot cells with no beds, no lights, no running water, and a hole in the floor for a toilet which could only be flushed

(continued)

from the outside. The infamous Draper "dog-house" is a separate building, locked from the outside, with no guard stationed inside. Inmates in punitive isolation received only one meal per day, frequently without utensils. They were permitted no exercise or reading material and could shower only every 11 days. Punitive isolation has been used to punish inmates for offenses ranging from swearing at a guard and failing to report to work on time, to murder.

In light of the foregoing facts, this Court has a clear duty to require the defendants in these cases to remedy the massive constitutional infirmities which plague Alabama's prisons. It is with great reluctance that federal courts intervene in the day-to-day operation of state penal systems, . . . a function they are increasingly required to perform. While this Court continues to recognize the broad discretion required for prison officials to maintain orderly and secure institutions, . . . constitutional deprivations of the magnitude presented here simply cannot be countenanced, and this Court is under a duty to, and will, intervene to protect incarcerated citizens from such wholesale infringements of their constitutional rights. . . .

Prisoners are entitled to be free of conditions which constitute cruel and unusual punishment in violation of the Eighth and Fourteenth Amendments. The content of the Eighth Amendment is not static but "must draw its meaning from the evolving standards of decency that mark the progress of a maturing society." *Trop v. Dulles.* . . . There can be no question that the present conditions of confinement in the Alabama penal system violate any current judicial definition of cruel and unusual punishment, a situation evidenced by the defendants' admission that serious Eighth Amendment violations exist. In these circumstances, it is the very confinement itself which impermissibly contravenes the Eighth and Fourteenth Amendment rights of the plaintiff classes. . . .

established aggravated and existing violations of plaintiffs' Eighth Amendment rights." Some observers believe that many of Judge Johnson's critics have never actually read his opinion. Instead, because these critics believe that judges should not be able to tell corrections officials how to run prisons, they automatically use the famous Alabama case as a symbol of improper judicial activism. In essence, then, the controversy about Judge Johnson's decision seems to stem more from the remedies that he imposed than from his finding that Alabama violated the Constitution.

Remedies for Unconstitutional Prison Conditions

Box 8-2 contains the portion of Judge Johnson's opinion that ordered Alabama to fix its prisons. Do his orders go too far in telling prison officials how to run their prisons? Could Judge Johnson have used any other approaches to avoid having such a powerful influence over the decisions about policies and practices within the prisons?

Judge Johnson noted at the beginning of his **remedial orders** that it was not his intent to make Alabama's prisons comfortable for inmates. Instead, he intended merely to ensure that conditions in the prisons met minimum constitutional standards. As you can see, Johnson gave very detailed orders about changes in the prisons' facilities and operations. As his critics have noted, he

BOX 8-2   *Pugh v. Locke:* Remedial Orders

. . . The Court now acts in these cases with a recognition that prisoners are not to be coddled, and prisons are not to be operated as hotels or country clubs. However, this does not mean that responsible state officials, including the Alabama Legislature, can be allowed to operate prison facilities that are barbaric and inhumane. Let the defendant state officials now be placed on notice that failure to comply with the minimum standards set forth in the order of this Court filed with this opinion will necessitate the closing of those several prison facilities herein found to be unfit for human confinement. . . .

ORDER

. . .

2. A Human Rights Committee for the Alabama Prison System is hereby designated and appointed. The function of the Human Rights Committee, acting as a Committee of the whole or through standing subcommittees appointed by the Committee chairman, shall be to monitor implementation of the standards set forth in Appendix A of this decree.

3. The defendants, within six months from this date, shall submit to the Court a comprehensive report setting forth their progress in the implementation of each and every standard. The report shall set forth reasons for the incomplete implementation of any standard. The report shall also include a time-table for full compliance. . . .

APPENDIX A
MINIMUM CONSTITUTIONAL
STANDARDS FOR INMATES
OF THE ALABAMA PENAL SYSTEM

I.   Overcrowding

1. The number of inmates in each institution in the Alabama penal system shall

not exceed the design capacity for that institution. . . .

II.   Segregation and Isolation

1. No more than one prisoner shall be confined in a single cell, and each cell shall be a minimum of 40 square feet. Within six months, the area of each single occupancy isolation cell shall be no less than 60 square feet.

2. Each cell shall be equipped with a toilet that can be flushed from the inside, a sink with hot and cold running water, ventilation and lighting which meet minimum standards of the United States Public Health Service, clean linen, and a bed off the floor.

3. Each inmate confined in isolation shall be

(a) permitted to bathe at least every other day;
(b) provided three wholesome and nutritious meals per day, served with eating and drinking utensils;
(c) supplied the same toilet articles and linens as are required to be supplied to the general population;
(d) provided reading and writing materials . . . ;
(e) allowed at least 30 minutes of outdoor exercise per day; and
(f) afforded adequate medical and mental health care . . .

4. . . . Any period of confinement for the purpose of punishment shall not exceed 21 days. . . .

III.   Classification

1. By April 15, 1976, the defendants shall file with the Court a plan for the classification of all inmates incarcerated in the Alabama penal system [including methods for identifying aged, infirm, disturbed, and mentally retarded prisoners]. . . .

(continued)

IV. Mental Health Care

[Corrections officials must hire mental health professionals and provide mental health care for those prisoners who need it.]

V. Protection Against Violence

. . .

5. With the exception of isolation units, guards shall be stationed inside living areas, including dormitories, at all times. There shall be at least one guard inside and one guard outside all living areas at all times. As to isolation units, guards must be stationed at all times so as to have visual and voice contact with the isolated prisoners.

6. At no time shall prisoners be used to guard other prisoners, nor shall prisoners be placed in positions of authority over other inmates. . . .

VI. Living Conditions

1. Prisoners shall be supplied, without charge, toothbrushes, toothpaste, shaving cream, razors and razor blades, soap, shampoo, and combs. . . .

2. Each prisoner shall be supplied weekly with clean bed linen and towels.

3. Each inmate shall have access to household cleaning supplies in order to maintain living areas, and sanitary conditions within the institution shall meet minimum public health standards. The defendants shall be responsible for implementing a regular an effective program of insect and rodent control.

4. All institutions shall be adequately heated, lighted, and ventilated. Windows and doors shall be properly screened and otherwise properly maintained. Electrical wiring must be safe.

5. Each prisoner shall have a bed off the floor, a clean mattress, and blankets as needed.

6. Each institution shall maintain in working order one toilet per 15 inmates, one urinal or one foot of urinal trough per 15 inmates, one shower per 20 inmates, and one lavatory per 10 inmates.

7. Each inmate shall have a minimum of 60 square feet of living space.

VII. Food Service

1. Every prisoner is entitled to three wholesome and nutritious meals per day, served with proper eating and drinking utensils.

. . .

3. Food shall be stored, prepared and served under sanitary conditions which meet minimum public health standards. . . .

4. Each inmate who requires a special diet for reasons of health or religion shall be provided a diet to meet his or her individual need.

VIII. Correspondence and Visitation

[No limit to the number of letters each week. Visits permitted at least once per week.]

IX. Educational, Vocational, Work and Recreational Opportunities

[Each inmate will be assigned a meaningful job and have opportunities for educational programs.]

X. Physical Facilities . . .

XI. Staff

[Must hire a sufficient number of staff, train staff, and "institute an affirmative hiring program designed to reduce and having the effect of reducing the racial and cultural disparity between the staff and inmate population."]

went so far as to specify the details of bathing schedules and the number of toilets to be made available. There is no doubt that this remedial order, through its detailed instructions, removed from corrections officials the authority to make discretionary decisions about how to handle a variety of management issues. But the question that is often debated remains: Even if the conditions in Alabama's prisons violated the Constitution (and not everyone agrees that they did), were there any other approaches that would have kept the judge from being so deeply involved in the day-to-day aspects of prison administration?

Other judges who handle prison reform cases or cases affecting the management of other institutions in society use the litigation process as a means to pressure officials into developing their own remedies. In other words, the judges preside over a negotiation process in which the court's power is used to pressure corrections officials to reach agreements with prisoners' attorneys about how to fix problems without spending unnecessary funds or ignoring corrections officials' expertise about how prisons should be run.[4] For example, a judge's order may say to prison officials, "You have six months to tell me how you will fix this list of problems," while simultaneously maintaining ongoing discussions between prison officials and prisoners' attorneys about how to solve the problems revealed by the lawsuit. The judge can always use the threat of direct orders if prison officials do not cooperate in developing their own solutions. The goal of this approach usually is the development of a **consent decree,** or a voluntary, negotiated resolution that becomes law as the order is issued by the judge.

In one respect, Judge Johnson's orders drew upon the court's ability to pressure officials to discuss and develop workable solutions. As one study has shown, the appointment of a citizens' Human Rights Committee to oversee the process of implementing remedies provided a means for negotiation and interaction between prison officials and outsiders interested in improving prison conditions. Moreover, the use of a citizens' committee helped to publicize the problems of Alabama's prisons so that the state's citizens would take greater interest in monitoring the development of remedies.[5]

In the lawsuit that challenged conditions in Georgia's prisons, the U.S. district court judge appointed a **special master**—an outside attorney—to supervise and facilitate pretrial negotiations and interactions between the two sides in the case. The special master conducted fact-finding hearings, and the judge accepted the special master's report on the nature of prison conditions as establishing the relevant facts of the case.[6]

The judge in the Georgia case also appointed a law professor to serve as "special monitor," a kind of special master for the remedy phase of the lawsuit. The special monitor "was given broad powers beyond mere oversight of decree implementation and acted as fact-finder, mediator, manager, and planner."[7] The approach used by a special monitor (or special master) can affect whether these representatives of the judge encourage the development of negotiated solutions or merely enforce orders imposed by the judge on a prison system. The first special monitor in the Georgia case "would surprise the [corrections officials] and wait to notify them of potential problems" by announcing inadequate compliance or violations of court orders in formal reports given to the judge and each side in the case.[8] By contrast, the second special monitor "would tell [corrections officials] of any concerns or problems he observed and not wait until he issued his report to [the judge]."[9] This second approach would appear to create more opportunities for corrections officials to make adjustments and solve problems themselves before being subject to additional specific orders from the judge.

Judge Johnson may have believed that he could not trust Alabama officials to develop remedies on their own. He may have had doubts about "whether the [fulfillment] of prisoners' constitutional rights can rest in the hands of the same elective legislative and executive branches that created and maintained the civil rights violations in the first place."[10] Johnson had faced strong resistance from Alabama's governor, George Wallace. However, when Johnson was elevated to the federal court of appeals, his successor in the case, Judge Robert Varner, enjoyed strong cooperation from the next Alabama governor, Fob James, and this cooperation facilitated progress in improving prison conditions.[11] The success of prison reform remedies depends on many factors, including the availability of funds to pay for improvements, the attitudes of the two sides in the case (i.e., will they cooperate to solve problems or continually fight about every issue?), and the judge's approach to developing remedies and monitoring compliance.

Although Eighth Amendment litigation has been the most controversial approach to conditions of confinement because of the many cases in which judges intervened in prison administration, it is not the only part of the Constitution that can affect prison conditions. Box 8-3 contains excerpts from a case involving another constitutional right. What claim is at issue in this case? How might claims based on this right produce judicial decisions which alter prison programs and practices?

The Results of Prison Reform Litigation

There have been several consequences of prison reform litigation's focus on conditions of confinement. One result is a reduction in severe problems, such as lack of heat, unsanitary food preparation conditions, failure to classify prisoners, and reliance on prisoners to guard and supervise other prisoners. Litigation has not eliminated such problems. But it has moved the nation closer to shared understandings about minimal acceptable conditions inside prisons. Individual states no longer can treat prisoners however they want to, beyond the scrutiny of courts and the public. Abusive treatment and inadequate standards still exist in some institutions, but now there are established procedures for petitioning courts to examine and remedy such problems.

Prison reform litigation has had especially dramatic effects on southern prisons. Southern states, in particular, experienced dramatic increases in public funding for corrections in the aftermath of court orders to remedy problems.[12] Thus, these states no longer were permitted to run their prisons however they saw fit. They were forced to join the mainstream of nationally accepted corrections practices by hiring guards, classifying inmates, ending reliance on prisoners to supervise other inmates, and generally spending more money on corrections—instead of trying to make prisons financially self-supporting.

| BOX 8-3 | *Glover v. Johnson,* **478 F.Supp. 1075 (E.D. Mich. 1978)** |

FEIKENS, Chief Judge.

On May 19, 1977, a civil rights suit was filed on behalf of present and future females incarcerated by the State of Michigan. . . . Plaintiffs sought a declaration by this Court that the State, through its Department of Corrections, had violated their rights under the Constitution. Plaintiffs also asked for injunctive relief to secure these rights. The original complaint focused on alleged inequalities apparent in the treatment and rehabilitation programs available to Plaintiffs at the Detroit House of Corrections when compared to those programs available to male offenders in various prison facilities throughout the States. . . .

. . . Plaintiffs argue that because the State has chosen to emphasize educational opportunities at three male facilities to which male prisoners may be assigned or transferred, the inmates at the single female facility are disadvantaged because they lack access to institutions with a similar emphasis. Evidence was introduced to show that the community college courses made available to them at Huron Valley are less adequate than those offered to males because the course selection is narrower, and often so limited as to make it difficult to complete successfully a course sequence leading to a major in a given field. . . .

Training in five broad occupational areas is currently available at Huron Valley: office occupations, food service, graphic arts, building maintenance, and general shop. . . . By way of comparison, male prisoners have access to some twenty different vocational programs, including automobile servicing, heating and air conditioning, machine shop, and drafting. Furthermore, evidence was taken indicating that the "male" versions of those programs . . . were often more extensive and more useful to the inmates. . . .

. . . The women inmates have a right to a range and quality of programming substantially equivalent to that offered the men, and the programs currently offered do not meet this standard. . . .

Litigation on conditions of confinement can involve a wide variety of issues, from food and medicine to recreational opportunities.[13] Prison reform litigation based on these issues led states to spend enormous sums of money on attorneys' fees and legal expenses—especially because states frequently were ordered to pay the fees of prisoners' attorneys when prisoners won a case. At the same time, litigation reduced the discretion and authority of wardens and other corrections officials. They often had to check with the state's attorneys before they could initiate or change policies and programs, for fear that they would affect litigation or violate a court order if they went ahead on their own.

One of the most highly debated results of prison reform litigation is its effect on violence within prisons. A study of Texas prisons after their major federal case (*Ruiz v. Estelle,* 1980), in which the district court ordered significant operational changes, found that judicial involvement actually increased violence within the prisons.[14] According to this study, under the old system, corrections officials gained the cooperation of the strongest inmates and gave them authority over other prisoners. This helped to maintain order within the institution. At the same time, guards and supervisory prisoners knew that they could choose specific actions to enforce discipline and order, even if it meant the use of violence. After prison litigation, the stronger inmates no longer could be used to maintain order, and they also no longer received special benefits. Relationships between guards and inmates changed as inmates' expectations and assertiveness about rights grew, often because they thought a judge was on their side. Guards no longer could beat prisoners or otherwise choose any means to maintain control. The result was a reduction in the traditional methods of enforcing order and in levels of obedience. Stronger prisoners still asserted authority over other inmates, but now it was on behalf of prison gangs, not to maintain order in the institutions. Consequently, prisoners became more fearful of one another, and violence among inmates increased.[15]

There are alternative explanations for increases in prison violence. For example, prison populations began rising during the 1980s due to tougher sentencing policies, thereby increasing overcrowding and conflict within institutions. Racial conflicts among prisoners sharpened, and race- and ethnicity-based gangs carried their violent rivalries from the streets into the cellblocks. Although these and other factors may have contributed to prison violence, prison reform litigation also likely contributed by raising prisoners' expectations while changing the traditional means of control.

Judges became deeply involved in the administration of many corrections institutions. This involvement could absorb significant portions of a judge's time, thus limiting a court's ability to handle other legal matters. In addition, judges' involvement in prisons sparked national debates about the proper role of judges and led to a political backlash against prisoner litigation. For example, the Violent Crime Control Act of 1994 sought to make it more difficult for inmates to prove that prison overcrowding constituted an Eighth Amendment violation and placed new requirements on judges' remedial orders to correct overcrowding.[16] When Republicans assumed control over both houses of Congress after the 1994 elections, Congress passed and President Clinton signed into law the Prison Litigation Reform Act of 1996 (PLRA). The law was incorporated into the Balanced Budget Downpayment Act without any hearings to permit critics of the PLRA to air their arguments. The PLRA limits the ability of federal judges to facilitate and supervise lasting consent decrees. It also limits other kinds of orders that judges may issue, including **preliminary injunctions.** A preliminary injunction is an immediate order to prevent corrections officials from taking a certain action until court hearings can be held to determine whether that action would be lawful. In addition, the PLRA limits the ability of judges to require states to pay for special masters and special monitors.

As you read the selected provisions of the Prison Litigation Reform Act presented in Box 8-4, think about how this legislation may affect prison litigation, prisoners' rights, and federal judges' control over the imposition of remedies in corrections settings. Do you agree with critics who contend that Congress has improperly attempted to limit the judiciary's appropriate power and responsibilities under the Constitution?[17]

The Prison Litigation Reform Act represents a political reaction to judges' involvement in prison administration. Stated another way, prison litigation reform has produced a political backlash that has imposed limitations on both

BOX 8-4 | **Prison Litigation Reform Act of 1996**
Pub. L. No. 104-134, Section 801, 110 STAT. 1321

18 U.S.C. [SECTION] 3626

(a)(1) Prospective Relief

(A) Prospective relief in any civil action with respect to prison conditions shall extend no further than necessary to correct the violation of the Federal right of a particular plaintiff or plaintiffs. The court shall not grant or approve any prospective relief unless the court finds that such relief is narrowly drawn, extends no further than necessary to correct the violation of the Federal right, and is the least intrusive means necessary to correct the violation of the Federal right. The court shall give substantial weight to any adverse impact on public safety or the operation of a criminal justice system caused by the relief.

(B) The court shall not order any prospective relief that requires or permits a government official to exceed his or her authority under State or local law or otherwise violates State or local law, unless—

(i) Federal law permits such relief to be ordered in violation of State or local law;

(ii) the relief is necessary to correct the violation of a Federal right; and

(iii) no other relief will correct the violation of the Federal right.

(C) Nothing in this section shall be construed to authorize the courts, in exercising their remedial powers, to order the construction of prisons or the raising of taxes, or to repeal or detract from otherwise applicable limitations on the remedial powers of the courts.

(2) Preliminary Injunctive Relief

In any civil action with respect to prison conditions, to the extent otherwise authorized by law, the court may enter a temporary restraining order or an order for preliminary injunctive relief. Preliminary injunctive relief must be narrowly drawn, extend no further than necessary to correct the harm the court finds requires preliminary relief, and be the least intrusive means necessary to correct that harm. The court shall give substantial weight to any adverse impact on public safety or the operation of a criminal justice system caused by the preliminary relief and shall respect the principles of comity set out in paragraph (1)(B) in tailoring any preliminary relief. Preliminary injunctive relief shall automatically expire on the date that is 90 days after its entry, unless the court makes the findings required under section (a)(1) for the entry of prospective relief and makes the order final before the expiration of the 90-day period.

(3) Prisoner Release Order

(A) In any civil action with respect to prison conditions, no prisoner release order shall be entered unless—

(i) a court has previously entered an order for less intrusive relief that has failed to remedy the deprivation of the Federal right sought to be remedied through the prisoner release order; and

(ii) the defendant has had a reasonable amount of time to comply with the previous court orders.

(B) In any civil action in Federal court with respect to prison conditions, a prisoner release order shall be entered only by a three-judge court in accordance with section 2284 of title 28, if the requirements of subparagraph (E) have been met.

(C) A party seeking a prisoner release order in Federal court shall file with any request for such relief, a request for a

(continued)

three-judge court and materials sufficient to demonstrate that the requirements of subparagraph (A) have been met.

(D) If the requirements under subparagraph (A) have been met, a Federal judge before whom a civil action with respect to prison conditions is pending who believes that a prison release order should be considered sua sponte shall request the convening of a three-judge court to determine whether a prisoner release order should be entered.

(E) The three-judge court shall enter a prisoner release order only if the court finds by clear and convincing evidence that—

(i) crowding is the primary cause of the violation of a Federal right; and

(ii) no other relief will remedy the violation of the Federal right.

(F) Any State or local official or unit of government whose jurisdiction or function includes the appropriation of funds for the construction, operation, or maintenance of program facilities, or the prosecution or custody of persons who may be released from, or not admitted to, a prison as a result of a prisoner release order shall have standing to oppose the imposition or continuation in effect of such relief and to seek termination of such relief, and shall have the right to intervene in any proceeding relating to such relief.

(b) Termination of Relief

(1) Termination of Prospective Relief

(A) In any civil action with respect to prison conditions in which prospective relief is ordered, such relief shall be terminable upon the motion of any party or intervener—

(i) 2 years after the date the court granted or approved prospective relief;

(ii) 1 year after the date the court has entered an order denying termination of prospective relief under this paragraph; or

(iii) in the case of an order on or before the date of enactment of the Prison Litigation Reform Act, 2 years after such date of enactment

(B) Nothing in this section shall prevent the parties from agreeing to terminate or modify relief before the relief is terminated under subparagraph (A).

(2) Immediate Termination of Prospective Relief: In any civil action with respect to prison conditions, a defendant or intervener shall be entitled to the immediate termination of any prospective relief if the relief was approved or granted in the absence of a finding by the court that the relief is narrowly drawn, extends no further than necessary to correct the violation of the Federal right, and is the least intrusive means necessary to correct the violation of the Federal right.

(3) Limitation: Prospective relief shall not terminate if the court makes written findings based on the record that prospective relief remains necessary to correct a current or ongoing violation of the Federal right, extends no further than necessary to correct the violation of the Federal right, and that the prospective relief is narrowly drawn and the least intrusive means to correct the violation.

(4) Termination or Modification of Relief: Nothing in this section shall prevent any party or intervener from seeking modification or termination before the relief is terminable under paragraph (1) or (2), to the extent that modification or termination would otherwise be legally permissible.

(c) Settlements

(1) Consent Decrees: In any civil action with respect to prison conditions, the court shall not enter or approve a consent decree unless it complies with the limitations on relief set forth in subsection (a).

(2) Private Settlement Agreements

(A) Nothing in this section shall preclude parties from entering into a private settlement agreement that does not comply with the limitations on relief set forth in subsection (a), if the terms of that agreement are not subject to court enforcement other than the reinstatement of the civil proceeding that the agreement settled.

(B) Nothing in this section shall preclude any party claiming that a private settlement agreement has been breached from seeking in State court any remedy available under State law.

(d) State Law Remedies

The limitations on remedies in this section shall not apply to relief entered by a State court based solely upon claims arising under State law.

(e) Procedure for Motions Affecting Prospective Relief

(1) Generally: The court shall promptly rule on any motion to modify or terminate prospective relief in a civil action with respect to prison conditions.

(2) Automatic Stay: Any prospective relief subject to a pending motion shall be automatically stayed during the period—

(A)(i) beginning on the 30th day after such motion is filed, in the case of a motion made under paragraph (1) or (2) of subsection (b); or

(ii) beginning on the 180th day after such motion is filed, in the case of a motion made under any other law; and

(B) ending on the date the court enters a final order ruling on the motion.

(f) Special Masters

(1) In General

(A) In any civil action in a Federal court with respect to prison conditions, the court may appoint a special master who shall be disinterested and objective and who will give due regard to the public safety, to conduct hearings on the record and prepare proposed findings of fact.

(B) The court shall appoint a special master under this subsection during the remedial phase of the action only upon a finding that the remedial phase will be sufficiently complex to warrant the appointment.

(2) Appointment

(A) If the court determines that the appointment of a special master is necessary, the court shall request that the defendant institution and the plaintiff each submit a list of not more than 5 persons to serve as a special master.

(B) Each party shall have the opportunity to remove up to 3 persons from the opposing party's list.

(C) The court shall select the master from the persons remaining on the list after the operation of subparagraph (B).

(3) Interlocutory Appeal: Any party shall have the right to an interlocutory appeal of the judge's selection of the special master under this subsection, on the ground of partiality.

(4) Compensation: The compensation to be allowed to a special master under this section shall be based on an hourly rate not greater than the hourly rate established under section 3006A for payment of court-appointed counsel, plus costs reasonably incurred by the special master. Such compensation and costs shall be paid with funds appropriated to the Judiciary.

(5) Regular Review of Appointment: In any civil action with respect to prison conditions in which a special master is appointed under this subsection, the court shall review the appointment of the special master every 6 months to determine whether the services of the special master continue to be required under paragraph (1). In no event shall the appointment of a special master extend beyond the termination of the relief.

(6) Limitations on Powers and Duties: A special master appointed under this subsection—

(A) may be authorized by a court to conduct hearings and prepare proposed findings of fact, which shall be made on the record;

(B) shall not make any findings or communications ex parte;

(continued)

(C) may be authorized by a court to assist in the development of remedial plans; and

(D) may be removed at any time, but shall be relieved of the appointment upon the termination of relief. . . .

42 U.S.C. [SECTION] 1997e

(a) Applicability of Administrative Remedies: No action shall be brought with respect to prison conditions under section 1979 of the Revised Statutes of the United States (42 U.S.C. 1983), or any other Federal law, by a prisoner confined in any jail, prison, or other correctional facility until such administrative remedies as are available are exhausted. . . .

(b)(2) In the event that a claim is, on its face, frivolous, malicious, fails to state a claim upon which relief can be granted, or seeks monetary relief from a defendant who is immune from such relief, the court may dismiss the underlying claim without first requiring the exhaustion of administrative remedies. . . .

28 U.S.C. [SECTION] 1915

(a)(1)(F)(2) A prisoner seeking to bring a civil action or appeal a judgment in a civil action or proceeding without prepayment of fees or security therefor, in addition to filing the affidavit filed under paragraph (1), shall submit a certified copy of the trust fund account statement (or institutional equivalent) for the prisoner for the 6-month period immediately preceding the filing of the complaint or notice of appeal, obtained from an appropriate official of each prison at which the prisoner is or was confined; and . . .

(b)(1) Notwithstanding subsection (a), if a prisoner brings a civil action or files an appeal in forma pauperis, the prisoner shall be required to pay the full amount of a filing fee. The court shall assess and, when funds exist, as a partial payment of any court fees required by law, an initial partial filing fee of 20 percent of the greater of—

(A) the average monthly deposits to the prisoner's account; or

(B) the average monthly balance in the prisoner's account for the 6-month period immediately preceding the filing of the complaint or notice of appeal.

(2) After payment of the initial partial filing fee, the prisoner shall be required to make monthly payments of 20 percent of the preceding month's income credited to the prisoner's account. The agency having custody of the prisoner shall forward payments from the prisoner's account to the clerk of the court each time the amount in the account exceeds $10 until the filing fees are paid. . . .

(3) In no event shall a prisoner be prohibited from bringing a civil action or appealing a civil or criminal judgment for the reason that the prisoner has no assets and no means by which to pay the initial partial filing fee . . .

. . .

(d) Successive Claims . . .

(g) In no event shall a prisoner bring a civil action or appeal a judgment in a civil action or proceeding under this section if the prisoner has, on 3 or more prior occasions, while incarcerated or detained in any facility, brought an action or appeal in a court of the United States that was dismissed on the grounds that it was frivolous, malicious, or fails to state a claim upon which relief may be granted, unless the prisoner is under imminent danger of serious physical injury. . . .

28 U.S.C. [SECTION] 1346

(b)(2) No person convicted of a felony who is incarcerated while awaiting sentencing or while serving a sentence may bring a civil action against the United States or an agency, officer, or employee of the Government, for mental or emotional injury while in custody without a prior showing of physical injury.

judges and prisoners. Some of the statute's most significant provisions include the following:

1. The establishment of specific requirements for findings that judges must make before relief can be granted or consent decrees can be imposed

2. A reduction in judges' authority to order the release of prisoners in response to overcrowding

3. Short time limits on the effective period for judges' remedial orders

4. A new requirement that prisoners must exhaust administrative remedies before filing civil rights lawsuits

5. Increased influence by corrections officials over the appointment of special masters to supervise the implementation of remedies

6. The definition and limitation of special masters' powers

7. The imposition of the special master's costs upon the court rather than on the state whose officials were sued in the case

8. Stricter procedures for filing fees by requiring partial payment of fees by prisoners with very limited resources instead of the waiver of fees, as usually occurred in the past

It remains to be seen how all of these new changes will affect prison litigation. It is possible that some portions of the statute will be declared unconstitutional if judges believe that Congress exceeded its authority in limiting judicial power for prison cases and thereby violated the constitutional principle of separation of powers.

SUMMARY

- Prisons' conditions of confinement that fall below society's contemporary standards of decency—as interpreted by judges—may violate the Eighth Amendment prohibition against cruel and unusual punishments.

- Judges' decisions affecting prison conditions often require large sums of money to remedy deficient conditions. They also may involve judges in the day-to-day management of prisons. Thus, these cases raise the greatest controversies about the proper role of judges in affecting prisons and prison reform.

- Lower federal courts became deeply involved in evaluating and remedying problems in state prisons during the 1960s and 1970s. Southern prisons in particular, such as those in Alabama, Georgia, and Texas, were required to spend large sums of money to become more like prisons elsewhere in the country, with professional staff and minimum standards for food, classification, and living conditions.

- Judges take different approaches in developing remedies for prison conditions. Some judges impose detailed orders.

Others facilitate interactions and negotiations between the opposing parties in each case. Alternatively, judges use special masters to help process the disputes or special monitors to oversee implementation of remedies.

- The Prison Litigation Reform Act enacted by Congress in 1996 places limits on judges' ability to impose remedial orders, imposes stricter requirements on prisoners regarding filing fees, and creates restrictions on the use of special masters.

Key Terms

consent decree
executive branch
judicial activism
preliminary injunction

Pugh v. Locke (1976)
remedial orders
special master (or special monitor)

Additional Readings

Chilton, Bradley. 1991. *Prisons Under the Gavel.* Columbus: Ohio State University Press.

Crouch, Ben M., and James W. Marquart. 1989. *Appeal to Justice: Litigated Reform of Texas Prisons.* Austin: University of Texas Press.

Feeley, Malcolm M., and Edward L. Rubin. 1998. *Judicial Policy Making and the Modern State: How the Courts Reformed America's Prisons.* New York: Cambridge University Press.

Smith, Christopher E. 1993. *Courts and Public Policy.* Chicago: Nelson-Hall.

Yackle, Larry. 1989. *Reform and Regret: The Story of Federal Judicial Involvement in the Alabama Prison System.* New York: Oxford University Press.

Notes

1. Donald H. Wallace, "Prisoners' Rights: Historical Views," in James W. Marquardt and Jonathan R. Sorenson, eds., *Correctional Contexts: Contemporary and Classical Readings* (Los Angeles: Roxbury, 1997), p. 249.

2. Cooper v. Pate, 378 U.S. 546 (1964).

3. Malcolm Feeley and Edward Rubin, *Judicial Policy Making and the Modern State: How the Courts Reformed America's Prisons.* (New York: Cambridge University Press, 1998), pp. 51, 81, 150–171.

4. Christopher E. Smith, *Courts and Public Policy* (Chicago: Nelson-Hall, 1993), pp. 99–101.

5. Tinsley Yarbrough, "The Alabama Prison Litigation," *The Justice System Journal* 9 (1984): 278–280.

6. Bradley S. Chilton and Susette M. Talarico, "Politics and Constitutional Interpretation in Prison Reform Litigation: The Case of *Guthrie v. Evans,*" in John DiIulio, Jr., ed., 1991. *Courts, Corrections, and the Constitution* (New York: Oxford University Press, 1990), p. 118.

7. Ibid., p. 119.

8. Ibid., p. 120.

9. Ibid.

10. Christopher E. Smith, "Federal Judges' Role in Prisoner Litigation: What's Necessary? What's Proper?" *Judicature* 70 (1986): 150.

11. John DiIulio, Jr., "Conclusion: What Judges Can Do to Improve Prisons and Jails," in DiIulio, ed., *Courts, Corrections, and the*

Constitution (New York: Oxford University Press, 1990), pp. 287–288.

12. Malcolm Feeley, "The Significance of Prison Conditions Cases: Budgets and Regions," *Law and Society Review* 23 (1989): 278.

13. Robert D. Lee, Jr., "Prisoners' Rights to Recreation: Quantity, Quality, and Other Aspects," *Journal of Criminal Justice* 24 (1996): 167–178.

14. Ben W. Crouch and James W. Marquart, *An Appeal to Justice: Litigated Reform of Texas Prisons* (Austin: University of Texas Press, 1989), pp. 213–220; Ruiz v. Estelle, 503 F.Supp. 1265 (S.D. Tex. 1980).

15. Ibid.

16. Jack E. Call and Richard Cole, "Assessing the Possible Impact of the Violent Crime Control Act of 1994 on Prison and Jail Overcrowding Suits," *The Prison Journal* 76 (1996): 92–106.

17. Ricardo Solano, Jr., "Is Congress Handcuffing Our Courts?" *Seton Hall Law Review* 28 (1997): 282–311.

CHAPTER NINE

Conditions of Confinement: Legal Doctrines

Imagine you are a justice on the U.S. Supreme Court. The Court reviews a case in which a prisoner claims that poor medical care provided in a corrections institution violates his Eighth Amendment rights. Because the Eighth Amendment prohibits "cruel and unusual punishments" but says nothing about medical care for prisoners, you must decide whether the prisoner has any rights at issue in the case. How will you approach this prisoner's claim? If you rule that medical care is unrelated to the "punishments" mentioned in the Eighth Amendment, does that mean that corrections officials are not obligated to provide medical care for prisoners? Is there another part of the Constitution that seems more relevant to the issue of medical care for prisoners? Just as in your other cases, you know that your decision here will establish law for the entire country and thereby potentially affect the lives of the million-plus individuals incarcerated in corrections institutions. What will you decide?

THE U.S. SUPREME COURT AND CONDITIONS OF CONFINEMENT

The foregoing scenario is not entirely hypothetical. The U.S. Supreme Court's first case applying the Eighth Amendment to prison conditions focused on a single issue: medical care. Lower federal courts handled the initial cases concerning a broad range of conditions within the prisons, and the Supreme Court eventually developed standards for applying the Eighth Amendment to such cases. However, the justices did not decide many cases concerning prison conditions.

Prison Medical Care and the Eighth Amendment

The initial U.S. Supreme Court case was *Estelle v. Gamble* (1976). As you will read in Box 9-1, Gamble injured his back when a bale of cotton fell on him while he was working at his prison job. Corrections officials responded to his complaints by giving him muscle relaxants and painkillers. But after a certain point, officials also punished him for failing to work, despite his continued claims that the back injury prevented him from working. He filed a lawsuit against the prison officials based on the claim that his right to protection against cruel and unusual punishments had been violated because he was not given adequate and appropriate medical care for his injury. As you read the case, identify the test developed by the Court for determining Eighth Amendment violations. Does this test prevent prisoners from experiencing any harm?

Although Gamble lost his case, the decision helped establish the legal standard for judges to apply in Eighth Amendment medical treatment cases. Justice Thurgood Marshall's majority opinion concluded that "deliberate indifference to serious medical needs of prisoners constitutes the 'unnecessary and wanton infliction of pain,' . . . proscribed by the Eighth Amendment." Notice that this rule does not guarantee prisoners medical treatment whenever they ask for it; in fact, it does not even guarantee them good medical treatment. Indeed, Marshall's opinion asserts that a prisoner victimized by medical malpractice does not necessarily experience a rights violation. Such a prisoner must pursue a tort action under state law. The rule in *Estelle v. Gamble* merely bars corrections officials from being "deliberate[ly] indifferent" to the medical needs of prisoners. As in cases concerning other kinds of rights, the Supreme Court appeared intent on ensuring that minimum human needs are met in providing medical care for prisoners. However, the justices did not establish a broad right that would encourage prisoners to file lawsuits simply because they were unhappy with the medical services provided. Indeed, prisoners' options for medical care are so limited that the Court has approved forcibly medicating mentally ill prisoners who do not wish to be so treated.[1]

The majority opinion cited the relevant Eighth Amendment precedents about applying contemporary standards and preventing the wanton infliction of pain. Ask yourself, however, if inadequate medical care should really be considered a violation of the Eighth Amendment? That is, is medical care truly a component

| BOX 9-1 | *Estelle v. Gamble,* 429 U.S. 97 (1976) |

JUSTICE MARSHALL delivered the opinion of the Court.

. . . According to the complaint, Gamble was injured November 9, 1973, when a bale of cotton fell on him while he was unloading a truck. He continued to work but after four hours he became stiff and was granted a pass to the unit hospital. At the hospital a medical assistant . . . checked him for a hernia and sent him back to his cell. Within two hours the pain became so intense that Gamble returned to the hospital where he was given pain pills by an inmate nurse and then was examined by doctor. The following day, Gamble saw a Dr. Astone who diagnosed the injury as a lowerback strain. [He prescribed a painkiller and a muscle relaxant] . . . and placed respondent on "cell-pass, cell-feed" status for two days, allowing him to remain in his cell at all times except for showers. . . . [The doctor later extended the cell-bound status for another seven days.] He also ordered that respondent be moved from an upper to a lower bunk for one week, but the prison authorities did not comply with that directive. . . . [The doctor subsequently extended the muscle relaxant, prescribed a new pain reliever, and continued the cell-bound status.]

On December 3, despite Gamble's statement that his back hurt as much as it had the first day, Dr. Astone took him off cell-pass, thereby certifying him to be capable of light work. At the same time, Dr. Astone prescribed [the new pain reliever] for seven days. Gamble then went to a [supervisory corrections officer] and told him that he was in too much pain to work. [The officer] had [Gamble] moved to "administrative segregation." On December 5, Gamble was taken before the prison disciplinary committee, apparently because of his refusal to work.

[During the remainder of December and January, Gamble was prescribed various medications for pain and high blood pressure. He was also threatened with discipline if he refused to work. However, he continued to claim that he was too ill to work.]

On January 31, Gamble was brought before the prison disciplinary committee for his refusal to work in early January. He told the committee that he could not work because of his severe back pain and his high blood pressure. [The medical assistant] testified that Gamble was in "first class" medical condition. The committee, with no further medical examination or testimony, placed [Gamble] in solitary confinement.

Four days later, on February 4, at 8 a.m. respondent asked to see a doctor for chest pains and "blank outs." It was not until 7:30 that night that a medical assistant examined him and ordered him hospitalized. The following day a Dr. Heaton performed an electrocardiogram; one day later [Gamble] was placed on Quinidine for treatment of irregular cardiac rhythm and moved to administrative segregation. On February 7, [Gamble] again experienced pain in his chest, left arm, and back and asked to see a doctor. The guards refused. He asked again the next day. The guards again refused. Finally, on February 9, he was allowed to see Dr. Heaton, who ordered the Quinidine continued for three more days. On February 11, he swore out his complaint.

The gravamen of respondent's [section] 1983 complaint is that petitioners have subjected him to cruel and unusual punishment in violation of the Eighth Amendment, made applicable to the States by the Fourteenth. . . . We therefore base our evaluation of respondent's complaint on those Amendments and our decisions interpreting them. . . .

Our more recent cases . . . have held that the Amendment proscribes more than physically barbarous punishments. *Trop v. Dulles* [1958] . . . ; *Weems v. United States* [1910] . . . The [Eighth] Amendment embodies "broad and idealistic concepts of dignity, civilized standards, humanity, and decency," *Jackson v. Bishop* [8th Cir. 1968] . . . against which we must evaluate penal measures. Thus we have held repugnant to the Eighth Amendment punishments which

(continued)

are incompatible with "the evolving standards of decency that mark the progress of a maturing society," *Trop v. Dulles*. . . , or which "involve the unnecessary and wanton infliction of pain," *Gregg v. Georgia* [1972]. . . .

These elementary principles establish the government's obligation to provide medical care for those whom it is punishing by incarceration. An inmate must rely on prison authorities to treat his medical needs; if the authorities fail to do so, those needs will not be met. In the worst cases, such a failure may actually produce physical "torture or a lingering death,". . . the evils of most concern to the drafters of the Amendment. In less serious cases, denial of medical care may result in pain and suffering which no one suggests would serve any penological interests. . . . The infliction of such unnecessary suffering is inconsistent with contemporary standards of decency as manifested in modern legislation codifying the common-law view that "it is but just that the public be required to care for the prisoner, who cannot by reason of the deprivation of his liberty, care for himself."

We therefore conclude that deliberate indifference to serious medical needs of prisoners constitutes the "unnecessary and wanton infliction of pain," . . . proscribed by the Eighth Amendment. This is true whether the indiffer-

ence is manifested by prison doctors in their response to the prisoner's needs or by prison guards in intentionally denying or delaying access to medical care or intentionally interfering with the treatment once prescribed. Regardless of how evidenced, deliberate indifference to a prisoner's serious illness or injury states a cause of action under [section] 1983.

This conclusion does not mean, however, that every claim by a prisoner that he has not received adequate medical treatment states a violation of the Eighth Amendment. An accident, although it may produce added anguish, is not the basis alone to be characterized as wanton infliction of unnecessary pain. . . .

Similarly, in the medical context, an inadvertent failure to provide adequate medical care cannot be said to constitute "an unnecessary and wanton infliction of pain" or to be "repugnant to the conscience of mankind." Thus, a complaint that a physician has been negligent in diagnosing or treating a medical condition does not state a valid claim of medical mistreatment under the Eighth Amendment. . . . In order to state a cognizable claim, a prisoner must allege acts or omissions sufficiently harmful to evidence deliberate indifference to serious medical needs. . . .

of the "punishment" referred to by the Eighth Amendment? The Supreme Court decided that medical care is among the services that states are required to supply for their prison inmates. In effect, contemporary standards of decency require that the government provide medical services for prisoners, who, by virtue of their incarceration, could not obtain such services for themselves. In addition, the deprivation of medical care can inflict pain and, in worst-case situations, lead to "physical 'torture or a lingering death'"—situations that the justices believed were clearly covered by the Eighth Amendment.

The lone dissenter, Justice John Paul Stevens, agreed that prisoners ought to be protected by the Eighth Amendment. He dissented, however, because he believed that the other justices were not providing enough protection for prisoners. Stevens was concerned that the "deliberate indifference" rule used by the Court incorrectly focused on the motives of corrections officials rather than on the conditions affecting the health and well-being of prisoners.

Stevens' analysis, in effect, raises the possibility that two prisoners suffering an identical harm—such as blurred vision and headaches—from a lack of medical services would receive different results in civil rights lawsuits. Suppose one pris-

Even applying these liberal standards, however, Gamble's claims against Dr. Gray, both in his capacity as treating physician and as medical director of the Corrections Department, are not cognizable under [section] 1983. [T]he question whether an X-ray or additional diagnostic techniques or forms of treatment is indicated is a classic example of a matter for medical judgment. A medical decision not to order an X-ray, or like measures, does not represent cruel and unusual punishment. At most it is medical malpractice, and as such the proper forum is the state court under the Texas Tort Claims Act.

JUSTICE STEVENS, dissenting:

Most of what is said in the Court's opinion is entirely consistent with the way the lower federal courts have been processing claims that the medical treatment of prison inmates is so inadequate as to constitute the cruel and unusual punishment prohibited by the Eighth Amendment. I have no serious disagreement with the way this area of the law has developed thus far, or with the probable impact of this opinion. Nevertheless, there are three reasons why I am unable to join it. First, insofar as the opinion orders the dismissal of the complaint against the chief medical officer of the prison, it is not faithful to the rule normally applied in construing allegations in a pleading prepared by an uncounseled inmate. Second, it does not adequately explain why the Court granted certiorari in this case. Third, it describes the state's duty to provide adequate medical care to prisoners in ambiguous terms which incorrectly relate to the subjective motivation of persons accused of violating the Eighth Amendment rather than to the standard of care required by the Constitution. . . .

[With respect to the third issue,] . . . by its repeated references to "deliberate indifference" and the "intentional" denial of adequate medical care, I believe the Court improperly attaches significance to the subjective motivation of the [prison officials] as a criterion for determining whether cruel and unusual punishment has been inflicted. Subjective motivation may well determine what, if any, remedy is appropriate against a particular defendant. However, whether the constitutional standard has been violated should turn on the character of the punishment rather than the motivation of the individual who inflicted it. Whether the conditions in Andersonville [a Civil War prison in which hundreds of Union troops held as prisoners of war died from disease and starvation] were the product of design, negligence, or mere poverty, they were cruel and unusual. . . .

oner was told, "We are concerned about your health so we called the doctor, who will be out to see you next week." That prisoner could not claim a rights violation—even if the prisoner became paralyzed two days later due to an undiagnosed stroke that was causing the blurred vision and headaches. By contrast, another prisoner suffering from the same symptoms and same outcome would experience a rights violation if prison officials had failed to take any action at all. Although the harm is the same—paralysis from an untreated stroke when officials did not respond immediately to reported symptoms—the legal situations are very different. But what if prison officials had given the second prisoner some aspirin? Would this simple act defeat an Eighth Amendment claim because the provision of aspirin showed that officials were not deliberately indifferent? In any case, Stevens believed that the Eighth Amendment analysis should focus on the harm suffered by the prisoner, not on the thoughts and motivation of prison officials.

In light of the majority opinion in *Estelle v. Gamble,* would a prisoner prevail in a lawsuit based on the hypothetical situation described in Box 9-2?

Before we examine other issues concerning prison conditions, you may want to look back at Box 3-1, which contained an actual complaint filed by a jail

A prisoner goes to the prison doctor complaining of back pains. The doctor examines the prisoner and gives him some aspirin. The next day, the prisoner returns with the same complaints and pleads, "Please take me to see a back specialist."

The doctor replies, "Just rest and take the aspirin. You'll be fine."

The prisoner responds, "But what if it doesn't get better?"

The doctor reacts angrily: "Look, I don't really care. I've got a lot of other prisoners who are much sicker than you. I don't have time for this. Rest and take the aspirin. Do as I say and stop bothering me."

Every day the prisoner asks to be taken to a specialist. Each request is denied. The prisoner writes to the warden, the state director of cor-

rections, federal judges, and even the governor of the state. Finally, after six months of constant complaining, the warden agrees to arrange for an examination by a back specialist.

After the examination, the specialist says to the prisoner, "You need major surgery on your back. If only you had come to see me several months ago, we might have been able to fix this with exercise and medication. However, you let it go too long, and now it will take surgery—and you still may have pain and mobility problems for the rest of your life."

The prisoner files a section 1983 action against prison officials charging deliberate indifference in denying him appropriate medical treatment. If you were the judge, based on *Estelle v. Gamble,* would you rule in favor of the prisoner?

inmate concerning inadequate medical treatment. Then reread the U.S. magistrate judge's report and recommendations in Box 3-2. Can you see how influential the decision in *Estelle v. Gamble* remains in determining the outcomes to prisoners' medical claims in the 1990s?

Prison Conditions

The U.S. Supreme Court addressed prison conditions in *Hutto v. Finney* (1978) (see Box 1-2).[2] The Court's opinion described the horrible conditions in punishment cells in Arkansas prisons. As many as ten or eleven prisoners were crowded into eight- by ten-foot cells with no furniture and a toilet that could only be flushed from outside the cell. The "grue" served to the prisoners each day for food did not provide enough calories to sustain even people who lie still all day, and thus the prisoners were effectively being starved. The justices endorsed the district judge's authority to issue orders to correct the unconstitutional conditions in the punishment cells. Amid the controversy over judicial action in prison reform cases, especially debates generated by Judge Frank Johnson's 1976 decision in *Pugh v. Locke,* the Supreme Court's first statement on such cases in 1978 provided support for continued action by federal judges. The Court's decision in *Hutto* demonstrated that the justices agreed that the Eighth Amendment applies to protect prisoners against overly harsh or otherwise inadequate living conditions.

The Court's next case involving conditions of confinement came in *Bell v. Wolfish* (1979), which will be discussed in greater detail in Chapter 11.[3] Because *Bell v. Wolfish* concerned living conditions and other practices affecting pretrial detainees at a federal jail, the Court applied Eighth Amendment–type standards in determining whether the detainees' right to due process was violated by the conditions. The Eighth Amendment itself could not be applied because the unconvicted pretrial detainees were not being "punished," and therefore the prohibition on "cruel and unusual punishments" did not apply. The Court examined whether "double bunking"—placing two detainees in rooms designed to hold one person—constituted "punishment" being applied to unconvicted detainees and therefore violated the right to due process. The Court applied the reasonableness test to conclude that no rights were violated. Because the Court's opinion emphasized that most detainees experienced double bunking for no more than sixty days, many observers took this to mean that the Court approved only short-term double bunking. The Court's next decision concerning conditions of confinement proved that interpretation to be incorrect.

In *Rhodes v. Chapman* (1981), prisoners in Ohio challenged the practice of "double celling"—housing two prisoners in cells designed to hold only one inmate.[4] The prisoners claimed that the double celling represented unconstitutional conditions of confinement because the inmates each had so few feet of living space within the crowded cells. How did the justices handle this claim? As you read the majority decision, which is excerpted in Box 9-3, see if the justices applied the same analysis as in *Estelle v. Gamble*?

In *Rhodes v. Chapman,* the Court rejected the Eighth Amendment claim. The district court decision rejected by the justices had relied, in part, on standards recommended by professional associations: "[T]he [district] court accepted as contemporary standards of decency several studies recommending that each person in an institution have at least 50–55 square feet of living space. In contrast, the double-celled inmates at SOCF share 63 square feet." The district court had cited the American Correctional Association's *Manual of Standards for Adult Correctional Institutions,* the National Sheriffs Association's *Handbook on Jail Architecture,* and the National Council on Crime and Delinquency's "Model Act for the Protection of the Rights of Prisoners." By rejecting the district court's decision favoring the prisoners' claims, the Supreme Court made it clear that professional associations do not define contemporary Eighth Amendment standards.

Justice Lewis Powell's opinion concluded that complaints about pain or discomfort do not establish Eighth Amendment violations. Powell stated that there is no fixed test for Eighth Amendment violations because *Trop v. Dulles* commands that judges apply society's evolving values. Thus, to show a constitutional violation, prison conditions must violate one of several tests that the Court employed itself or endorsed in lower court decisions. There must be "unnecessary and wanton inflictions of pain." Alternatively, the punishment must be "grossly disproportionate to the crime." Also, in reference to *Estelle v. Gamble,* an Eighth Amendment violation might be based on a prison condition producing "physical torture" or "pain without any penological purpose." Another possibility, established in *Hutto v. Finney,* was to show that conditions "resulted in unquestioned and serious deprivations of basic human needs."

JUSTICE POWELL delivered the opinion of the Court [joined by Chief Justice Burger and Justices Stewart, White, and Rehnquist].

The question presented is whether the housing of two inmates in a single cell at the Southern Ohio Correctional Facility (SOCF) is cruel and unusual punishment prohibited by the Eighth and Fourteenth Amendment. . . .

Each cell at SOCF measures approximately 63 square feet. Each contains a bed measuring 36 by 80 inches, a cabinet-type night stand, a wall-mounted sink with hot and cold running water, and a toilet that the inmate can flush from inside the cell. Cells housing two inmates have a two tiered bunk bed. Every cell has a heating and air circulation vent near the ceiling and 960 of the [1620] cells have a window that inmates can open and close. All of the cells have a cabinet, shelf, and radio built into one of the walls, and in all of the cells one wall consists of bars through which inmates can be seen. [In addition, there are dayrooms near the cells containing televisions and card tables where inmates, except those restricted to their cells, can spend most of the day.] . . .

[The district court found double celling unconstitutional because the prison exceeded its de-sign capacity, each inmate in a double cell had less than the recommended 50–55 square feet of living space to himself, and double celling had become a standard practice rather than a temporary condition.]

. . . Until this case, we have not considered a disputed contention that the conditions of confinement at a particular prison constituted cruel and unusual punishment. Nor have we had an occasion to consider specifically the principles relevant to assessing claims that conditions of confinement violate the Eighth Amendment. . . .

. . . Today the Eighth Amendment prohibits punishments which, although not physically barbarous, "involve the unnecessary and wanton infliction of pain," . . . or are grossly disproportionate to the severity of the crime. . . . Among "unnecessary and wanton" inflictions of pain are those that are "totally without penological justification." . . .

No static "test" can exist by which courts determine whether conditions of confinement are cruel and unusual, for the Eighth Amendment "must draw its meaning from the evolving standards of decency that mark the progress of a maturing society." *Trop v. Dulles* . . .

Note that the Court's reference to *Estelle v. Gamble* focused on the harm suffered by the prisoner, not on the attitudes and motives of the corrections officials. This point is even clearer in *Hutto,* where the Court's test looks solely at the nature of the conditions and does not depend at all on whether corrections officials were deliberately indifferent. In light of the various tests suggested by the *Rhodes* opinion, think back to the example at the beginning of Chapter 8. Does the prisoner's complaint about asbestos insulation establish an Eighth Amendment violation?

A Defense of Judicial Action in Prison Reform Cases

Several justices feared that the majority opinion in *Rhodes* would be interpreted as urging lower court judges to be less actively involved in overseeing and reme-dying unconstitutional conditions in prisons. Thus, Justice William Brennan, joined by Justices Harry Blackmun and John Paul Stevens, wrote a concurring

These principles apply when the conditions of confinement compose the punishment at issue. Conditions must not involve the wanton and unnecessary infliction of pain, nor may they be grossly disproportionate to the severity of the crime warranting imprisonment. In *Estelle v. Gamble,* . . . we held that the denial of medical care is cruel and unusual because, in the worst case, it can result in physical torture, and, even in less serious cases, it can result in pain without any penological purpose. . . . In *Hutto v. Finney,* . . . , the conditions of confinement in two Arkansas prisons constituted cruel and unusual punishment because they resulted in unquestioned and serious deprivations of basic human needs. Conditions other than those in *Gamble* and *Hutto,* alone or in combination, may deprive inmates of the minimal civilized measure of life's necessities. Such conditions could be cruel and unusual under the contemporary standard of decency that we recognized in *Gamble.* . . . But conditions that cannot be said to be cruel and unusual under contemporary standards are not unconstitutional. To the extent that such conditions are restrictive and even harsh, they are part of the penalty that criminal offenders pay for their offenses against society. . . .

. . . [The District Court's] general considerations fall far short in themselves of proving cruel and unusual punishment, for there is no evidence that double celling under these circumstances either inflicts unnecessary or wanton pain or is grossly disproportionate to the severity of crimes warranting imprisonment. At most, these considerations amount to a theory that double celling inflicts pain. Perhaps they reflect an aspiration toward an ideal environment for long-term confinement. But the Constitution does not mandate comfortable prisons, and prisons of SOCF's type, which house persons convicted of serious crimes, cannot be free of discomfort. . . .

. . . When conditions of confinement amount to cruel and unusual punishment, "federal courts will discharge their duty to protect constitutional rights." . . . In discharging this oversight responsibility, however, courts cannot assume that state legislatures and prison officials are insensitive to the requirements of the Constitution or to the perplexing sociological problems of how best to achieve the goals of the penal function in the criminal justice system: to punish justly, to deter future crime, and to return imprisoned persons to society with an improved chance of being useful, law-abiding citizens. . . .

opinion to encourage federal court judges to remain active and on guard against constitutional violations. Brennan agreed that the prisoners in *Rhodes* had not proved that their rights were violated, but he did not want this decision to signal a change of course for the federal courts in their protection of prisoners' rights. As you read Brennan's concurring opinion, excerpted in Box 9-4, consider why it is regarded by some observers as a straightforward response to all the critics who accused judges of improper judicial activism in prison reform cases.

Justice Brennan's opinion provided several of the primary justifications commonly presented to support judges' actions to safeguard prisoners' rights. First, prisoners are a politically powerless and despised minority within society. The public does not care what happens to them, and so there is little reason for elected officials to care about prison conditions and other aspects of prisoners' rights. Thus, the courts, and especially the federal courts with their tenured judges, are best positioned to make sure that the Constitution's protections apply to *all* people, even those who have earned their despised status by committing crimes.

BOX 9-4

Rhodes v. Chapman (1981) [concurring opinion]

JUSTICE BRENNAN, with whom JUSTICE BLACKMUN and JUSTICE STEVENS join, concurring in judgment.

Today's decision reaffirms that "[c]ourts certainly have a responsibility to scrutinize claims of cruel and unusual punishment." With that I agree. I also agree that the District Court's findings in this case do not support a judgment that the practice of double celling in the Southern Ohio Correctional Facility is in violation of the Eighth Amendment. I write separately, however, to emphasize that today's decision should in no way be construed as a retreat from careful judicial scrutiny of prison conditions, and to discuss the factors courts should consider in undertaking such scrutiny.

Although this Court has never before considered what prison conditions constitute "cruel and unusual punishment" within the meaning of the Eighth Amendment, . . . such questions have been addressed repeatedly by the lower courts. In fact, individual prisons or entire prison systems in at least 24 States have been declared unconstitutional under the Eighth and Fourteenth Amendments, with litigation underway in many others. Thus, the lower courts have learned from repeated investigation and bitter experience that judicial intervention is *indispensable* if constitutional dictates—not to mention considerations of basic humanity—are to be observed in the prisons.

No one familiar with litigation in this area could suggest that courts have been overeager to usurp the task of running prisons, which, as the Court today properly notes, is entrusted in the first instance to the "legislature and prison administration rather than a court." . . . And certainly, no one could suppose that the courts have ordered creation of "comfortable prisons," . . . on the model of country clubs. To the contrary, "the soul-chilling inhumanity of conditions in American prisons has been thrust upon the judicial conscience." . . .

Public apathy and the political powerlessness of inmates have contributed to the pervasive neglect of prisons. . . . [T]he courts have emerged as a critical force behind efforts to ameliorate inhumane conditions. Insulated as they are from political pressures, and charged with the duty of enforcing the Constitution, courts are in the strongest position to insist that unconstitutional conditions be remedied, even at significant financial cost. Justice Blackmun, then serving on the Court of Appeals, set the tone in *Jackson v. Bishop* . . . : "Humane considerations and constitutional requirements are not, in this day, to be measured or limited by dollar considerations. . . ."

Second, judges have learned through experience with prisoners' cases that the other branches of government cannot be relied upon to ensure the existence of constitutional protections and proper conditions within corrections institutions. Indeed, Brennan noted that some corrections officials privately welcome judicial action because it can help push legislative and executive branch officials to provide needed funds for creating and maintaining professionally managed prisons.

Third, Brennan indicated that constitutional rights are such valued possessions under our system of government that they must be protected, no matter what the financial cost. A state's claim that "it will cost too much to fix" should not be permitted to prevent prisoners from receiving the Constitution's protections.

Justice Blackmun's concurring opinion reinforced the view that judges cannot defer to the judgment of other government officials about how prisons

Progress toward constitutional conditions of confinement in the Nation's prisons has been slow and uneven, despite judicial pressure. Nevertheless, it is clear that judicial intervention has been responsible, not only for remedying some of the worst abuses by direct order, but also for "forcing the legislative branch of government to reevaluate correction policies and to appropriate funds for upgrading penal institutions."

Even prison officials have acknowledged that judicial intervention has helped them to obtain support for needed reform. . . .

. . . [A] court considering an Eighth Amendment challenge to conditions of confinement must examine the totality of circumstances. Even if no single condition of confinement would be unconstitutional in itself, "exposure to the cumulative effect of prison conditions may subject inmates to cruel and unusual punishment." . . .

In determining when prison conditions pass beyond legitimate punishment and become cruel and unusual punishment, the "touchstone is the effect upon the imprisoned." . . . The court must examine the effect upon inmates of the physical plant, . . . ventilation, . . . sanitation, . . . safety, . . . inmate needs and services, . . . and staffing. . . . When "the cumulative impact of the conditions of incarceration threatens the physical, mental, and emotional health and well-being of the inmates and/or creates a probability of recidivism and future incarceration," the court must conclude that the conditions violate the Constitution. . . .

JUSTICE BLACKMUN, concurring in judgment.

. . . I perceive, as Justice Brennan obviously does in view of his separate writing, a possibility that the Court's opinion in this case today might be regarded, because of some of its language, as a signal to prison administrators that the federal courts are now to adopt a policy of general deference to such administrators and to state legislatures, deference not only for the purpose of determining contemporary standards of decency, . . . but for the purpose of determining whether conditions at a particular prison are cruel and unusual within the meaning of the Eighth Amendment. . . . That was perhaps the old attitude prevalent several decades ago. I join Justice Brennan's opinion because I, too, feel that the federal courts must continue to be available to those state inmates who sincerely claim that the conditions to which they are subjected are violative of the [Eighth] Amendment. . . .

JUSTICE MARSHALL, dissenting.

. . . In a doubled cell, each inmate has only 30–35 square feet of floor space. Most of the windows in the Supreme Court building are larger than that. The conclusion of every expert who testified at trial and of every serious study of which I am aware is that a long-term inmate must have to himself, at the very least, 50 square feet of floor space—an area smaller than that occupied by a good-sized automobile—in order to avoid serious mental, emotional, and physical deterioration. . . .

should be run. Judges are responsible for protecting individual rights, and they must make sure that corrections officials respect those rights in managing their prisons.

In his dissenting opinion, Justice Marshall agreed with Brennan's ideas but disagreed with the conclusion that the prisoners in this case had not demonstrated that their rights were violated. Marshall believed that the lack of living space for each prisoner within the double cells created crowded conditions that violated the Eighth Amendment.

Recent Developments

In the decade after the *Rhodes* decision, the Supreme Court's composition changed significantly. In the 1980s, president Ronald Reagan appointed three new justices—Sandra Day O'Connor, Antonin Scalia, and Anthony Kennedy—and elevated William Rehnquist to chief justice upon the retirement of Chief Justice Warren Burger. Then, in 1990, President George Bush appointed David Souter to replace the retiring Justice William Brennan. As Republicans, both Reagan and Bush sought to appoint conservative justices who would be less willing to recognize rights for criminal defendants and prisoners. As a result, the Court's decisions concerning many constitutional rights issues tended to favor the government instead of individual claimants.

In *Wilson v. Seiter* **(1991),** the Court shifted direction in analyzing cases involving conditions of confinement. Pearly Wilson raised a number of claims against an Ohio prison, including overcrowding, excessive noise, poor ventilation, and unsanitary food preparation. As you read the Court's opinion in Box 9-5, look carefully to the test applied by the majority of justices to determine whether conditions of confinement violate the Eighth Amendment.

Notice that the five-member majority in *Wilson v. Seiter* consisted entirely of justices appointed to the Court or elevated to chief justice by Presidents Reagan and Bush. Clearly, the new appointees since the *Rhodes* decision in 1981 determined the outcome of the case.

In *Wilson v. Seiter,* Justice Scalia's majority opinion draws from the test for inadequate medical care in *Estelle v. Gamble* and expands that test to cover all Eighth Amendment conditions-of-confinement situations. Thus, after *Wilson,* the courts may not merely look to see if prison conditions are inhumane and horrible. Instead, to establish an Eighth Amendment violation, prisoners must show inadequate conditions *and* "deliberate indifference" on the part of corrections officials. Horrible conditions alone no longer constitute an Eighth Amendment violation. As we saw in *Estelle,* the introduction of a "deliberate indifference" test makes it much more difficult for prisoners to win cases concerning conditions of confinement. Now they must present proof of the corrections officials' thoughts or motives.

Scalia's opinion seems to claim that the application of the "deliberate indifference" test to all conditions-of-confinement situations is merely the natural extension of the Court's existing precedents. The opinion cited *Estelle v. Gamble* and *Whitley v. Albers* to show that other Eighth Amendment cases required a showing of corrections officials' thinking or motives in order to prove a constitutional violation. Is this a correct and complete review of the relevant precedents?

What about *Hutto v. Finney* (1978), a key case—unlike *Estelle v. Gamble* (medical care) and *Whitley v. Albers* (use of force)—that is similar to *Wilson v. Seiter* in raising claims about *living conditions* within a prison? Justice Powell's majority opinion in *Rhodes v. Chapman* (1981) had noted that "In *Hutto v. Finney*, . . . , the conditions of confinement in two Arkansas prisons constituted cruel and unusual punishment because they resulted in unquestioned and serious deprivations of basic human needs." This *Hutto* test focused exclusively on the actual conditions and did not examine the thoughts or motives of corrections officials. Scalia's opinion appears to ignore *Hutto* in favor of prior cases that were more supportive of the "deliberate indifference" test that he wished to apply to prison conditions cases. Did he forget about *Hutto?* Did he ignore *Hutto?* Or is *Hutto* not actually a relevant precedent for the *Wilson* case?

B O X 9 - 5	***Wilson v. Seiter*, 501 U.S. 294 (1991)**

JUSTICE SCALIA delivered the opinion of the Court [joined by Chief Justice Rehnquist and Justices O'Connor, Kennedy, and Souter].

This case presents the question whether a prisoner claiming that conditions of confinement constitute cruel and unusual punishment must show a culpable state of mind on the part of prison officials and, if so, what state of mind is required.

Petitioner Pearly L. Wilson is a felon incarcerated at the Hocking Correctional Facility (HCF) in Nelsonville, Ohio. Alleging that a number of the conditions of his confinement constituted cruel and unusual punishment in violation of the Eighth and Fourteenth Amendment, he brought this action under 42 U.S.C. [section] 1983. . . . The complaint alleged overcrowding, excessive noise, insufficient ventilation, unclean and inadequate restrooms, unsanitary dining facilities and food preparation, and housing with mentally and physically ill inmates. Petitioner sought declaratory and injunctive relief, as well as $900,000 in compensatory and punitive damages. . . .

The District Court granted summary judgment for respondents [the prison officials]. The Court of Appeals for the Sixth Circuit affirmed . . . , and we granted certiorari . . .

The Eighth Amendment, which applies to the States through the Due Process Clause of the Fourteenth Amendment, . . . prohibits the infliction of "cruel and unusual punishments" on those convicted of crimes. In *Estelle v. Gamble*, . . . we first acknowledged that the provision could be applied to some deprivations that were not specifically part of the sentence but were suffered during imprisonment. We rejected, however, the inmate's claim in that case that prison doctors had inflicted cruel and unusual punishment by inadequately attending to his medical needs—because he had failed to establish that they possessed a sufficiently culpable state of mind. Since, we said, only the "'unnecessary and *wanton* infliction of pain'"

implicates the Eighth Amendment, . . . a prisoner advancing such a claim must, at a minimum, allege "deliberate indifference" to his "serious" medical needs. . . .

Our holding in *Rhodes [v. Chapman]* turned on the objective component of an Eighth Amendment prison claim (was the deprivation sufficiently serious?), and we did not consider the subjective component (did the officials act with a sufficiently culpable state of mind?). That *Rhodes* had not eliminated the subjective component was made clear by our next relevant case, *Whitley v. Albers* [1986]. . . . There an inmate shot by a guard during an attempt to quell a prison disturbance contended that he had been subjected to cruel and unusual punishment. We stated:

>"*After incarceration, only the unnecessary and wanton infliction of pain . . . constitutes cruel and unusual punishment forbidden by the Eighth Amendment. To be cruel and unusual punishment, conduct that does not purport to be punishment at all must involve more than ordinary lack of due care for the prisoner's interests or safety. . . . It is* obduracy and wantonness, not inadvertence or error in good faith, *that characterize the conduct prohibited by the Cruel and Unusual Punishments Clause, whether that conduct occurs in connection with establishing conditions of confinement, supplying medical needs, or restoring official control over a tumultuous cellblock. . . .*

These cases mandate inquiry into a prison official's state of mind when it is claimed that the official has inflicted cruel and unusual punishment. . . . Petitioner concedes that this is so with respect to *some* claims of cruel and unusual prison conditions. He acknowledges, for instance, that, if a prison boiler malfunctions accidentally during a cold winter, an inmate would have no basis for an Eighth Amendment

(continued)

claim, even if he suffers objectively significant harm. . . . Petitioner, and the United States [government] as *amicus curiae* in support of petitioner, suggests that we should draw a distinction between "short-term" or "one-time" conditions (in which a state of mind requirement would apply) and "continuing" or "systemic" conditions (where official state of mind would be irrelevant). We perceive neither a logical nor a practical basis for that distinction. The source of the intent requirement is not the predilections of this Court, but the Eighth Amendment itself, which bans only cruel and unusual *punishment*. If the pain inflicted is not formally meted out as *punishment* by the statute or the sentencing judge, some mental element must be attributed to the inflicting officer before it can qualify. . . .

The United States [government] suggests that a state of mind inquiry might allow officials to interpose the defense that, despite good faith efforts to obtain funding, fiscal constraints, beyond their control prevent the elimination of inhumane conditions. Even if that were so, it is hard to understand how it could control the meaning of "cruel and unusual punishment" in the Eighth Amendment. An intent requirement is either implicit in the word "punishment" or is not; it cannot be alternately required and ignored as policy considerations might dictate. At any rate, the validity of a "cost" defense as negating the requisite intent is not at issue in this case, since respondents have never advanced it. Nor, we might note, is there any indication that other officials have sought to use such a defense to avoid the holding of *Estelle v. Gamble*. . . .

. . . *Whitley* makes clear, however, that, in this context, wantonness does not have a fixed meaning, but must be determined with "due regard for differences in the kind of conduct against which an Eighth Amendment objection is lodged." . . . Where (as in *Whitley*) officials act in response to a prison disturbance, their actions are necessarily taken "in haste, under pressure," and balanced against "competing institutional concerns for the safety of prison staff or other inmates." . . . In such an emergency situation, we found that wantonness consisted of acting "'maliciously and sadistically for the very purpose of causing harm.'" . . . In contrast, "the State's responsibility to attend to the medical needs of prisoners does not ordinarily clash with other equally important governmental responsibilities," . . . so that, in that context, as *Estelle* held, "deliberate indifference" would constitute wantonness. . . .

. . . Some conditions of confinement may establish an Eighth Amendment violation "in combination" when each would not do so alone but only when they have a mutually enforcing effect that produces the deprivation of a single, identifiable human need such as food, warmth, or exercise—for example, a low cell temperature at night combined with a failure to issue blankets. . . . To say that some prison conditions may interact in this fashion is a far cry from saying that all prison conditions are a seamless web for Eighth Amendment purposes. Nothing so amorphous as "overall conditions" can rise to the level of cruel and unusual punishment when no specific deprivation of a single human need exists. . . .

Scalia's opinion also rejected potential claims based on the "totality of conditions" in institutions. Instead, claimants must demonstrate the "deprivation of a single, identifiable human need such as food, warmth, or exercise—for example, a low cell temperature at night combined with a failure to issue blankets."

Among justices in the *Wilson* majority, only Chief Justice Rehnquist was on the Supreme Court when it made its prior decisions about general conditions of confinement in *Hutto v. Finney* and *Rhodes v. Chapman*. By contrast, all four of the justices in *Wilson* who disagreed with the majority were on the Court when the previous conditions-of-confinement cases were decided. They disagreed

BOX 9-6   *Wilson v. Seiter* (1991) [opinion concurring only with the judgment]

JUSTICE WHITE, with whom JUSTICE MARSHALL, JUSTICE BLACKMUN, and JUSTICE STEVENS join, concurring in the judgment.

The majority holds that prisoners challenging the conditions of their confinement under the Eighth Amendment must show "deliberate indifference" by the responsible officials. Because that requirement is inconsistent with our prior decisions, I concur only in the judgment.

It is well established, and the majority does not dispute, that pain or other suffering that is part of the punishment imposed on convicted criminals is subject to Eighth Amendment scrutiny without regard to an intent requirement. The linchpin of the majority's analysis therefore is its assertion that "[i]f the pain inflicted is not formally meted out *as punishment by the statute or the sentencing judge,* some mental element must be attributed to the influencing official before it can qualify". . . [emphasis added]. That reasoning disregards our prior decisions that have involved challenges to conditions of confinement, where we have made it clear that the conditions are themselves *part of the punishment,* even though not specifically "meted out" by a statute or judge.

We first considered the relationship between the Eighth Amendment and conditions of confinement in *Hutto v. Finney* [1978]. . . . There the District Court had entered a series of remedial orders after determining that the conditions

in the Arkansas prison system violated the Eighth Amendment. The prison officials, while conceding that the conditions were cruel and unusual, challenged two aspects of the District Court's relief: (1) an order limiting punitive isolation to 30 days; and (2) an award of attorneys' fees [to the prisoners' attorneys].

In upholding the District Court's limitation on punitive isolation, we first made clear that the conditions of confinement are part of the punishment that is subject to Eighth Amendment scrutiny. Focusing only on the objective conditions of confinement, we then explained that we found "no error in the [district] court's conclusion that, taken as a whole, conditions in the isolation cells continued to violate the prohibition against cruel and unusual punishment."

In *Rhodes v. Chapman* [1981] . . . [we stated that] "No static 'test' can exist by which courts determine whether conditions of confinement are cruel and unusual, for the Eighth Amendment "must draw its meaning from the evolving standards of decency that mark the progress of a maturing society." *Trop v. Dulles.* . . .

We then explained how those principles operate in the context of a challenge to conditions of confinement:

"*These principles apply when the conditions of confinement compose the punishment at issue.* Conditions must not involve wanton and

(*continued*)

with the majority's reasoning in *Wilson,* but they agreed that the prisoner should not prevail in this case. Thus, their disagreement was expressed in an opinion concurring with the judgment but not with the legal rule applied. They obviously disagreed with the newer justices' descriptions of the cases that they—the experienced justices—had decided prior to the newcomers' appointments. As you read Box 9-6, which excerpts the experienced justices' opinion, ask yourself: Who has a more accurate view of the meaning of the Supreme Court's earlier decisions on the Eighth Amendment and conditions of confinement—the newcomers in the *Wilson* majority or the four veteran justices who joined a different opinion?

unnecessary infliction of pain, nor may they be grossly disproportionate to the severity of the crime warranting imprisonment. In *Estelle v. Gamble* . . . we held that the denial of medical care is cruel and unusual because, in the worst case, it can result in physical torture, and, even in less serious cases, it can result in pain without any penological purpose. . . . In *Hutto v. Finney,* . . . the conditions of confinement in two Arkansas prisons constituted cruel and unusual punishment because they resulted in unquestioned and serious deprivations of basic human needs. Conditions other than those in *Gamble* and *Hutto,* alone or in combination, may deprive inmates of the minimal civilized measure of life's necessities. Such conditions could be cruel and unusual under the contemporary standard of decency that we recognized in *Gamble."*

. . . *Rhodes* makes it crystal clear, therefore, that Eighth Amendment challenges to conditions of confinement are to be treated like Eighth Amendment challenges to punishment that is "formally meted out *as punishment* by the statute or the sentencing judge," . . . —we examine only the objective severity, not the subjective intent of government officials.

The majority relies upon our decisions in *Louisiana ex rel. Francis v. Resweber* [1947, concerning a malfunctioning electric chair that caused a prisoner to face a second attempt at execution]; *Estelle v. Gamble* [1976, concerning a claim about the deprivation of medical care]; and *Whitley v. Albers* [1986, concerning a prisoner who was shot when officers attempted to quell a disturbance], but none of those cases involved a challenge to conditions of confinement. . . . The distinction is crucial because unlike "conduct that does not purport to be punishment at all," as in *Gamble* and *Whitley,* the Court has not made intent an element of a cause of action challenging unconstitutional conditions of confinement." . . .

Moreover, *Whitley* expressly supports an objective standard for challenges to conditions of confinement. There, in discussing the Eighth Amendment, we stated:

> . . . [H]*arsh conditions of confinement" may constitute cruel and unusual punishment unless such conditions "are part of the penalty that criminal offenders pay for their offenses against society."* . . .

Not only is the majority's intent requirement a departure from precedent, it likely will prove impossible to apply in many cases. Inhumane prison conditions often are the result of cumulative actions and inactions by numerous officials inside and outside a prison, sometimes over a long period of time. In those circumstances, it is far from clear whose intent should be examined, and the majority offers no real guidance on this issue. In truth, intent simply is not very meaningful when considering a challenge to an institution, such as a prison system.

The majority's approach is also unwise. It leaves open the possibility, for example, that prison officials will be able to defeat a [section] 1983 action challenging inhumane prison conditions simply by showing that the conditions are caused by insufficient funding from the state legislature, rather than by any deliberate indifference on the part of prison officials. . . . In my view, having chosen to use imprisonment as a form of punishment, a state must ensure that the conditions in its prisons comport with the "contemporary standards of decency" required by the Eighth Amendment. . . . As the United States [government] argues: "[S]eriously inhumane, pervasive conditions should not be insulated from constitutional challenge because the officials managing the institution have exhibited a conscientious concern for ameliorating its problems, and have made efforts (albeit unsuccessful) to that end. . . . *The ultimate result of today's decision, I fear, is that "serious deprivations of basic human needs,"* . . . will go unredressed due to an unnecessary and meaningless search for "deliberate indifference."

These justices disagreed with the majority's presentation of prior Supreme Court decisions. They not only questioned why *Hutto v. Finney* was omitted from Scalia's discussion in the majority opinion but also disagreed with how the other cases were described. These justices clearly believed that conditions of confinement alone can violate the Eighth Amendment, no matter what corrections officials were thinking—just as Justice Stevens had argued in the dissenting opinion in *Estelle v. Gamble* (1976). Justice White's dissenting opinion expressed concerns that corrections officials would escape responsibility for violations simply by saying, "We were concerned about the poor prison conditions, but we just didn't have the money to fix things." This kind of statement would show that there was no "deliberate indifference," yet the prisoners would still suffer from inadequate conditions.

Justice White also raised the possibility that the search for "deliberate indifference"—evidence of a specific thought or motive on the part of corrections officials—would ignore the actual manner in which inadequate conditions develop. White noted that conditions may be produced by "cumulative action" over a long period of time. For example, one official may decide that a prison should not be expanded or renovated. Subsequently, another official may decide to send more prisoners into the institution. Still later, yet another official may decide that four prisoners must occupy each cell because there is no place else to put all of the prisoners who have been sent to the institution. No single decision "caused" excessive overcrowding, yet a series of decisions over a number of years can produce inadequate living conditions—even without any specific individual demonstrating "deliberate indifference." However, if section 1983 actions must show that a "person . . . cause[d]" a constitutional violation, does White's argument about cumulative decisions effectively expand section 1983 beyond its intended purpose?

The other key difference highlighted by White's opinion is the disagreement among the justices about the nature of "punishment" in assessing what constitutes "cruel and unusual punishment." Scalia's majority opinion claimed that conditions of confinement are not "punishment," because they are not formally imposed by a legislature or judge in defining a sentence. Therefore, for conditions of confinement to be considered "punishment" covered by the Eighth Amendment, there must be some motive or intention (i.e., "deliberate indifference") on the part of corrections officials to impose inadequate conditions on prisoners as part of punishing them for their crimes. The four senior justices disagreed. They argued that the conditions themselves were automatically part of the punishment experienced by incarcerated prisoners; therefore, improper conditions by themselves can violate the Eighth Amendment.

After the decision in *Wilson v. Seiter,* interested observers waited to see if the Court would make it even more difficult for prisoners to win conditions-of-confinement lawsuits. The next indication of the Court's approach came in *Helling v. McKinney* (1993), in which a prisoner sued corrections officials for placing him in a small cell with a chain-smoking inmate. He claimed that the exposure to second-hand smoke in the cell was harmful to his health. In its decision, which is excerpted in Box 9-7, does the Court use *Helling* as an opportunity

BOX 9-7

Helling v. McKinney, 509 U.S. 25 (1993)

JUSTICE WHITE delivered the opinion of the Court.

This case requires us to decide whether the health risk posed by involuntary exposure of a prison inmate to environmental tobacco smoke (ETS) can form the basis of a claim for relief under the Eighth Amendment.

Respondent is serving a sentence of imprisonment in the Nevada prison system. . . . The complaint . . . alleged that respondent was assigned to a cell with another inmate who smoked five packs of cigarettes a day. The complaint also stated that cigarettes were sold to inmates without properly informing of the health hazards nonsmoking inmates would encounter by sharing a room with an inmate who smoked, . . . and that certain cigarettes burned continuously, releasing some type of chemical. . . . Respondent complained of certain health problems allegedly caused by exposure to cigarette smoke. . . .

We have great difficulty agreeing [with the prison officials' argument] that prison authorities may not be deliberately indifferent to an inmate's current health problems but may ignore a condition of confinement that is sure or very likely to cause serious illness and needless suffering the next week or month or year. In *Hutto v. Finney ,* . . . we noted that inmates in punitive isolation were crowded into cells and that some of them had infectious maladies such as hepatitis and venereal disease. This was one of the prison conditions for which the Eighth Amendment required a remedy, even though it was not

alleged that the likely harm would occur immediately and even the possible infection might not affect all of those exposed. We would think that a prison inmate also could successfully complain about demonstrably unsafe drinking water without waiting for an attack of dysentery. Nor can we hold that prison officials may be deliberately indifferent to the exposure of inmates to a serious communicable disease on the ground that the complaining inmates show no serious current symptoms.

That the Eighth Amendment protects against future harm to inmates is not a novel proposition. The Amendment, as we have said, requires that inmates be furnished with the basic human needs, one of which is "reasonable safety,". . . It is "cruel and unusual punishment to hold convicted criminals in unsafe conditions." . . . It would be odd to deny an injunction to inmates who plainly proved an unsafe, life-threatening condition in their prison on the ground that nothing yet had happened to them. . . . We thus reject petitioners' central thesis that only deliberate indifference to current serious health problems of inmates is actionable under the Eighth Amendment. . . .

We affirm the holding of the Court of Appeals that McKinney states a cause of action under the Eighth Amendment by alleging that petitioners have, with deliberate indifference, exposed him to levels of ETS that pose an unreasonable risk of serious damage to his future health. . . .

to make it even more difficult for prisoners to pursue lawsuits alleging unconstitutional conditions of confinement?

As you can see, the majority of justices decided not to make prisoner lawsuits more difficult. The *Helling* decision applied the standard established in *Wilson v. Seiter*—namely, the requirement that "deliberate indifference" by corrections officials be demonstrated. However, the justices did not insist that the prisoner prove that he had already suffered a serious injury from breathing his cellmate's cigarette smoke. As Justice Byron White pointed out, when prisoners are exposed to dangerous or unhealthy conditions, they need not wait until they suffer from a serious or life-threatening illness before asserting claims about improper conditions of confinement. As a practical matter, the potential risk of liability from this situation cannot help but force prison administrators to consider smoking bans or other strategies to address this potential problem.[5] What impact does this case have, if any, upon your analysis of the asbestos insulation example at the beginning of Chapter 8?

In a dissenting opinion, Justices Clarence Thomas and Antonin Scalia took the opportunity to express openly their view that the Eighth Amendment does not protect prisoners from unhealthy or unsafe conditions of confinement. You may recall from Chapter 7 that Thomas and Scalia expressed doubts about prisoners' Eighth Amendment rights in their dissenting opinion in *Hudson v. McMillian* (1992) the preceding year. That was the case in which the guards beat up the shackled prisoner and the prisoner was permitted to sue even though he did not suffer from "serious" injuries. In their *Helling* dissent, Thomas and Scalia openly stated that the Eighth Amendment does not protect prisoners inside corrections institutions. They have two primary justifications for this conclusion. First, conditions of confinement are not "punishment" under the Eighth Amendment. This idea was raised in Scalia's majority opinion in *Wilson v. Seiter,* but Scalia and Thomas did not pursue its full implications until the *Helling* decision. Thus, the Eighth Amendment limits the kinds of sentences judges can pronounce in court, but it does not protect incarcerated offenders as those sentences are carried out over succeeding days, months, and years. Second, Thomas and Scalia believe that the Eighth Amendment (and other parts of the Constitution) should be interpreted according to the intentions of the framers (1789–1791) who wrote and ratified the Bill of Rights. According to their analysis, the people who wrote and ratified the Eighth Amendment did not intend for it to protect people in prison against unpleasant or inhumane conditions of confinement.

As you read Justice Thomas's opinion in Box 9-8, ask yourself: What would be the results for prison conditions and prisoners' rights generally if a majority of justices adopted the views of Thomas and Scalia?

The views expressed by Thomas and Scalia have several important implications. First, they would reject the *Trop v. Dulles* approach of interpreting the Eighth Amendment according to society's evolving standards of decency. Instead, they would define "cruel and unusual punishments"—now and forever—as they believe it was defined in 1791. Second, they would overturn all Supreme Court decisions recognizing Eighth Amendment rights for prisoners, including *Estelle v. Gamble, Hutto v. Finney, Hudson v. McMillian,* and *Helling v. McKinney.* Third, they would effectively prohibit federal judges from examining and remedying problems with conditions of confinement in corrections institutions.[6] Instead, they would leave such matters to the states, presumably permitting corrections officials to handle all management decisions in prisons unless state law provided an opportunity for state judges to supervise and intervene. This approach, of course, raises questions about whether elected officials, including elected state judges, have sufficient independence from and immunity to political pressure to make courageous decisions on behalf of society's most despised

JUSTICE THOMAS, with whom JUSTICE SCALIA joins, dissenting.

The Eighth Amendment provides that "[e]xcessive bail shall not be required, nor excessive fines imposed, nor cruel and unusual punishments inflicted." The Court holds that a prisoner states a cause of action under the Cruel and Unusual Punishments Clause by alleging that prison officials, with deliberate indifference, have exposed him to an unreasonable risk of harm. This decision, like every other "conditions of confinement" case since *Estelle v. Gamble* . . . rests on the premise that deprivations suffered by a prisoner constitute "punishmen[t]" for Eighth Amendment purposes, even when the deprivations have not been inflicted as part of a criminal sentence. . . . I have serious doubts about this premise.

At the time the Eighth Amendment was ratified, the word "punishment" referred to the penalty imposed for the commission of a crime. . . . That is also the primary definition of the word today. . . . And this understanding of the word, of course, does not encompass a prisoner's injuries that bear no relation to his sentence.

Nor, as far as I know, is there any historical evidence indicating that the framers and ratifiers of the Eighth Amendment had anything other than this common understanding of "punishment" in mind. . . . Just as there was no suggestion in English constitutional history that harsh prison conditions might otherwise constitute cruel and unusual (or otherwise illegal) "punishment," the debates surrounding the framing and ratification of our own Constitution and Bill of Rights were silent regarding this possibility. . . .

Judicial interpretations of the Cruel and Unusual Punishments Clause were, until quite recently, consistent with its text and history. . . . This Court did not so much as intimate that the Cruel and Unusual Punishments Clause might reach prison conditions for the first 185 years of the provision's existence. It was not until the 1960s that lower courts began applying the Eighth Amendment to prison deprivations . . . , and it was not until 1976, in *Estelle v. Gamble,* that this Court first did so.

Thus, although the evidence is not overwhelming, I believe that the text and history of the Eighth Amendment, together with the decisions interpreting it, support the view that judges or juries—but not jailers—impose "punishment." At a minimum, I believe that the original meaning of "punishment," the silence in the historical record, and the 185 years of uniform precedent shift the burden of persuasion to those who would apply the Eighth Amendment to prison conditions. In my view, that burden has not yet been discharged. It was certainly not discharged in *Estelle v. Gamble.* . . .

To state a claim under the Cruel and Unusual Punishments Clause, a party must prove not only that the challenged conduct was both cruel and unusual, but also that it constitutes *punishment*. The text and history of the Eighth Amendment, together with pre-*Estelle* precedent, raise substantial doubts in my mind that the Eighth Amendment proscribes a prison deprivation that is not inflicted as part of a sentence. And *Estelle* itself has not dispelled these doubts. Were the issue squarely presented, therefore, I might vote to overrule *Estelle*. I need not make that decision today, however, because this case is not a straightforward application of *Estelle*. It is, instead, an extension.

In *Hudson,* the Court extended *Estelle* to cases in which the prisoner has suffered only minor injuries; here it extends *Estelle* to cases in which there has been no injury at all. Because I seriously doubt that *Estelle* was correctly decided, I decline to join the Court's holding. *Stare decisis* [obedience to case precedents] may call for hesitation in overruling a dubious precedent, but it does not demand that such a precedent be expanded to its outer limits. I would draw the line at actual, serious injuries and reject the claim that exposure to the *risk* of injury can violate the Eighth Amendment.

political minority—convicted offenders. This approach clearly clashes with the trend established by Judge Frank Johnson's decision in *Pugh v. Locke,* which apparently was based on the view that the legislative and executive officials who created inhumane conditions in prisons cannot be trusted to monitor, identify, and correct those conditions on their own.

Even if one accepts the Thomas–Scalia view that original intentions should determine how the Constitution is interpreted—and the other justices obviously do not accept that view, especially with respect to the Eighth Amendment—there are potential problems with the analysis presented by Thomas and Scalia. For example, Scalia has admitted in a published article that he would not follow original intent in all circumstances involving the Eighth Amendment. For example, he would not permit whipping even though it was an acceptable punishment in 1791.[7] If he is selective in his application of original intent interpretation, why apply it to prisoners' rights and not to all other Eighth Amendment situations?

In addition, Thomas takes a questionable approach to interpreting history when he claims that the framers of the Eighth Amendment did not intend for it to apply to prisons. In fact, there were no institutions like our modern prisons in 1791. Incarceration was just being developed as a means of punishment, and prisons did not even exist in the United States until the nineteenth century.[8] For example, one study found that only nineteen criminal offenders were sentenced to jail as a form of punishment in New York during the entire period from 1691 to 1776.[9] How can original intent be applied as an approach to constitutional interpretation when discussing an institution—the modern prison—that was unknown to the Eighth Amendment's authors and ratifiers? How can anyone know what the Eighth Amendment's framers would have thought about the issue of prison conditions when they only had knowledge of conditions in local jails that were used for short-term confinement? Although Thomas may, in fact, be correct in assessing what the framers would have thought about prisons, how can we know for sure? He does not confront the difficulty involved in applying original intent to prisons because he simply assumes—inaccurately—that prisons were a common form of punishment when the Eighth Amendment was drafted and ratified.

After *Helling,* the U.S. Supreme Court decided *Farmer v. Brennan* (1994).[10] Farmer was a transsexual prisoner with feminine characteristics (he had taken female hormone injections) who was transferred to a higher-security prison for disciplinary reasons. The higher-security prison contained inmates with records of serious, violent crimes, and Farmer was beaten and raped by a fellow inmate. He filed suit against corrections officials claiming that they showed "deliberate indifference" to his safety by placing him among violent prisoners likely to victimize him because of his feminine appearance and characteristics. The case concerned the precise definition of "deliberate indifference." Decisions by circuit courts of appeals were in conflict on the issue. One court said that to show "deliberate indifference," a prisoner in Farmer's position must demonstrate that corrections officials *actually knew* that his or her safety was threatened by his placement with higher-security prisoners.[11] Another court said that officials could be liable if a prisoner could demonstrate that the officials *should have known* about a serious danger to an inmate.[12] The U.S. Supreme Court endorsed the standard requiring proof that officials actually knew about excessive risks to inmates' health and safety. This standard is more difficult for prisoners to prove and provides corrections officials with greater protection against liability. As stated in Justice David Souter's majority opinion:

> We reject petitioner's invitation to adopt an objective test for deliberate indifference. We hold instead that a prison official cannot be found liable under the Eighth Amendment for denying an inmate humane conditions of confinement unless the official knows of and disregards an excessive risk to inmate health or safety; the official must both be aware of facts from which the inference could be drawn that a substantial risk of serious harm exists, and he must also draw the inference.

Although the Supreme Court imposed the more difficult standard of proof on prisoners, Souter's opinion indicated that the justices did not intend to permit corrections officials to hide behind claims of ignorance. The justices invited trial court judges and jurors to draw conclusions about the officials' knowledge based on facts defining the circumstances in which the officials worked:

> [I]f an Eighth Amendment plaintiff presents evidence showing that a substantial risk of inmate attacks was "longstanding, pervasive, well-documented, or expressly noted by prison official in the past, and the circumstances suggest that the defendant-official being sued had been exposed to information concerning the risk and thus 'must have known' about it, then such evidence could be sufficient to permit a trier of fact to find that the defendant-official had actual knowledge of the risk."

As in *Helling,* the majority did not follow Thomas's suggestion to curtail prisoners' conditions-of-confinement lawsuits. In a concurring opinion, Thomas repeated his view that the Eighth Amendment does not regulate prison conditions. In his mind, it applies only to punishments imposed as part of a sentence, and not to circumstances involved in carrying out the sentence.

SUMMARY

- The U.S. Supreme Court endorsed the lower courts' authority to remedy prison conditions under the Eighth Amendment in *Hutto v. Finney.* The Court included medical services under Eighth Amendment protections, but prisoners are entitled only to be free of "deliberate indifference" in depriving them of medical care for serious needs.

- When the Supreme Court decided that double celling did not violate the Eighth Amendment, several justices expressed concern that the Supreme Court should continue to encourage lower court judges to watch carefully for constitutional violations.

- After the Supreme Court's composition changed from appointments made by

Presidents Reagan and Bush, those appointees formed a five-member majority to limit opportunities for successful conditions-of-confinement lawsuits. In *Wilson v. Seiter,* these justices changed the Court's approach by requiring a showing of "deliberate indifference" for all conditions-of-confinement cases.

- In *Wilson v. Seiter,* the four senior justices disagreed with the majority opinion and argued that inadequate conditions themselves can violate the Eighth Amendment, regardless of the thoughts or motives of corrections officials.

- A majority of justices believe that prisoners should be able to challenge conditions of confinement, even in cases involving minor injuries (*Hudson v. McMillian*) or potential future harms (*Helling v. McKinney*). Meanwhile, Justices Thomas and Scalia have begun to argue that the Eighth Amendment should not protect prisoners inside the walls of prisons.

Key Terms

Estelle v. Gamble (1976)
Helling v. McKinney (1993)

Rhodes v. Chapman (1981)
Wilson v. Seiter (1991)

Additional Readings

Buterin, Stephen. 1993. "The Eighth Amendment and the State of Mind Requirement." *Hamline Law Review* 16: 417–445.

Newman, Amy. 1992. "Eighth Amendment: Cruel and Unusual Punishment and Conditions Cases." *Journal of Criminal Law and Criminology* 82: 979–999.

Oglivie, Ian. 1994. "Cruel and Unusual Punishment: The Ninth Circuit Analyzes Prison Security Policy with 'Deliberate Indifference' to Penological Needs." *St. John's Law Review* 68: 259–281.

Notes

1. Washington v. Harper, 494 U.S. 210 (1990).
2. Hutto v. Finney, 437 U.S. 678 (1978).
3. Bell v. Wolfish, 441 U.S. 520 (1979).
4. Rhodes v. Chapman, 452 U.S. 337 (1981).
5. Michael S. Vaughn and Rolando V. del Carmen, "Smoke-Free Prisons: Policy Dilemmas and Constitutional Issues," *Journal of Criminal Justice* 21 (1993): 151–171.
6. Christopher E. Smith, "The Constitution and Criminal Punishment: The Emerging Visions of Justices Scalia and Thomas," *Drake Law Review* 43 (1995): 611.
7. Antonin Scalia, "Originalism: The Lesser Evil," *University of Cincinnati Law Review* 57 (1989): 861–864.
8. Lawrence M. Friedman, *Crime and Punishment in American History* (New York: Basic Books, 1993), pp. 48–49.
9. Ibid., p. 48.
10. Farmer v. Brennan, 114 S.Ct. 1970 (1994).
11. McGill v. Duckworth, 944 F.2d 344 (7th Cir. 1992).
12. Young v. Quinlan, 960 F.2d 351 (3rd Cir. 1992).

CHAPTER TEN

Probation, Parole, and Release

Imagine you are a parole officer. You are responsible for monitoring the behavior of convicted offenders who have served most of their sentences in prison but have been released on parole to complete their sentences living in the community under strict conditions. You have suspicions that one parolee, Bill Smith, is hiding something from you. He seems evasive when he talks to you at your office. He constantly manufactures excuses for why you should not drop in on him at his home or job. Prior to his conviction for drug trafficking, he had been involved in a local gang. You fear that he is becoming involved with his old gang friends, even though the conditions of his parole release clearly forbid him from associating with gang members.

One day you stop by the factory where Smith works. You learn that he did not show up for work that day. When you phone his house, his mother tells you that he is too sick to come to the phone. You spend the next few hours meeting with other parolees in their scheduled appointments, and then the telephone rings. A voice says, "Bill Smith is over at the corner of 28th Street and Third Avenue selling drugs with his gang buddies right now." The unidentified caller quickly hangs up.

You jump in your car and drive over to 28th Street. You find Bill Smith walking down the street in your direction. On the other side of the street, you see a small group of men wearing gang jackets and colors.

"What do you think you're doing?" you say angrily to Smith.

"I didn't do anything," Smith replies defensively. "I was just out for some fresh air since I didn't feel well today."

"I know what you were doing," you say. "You were back with your old drug-dealing gang friends. That's a violation of your parole conditions, so I'm having you sent back to prison."

"That's not fair!" he exclaims. "Besides, you can't prove anything anyway."

Should you be able to send him back to prison on the basis of what you've seen and heard? Because he is a convicted criminal still serving a sentence under correctional supervision, should he have any rights protecting his ability to remain on parole instead of going back to prison?

PROBATION AND PAROLE

Although people sometimes confuse the two, probation and parole are different concepts. **Probation** is a sentence served within the community under restrictive conditions and the supervision of a probation officer. During probation, a sentence of incarceration is suspended, but the offender may be imprisoned for violating probation conditions or committing a new crime. Probation is a very common sentence for lesser offenses, but sometimes people who commit serious or even violent crimes are sentenced to probation. An individual who receives probation despite committing a serious crime may be viewed as unlikely to commit another crime or may simply benefit from overcrowded prisons. It's important to understand the rights of probationers because of the large numbers of offenders on probation; currently, two-thirds of all people under criminal sentence in the United States are on probation.

By contrast, **parole** is a status attained by incarcerated prisoners who serve a major portion of their sentence in prison before being granted release into the community. They serve the remainder of their sentence in the community under restrictive conditions and the supervision of a parole officer. The federal government and several states have abolished parole release, but most states still have parole as a means to release offenders back into the community prior to completion of the sentence. Whereas probationers, especially those convicted of minor offenses, typically require little supervision and cause few problems, it is a different story for many parolees. Parolees must make significant adjustments in returning to society after living for years in a prison. Many parolees are also people who never functioned successfully in free society prior to imprisonment, so it may be especially difficult to help them become productive, law-abiding citizens.

Each probationer and parolee must abide by a specific set of conditions. Some conditions are common to both groups, such as not being allowed to drink alcohol or take drugs and having to meet regularly with a supervising officer (either a probation officer or a parole officer). Other conditions may be specific to a particular individual, such as regular drugs tests, curfews, and rules against being in certain parts of town or associating with specific individuals. Some courts also have approved periodic polygraph exams to make sure conditions are being obeyed and no further crimes are being committed.[1]

There are other differences between probation and parole. Probation is a sentence imposed by a judge, and it frequently is administered by probation officers who work for the court rather than for the state department of corrections. By contrast, parole is determined by a decision of a parole board. Such boards often are composed of political appointees drawn from the community, such as a businessperson, a minister, a teacher, and someone active in the governor's political campaigns. Alternatively, the parole board may include corrections department officials or treatment professionals, such as psychologists. Although the parole board may be an independent agency, it usually has close connections with the department of corrections. Moreover, prisoners released on parole are supervised in the community by parole officers who generally work for the state department of corrections.

There is no right to parole. In *Greenholtz v. Inmates of the Nebraska Penal and Correction Complex* (1979),[2] the Supreme Court made it quite clear that parole release is granted by the state and is not an entitlement that a prisoner can demand: "There is no constitutional right or inherent right of a convicted person to be conditionally released before the expiration of a valid sentence." In another case, *Connecticut Board of Pardons v. Dumschat* (1981),[3] the Court rejected a life-sentenced inmate's claim that a state board of pardons must explain why they did not commute his sentence when three-fourths of lifers in that state have their sentences commuted and thereby become eligible for parole. The Court rejected the claim because the state's statute gave the board of pardons discretion to make commutation decisions and did not require the board to explain its decisions. As discussed in Chapter 6, states may create liberty interests that trigger protections and entitlements for prisoners. However, the Supreme Court appears less likely to recognize and protect such interests in light of the 1995 decision in *Sandin v. Conner* (discussed in Chapter 6), which changed the rules for identifying state-created liberty interests. Thus, it seems unlikely the Supreme Court will recognize a state-created liberty interest that triggers an entitlement to release. Rather, the Court will make states follow through on the procedures that they put forth in their statutes and regulations for granting parole. In sum, the Court has never sought a role in defining when prisoners must gain release.

A related issue concerns clemency for death row inmates. A grant of clemency will not necessarily result in release because it often simply changes a death sentence to a life sentence. In *Ohio Adult Parole Authority v. Woodard* (1998),[4] the Supreme Court rejected the argument that a "life" interest in clemency for death row inmates under the Due Process Clause was different from and more compelling than the asserted "liberty" interest that the Court declined to recognize for lifers in *Connecticut Board of Pardons v. Dumschat* (1981). The Court concluded that no protected interest was created because clemency is a discretionary decision of the governor. The Court reiterated its conclusion in

Dumschat that "pardon and commutation decisions have not traditionally been the business of the courts; as such, they are rarely, if ever appropriate subjects for judicial review." The Court also concluded that voluntary interviews conducted with offenders as part of the clemency decision-making process do not violate the Fifth Amendment privilege against compelled self-incrimination.

Rights of Probationers and Parolees

Despite their differences, probation and parole have important aspects in common, especially from the viewpoint of the offender. In both situations, offenders walk relatively freely among the other citizens in society, yet they remain in the custody of the corrections system. They remain under a criminal sentence that must be completed before they regain the same freedom enjoyed by others in society. Because they are under criminal sanction, probationers and parolees do not enjoy the same rights as law-abiding citizens. They must abide by the conditions of their release, and they must remain aware that they can be sent to prison for violating the conditions of their release.

Obviously, offenders serving their sentences in prison have significant limitations on their rights. As discussed in previous chapters, courts often define prisoners' limited rights by giving first priority to correctional institutions' need to maintain security and order. Thus, prisoners are not free to exercise their religious practices if such practices (or the schedule for such practices) clash with the prison's overriding interest in security and order. Similarly, prisoners cannot exercise freedom of speech and freedom of the press if their actions might endanger a prison's security and order. By contrast, probationers and parolees are not confined within corrections institutions. Therefore, their actions are much less likely to disrupt any corrections programs. The courts remain concerned that activities by probationers and parolees not lead to crime or disrupt society. But there is less reason to limit certain constitutionally protected activities, such as speech and religion, for those outside institutions than there is for prison inmates.

For example, recall the Muslim prisoners in *O'Lone v. Shabazz*, discussed in Chapter 5. They were denied the opportunity to attend Friday religious services inside the prison because, according to prison officials and the U.S. Supreme Court majority, moving them from their outside work detail into the prison would disrupt safety and security. By contrast, if a probationer or parolee wanted to attend religious services, the only questions would be whether such activities violated a condition of release and whether such conditions were proper. If, for example, a parolee is barred from associating with certain people because of their prior involvement in criminal activities with the parolee, then the parolee may not be able to attend a specific church if those people also attend the church. However, a court should not permit probation or parole conditions to prevent someone from attending religious services if there are not strong reasons for keeping that individual from either going to a particular religious institution or going out at a particular time during the week. Offenders on release cannot be barred from practicing their religion simply because authorities want to maintain additional control over them. There must be a strong reason to outweigh the offender's First Amendment religious exercise right.

The courts have struck down conditions imposed by corrections officials that attempted to prevent parolees from giving public speeches.[5] The primary situation in which probation or parole conditions could interfere with First Amendment rights with respect to speeches and writing is when such activities are related to the offender's crime. For example, a probationer convicted of kicking a police officer at a public demonstration was prohibited from speaking at and participating in public demonstrations during the probationary period.[6] With respect to other kinds of speaking and writing activities, offenders obviously could be barred from communicating with or harassing crime victims and witnesses connected to their cases.

With respect to Fourth Amendment rights concerning searches and seizures, there may be stronger reasons to limit probationers' and parolees' rights. The government designs the criminal justice system, in part, to protect the public from people who would harm their fellow citizens. When convicted offenders are released into the community on probation or parole, the government is providing less supervision and control than it does for offenders who are locked up. There are always concerns, especially with parolees who have committed violent crimes, that parole officials will make mistakes in deciding whom it is safe to release. In recent years, there have been several highly publicized incidents in which parolees murdered people, including small children. Such incidents create tremendous public outcry as citizens and the media clamor, "Why wasn't this person in prison? How could such a violent person possibly be released?" Because of the potential risk to public safety posed by convicted offenders living in the community, the courts have permitted officials to assume significant authority to search and detain probationers and parolees. That is, the courts have agreed that probation and parole officials must be able to discover if offenders are hiding guns, drugs, or evidence of criminal activity. Specifically, in ***Griffin v. Wisconsin*** (1987), the Supreme Court examined the authority of probation officers to conduct warrantless searches of probationers' homes. As you read the case, which is excerpted in Box 10-1, ask yourself: Should probationers and parolees receive any Fourth Amendment protections, and if so, in what situations?

There are several important points to note about the Supreme Court's opinion in *Griffin*. The opinion emphasized that probationers and parolees do not enjoy the same rights as other citizens. However, the justices also stressed that people do not lose all rights, including Fourth Amendment protections for their homes, simply because they are convicted offenders serving sentences within the community. Thus, probationers and parolees are not subject to every kind of search that supervising officials may choose to undertake. The Fourth Amendment bars "unreasonable" searches and seizures aimed at convicted offenders as well as everyone else. The Court's primary task in this opinion was to determine when it is "reasonable" to search a probationer's home without a warrant.

In this decision, the Supreme Court did not endorse warrantless searches of probationers' homes whenever there are reasonable grounds for such searches. The Wisconsin Supreme Court attempted to apply such a rule, but the U.S. Supreme Court declined to endorse it. If the Wisconsin Supreme Court had created the rule under the Wisconsin Constitution, it would have rested its decision on state law, and the U.S. Supreme Court would have left the case alone (unless

BOX 10-1   *Griffin v. Wisconsin*, 483 U.S. 868 (1987)

JUSTICE SCALIA delivered the opinion of the Court.

Petitioner Joseph Griffin, who was on probation, had his home searched by probation officers acting without a warrant. The officers found a gun that later served as the basis for Griffin's conviction of a state-law weapons offense. We granted certiorari . . . to consider whether this search violated the Fourth Amendment. . . .

. . . One of the [Wisconsin State Department of Health and Social Services'] regulations permits any probation officer to search a probationer's home without a warrant as long as his supervisor approves and as long as there are "reasonable grounds" to believe the presence of contraband—including any item that the probationer cannot possess under the probation conditions. . . . The rule provides that an officer should consider a variety of factors in determining whether "reasonable grounds" exist, among which are information provided by an informant, the reliability and specificity of that information, the reliability of the informant, . . . the officer's own experience with the probationer, and the "need to verify compliance with rules of supervision and state and federal law." . . . Another regulation makes it a violation of the terms of probation [for a probationer] to refuse to consent to a home search. . . . And still another [regulation] forbids a probationer to possess a firearm without advance approval from a probation officer. . . .

[A probation officer supervisor received a report from the police department that Griffin may have guns in his apartment. The supervisor, a probation officer, and three police officers went to Griffin's apartment and informed him that they were going to conduct a search. During the course of the search, they found a handgun, which led to Griffin's conviction on a felony firearms charge: possession of a firearm by a convicted felon.]

We think the Wisconsin Supreme Court correctly concluded that this warrantless search did not violate the Fourth Amendment. To reach that result, however, we find it unnecessary to embrace a new principle of law, as the Wisconsin court evidently did, that any search of a probationer's home by a probation officer satisfies the Fourth Amendment as long as the information possessed by the officer satisfies a federal "reasonable grounds" standard. . . . The search of Griffin's home satisfied demands of the Fourth Amendment because it was carried out pursuant to a regulation that itself satisfies the Fourth Amendment's reasonableness requirement under well-established principles.

A probationer's home, like anyone else's, is protected by the Fourth Amendment's requirement that searches be "reasonable." Although we usually require that a search be undertaken only pursuant to a warrant (and thus supported by probable cause, as the Constitutions says warrants must be), . . . we have permitted exceptions when "special needs, beyond the normal need for law enforcement, make the warrant and probable-cause requirement

the justices believed the decision violated the Fourth Amendment to the U.S. Constitution). State court decisions that rest on independent and adequate state law grounds with no implications for federal law are not reviewable by the U.S. Supreme Court. State supreme courts are the final judicial interpreters of issues that concern state law exclusively. Here, however, the Wisconsin Supreme Court based its decision on the Fourth Amendment to the U.S. Constitution. As a result, the U.S. Supreme Court—the final authority over judicial interpretations of the federal constitution—reviewed the decision.

impracticable.". . . Thus, we have held that government employers and supervisors may conduct warrantless, work-related searches of employees' desks and offices without probable cause, . . . and that school officials may conduct warrantless searches of some student property [e.g., students' lockers] also without probable cause. . . .

A State's operation of a probation system, like its operation of a school, government office or prison, or its supervision of a regulated industry, likewise presents "special needs" beyond normal law enforcement that may justify departures from the usual warrant and probable-cause requirements. Probation, like incarceration, is "a form of criminal sanction imposed by a court upon an offender after verdict, finding, or plea of guilty." . . . [T]o a greater or lesser degree, it is always true of probationers (as we have said it to be true of parolees) that they do not enjoy "the absolute liberty to which every citizen is entitled, but only . . . conditional liberty properly dependent on observance of special restrictions." *Morrissey v. Brewer,* 408 U.S. 471, 480 (1972).

. . . Supervision [of probationers], then, is a "special need" of the State permitting a degree of impingement upon privacy that would not be constitutional if applied to the public at large. That permissible degree is not unlimited, however, so we next turn to whether it has been exceeded here.

. . . We think it clear that the special needs of Wisconsin's probation system make the warrant requirement impracticable and justify replacement of the standard probable cause by "reasonable grounds," as defined by the Wisconsin Supreme Court.

A warrant requirement would interfere to an appreciable degree with the probation system, setting up a magistrate rather than the probation officer as the judge of how close a supervision the probationer requires. Moreover, the delay inherent in obtaining a warrant would make it more difficult for probation officials to respond quickly to evidence of misconduct. . . .

. . . [W]e think it reasonable to permit information provided by a police officer, whether or not on the basis of firsthand knowledge, to support a probationer search. The same conclusion is suggested by the fact that the police may be unwilling to disclose their confidential sources to probation personnel. For the same reason, and also because it is the very assumption of the institution of probation that the probationer is in need of rehabilitation and is more likely than the ordinary citizen to violate the law, we think it enough if the information provided indicates, as it did here, only the likelihood ("had or might have guns") of facts justifying the search.

The search of Griffin's residence was "reasonable" within the meaning of the Fourth Amendment because it was conducted pursuant to a valid regulation governing probationers. This conclusion makes it unnecessary to consider whether, as the court below held and the State urges, any search of a probationer's home by a probation officer is lawful when there are "reasonable grounds" to believe contraband is present. . . .

The U.S. Supreme Court found warrantless searches of probationers' homes to be reasonable when such searches are conducted pursuant to valid state regulations. Here, the Wisconsin regulation set certain requirements for the search, including the factors to consider in deciding if a search is justified and the approval of a supervisor. These requirements provided a basis for permitting warrantless searches because the existence of these regulations prevented the worst-case situation—probation officers conducting searches on their own whenever they want to. The Court left open the question of whether any warrantless search of a probationer's home is permissible so long as it has a reasonable basis. Thus, states were sent a message that if they provide valid regulations to guide such searches, the Court is prepared to permit such searches to go forward.

In 1998, the Supreme Court addressed a related issue concerning the Fourth Amendment rights of parolees. In *Griffin,* the Supreme Court determined that the probationer's rights were not violated by the warrantless search. But if a court decides that a parolee's Fourth Amendment rights definitely were violated by an improper search, can the government still use the evidence against the parolee? In *Pennsylvania Board of Probation and Parole v. Scott,* (1998), the Supreme Court addressed this issue. As you read this case, which is excerpted in Box 10-2, ask yourself if you believe the Court answered these questions properly. What are the implications of the Court's decisions for the lives of parolees on release from prison?

In the *Scott* decision, the authors of majority and dissenting opinions disagreed about how to characterize parole revocation proceedings. Are they comparable to criminal trials or not? Moreover, they disagreed about the role of parole officers. Are they more comparable to police officers or to social workers (or to both)? Fundamentally, the decision confirms that parolees have significantly less protection than other citizens when it comes to Fourth Amendment rights. The decision also reflects continuing divisions among the justices about the necessity of the exclusionary rule as a means to uphold the Fourth Amendment.

Revocation of Probation and Parole

Probationers and parolees must obey their conditions of release in order to avoid being sent to prison. If they repeatedly fail drug tests or commit another crime, they are likely to be locked up. If they break curfew or miss meetings with their supervising officers, those officers make discretionary decisions about whether these violations are sufficient to justify sending them to prison. Probation and parole officers have significant discretion in deciding when to initiate the process of putting offenders behind bars for violating release conditions. They do not make the final decision on revocation, but they set the wheels in motion. Almost any violation of a probation or parole condition can lead to a loss of freedom. One potential exception is failure to pay a fine or restitution as part of probation conditions. If an indigent probationer makes a good-faith effort to pay but is unable to do so for lack of money, the Supreme Court says that probation should not be revoked.[7] Instead, judges should try to create community service requirements or other alternatives to replace the fine.

Review the scenario at the beginning of the chapter. Obviously, one of the biggest concerns about probation and parole—for offenders and corrections officials alike—is how easy (or difficult) it is to send an offender to prison when conditions of probation or parole allegedly have been violated. On the one hand, probationers and parolees certainly do not want to be shipped off to prison on the whim of a suspicious or vindictive official. On the other hand, law enforcement and corrections officials want the authority to move offenders quickly into incarceration when the conditions of release are violated.

| **BOX 10-2** | ***Pennsylvania Board of Probation and Parole v. Scott*, 118 S.Ct. 2014 (1998)** |

JUSTICE THOMAS delivered the opinion of the Court, in which CHIEF JUSTICE REHNQUIST and JUSTICES O'CONNOR, SCALIA, and KENNEDY joined.

This case presents the question whether the exclusionary rule, which generally prohibits the introduction at criminal trial of evidence obtained in violation of a defendant's Fourth Amendment rights, applies in parole revocation hearings. We hold that it does not.

Respondent Keith M. Scott pleaded nolo contendere to a charge of third-degree murder and was sentenced to a prison term of 10 to 20 years, beginning on March 31, 1983. On September 1, 1993, just months after completing the minimum sentence, respondent was released on parole. One of the conditions of respondent's parole was that he would refrain from "owning or possessing any firearms or other weapons." . . . The parole agreement, which respondent signed, further provided:

> I expressly consent to the search of my person, property and residence, without a warrant by agents of the Pennsylvania Board of Probation and Parole. Any items, in [sic] the possession of which constitutes a violation of parole/reparole shall be subject to seizure, and may be used as evidence in the parole revocation process.

About five months later, after obtaining an arrest warrant based on evidence that respondent had violated several conditions of his parole by possessing firearms, consuming alcohol, and assaulting a co-worker, three parole officers arrested respondent at a local diner. Before being transferred to a correctional facility, respondent gave the officers the keys to his residence. The officers entered the home, which was owned by his mother, but did not perform a search for parole violations until respondent's mother arrived. The officers neither requested nor obtained consent to perform the search, but respondent's mother did direct them to his bed-

room. After finding no relevant evidence there, the officers searched an adjacent sitting room in which they found five firearms, a compound bow, and three arrows.

At his parole violation hearing, respondent objected to the introduction of the evidence obtained during the search of his home on the ground that the search was unreasonable under the Fourth Amendment. The hearing examiner, however, rejected the challenge and admitted the evidence. As a result, the Pennsylvania Board of Probation found sufficient evidence in the record to support the weapons and alcohol charges and recommitted respondent to serve 36 months' backtime.

The Commonwealth Court of Pennsylvania reversed and remanded, holding, inter alia, that the hearing examiner had erred in admitting the evidence obtained during the search of respondent's residence.

The court ruled that the search violated respondent's Fourth Amendment rights because it was conducted without the owner's consent and was not authorized by any state statutory or regulatory framework ensuring the reasonableness of searches by parole officers. . . . The court further held that the exclusionary rule should apply because, in the circumstances of respondent's case, the deterrence benefits of the rule outweighed the costs. . . .

The Pennsylvania Supreme Court affirmed. . . . The court stated that respondent's Fourth Amendment right against unreasonable searches and seizures was "unaffected" by his signing of the parole agreement giving parole officers permission to conduct warrantless searches. . . . It then held that the search in question was unreasonable because it was supported by "mere speculation" rather than a "reasonable suspicion" of a parole violation. . . . Carving out an exception to its per se bar against application of the exclusionary rule in parole revocation hearings, . . . the court further ruled that the federal

(continued)

exclusionary rule applied to this case because the officers who conducted the search were aware of respondent's parole status. . . . The court reasoned that, in the absence of the rule, illegal searches would be undeterred when officers know that the subjects of their searches are parolees and that illegally obtained evidence can be introduced at parole hearings. . . .

We have emphasized repeatedly that the State's use of evidence in violation of the Fourth Amendment does not itself violate the Constitution. . . . Rather, a Fourth Amendment violation is "fully accomplished" by the illegal search or seizure, and no exclusion from a judicial or administrative proceeding can "cure the invasion of the defendant's rights which he has already suffered.". . . The exclusionary rule is instead a judicially created means of deterring illegal searches and seizures. . . . As such, the rule does not "proscribe the introduction of illegally seized evidence in all proceedings or against all persons," . . . but applies only in contexts "where its remedial objectives are thought most efficaciously served." . . . Moreover, because the rule is prudential rather than constitutionally mandated, we have held it to be applicable only where its deterrence benefits outweigh its "substantial social costs." . . .

Recognizing these costs, we have repeatedly declined to extend the exclusionary rule to proceedings other than criminal trials. . . . For example, in *United States v. Calandra* [1974], we held that the exclusionary rule does not apply to grand jury proceedings; in so doing, we emphasized that such proceedings play a special role in the law enforcement process and that the traditionally flexible, nonadversarial nature of those proceedings would be jeopardized by application of the rule. . . . Likewise, in *United States v. Janis* [1976], we held that the exclusionary rule did not bar the introduction of unconstitutionally obtained evidence in a civil tax proceeding because the costs of excluding relevant and reliable evidence would outweigh the marginal deterrence benefits, which, we noted, would be minimal because the use of the exclusionary rule in criminal trials already deterred illegal searches. . . . Finally, in *INS v. Lopez-Mendoza*. . . (1984), we refused to extend the exclusionary rule to civil deportation proceedings, citing the high social costs of allowing an immigrant to remain illegally in this country and noting the incompatibility of the rule with the civil, administrative nature of those proceedings. . . .

As in *Calandra, Janis,* and *Lopez-Mendoza,* we are asked to extend the operation of the exclusionary rule beyond the criminal trial context. We again decline to do so. Application of the exclusionary rule would both hinder the functioning of state parole systems and alter the traditionally flexible, administrative nature of parole revocation proceedings. The rule would provide only minimal deterrence benefits in this context, because application of the rule in the criminal trial context already provides significant deterrence of unconstitutional searches. We therefore hold that the federal exclusionary rule does not bar the introduction at parole revocation hearings of evidence seized in violation of parolees' Fourth Amendment rights.

Because the exclusionary rule precludes consideration of reliable, probative evidence, it imposes significant costs: it undeniably detracts from the truthfinding process and allows many who would otherwise be incarcerated to escape the consequences of their actions. . . . Although we have held these costs to be worth bearing in certain circumstances, our cases have repeatedly emphasized that the rule's "costly toll" upon truth-seeking and law enforcement objectives presents a high obstacle for those urging application of the rule. . . .

. . . In most cases, the State is willing to extend parole only because it is able to condition it upon compliance with certain requirements. The State thus has an "overwhelming interest" in ensuring that a parolee complies with those requirements and is returned to prison if he fails to do so. . . .

[Because of the litigation involved in exclusionary rule issues, the application of the rule to parole revocation hearings would adversely affect the nature of parole revocation hearings.]. . . Such litigation is inconsistent with the nonadversarial, administrative processes established by the States. . . . Such a transformation [in the nature of parole hearings] might disadvantage parolees because in an adversarial proceeding, "the hearing body may be less tolerant of marginal deviant behavior and feel more pressure to incarcerate than to continue nonpunitive rehabilitation.". . . And the financial costs of such a system could reduce the State's incentive to extend parole in the first place. . . .

. . . [Parole officers'] primary concern is whether their parolees should remain free on parole. Thus their relationship with parolees is more supervisory than adversarial. . . . It is thus "unfair to assume that the parole officer bears hostility against the parolee that destroys his neutrality; realistically the failure of the parolee is in a sense a failure for his supervising officer.". . . Although this relationship does not prevent parole officers from ever violating the Fourth Amendment rights of their parolees, it does mean that the harsh deterrent of exclusion is unwarranted, given such other deterrents as departmental training and discipline and the threat of damages actions. . . .

JUSTICE SOUTER, with whom JUSTICES GINSBURG and BREYER join, dissenting

The Court's holding that the exclusionary rule of *Mapp v. Ohio* . . . (1961) has no application to parole revocation proceedings rests upon the mistaken conceptions of the actual function of revocation, of the objectives of those who gather evidence in support of petitions to revoke, and, consequently, of the need to deter violations of the Fourth Amendment that would tend to occur in administering parole laws. In reality a revocation proceeding often serves the same function as a criminal trial, and the revocation hearing may very well present the only forum in which the State will seek to use evidence of a parole violation, even when the evidence would support an independent criminal charge. The deterrent function of the exclusionary rule is therefore implicated as much by a revocation proceeding as by a conventional trial, and the exclusionary rule should be applied accordingly. From the Court's conclusion to the contrary, I respectfully dissent. . . .

As these [prior] cases show, the police very likely do know a parolee's status when they go after him, and (contrary to the majority's assumption) this fact is significant for three reasons. First, and most obviously, the police have reason for concern with the outcome of a parole revocation proceeding which is just as foreseeable as the criminal trial and at least as likely to be held. Police officers, especially those employed by the same sovereign that runs the parole system, therefore have every incentive not to jeopardize a recommitment by rendering evidence inadmissible . . . . Second, . . . the likelihood of trial is often far less than the probability of a petition for parole revocation, with the consequence that the revocation hearing will be the only forum in which the evidence will ever be offered. Often, therefore, there will be nothing "marginal" about the deterrence provided by an exclusionary rule operating there. . . . Finally, the cooperation between parole officers and police officers, as in the instances shown in [prior] cases, casts serious doubt upon the aptness of treating police officers differently from parole officers, doubt that is confirmed by the following attention to the Court's characterization of the position of the parole officer.

. . . As the Court describes him, the parole officer is less interested in catching a parole violator than in making sure that the parolee continues to go straight. . . . This view of the parole officer suffers, however, from its selectiveness. Parole officers wear several hats; while they are indeed the parolees' counselor and social workers, they also "often serve as both prosecutors and law enforcement officials in their relationship with probationers and parolees." . . .

As to the benefit of an exclusionary rule in revocation proceedings, the majority does not see that in the investigation of criminal conduct by someone known to be on parole, Fourth Amendment standards will have very little deterrent sanction unless evidence offered for parole revocation is subject to suppression for unconstitutional conduct. It is not merely that parole revocation is the government's consolation prize when, for whatever reason, it cannot obtain a

(continued)

further criminal conviction, though that will sometimes be true. . . . What is at least equally telling is that parole revocation will frequently be pursued instead of prosecution as the course of choice. . . .

JUSTICE STEVENS, dissenting.

Justice Souter has explained why the deterrent function of the exclusionary rule is implicated as much by a parole revocation proceeding as by a conventional trial. I agree with that explanation. I add this comment merely to endorse [the late] Justice Stewart's conclusion that the "rule is constitutionally required, not as a 'right' explicitly incorporated in the Fourth Amendment's prohibitions, but as a remedy necessary to ensure that those prohibitions are observed in fact." . . .

The U.S. Supreme Court first addressed the issue of parole revocation in *Morrissey v. Brewer* (1972). As you read the *Morrissey* opinion, excerpted in Box 10-3, see if you can identify any requirements imposed by the Supreme Court before a parolee can be sent back to prison.

How would you apply the *Morrissey* decision to the hypothetical case at the beginning of the chapter? Obviously, the U.S. Supreme Court believes that parole officers should not have the power to decide, on their own, that a parolee will be returned to prison. If parole officers had that power, they could end someone's liberty (enjoyed under specified conditions) and have him or her incarcerated for years based on a discretionary judgment and without any safeguards against abuse of the process. As we saw in the discussion of disciplinary proceedings in Chapter 6, the Supreme Court wants to protect legitimate "liberty interests." Here, parolees stand to lose significant liberty if they are returned to prison, so the law and legal process must ensure that a fair decision is made if this liberty is to be lost.

In *Morrissey*, the Supreme Court outlined a two-stage process. In the first stage, after the parole officer has the parolee taken into custody, a preliminary hearing must be held to establish that reasonable grounds exist for revocation. This preliminary hearing must be before some official other than the parole officer who initiated the arrest, and the parolee must be informed, or given "notice," of the conditions of parole that he or she allegedly violated. At the hearing, the parolee is permitted to appear and present his or her side of the story, including the presentation of documents and witnesses. The parolee also may cross-examine anyone who is supplying evidence that a parole violation occurred, although this confrontation of adverse witnesses may be blocked if the hearing officer determines that the informant would risk harm by being revealed and presented at the hearing. The hearing officer then summarizes what occurs at the hearing and determines whether there is probable cause to hold the parolee for the final decision of the parole board on revocation. The entire process is supposed to be more informal than courtroom proceedings.

At the second stage, the revocation hearing, the parolee must receive notice of charges, and the evidence of violations must be disclosed. The parolee can present his or her version of events, supported by evidence and witnesses, and

BOX 10-3   *Morrissey v. Brewer, 408 U.S. 471 (1972)*

[Morrissey was on parole after serving time in prison for forging a check. At the direction of his parole officer, he was arrested and, based on the parole officer's written report, returned to prison when the state Board of Parole revoked his parole. He filed a habeas corpus action alleging that he was denied due process because his parole was revoked without a hearing.]

CHIEF JUSTICE BURGER delivered the opinion of the Court.

. . . Implicit in the system's concern with parole violations is the notion that the parolee is entitled to retain his liberty as long as he substantially abides by the conditions of his parole. The first step in a revocation decision thus involves a wholly retrospective factual question: whether the parolee has in fact acted in violation of one or more conditions of his parole. Only if it is determined that the parolee did violate the conditions does the second question arise: should the parolee be recommitted to prison or should other steps be taken to protect society and improve chances of rehabilitation? . . .

We see, therefore, that the liberty of a parolee, although indeterminate, includes many of the core values of unqualified liberty and its termination inflicts a "grievous loss" on the parolee and often on others. It is hardly useful any longer to try to deal with this problem in terms of whether the parolee's liberty is a "right" or a "privilege." By whatever name, the liberty is valuable and must be seen as within the protection of the Fourteenth Amendment. Its termination calls for some orderly process, however informal. . . .

We now turn to the nature of the process that is due, bearing in mind that the interest of both State and parolee will be furthered by an effective but informal hearing. In analyzing what is due, we see two important stages in the typical process of parole revocation:

(a) ARREST OF PAROLEE AND PRELIMINARY HEARING

. . . In our view, due process requires that after the arrest, the determination that reasonable ground exists for revocation of parole should be made by someone not directly involved in the case. . . . The officer directly involved in making recommendations cannot always have complete objectivity in evaluating them. . . .

This independent officer need not be a judicial officer. The granting and revocation of parole are matters traditionally handled by administrative officers. . . . It will be sufficient, therefore, in the parole revocation context, if an evaluation of whether reasonable cause exists to believe that conditions of parole have been violated is made by someone such as a parole officer other than the one who has made the report of parole violations or has recommended revocation. A State could certainly choose some other independent decisionmaker to perform this preliminary function.

With respect to the preliminary hearing before this officer, the parolee should be given notice that the hearing will take place and that its purpose is to determine whether there is probable cause to believe he has committed a parole violation. The notice should state what parole violations have been alleged. At the hearing the parolee may appear and speak in his own behalf; he may bring letters, documents, or individuals who can give relevant information to the hearing officer. On request of the parolee, a person who has given adverse information on which parole revocation is to be based is to be made available for questioning in his presence. However, if the hearing officer determines that an informant would be subjected to risk of harm if his identity were disclosed, he need not be subjected to confrontation and cross-examination.

The hearing officer shall have the duty of making a summary, or digest, of what occurs at

(continued)

the hearing in terms of the responses of the parolee and the substance of the documents or evidence given in support of parole revocation and of the parolee's position. Based on the information before him, the officer should determine whether there is probable cause to hold the parolee for the final decision of the parole board on revocation. Such a determination would be sufficient to warrant the parolee's continued detention and return to the state correctional institution pending the final decision. As in [a prior precedent concerning forfeiture of welfare benefits], "the decisionmaker should state the reasons for his determination and indicate the evidence he relied on . . ." but it should be remembered that this is not a final determination calling for "formal findings of fact and conclusions of law.". . . No interest would be served by formalism in this process; informality will not lessen the utility of this inquiry in reducing the risk of error.

(b) THE REVOCATION HEARING

There must also be an opportunity for a hearing, if it is desired by the parolee, prior to the final decision on revocation by the parole authority. This hearing must be the basis for more than determining probable cause; it must lead to a final evaluation of any contested relevant facts and consideration of whether the facts as determined warrant revocation. The parolee must have an opportunity to be heard and to show, if he can, that he did not violate the conditions, or, if he did, that circumstances in mitigation suggest that the violation does not warrant revocation. The revocation hearing must be tendered within a reasonable time after the parolee is taken into custody. A lapse of two months, as respondent suggests occurs in some cases, would not appear to be unreasonable.

We cannot write a code of procedure; that is the responsibility of each State. Most States have done so by legislation, others by judicial decision usually on due process grounds. Our task is limited to deciding the minimum requirements of due process. They include (a) written notice of the claimed violations of parole; (b) disclosure to the parolee of evidence against him; (c) opportunity to be heard in person and to present witnesses and documentary evidence; (d) the right to confront and cross-examine adverse witnesses (unless the hearing officer specifically finds good cause for not allowing confrontation); (e) a "neutral and detached" hearing body such as a traditional parole board, members of which need not be judicial officers or lawyers; and (f) a written statement by the factfinders as to the evidence relied on and reasons for revoking parole. We emphasize there is no thought to equate this second stage of parole revocation to a criminal prosecution in any sense. It is a narrow inquiry; the process should be flexible enough to consider evidence including letters, affidavits, and other material that would not be admissible in an adversary criminal trial.

We do not reach or decide the question whether the parolee is entitled to the assistance of counsel or to appointed counsel if he is indigent. . . .

can cross-examine opposing witnesses unless there is good reason to prevent such a confrontation. The hearing must be before a neutral and detached hearing body, but that body need not be composed of judges or lawyers. The hearing body must provide a written statement of the evidence and reasoning that support any decision to revoke parole. The revocation hearing need not take place immediately after the preliminary hearing, but merely within a reasonable time period. Note that the Court said a two-month delay "would not appear to be unreasonable."

Thus, the entire parole revocation process provides procedural protections for the parolee, but not at the same level of formality as a criminal trial. The decision makers in parole revocation hearings need not be trained in law. Parolees can present their side of the story and cross-examine witnesses, but in reality, they may not be able to undertake these tasks effectively without the assistance of an attorney. However, unlike in a criminal court proceeding, the Court left open the question about whether attorneys are required. Obviously, the introduction of defense attorneys could make parole revocation proceedings more formal and combative. But the involvement of such attorneys also would enable parolees to make stronger presentations to counteract the allegations of violations.

The following year, the Supreme Court applied the *Morrissey* procedural protections to probation revocation proceedings in ***Gagnon v. Scarpelli*** (1973). If the government wishes to send probationers to prison for violating their conditions of probation, they must provide notice of alleged violations, hold hearings, and provide an opportunity to present arguments and evidence—just as they do in parole revocation proceedings under the *Morrissey* requirements. In *Gagnon,* however, the Supreme Court tackled the question of whether parolees and probationers facing revocation and imprisonment are entitled to be represented by an attorney in the revocation proceedings. As you read the portion of the *Gagnon* opinion in Box 10-4, ask yourself whether Bill Smith, our parolee in the chapter opener, would be entitled to an attorney at his parole revocation hearings.

Parolees and probationers do not have a right to counsel during revocation hearings, unless the revocation hearing is combined with a sentencing proceeding because imposition of the actual sentence was deferred when the probation was imposed.[8] In *Gagnon* (and many other cases), by contrast, the sentence of incarceration has already been set and then suspended while the offender is on probation. Therefore, the revocation proceeding is not combined with a sentencing proceeding.

According to the Supreme Court, defense attorneys may be necessary for some of these nonsentencing-revocation cases. But probationers and parolees must request representation, and their requests are judged on a case-by-case basis. Counsel may be appropriate if cases are too complicated to be presented by probationers or parolees, or if probationers or parolees are otherwise incapable of representing themselves effectively. Certainly, many probationers and parolees are capable of standing before a hearing officer or board and describing their own version of events. However, when it comes to gathering evidence, locating witnesses, and especially cross-examining opposing witnesses, few probationers or parolees have any hope of preparing and presenting a case as effectively as an attorney. Case preparation tasks are even more difficult for probationers and parolees facing revocation because they have been arrested and are in jail while they await their hearings. It can be extraordinarily difficult to gather evidence and find witnesses while sitting in jail.

A particularly interesting aspect of the Court's justification for denying a general right to counsel is the claim that hearing boards will be more sympathetic to parolees and probationers—and their need for rehabilitation—*without* attorneys present. According to the *Gagnon* opinion, the introduction of attorneys would make hearing officials more inclined to send offenders back to prison. But why

BOX 10-4

Gagnon v. Scarpelli, 411 U.S. 778 (1973)

JUSTICE POWELL delivered the opinion of the Court.

. . . The introduction of counsel into a revocation proceeding will alter significantly the nature of the proceeding. If counsel is provided for the probationer or parolee, the State in turn will normally provide its own counsel; lawyers, by training and disposition, are advocates and bound by professional duty to present all available evidence and arguments in support of their clients' positions and to contest with vigor all adverse evidence and views. The role of the hearing body itself, aptly described in *Morrissey* as being "predictive and discretionary" as well as factfinding, may become more akin to that of a judge at a trial, and less attuned to the rehabilitative needs of the individual probationer or parolee. In the greater self-consciousness of its quasi-judicial role, the hearing body may be less tolerant of marginal deviant behavior and feel more pressure to reincarcerate than to continue nonpunitive rehabilitation. Certainly, the decisionmaking process will be prolonged, and the financial cost to the State—for appointed counsel, counsel for the State, a longer record, and the possibility of judicial review—will not be insubstantial.

In some cases, these modifications in the nature of the revocation hearing must be endured and the costs borne because, as we have indicated above, the probationer's or parolee's version of a disputed issue can fairly be represented only by a trained advocate. But due process is not so rigid as to require that the significant interests in informality, flexibility, and economy must always be sacrificed. . . .

We thus find no justification for a new inflexible constitutional rule with respect to the requirement of counsel. We think, rather, that the decision as to the need for counsel must be

---

didn't the Court conclude just the opposite—that boards would be less inclined to revoke probation and parole if an attorney made the strongest possible presentation of the client's case? Is it really so clear that the introduction of attorneys will shift decision making in one direction or another? Without attorneys, many probationers and parolees certainly are not able to present the strongest possible arguments and evidence on their own behalf. But at the same time, as the Court's opinion describes, the cost of revocation hearings certainly would increase if attorneys were involved. In rejecting the right to counsel, is the Court striking the appropriate balance between the financial costs to the legal system and the liberty interests of offenders facing imprisonment through revocation of probation or parole?

Return once again to the case at the beginning of the chapter. Are there any apparent reasons that Bill Smith should be entitled to representation by an attorney at his revocation hearing? Is the case complicated? Does Smith appear incapable of presenting his own side? Although it seems unlikely that Smith would receive an attorney under the rule of the *Gagnon* decision, an attorney might actually make a big difference in the case. When the parole officer describes seeing Smith walking down the street and gang members loitering on the other side of the street, who will do a more effective job of cross-examining the officer about whether he actually saw Smith selling drugs or associating with gang mem-

made on a case-by-case basis in the exercise of a sound discretion by the state authority charged with responsibility for administering the probation and parole system. Although the presence and participation of counsel will probably be both undesirable and constitutionally unnecessary in most revocation hearings, there will remain certain cases in which fundamental fairness—the touchstone of due process—will require that the State provide at its expense counsel for indigent probationers or parolees.

It is neither possible nor prudent to attempt to formulate a precise and detailed set of guidelines to be followed in determining when the providing of counsel is necessary to meet the applicable due process requirements. The facts and circumstances in preliminary and final hearings are susceptible of almost infinite variation, and a considerable discretion must be allowed the responsible agency in making the decision. Pre-

sumptively, it may be said that counsel should be provided in cases where, after being informed of his right to request counsel, the probationer or parolee makes such a request, based on a timely and colorable claim (i) that he has not committed the alleged violation of the conditions upon which he is at liberty; or (ii) that, even if the violation is a matter of public record or is uncontested, there are substantial reasons which justified or mitigated the violation and make revocation inappropriate, and that the reasons are complex or otherwise difficult to develop or present. In passing on a request for the appointment of counsel, the responsible agency also should consider, especially in doubtful cases, whether the probationer appears to be capable of speaking for himself. In every case in which a request for counsel at a preliminary or final hearing is refused, the grounds for refusal should be stated succinctly in the record. . . .

bers? Smith may be able to bring forth this information in questioning the parole officer, but an attorney undoubtedly would be able to question the officer more effectively.

In 1997, the U.S. Supreme Court examined Oklahoma's Preparole Conditional Supervision Program. In an effort to address the problems of prison overcrowding, Oklahoma's program permitted the Pardon and Parole Board to approve prisoners for release, but the final decision on parole was made by the governor. Ernest Harper was released through the program after serving fifteen years of a life sentence for murder. He spent five uneventful months in free society before the governor denied his parole and he was returned to prison. The Court rejected Oklahoma's arguments that preparole decisions should remain at the discretion of government officials. Instead, the Court declared that the preparole program must adhere to the procedural revocation requirements established by *Morrissey* because the program was so similar to regular parole and thereby created an important liberty interest for offenders released into the community.[9]

In contrast to revocations involving parole, preparole release, and probation in which there are procedural requirements, there is no requirement of hearings if a parole decision is rescinded before the inmate is ever released. The test case for this issue concerned an inmate who was approved for parole and who attended prison classes to prepare for release. But parole authorities reversed their decision because they discovered the inmate was not truthful in his parole application and interview. Because the inmate had not yet been released, he did not possess and thereby lose a liberty interest that would trigger the requirements of hearings prior to revocation.[10]

RELEASE FROM CORRECTIONAL SUPERVISION

Entitlement to Freedom

Release from correctional supervision is determined by the sentencing authorities of federal and state criminal justice systems. When prisoners complete their sentences, they expect to be released. If corrections officials attempted to hold someone beyond the release date, a habeas corpus action likely would be filed. The prisoner would seek a judicial ruling that he or she was illegally detained by criminal justice officials. In modern times, most such situations likely are due to bureaucratic errors rather than intentional actions by corrections officials. Many prison systems are so overcrowded that they need to free up cell space to make room for new inmates. Thus, release from correctional supervision generally is handled by state or federal authorities according to their own sentencing guidelines, mandatory sentencing statutes, discretionary sentences imposed by judges, and regulations concerning "good time"—time deducted from a sentence for good behavior. Although states generally control the release of their own offenders, circumstances arise in which the Supreme Court examines states' practices and procedures.

For example, during the 1980s, Florida addressed its prison overcrowding problems through a series of statutes authorizing the state Department of Corrections to grant early release credits to prison inmates. In 1992, a new statute was enacted that canceled credits that had already been awarded to certain classes of offenders. In 1986, Kenneth Lynce had been sentenced to twenty-two years in prison for attempted murder. Through Florida's various early release credit program, Lynce earned credits that shaved more than fifteen years off his sentence, and so he was released in 1992. Shortly thereafter, Florida's attorney general issued a new interpretation of a 1992 statute that effectively canceled some credits—in Lynce's case, more than five years' worth—for offenders convicted of murder or attempted murder. Lynce was rearrested and returned to prison. He filed a habeas corpus petition claiming that his rights were violated when he was returned to prison after being released from correctional supervision.

The U.S. Supreme Court decided *Lynce v. Mathis* in 1997.[11] In a unanimous decision, the justices ruled that retroactive cancellation of release credits already used to obtain a prisoner's freedom violated the ***Ex Post Facto*** **Clause** of the Constitution. The Constitution's protection against *ex post facto* laws prohibits the government from defining crimes or increasing punishments after a crime has already been committed. The purpose of the provision is to make sure that the government gives people fair notice about what behaviors are illegal and what the punishments are for illegal behaviors—before those criminal behaviors are committed. Here, the Court viewed the 1992 statute and its interpretation by the attorney general as clearly retroactive—that is, after the fact with regard to Lynce's crime, sentence, and earned release credits. Thus, the new application of the law had the effect of "changing the rules of the game" and imposing extra punishment on him after he had been released.

One certainly could argue that a person sentenced to twenty-two years in prison for attempted murder should not be entitled to have that sentence reduced by more than fifteen years simply because prisons are overcrowded. Indeed, Lynce had no constitutional right to a reduced sentence. However, when Florida reduced his sentence by fifteen years and then released him, the U.S. Supreme Court required Florida to live by the rules that it established for its own corrections system. Once having released Lynce—and 164 other early releasees convicted of murder and attempted murder—Florida could not simply change its mind and deprive these people of their liberty again through an after-the-fact (*ex post facto*) rule.

A different issue concerning entitlement to release arose in *Foucha v. Louisiana* (1992).[12] Under American law, people found to be insane are not held responsible for their crimes. For example, John Hinckley, who shot President Ronald Reagan in 1981, was found not guilty by reason of insanity. But people who are acquitted of crimes because of insanity do not automatically go free. Usually, due to civil commitment statutes, they are confined in secure psychiatric hospitals, where they presumably receive treatment for their mental illnesses. Sometimes, a person acquitted of a crime due to insanity may be locked in a mental hospital for a longer period of time than he or she would have spent in prison if convicted of the crime.

Under Louisiana's law, people found not guilty of crimes by reason of insanity could be committed to psychiatric hospitals. If a hospital review committee recommended that the person be released because he or she had recovered from the mental illness, a court hearing was held to determine whether the person was a danger to him- or herself or others. If the court determined that the person posed a danger, the person could be returned to the psychiatric hospital *whether or not the person was still mentally ill*. Some observers saw the Louisiana law as a means to get around the legal prohibition on convicting and imprisoning people acquitted by reason of insanity by confining them in mental health institutions. This seemed especially true because, under this statute, people could be held in psychiatric hospitals even when they were no longer mentally ill.

If this was Louisiana's purpose, one can understand its underlying motive. People acquitted by reason of insanity are *factually guilty*—that is, they did, in fact, commit the crime. However, they are not *legally guilty*—and therefore cannot be punished in the criminal justice system—because of a long tradition of holding people legally responsible for their misdeeds only when they have a sufficient level of understanding of the nature and consequences of their actions. A statute seeking to detain such people further, even after they are no longer insane, may intend to protect society from people whose past actions lead us to fear what they may do in the future, or it may seek merely to punish people who escaped the usual criminal punishment through the insanity defense.

In a five-to-four decision, the Supreme Court ruled that the Louisiana law violated the Constitution. According to the majority opinion, states have the authority to commit insanity acquittees to mental institutions. However, it violates the right to due process for a state to hold such people after they have recovered their sanity or are no longer dangerous. Under the Court's 1992 decision, insanity acquittees are entitled to release when they regain their sanity.

A different twist on the problem of mentally-troubled offenders arose in 1997 in *Kansas v. Hendricks.* Hendricks had a forty-year record of sexually abusing children. After spending years shuttling between prisons and state psychiatric hospitals, he was convicted in 1984 of his seventh offense—taking "indecent liberties" with two thirteen-year-old boys. He was sentenced to serve ten years in prison. In 1994, shortly before Hendricks was scheduled to begin the release process by moving to a halfway house, the Kansas legislature enacted the Sexually Violent Predator Act—a new law undoubtedly influenced by the public outrage concerning publicized incidents of paroled sex offenders committing new crimes. Under the law, the state could use civil commitment to hospitalize persons likely to commit "predatory acts of sexual violence" due to a "mental abnormality" or a "personality disorder." The act was aimed at sex offenders who were scheduled for release from prison, who were found to be mentally unfit to stand trial, or who were acquitted of criminal charges by reason of insanity. In other words, the law was aimed at categories of sex offenders who could not be imprisoned or could not be imprisoned any longer. The state applied the law to Hendricks, and after a jury trial in which he was found to be a sexually violent predator, he was committed to the mental health system.

Hendricks challenged the law on three grounds. First, he claimed that it violated his right to due process, much the same as the Supreme Court had applied the right to due process for insanity acquittees in *Foucha v. Louisiana,* except here the state was using the law to detain someone further *after* he had served his entire criminal sentence. Second, he also raised a double jeopardy challenge, claiming that he was being punished twice for the same crime. Third, he cited the *Ex Post Facto* Clause, because Kansas created this new detention program *after* he had committed his crime and served most of his criminal sentence. As you read the case excerpt in Box 10-5, think about which claim produced the significant disagreement among the justices on the U.S. Supreme Court.

The debate among the justices about the *Ex Post Facto* Clause and its application to this situation highlights the different views of the case. The majority accepted the state's argument that the new statute was intended to provide treatment for sex offenders. The dissenters interpreted the statute as finding a new way to further punish sex offenders, especially since no treatment was provided for Hendricks while he was in prison or even when he was initially committed under the new statute.

Is this case consistent with *Foucha v. Louisiana,* in which the state was not allowed to hold insanity acquittees further even when it found them to pose a danger? Clearly, there are differences between the two cases. One case concerned insanity acquittees, and the other concerned sex offenders—although the Kansas statute would apply to acquittees in other cases. One case focused on the right to

BOX 10-5   *Kansas v. Hendricks,* 117 S.Ct. 2072 (1997)

JUSTICE THOMAS delivered the opinion of the Court.

. . . We granted Hendricks' cross petition to determine whether the Act violates the Constitution's double jeopardy prohibition or its ban on *ex post-facto* lawmaking. The thrust of Hendricks' argument is that the Act establishes criminal proceedings; hence confinement under it necessarily constitutes punishment. He contends that where, as here, newly enacted "punishment" is predicated upon past conduct for which he has already been convicted and forced to serve a prison sentence, the Constitution's Double Jeopardy and *Ex Post Facto* Clauses are violated. We are unpersuaded by Hendricks' argument that Kansas has established criminal proceedings.

The categorization of a particular proceeding as civil or criminal "is first of all a question of statutory construction." . . . We must initially ascertain whether the legislature meant the statute to establish "civil" proceedings. If so, we ordinarily defer to the legislature's stated intent. Here, Kansas' objective to create a civil proceeding is evidenced by its placement of the Sexually Violent Predator Act within the Kansas probate code, instead of the criminal code, as well as its description of the Act as creating a "*civil commitment procedure.*" . . . Nothing on the face of the statute suggests that the legislature sought to create anything other than a civil commitment scheme designed to protect the public from harm.

. . . [W]e will reject the legislature's manifest intent only where a party challenging the statute provides "the clearest proof" that "the statutory scheme [is] so punitive either in purpose or effect as to negate [the State's] intention" to deem it "civil.". . . In those limited circumstances, we will consider the statute to have established criminal proceedings for constitutional purposes. Hendricks, however, has failed to satisfy this heavy burden.

As a threshold matter, commitment under the Act does not implicate either of the two primary objectives of criminal punishment: retribution or deterrence. The Act's purpose is not retributive because it does not affix culpability for prior criminal conduct. Instead, such conduct is used solely for evidentiary purposes, either to demonstrate that a "mental abnormality" exists or to support a finding of future dangerousness. . . .

Hendricks focuses on his confinement's potentially indefinite duration as evidence of the State's punitive intent. That focus, however, is misplaced. Far from any punitive objective, the confinement's duration is instead linked to the stated purposes of the commitment, namely, to hold the person until his mental abnormality no longer causes him to be a threat to others. . . .

Finally, Hendricks argues that the Act is necessarily punitive because it fails to offer any legitimate "treatment." . . .

Although the treatment program initially offered to Hendricks may have seemed somewhat meager, it must be remembered that he was the first person committed under the Act. That the State did not have all of its treatment procedures in place is thus not surprising. . . . [B]efore this Court, Kansas declared "[a]bsolutely" that persons committed under the Act are now receiving in the neighborhood of "31.5 hours of treatment per week." . . .

Where the State has "disavowed any punitive intent"; limited confinement to a small segment of particularly dangerous individuals; provided strict procedural safeguards; directed that confined persons be segregated from the general prison population and afforded the same status as others who have been civilly committed; recommended treatment if such is possible; and permitted immediate release upon a showing that the individual is no longer dangerous or mentally impaired, we cannot say that it acted with punitive intent. We therefore hold that the Act does not establish criminal proceedings and

(continued)

that involuntary confinement pursuant to the Act is not punitive. Our conclusion that the Act is nonpunitive thus removes an essential prerequisite for both Hendricks' double jeopardy and *ex post-facto* claims. . . .

We hold that the Kansas Sexually Violent Predator Act comports with due process requirements and neither runs afoul of double jeopardy principles nor constitutes an exercise in impermissible *ex post-facto* lawmaking. Accordingly, the judgment of the Kansas Supreme Court is reversed.

It is so ordered.

JUSTICE BREYER, with whom JUSTICES STEVENS and SOUTER join, and with whom JUSTICE GINSBURG joins as to Parts II and III, dissenting.

. . . Kansas' 1994 Act violates the Federal Constitution's prohibition of "any . . . *ex post-facto* Law" if it "inflicts" upon Hendricks "a greater punishment" than did the law "annexed to" his "crime[s]" when he "committed" those crimes in 1984. . . . The majority agrees that the Clause "'forbids the application of any *new punitive measure* to a crime already consummated.'" . . . But it finds the Act is not "punitive." With respect to that basic question, I disagree with the majority.

Certain resemblances between the Act's "civil commitment" and traditional criminal punishments are obvious. Like criminal imprisonment, the Act's civil commitment amounts to "secure" confinement, . . . and "incarceration against one's will." . . .

Moreover, the Act, like criminal punishment, imposes its confinement (or sanction) only upon an individual who has previously committed a criminal offense. . . .

In this circumstance, with important features of the Act pointing in opposite directions [in light of its stated "civil" intentions but characteristics that look like punishment], I would place particular importance upon those features that would likely distinguish between a basically punitive and a basically nonpunitive purpose. . . . [F]or reasons that I will point out, when a State believes that treatment does exist, and then couples that admission with a legislatively required delay of such treatment until a person is at the end of a jail term (so that further incapacitation is therefore necessary), such a legislative scheme begins to look punitive. . . .

Several important treatment related factors . . . in this case suggest [that there is a punitive rather than civil purpose]. First, the State Supreme Court here . . . has held that treatment is not a significant objective of the Act. The Kansas court wrote that the Act's purpose is "segregation of sexually violent offenders," with "treatment" a matter that was "incidental at best." . . .

We have generally given considerable weight to the findings of state and lower federal courts regarding the intent or purpose underlying state officials' actions. . . .

The record provides support for the Kansas court's conclusion. The court found that, as of the time of Hendricks' commitment, the State had not funded treatment, it had not entered into treatment contracts, and it had little, if any, qualified treatment staff. . . . Hendricks, according to the commitment program's own director, was receiving "essentially no treatment." . . .

It is not surprising that some of the Act's official supporters had seen in it an opportunity permanently to confine dangerous sex offenders. . . .

Second, the Kansas statute insofar as it applies to previously convicted offenders, such as Hendricks, commits, confines, and treats those offenders *after* they have served virtually their

due process, and the other debated *ex post facto* law protections. However, underlying the two cases is a common issue: In a society increasingly fearful about crime, how much power does the state have to continue detaining offenders who can no longer be detained under the traditional rules of the criminal justice system—either because they completed their criminal sentence or because they were acquitted by reason of insanity? For the moment, the Supreme Court has treated

entire criminal sentence. That time related circumstance seems deliberate. . . . But why, one might ask, does the Act not commit and require treatment of sex offenders sooner, say soon after they begin to serve their sentences?

. . . [I]t is difficult to see why rational legislators who seek treatment would write the Act in this way—providing treatment years after the criminal act that indicated its necessity. . . . And it is particularly difficult to see why legislators who specifically wrote into the statute a finding that "prognosis for rehabilitating . . . in a prison setting is poor" would leave an offender in that setting for months or years before beginning treatment. This is to say, the timing provisions of the statute confirm the Kansas Supreme Court's view that treatment was not a particularly important legislative objective.

Third, the statute, at least as of the time Kansas applied it to Hendricks, did not require the committing authority to consider the possibility of using less restrictive alternatives, such as postrelease supervision, halfway houses, or other methods that *amici* supporting Kansas here have mentioned. . . .

This Court has said that a failure to consider, or to use, "alternative and less harsh methods" to achieve a nonpunitive objective can help to show that legislature's "purpose . . . was to punish." . . .

Fourth, . . . I have found 17 States with laws that seek to protect the public from mentally abnormal, sexually dangerous individuals through civil commitment or other mandatory treatment programs. Ten of those statutes, unlike the Kansas statute, begin treatment of an offender soon after he has been apprehended and charged with a serious sex offense. Only seven, like Kansas, delay "civil" commitment (and treatment) until the offender has served his criminal sentence (and this figure includes the Acts of Minnesota and New Jersey, both of which generally do not delay treatment). Of these seven, however, six (unlike Kansas) require consideration of less restrictive alternatives. . . . Only one State other than Kansas, namely Iowa, both delays civil commitment (and consequent treatment) and does not explicitly consider less restrictive alternatives. But the law of [Iowa] applies prospectively only [considering those committing offenses after July 1, 1997], thereby avoiding *ex post-facto* problems. . . .

To find a violation of [the *Ex Post Facto*] Clause here, however, is not to hold that the Clause prevents Kansas, or other States, from enacting dangerous sexual offender statutes. A statute that operates prospectively, for example, does not offend the *Ex Post-Facto* Clause. . . . Neither does it offend the *Ex Post-Facto* Clause for a State to sentence offenders to the fully authorized sentence, to seek consecutive, rather than concurrent, sentences, or to invoke recidivism statutes to lengthen imprisonment. Moreover, a statute that operates retroactively, like Kansas' statute, nonetheless does not offend the Clause *if the confinement that it imposes is not punishment*—if, that is to say, the legislature does not simply add a later criminal punishment to an earlier one.

The statutory provisions before us do amount to punishment primarily because, as I have said, the legislature did not tailor the statute to fit the nonpunitive civil aim of treatment, which it concedes exists in Hendricks' case. The Clause in these circumstances does not stand as an obstacle to achieving important protections for the public's safety; rather it provides an assurance that, where so significant a restriction of an individual's basic freedoms is at issue, a State cannot cut corners. Rather, the legislature must hew to the Constitution's liberty protecting line. . . .

I therefore would affirm the judgment below.

---

the two situations differently by denying states further detention powers with respect to recovered insanity acquittees (*Foucha*) but granting states additional power over sex offenders (*Hendricks*). In analyzing the practical dynamics of the Supreme Court's decision making, it is unclear whether this distinction will remain. Both cases were five-to-four decisions, which means that the change of a single vote could either deny or grant states' power in both circumstances. The future of these issues may depend on how the Supreme Court's composition changes in the future. In any case, the *Hendricks* decision certainly invites states to consider the possibility that statutes may be developed to permit continued detention of offenders feared by society because of their past actions—even when those people cannot be held under the usual criminal justice rules and processes.

Civil Disabilities

Upon completion of a criminal sentence, ex-offenders continue to suffer consequences from their past crimes. Sometimes, the consequences are informal—for example, when employers, credit agencies, educational institutions, and other important decision makers deny people opportunities and benefits because of a criminal record. In a highly publicized incident in 1995, a high school student's acceptance for admission to Harvard University was suddenly rescinded when the university learned that the young woman had been convicted of manslaughter for beating her mother to death five years earlier.[13] The woman had completed her criminal sentence in a juvenile detention facility. Despite the fact that she had served the punishment imposed on her by the state for her crime, however, the university arguably "punished" her further by denying her an opportunity for which she was otherwise apparently well qualified. This incident received national publicity because it involved prestigious Harvard University. But such things happen every day and affect the lives of many people with criminal records who have already paid the price imposed by the criminal justice system for committing a crime.

The continuing price of a criminal conviction is not limited to decisions by private institutions. States and the federal government have laws that impose continuing limitations on many ex-offenders in the form of **civil disabilities**—legal restrictions on rights and opportunities as a consequence of past criminal convictions. Depending on the jurisdiction, such restrictions may limit the right to vote, hold public office, obtain certain occupational licenses, or gain employment in certain jobs, such as law enforcement officers.

Table 10-1 lists the most frequent civil disabilities imposed on ex-offenders by various states.[14] For example, fourteen states permanently deny convicted felons the right to vote, while other states suspend the right until completion of sentence, release from prison, or good behavior during a postsentence waiting period.[15] Six states permanently deny convicted felons the opportunity to hold government jobs, while others limit employment opportunities if they are related to the crime committed by the person (e.g., embezzlement or fraud). Thirty-one states permanently restrict the right of convicted felons to serve on juries. Eighteen states prevent convicted felons from ever holding public office, and seven more states impose that limitation for those convicted of certain offenses.[16] Additional restrictions concern the ability to legally own firearms and an obligation to register with local law enforcement agencies. And many states permit a felony conviction to determine the outcome of child custody and divorce cases.[17] Although these family developments occur prior to release, they obviously have

| **TABLE 10-1** | **Common Civil Disabilities Imposed on Convicted Felons, 1996** |

Permanent Loss of Voting Rights

Alabama	Mississippi	Virginia
Arkansas	Nevada	Washington
Florida	New Mexico	Wisconsin
Iowa	Rhode Island	Wyoming
Kentucky	Tennessee	

Permanent Bar on Public Employment

Alabama	Iowa	Rhode Island
Delaware	Mississippi	South Carolina

Permanent Loss of Right to Hold Public Office

Alabama	Kentucky	Pennsylvania (some crimes)
Arkansas	Maine (some crimes)	South Carolina
California (some crimes)	Massachusetts (some crimes)	Tennessee
Delaware	Mississippi	Texas
District of Columbia (some crimes)	Nevada	Virginia
Florida	New Jersey	West Virginia (some crimes)
Georgia	New Mexico	Wisconsin
Indiana (some crimes)	New York	
Iowa	Ohio	

Permanent Bar on Jury Service

Alabama	Massachusetts	Rhode Island
Arkansas	Missouri	South Carolina
California	Montana	South Dakota
Delaware	Nebraska	Tennessee
Florida	Nevada	Texas
Georgia	New Jersey	Utah
Hawaii	New Mexico	Virginia
Idaho	New York	West Virginia
Iowa	Ohio	Wyoming
Kentucky	Oklahoma	
Maryland	Pennsylvania	

Source: Kathleen M. Olivares, Velmer S. Burton, Jr., and Francis T. Cullen, "The Collateral Consequences of a Felony Conviction: A National Study of State Legal Codes 10 Years Later," *Federal Probation* 60 (September 1996): 12.

effects on individuals and families that last long after the offender has completed a sentence.

What is the purpose of legal restrictions that extend beyond the completion of a sentence? If society says a certain crime is worth three years of incarceration and the offender serves those three years, why hasn't he or she paid the debt and gained the chance to start over as a full-fledged member of society? While some may argue that there is strong reason to prevent ex-felons from gaining power and serving as role models in elective office, how is society harmed by permitting ex-felons to vote?

Critics of civil disabilities argue that such legal restrictions help to defeat the goals of rehabilitation. Ex-felons continue to be punished and stigmatized—and told that they will never be permitted to be equal citizens in society, even after they have served their sentences. By excluding ex-felons from participating in key components of society, such as voting, society continues to humiliate individuals for past misdeeds. Many people will suffer lifelong civil disabilities from foolish actions taken as immature eighteen-year-olds. Ex-offenders who have straightened themselves out and learned a lesson from youthful mistakes are prevented from giving their communities the full benefit of the insight, maturity, and wisdom that they may have gained.

A particularly striking impact of civil disabilities is the weakened political power of African-Americans. One study estimated that 1.46 million African-American men out of a total voting-age population of 10.4 million have lost their right to vote.[18] The impact of civil disabilities weakens the voting power of African-Americans and deprives many men from the opportunity to be leaders in public life, even decades after the bad behavior of their youth. This impact is particularly troubling because of racial discrimination in the justice process. For example, evidence suggests that African-Americans are more likely to be subject to discretionary arrest decisions by police, more likely to be targeted in drug investigations, more likely to be affected by adverse decisions related to bail and juvenile court, and otherwise subjected to various forms of discrimination in the criminal justice system.[19] Thus, the adverse effects of civil disabilities extend and magnify the consequences of racial discrimination.

In light of the number of people affected, these rules may influence who is elected to be mayors, judges, and other important officials in certain cities. In a democracy that emphasizes the importance of permitting citizens to choose their leaders and use their votes to shape public policy, is it appropriate to maintain these civil disabilities—especially when they may serve to magnify the impact of racial discrimination?

In fact, ex-offenders have challenged many of these restrictions in court. However, the courts have upheld many restrictions, and so such restrictions are common in many states and not merely isolated laws in specific states. For example, the U.S. Supreme Court examined California's ban on voting by convicted felons in *Richardson v. Ramirez* (1974).[20] The Court concluded that states possess the authority to limit convicted felons' right to vote. In support of this conclusion, the Court pointed to a provision of the Fourteenth Amendment of the Constitution that refers to states' authority to deny voting rights to people "for participation in rebellion, *or other crimes*" (emphasis added). Although ex-offenders frequently say that they "paid their debt to society" by serving their term of punishment, they do not necessarily begin life again with a clean slate. By virtue of being convicted of a crime, there are continuing consequences, both formal and informal, including legal limitations on rights for those who have previously been convicted of felonies.

SUMMARY

- There is no right to probation or parole. Probation is a sentence determined by a judge or sentencing guidelines, and parole is determined by state authorities, usually a state parole board. Both probation and parole involve release of convicted offenders, subject to specific conditions, while they remain under the supervision of the corrections system.

- Probationers and parolees enjoy more freedom than people in prison, but their rights are limited nonetheless. They must obey the conditions of their release or face the prospect of imprisonment. States may not interfere with probationers' and parolees' rights to free speech and religion without valid reasons, but states have significant authority to monitor releasees and use warrantless searches to find weapons, contraband, or evidence of crimes.

- Probation and parole may not be revoked at the discretion of a probation or parole officer. These officers enjoy significant discretion in determining when to report alleged violations of release conditions, but the Supreme Court requires a two-stage hearing process before probation or parole is revoked.

- The two-stage hearing process begins after arrest with a preliminary hearing to determine if probable cause exists to believe that a violation occurred. The second stage is the revocation hearing. In both stages, officials must provide notice of alleged violations to the offender, an opportunity for the offender to present arguments and evidence, a neutral hearing officer or board, and an opportunity for the offender to cross-examine opposing witnesses.

- There is no right to counsel for revocation proceedings. Requests for representation by an attorney are decided on a case-by-case basis depending on the complexity of the case and the capabilities of the offender facing revocation.

- Prisoners may file habeas corpus petitions to challenge continued confinement beyond their date for release from the corrections system.

- States may not rescind early release credits after they have been granted and led to the early release of an offender.

- States may not continue to detain insanity acquittees who regain their sanity, but they may use civil commitment procedures to continue confining sex offenders who have completed their criminal sentences.

- After release from the corrections system, ex-offenders may be denied rights, benefits, and opportunities as a result of their criminal records. Some denials may stem from adverse decisions by employers, credit agencies, and other private decision makers. Other restrictions are imposed as civil disabilities under laws that limit the right to vote, hold public office, and gain certain employment opportunities.

Key Terms

civil disabilities
Ex Post Facto Clause
Gagnon v. Scarpelli (1973)
Griffin v. Wisconsin (1987)
Kansas v. Hendricks (1997)

Morrissey v. Brewer (1972)
parole
*Pennsylvania Board of Probation and Parole
v. Scott* (1998)
probation

Additional Readings

Filcik, Jeffrey. 1990. "Signs of the Times: Scarlet Letter Probation Conditions." *Washington University Journal of Urban and Contemporary Law* 37: 291–323.

Fogel, Sandra. 1993. "Retroactive Application of Illinois Statute Eliminating Opportunity for Annual Parole Hearings Violates Ex Post Facto Prohibition." *Southern Illinois University Law Journal* 17: 403–416.

Rosen, Cathy Jo. 1990. "The Fourth Amendment Implications of Urine Testing for Evidence of Drug Use in Probation." *Brooklyn Law Review* 55: 1195–1253.

Notes

1. State v. Travis, 967 P.2d 234 (Idaho 1994); see Risdon Slate and Patrick Anderson, "Lying Probationers and Parolees: The Issue of Polygraph Surveillance," *Federal Probation* 60 (September 1996): 54–59.

2. Greenholtz v. Inmates of the Nebraska Penal and Correction Complex, 442 U.S. 1 (1979).

3. Connecticut Board of Pardons v. Dumschat, 452 U.S. 458 (1981).

4. Ohio Adult Parole Authority v. Woodard, 118 S.Ct. 1244 (1998).

5. Sobell v. Reed, 327 F.Supp. 1294 (S.D. N.Y. 1971); Hyland v. Procunier, 311 F.Supp. 749 (N.D. Cal. 1970).

6. In re Mannino, 92 Cal. Rptr. 880 (Cal. Ct. App. 1971); John W. Palmer, *Constitutional Rights of Prisoners*, 5th ed. (Cincinnati: Anderson, 1997), p. 170.

7. Bearden v. Georgia, 461 U.S. 660 (1983).

8. Mempa v. Rhay, 389 U.S. 128 (1967).

9. Young v. Harper, 117 S.Ct. 1148 (1997).

10. Jago v. Van Curen, 454 U.S. 14 (1981).

11. Lynce v. Mathis, 117 S.Ct. 891 (1997).

12. Foucha v. Louisiana, 504 U.S. 71 (1992).

13. "Killers Need Not Apply," *Newsweek*, 17 April 1995, p. 39.

14. Kathleen M. Olivares, Velmer S. Burton, and Francis T. Cullen, "The Collateral Consequences of a Felony Conviction: A National Study of State Legal Codes 10 Years Later," *Federal Probation* 60 (1996): 10–17.

15. Ibid., p. 11.

16. Ibid., p. 12.

17. Ibid., p. 11.

18. Pierre Thomas, "Jail Time Endangers Black Vote, Study Shows," *Lansing State Journal* (*Washington Post* wire service), 31 January 1997, p. A5.

19. See Samuel Walker, Cassia Spohn, and Miriam DeLeone, *The Color of Justice: Race, Ethnicity, and Crime in America* (Belmont, CA: Wadsworth, 1996).

20. Richardson v. Ramirez, 418 U.S. 24 (1974).

CHAPTER ELEVEN

Jails

Imagine your uncle goes on a European vacation and gives you permission to use his car while he is away. On a Saturday afternoon, a police officer stops you for failing to use your turn signal while changing lanes. After the officer runs a computer check on the car's tags, she handcuffs you, places you in the backseat of the police car, and reads you your *Miranda* warnings. When the officer informs you that you are driving a stolen car, you remember that your uncle's car was stolen six months ago but was recovered and returned to him a month later. Apparently, the computer records were never updated to show that the car was recovered. Because your uncle is out of the country, there's no way you can prove that the car is not stolen.

During your weekend in jail, as you await your appearance before a judge on Monday morning, you endure repeated strip searches, you are beaten up by several rough characters sharing the same cell, the jail's heating system quits working in the middle of winter, and the greasy, undercooked eggs served for breakfast make you sick. When you complain about what has happened to you, a deputy sheriff pushes you against a brick wall and tells you to "shut up!"

On Monday morning, it turns out that the judge is a friend of your uncle's who knows about the stolen car being recovered, so the charges against you are dismissed. When your personal property is returned by jail personnel, you discover that all of your money is missing from your wallet, and no one seems to know anything about it. Thus, you find yourself on the sidewalk in front of the jail, penniless and with no way to get home because the car is still in the impound lot miles away. Angry and humiliated, you decide to sue the city for violating your rights. Have your Eighth Amendment rights to protection against cruel and unusual punishments been violated? What about your Fourth Amendment rights to protection against unreasonable searches and seizures?

THE CONTEXT OF JAILS

It is common for Americans to think of jails and prisons as holding people different from themselves. With respect to prisons, the conventional wisdom is accurate. People in prison typically are those who committed violent crimes or drug offenses. With respect to jails, however, the conventional wisdom is only partly accurate. Most of the half-million people in American jails on any given day are poor, which differentiates them from the majority of Americans. However, only about half of the people in jail have been convicted of a crime. The others are unconvicted arrestees awaiting trial—or release if the charges are dropped—many of whom are too poor to post bail. All of the unconvicted individuals in jail, whether poor or not, have one thing in common: A police officer decided to arrest them. People in this category are not limited to "bad" people who are locked up to protect the "good" people in society. Rather, they are individuals who found themselves in a place and a time when a police officer made a discretionary decision to make an arrest. Many of them are, in fact, guilty of crimes. But others may be arrested and detained through mistaken identity, an argument with a police officer, or bizarre behavior that officials wish to remove from public view.

Are unconvicted people in jail different from the majority of people in society? In one respect, yes—they are largely poor people. But in another respect, no—anyone can get arrested in American society, and anyone can go to jail. You do not have to commit a crime, and you do not have to do anything wrong. For example, someone might wrongly identify you as a purse snatcher. Or you might rush from home one morning and forget your purse or wallet; if you are stopped for a traffic violation, you could be arrested for driving without a license. Or there might be a mistake in the criminal justice system, as shown in the example that begins this chapter, which is based on real events. As you read Box 11-1, which describes conditions in New York City holding cells, imagine the possibility that you could end up in jail. Then ask yourself: If innocent people can end up in jail, what rights should protect people who are in jail? Should people in jail have more rights than, or at least the same rights as, convicted offenders serving in prison?

| BOX 11-1 | The Reality of Jail Conditions |

A nurse was arrested when a jealous woman, who thought the nurse was chasing her husband, accused the nurse of theft. A college student was arrested for disorderly conduct and resisting arrest. A broadcast production assistant was arrested for driving his uncle's car, which was wrongly listed on a police computer as stolen. All three individuals were released after a few days, and charges were dropped. However, during those few days in New York City's jail cells, they also saw and experienced unforgettable and frightening scenes.

Arrestees are brought to jail chained together in groups of up to twenty individuals, and these groups are transported in vans with only ten seats. By virtue of being arrested, someone could easily be chained to another arrestee who is vomiting or who smells as if he or she sleeps amid trash on the streets. Large cells may be filled with fifty or more people, standing or sitting on the concrete floor. There are no mattresses or clean clothing. If there are toilets, they are in wide-open view along the wall of the cell, and many of them are filthy and backed up. The typical meal served to inmates is a baloney and cheese sandwich.

Inside the cells, aggressive arrestees prey upon those who are weak or fearful, taking their watches and jewelry and threatening violence for any resistance. These holding facilities are designed to hold people for only a few hours, not for a few days. Yet people are detained for as long as seventy-two hours before they see a judge and then are either released or moved to the city's regular jail. In 1990, the average stay in the holding cells was forty hours. Imagine all of the things that could happen to someone in forty hours in such a situation.

The nurse remained standing for two nights, refusing to sit down or use the bathroom in order to avoid contact with the filth. The broadcast production assistant bluffed his way out of a confrontation with a cellmate who threatened to cut him with a razor blade; he gained his release after forty-four hours. The college student spent nearly forty-eight hours in custody before gaining release.

Sources: William Glaberson, "Trapped in the Terror of New York's Holding Pens," *New York Times,* 23 March 1990, pp. A1, B4, B5; Selwyn Raab, "Judge Orders Payments to 7 Inmates Without Beds," *New York Times,* 11 April 1991, p. B8; Douglas Martin, "Mounting Delays Hinder Arrest System," *New York Times,* 11 July 1987, p. 33.

The New York City holding cells described in Box 11-1 represent a worst-case scenario for jail conditions. Not all jails are that bad, and many jails are well-organized, professionally managed modern facilities. However, jails vary widely with respect to size, organization, and conditions. Jails are run by local governments, which frequently do not have the resources necessary to keep facilities in tiptop shape.

Most jails are administered by a county or city. The jail may be housed in a building designed and built especially for the purpose of detaining arrestees and punishing people serving short sentences. Or the jail may be merely a wing of cells or one large cell in a section of a courthouse or police station. Typically, the jail is administered by the county sheriff, an elected official who usually possesses a background in law enforcement rather than corrections. Corrections responsibilities are an extra set of duties that sheriffs and their deputies handle on the side. Thus, the people running local jails may not possess either the expertise or the interest to run these institutions professionally.

Given limited facilities and populations that may change on a daily basis, jail administrators face difficult challenges. Unlike prisons, jails typically do not have recreational, vocational, or educational programs to occupy inmates, so they may be idle throughout each day. As corrections administrators know, idleness and boredom can contribute to conflict as inmates take out their frustrations on one another. In addition, the population within jails changes constantly. Each day brings a new mix of detainees accused of murder and other violent crimes, arrested merely for being drunk and disorderly, or held for lack of space in mental institutions. Some scholars argue that jails are the facilities used by society to control people who are considered odd and unpleasant—such as alcoholics, homeless people, and mental patients—in order to keep them from "bothering" the public, even when they have committed no crimes.[1] In Mississippi, for example, mental patients may be held for months in jail—without being accused of any crime—as they wait for a bed to open up at a state mental hospital.[2] One survey found that 75 percent of Mississippi's jails contained mentally ill people being held without any criminal charges, a figure second only to the 81 percent of Kentucky's jails holding mentally ill people.[3] How can a local government possibly have the facilities, programs, and expertise to deal with the range of people—and problems—that are brought to their doors by police officers? Usually, they can do little more than detain these people and hope that they can prevent violence, suicides, and the other worst-case problems that arise in jails.

As you can see, jails present special challenges in terms of the protection of constitutional rights. On the one hand, jails hold many people who are presumed to be innocent and therefore should not automatically lose all of the rights lost by individuals convicted of violating criminal laws. On the other hand, jails do not necessarily have the resources and facilities to separate the unconvicted, presumably innocent arrestees from the convicted offenders who are serving short sentences or awaiting transfer to prison. This makes it very difficult to protect particular rights for one set of inmates that are being denied to another set. Moreover, the problems of jails can be complicated by the mix of inmates—and inmate problems—coming through the jailhouse doors every day. These problems may be compounded by the lack of interest and expertise that many local law enforcement officials bring to the business of jail administration. Unlike prison administrators, local sheriffs may not devote much attention to planning and developing the most effective practices and procedures for their local jails.

RIGHTS OF JAIL INMATES

With regard to the rights of prison inmates, we have seen that the courts usually seek to balance individuals' constitutional rights with corrections institutions' need to maintain order and security. The same holds true for the rights of people in jail. In fact, jail security may have special importance to officials because many jails are located in the centers of cities and towns while prisons often are located in rural areas. Escapes from jails thus may be especially unsettling to the public.

The U.S. Supreme Court produced its major precedent concerning jails in **Bell v. Wolfish (1979)**. A lawsuit was filed on behalf of all inmates in the Metropolitan Correctional Center (MCC), a jail in New York City holding many inmates awaiting trial on federal charges. The facility also housed inmates serving short sentences and convicted offenders awaiting transfer to federal prisons. This federal jail was different from the holding cells operated by the City of New York, which were described in Box 11-1. According to the Supreme Court's opinion, "The MCC differs markedly from the familiar image of a jail; there are no barred cells, dank, colorless corridors, or clanging steel gates." Instead, the twelve-story structure had residential units consisting of dormitory-type rooms connected to a central common room. Despite being designed to provide a more pleasant environment than the traditional bars-and-cells jail, detainees filed a lawsuit challenging many aspects of their confinement. As described by the Supreme Court,

> [The inmates'] petition served up a veritable potpourri of complaints that implicated virtually every facet of the institution's conditions and practices. [They] charged [among other things] that they had been deprived of their statutory and constitutional rights because of overcrowded conditions, undue length of confinement, improper searches, inadequate recreational, educational, and employment opportunities, insufficient staff, and objectionable restrictions on the purchase and receipt of personal items and books.

Overcrowding at the jail was a central feature of the legal complaint. The dormitory rooms had been designed to hold a single inmate. However, an unexpected influx of inmates had led not only to double bunking in each room but also to inmates sleeping on cots in the central common rooms.

The Constitution and Jail Conditions

The Supreme Court's approach to analyzing the complaints of unconvicted jail inmates differs in one significant respect from its analysis of claims filed by prison inmates: It does not apply the Eighth Amendment to protect unconvicted people in jails. The Eighth Amendment prohibits "cruel and unusual *punishments.*" However, unconvicted offenders are, in the eyes of the law, *not* being punished. In the criminal justice system, "punishment" is applied to people *after* they have been convicted of a crime. Prior to conviction, a suspect is merely being detained, not punished. Thus, the Eighth Amendment does not apply—except to those convicted offenders who are serving short sentences in jail or awaiting transfer to prison.

At first glance, it may appear odd that the Eighth Amendment does not apply to everyone in jail. Aren't jailed suspects suffering from the same pains of imprisonment as convicted offenders in prisons? They lose their liberty; they live under severely restricted conditions in which they are at the mercy of officials to feed them and provide for the necessities of life; they are deprived of free contact with family and friends; and they live among dangerous and unstable individuals. It certainly must feel like punishment to those who are in jail. Yet under the law, if they have not yet been convicted of a crime, they are not yet being punished. Therefore, the Eighth Amendment does not protect them.

At the same time, it may seem odd that *some* jail inmates are protected by the Eighth Amendment while others are not, even though they are living in the same conditions. Because jails lack the resources and facilities to house the unconvicted separately from the convicted, everyone is treated alike. In other words, those who are—under the law—not being punished are treated exactly the same as those who are being punished. Ironically, of course, only those inmates who have been convicted of violating society's criminal laws receive the benefits and protections of the Eighth Amendment. Those who are still "innocent" cannot claim the same constitutional protections.

As you will see, the courts deal with these apparent contradictions by applying another provision of the Constitution to provide unconvicted pretrial detainees with comparable protections to those offered by the Eighth Amendment for convicted offenders. As you read the excerpt of *Bell v. Wolfish* in Box 11-2, see if you can identify the constitutional right that protects unconvicted detainees. Did the Supreme Court reach the same conclusions that it would have reached if it had applied the Eighth Amendment?

Instead of applying the Eighth Amendment to unconvicted detainees, the courts apply the right to **due process of law.** Specifically, the Fifth Amendment Due Process Clause protects detainees in federal custody, while the Fourteenth Amendment Due Process Clause protects detainees in the custody of state and local officials. For purposes of evaluating the rights of jail inmates, the two clauses operate in the same manner. The clauses are located in different parts of the Constitution because the Fourteenth Amendment's clause was designed specifically to provide the right to protection against actions by state and local officials. Therefore, the key phrasing in the Fourteenth Amendment is, "[N]or shall any State deprive any person of life, liberty, or property, without due process of law." This is nearly identical to the language in the Fifth Amendment, which states, "No person shall . . . be deprived of life, liberty, or property, without due process of law." According to *Bell v. Wolfish,* any jail practices or conditions that impose "punishment" on pretrial detainees violate the right to protection against deprivations without due process.

In terms of the actual phrasing of both due process clauses, what is it that unconvicted inmates are losing if any jail practices or conditions constitute "punishment"? They have already lost liberty by virtue of being arrested and jailed. Jail inmates who file lawsuits are not complaining about losing their lives—although the families of inmates who die in jails might make that claim. They might file claims about lost property, but as indicated in *Bell v. Wolfish,* the Due Process Clause is not limited to such claims. It is also used to complain about overcrowding, food, and other issues concerning conditions of confinement. Where in either Due Process Clause does it say anything about conditions of confinement in jails? Obviously, these clauses do not refer specifically to jail conditions. Why, then, does the Supreme Court use the right to due process as the basis for guarding against improper practices and conditions in jails?

BOX 11-2   *Bell v. Wolfish*, 441 U.S. 520 (1979)

JUSTICE REHNQUIST delivered the opinion of the Court.

. . . In evaluating the constitutionality of conditions or restrictions of pretrial detention that implicate only the protection against deprivation of liberty without due process of law, we think that the proper inquiry is whether those conditions amount to punishment of the detainee. For under the Due Process Clause, a detainee may not be punished prior to an adjudication of guilt in accordance with due process of law. . . . A person lawfully committed to pretrial detention has not been adjudged guilty of any crime. He has had only a "judicial determination of probable cause as a prerequisite to [the] extended restraint of [his] liberty following arrest." . . . And, if he is detained for a suspected violation of a federal law, he also has had a bail hearing. . . . Under such circumstances, the Government concededly may detain him to ensure his presence at trial and may subject him to the restrictions and conditions of the detention facility so long as those conditions and restrictions do not amount to punishment, or otherwise violate the Constitution.

Not every disability imposed during pretrial detention amounts to "punishment" in the constitutional sense, however. Once the Government has exercised its conceded authority to detain a person pending trial, it obviously is entitled to employ devices that are calculated to effectuate this detention. Traditionally, this has meant confinement in a facility which, no matter how modern or how antiquated, results in restricting the movement of a detainee in a manner in which he would not be restricted if he simply were free to walk the streets pending trial. Whether it be called a jail, a prison, or a custodial center, the purpose of the facility is to detain. Loss of freedom of choice and privacy are inherent incidents of confinement in such a facility. And the fact that such detention interferes with the detainee's understandable desire to live as comfortably as possible and with as little restraint as possible during confinement

does not convert the conditions or restrictions of detention into "punishment." . . .

. . . A court must decide whether the disability is imposed for the purpose of punishment or whether it is but an incident of some other legitimate governmental purpose. . . . Absent a showing of an expressed intent to punish on the part of detention facility officials, that determination generally will turn on "whether an alternative purpose to which [the restriction] may rationally be connected is assignable for it, and whether it appears excessive in relation to the alternative purpose assigned [to it]." . . .

. . . We do not accept [the detainees'] argument that the Government's interest in ensuring a detainee's presence at trial is the *only* objective that may justify restraints and conditions once the decision is lawfully made to confine a person. . . . The Government also has legitimate interests that stem from its need to manage the facility in which the individual is detained. These legitimate operational concerns may require administrative measures that go beyond those that are, strictly speaking, necessary to ensure that the detainee shows up at trial. For example, the Government must be able to take steps to maintain security and order at the institution and make certain no weapons or illicit drugs reach detainees. Restraints that are reasonably related to the institution's interest in maintaining jail security do not, without more, constitute unconstitutional punishment, even if they are discomforting and are restrictions that the detainee would not have experienced had he been released while awaiting trial. We need not here attempt to detail the precise extent of the legitimate governmental interests that may justify conditions or restrictions of pretrial detention. It is enough simply to recognize that in addition to ensuring the detainees' presence at trial, the effective management of the detention facility once the individual is confined is a valid objective that may justify imposition of conditions and restrictions of pretrial detention and dispel any inference that such restrictions are intended as punishment. . . .

Historically, the Supreme Court has viewed the right to due process as the most flexible of all Constitutional rights. The Court has regularly interpreted the words "due process" as covering a wide range of rights that the justices believe exist but that are not mentioned explicitly in the Constitution. Over time, the Court has used the words "due process" as the basis for rights to enter into contracts, travel between states, obtain contraceptives, and make choices about abortion. With respect to jails, everyone seems to agree that unconvicted arrestees should be protected against excessive harms, yet the Constitution does not specifically provide for such protections. Thus, the Court employs the due process clauses to provide needed protection.

The Court is not always examining whether there is *literally* a loss of liberty (obviously there is such a loss in all cases of jailed detainees), a loss of life (which applies to relatively few cases), or a loss of property (which applies to only some cases). Instead, the Court has ruled that when practices and conditions in jail are excessive or harmful, pretrial detainees are losing *something* important, not simply "life, liberty, or property" as stated in the Constitution. Perhaps they are losing something related to the quality of their daily lives or to the extensiveness of their loss of liberty. Fundamentally, these losses, if excessive, are boiled down into the concept of "punishment."

As with other matters of legal interpretation, the Supreme Court's use of the right to due process does not work neatly if one focuses on the Constitution's words. In theory, people should not receive "punishment"—the full losses associated with restrictions on liberty and uncomfortable living conditions—until they have enjoyed the entire due process of law (i.e., hearings, trials, and so on) required to convict someone of a crime. In that respect, it makes sense to say that "punishment" applied to unconvicted detainees violates the right to due process of law. In practice, however, pretrial detainees suffer the same losses and experience the same conditions of confinement as their cellmates who are convicted offenders being punished. Thus, in the final analysis, the justices actually are using the due process clauses as straight substitutes for the Eighth Amendment. Because they defined the Eighth Amendment concept of "punishment" to apply only to conditions imposed after conviction, and not to conditions shared alike by unconvicted detainees and convicted offenders, the justices needed to find other constitutional provisions to prevent abuses in jails. The due process clauses are the provisions that fulfill this purpose.

How, then, does one know which practices or conditions in jail constitute "punishment" and thereby violate the right to due process? According to the Court's opinion in *Bell v. Wolfish,* there are three ways in which a practice or condition may constitute punishment. First, it is considered punishment if the inmates can prove that the jail officials clearly intended for the practice or condition to punish the pretrial detainees. Second, it can be considered punishment if it is not reasonably related to a legitimate government purpose. In other words, the practices and conditions in jails must be consistent with and advance the institution's proper interests. Among the proper interests recognized by the Supreme Court are making sure detainees appear for trial and maintaining security, order, and administrative efficiency at the jail. Third, the practices and con-

| **BOX 11-3** | **Jail Overcrowding** |

Imagine you are a federal judge presented with the following lawsuit. A local jail contains three large cells, each of which contains four bunk-beds, eight chairs, one toilet, and a television set. Inmates file suit alleging unconstitutional overcrowding. Two of the cells always contain between twelve and twenty inmates. Because there are only eight beds and eight chairs, some inmates must sleep on mattresses on the floor, and some inmates must stand up or sit on the floor during the day. There is not enough room to put additional bunkbeds into the cells. By contrast, the third cell, which is unofficially reserved for self-identified homosexual inmates, never has more than two or three inmates. A year earlier, a gay inmate had won a substantial lawsuit against jail officials because he was beaten and sexually assaulted when placed in a cell with the usual random mix of inmates. As a result of the lawsuit, the sheriff decided to use one cell to keep any gay inmates separate from other inmates. Inmates are asked if they are gay when they are brought to the jail. If they answer yes, they are placed in the reserved cell away from the other prisoners. Some inmates from the local area who are arrested regularly for public drunkenness and other offenses have learned to say that they are gay to ensure that they are placed in the cell where there are always bunkbeds available. The inmates who are crowded into the other two cells are angry about and envious of the nearly empty cell across the corridor. The pretrial detainees claim that the overcrowded conditions "punish" them improperly in light of the fact that additional beds, chairs, and living space are available in the third cell.

How would you analyze and decide this case?

---

ditions in jail may not be excessive in relation to their intended purposes, especially when alternative practices or conditions could have served the purpose just as well. For example, in making sure that inmates remain in custody, jail officials cannot chain each inmate to the wall within a locked cell when they could be held just as effectively if permitted to walk around within the locked cell.

When applying these standards in *Bell v. Wolfish* to the claim that it is unconstitutional to double bunk inmates in dormitory rooms designed for one person, the Supreme Court rejected the inmates' arguments. Because inmates were kept in the dormitory rooms only seven or eight hours each night for sleeping, the detainees were not actually confined in overcrowded quarters; they were free to walk around the large common rooms the rest of the day. Therefore, the Court concluded that the practice of double bunking was related to the administrative necessities of the jail and was not excessive in light of available alternatives.

In light of the standards established in *Bell v. Wolfish,* consider whether the hypothetical case presented in Box 11-3 involves any constitutional violations.

Other Rights

The decision in *Bell v. Wolfish* addressed a number of different rights issues. Because the Supreme Court examined the issues by asking whether they were reasonably related to legitimate goals of the jail, the justices focused on the institution's interests in security, order, and administrative efficiency, just as they do in cases concerning prisons.

For example, the justices endorsed the MCC's "publisher-only" rule for books and magazines. This is a common rule in corrections settings. Because of the fear that contraband—such as LSD on blotter paper—might be hidden inside books and magazines, corrections officials will only permit inmates to receive publications when they are sent directly from the publisher to inmate in the original packaging. This avoids the potential problem of friends and family members sending publications that might contain contraband. The Court acknowledged the serious security and administrative problems involved if publications come from sources other than the publishers, and noted that there was not enough staff available to search each publication page by page. Thus, the Court endorsed the publisher-only rule, despite the inmates' claim that this rule infringed on their First Amendment rights to receive literature. According to the majority opinion, the publisher-only rule "is a rational response by [jail] officials to an obvious security problem."

The Supreme Court also overruled the lower courts by allowing prison officials to restrict packages of personal property and food sent to inmates by friends and family. The MCC permitted inmates to receive one package of food at Christmas but barred other packages of food or property sent from the outside. The Supreme Court accepted the jail officials' arguments that packages of food and property would increase risks of gambling, theft, and fights among inmates. In addition, they noted that packages sent from the outside may be a way to send hidden contraband to inmates. Based on the MCC policy and the Supreme Court's decision, how would you handle the hypothetical claim described in Box 11-4?

In *Bell v. Wolfish*, the Supreme Court also approved unannounced "shakedown" room searches despite inmates' claims that these searches violated the Fourth Amendment prohibition on unreasonable searches and seizures. Nor are inmates permitted to observe the searches of their rooms. The inmates had alleged that officers were stealing their personal effects during the searches, but the Court did not agree that this provided a strong enough reason to alter the jail's rule against inmates being present.

As you may recall from Chapter 5, *Bell v. Wolfish* also raised a challenge to strip searches and body cavity inspections undertaken after detainees met with visitors. The Court applied the reasonableness test to conclude that the institution's interest in preventing contraband from being smuggled in outweighed the detainees' Fourth Amendment interest in being free from intrusive bodily searches. Justice Thurgood Marshall objected to searches unless they were justified by a reasonable suspicion of wrongdoing based on the actions of the detainee.

Other dissenters in the case argued that unconvicted, presumably innocent detainees should be not subjected to the identical treatment and conditions imposed on convicted offenders. According to Justice John Paul Stevens:

> *The fact that an individual may be unable to pay for a bail bond, however, is an insufficient reason for subjecting him to indignities that would be*

BOX 11-4	**Jailhouse Worship**

Muslim prisoners in the MCC file a lawsuit alleging that the jail's policies violate their freedom of religion. First, they claim that the MCC's policy of permitting one package of food at Christmas discriminates in favor of Christians, who have their most important religious holiday at that time of year. They claim that they should be able to receive food packages at the time of their most important religious holiday, and not just when the Christian majority has its important holiday. Second, they note that the jail officials' arguments about the risk of gambling, theft, fights, and contraband if packages are permitted must not be too strong because these very same officials allow packages in at Christmastime. Therefore, the Muslim inmates claim that they should be free to receive packages from the outside, especially during their two most important religious festivals—which do not occur at Christmastime.

If jail officials permit food packages for one religious holiday, can they really argue that they cannot permit food packages at other religious holidays? Is this improper religious discrimination?

appropriate punishment for convicted felons. Nor can he be subject on that basis to onerous restraints that might be properly regulatory with respect to particularly obstreperous or dangerous arrestees. An innocent man who has no propensity toward immediate violence, escape, or subversion may not be dumped into a pool of second- class citizens and subjected to restraints designed to regulate others who have [shown a propensity to violence, escape, or subversion].

Stevens' dissenting opinion demonstrated that some justices believe that unconvicted detainees should enjoy more liberty and more constitutional protections than people already convicted of crimes. However, the majority's concerns about institutional security led them to reject this argument and to effectively treat all detainees the same, whether convicted of a crime or not.

The U.S. Supreme Court has decided only a few other cases concerning jail inmates. Consistent with *Bell v. Wolfish,* the justices have not established constitutional protections for presumptively innocent, unconvicted detainees. Instead, they have emphasized the security interests of jails in justifying limitations on inmates' constitutional rights. Because there is no reasonable expectation of privacy in jail cells, officials can undertake surveillance of inmates, including eavesdropping through hidden microphones.[4] In *Block v. Rutherford* (1984),[5] as described in Chapter 4, the Court declared that inmates have no constitutional right to contact visits. A jail may forbid contact visits for all inmates, including unconvicted detainees who are not suspected of seeking contraband or otherwise misbehaving. In *Houchins v. KQED, Inc.* (1978),[6] the Court rejected a claim by news reporters that they were entitled to access to a jail to report on a suicide and the allegedly bad conditions in the jail.

Lower courts have decided other kinds of cases concerning jails. Inmates in jails may make the same types of claims as those by convicted offenders in prisons about rights related to religious exercise, access to the courts, and other issues. Jails, however, often have fewer resources and more difficult administrative problems (e.g., a population that changes on a daily basis, a mix of convicted and unconvicted inmates, and a mix of security classifications among inmates in the same facility) that interfere with their ability to organize programs and provide facilities such as law libraries and chapels. For example, jail inmates are entitled to access to the courts, including legal assistance or law library access. However, the jail law library materials need only be adequate; they do not have to match the library resources available in a state prison.[7] In light of the Supreme Court's decision in *Lewis v. Casey* (1996), discussed in Chapter 4, jail inmates must make a clear demonstration of the harm they have suffered from allegedly inadequate library materials in order to have any hope of judicial intervention.

Box 11-5 provides an illustration of the kinds of cases presented to the lower federal courts concerning jail conditions. Notice how the court is asked to address more than one issue in a single case. What does the case show us about the kinds of problems faced by jail officials? Does the court of appeals apply the U.S. Supreme Court's precedents properly?

In reflecting on this lower court ruling, consider several questions. Under the court's reasoning, could any safety cell conditions be found unconstitutional if those conditions are regarded as merely "temporary"? Is there any indication that unconvicted pretrial detainees have any greater rights while in administrative segregation than those possessed by convicted offenders in a jail? How might the court's opinion have differed if there had been no Spanish-speaking staff members at the jail? These questions help to illustrate the fact that the U.S. Supreme Court does not resolve all legal issues affecting prisons and jails through its decisions. Lower courts play an important role by filling in the missing pieces of corrections law as they confront a variety of situations that have never been directly addressed by the nation's highest court. U.S. Supreme Court decisions receive primary attention in corrections law because those decisions establish principles that must be followed throughout the country. However, many of the rules developed by judges for the corrections context actually come from the lower courts, which confront corrections issues on a more regular basis.

PROTECTING JAIL INMATES AGAINST HARM

As indicated by the discussion of safety cells in *Anderson v. County of Kern*, one of the biggest challenges facing jail administrators is protecting inmates against harm. Because jails contain such a changing mixture of detainees yet lack the facilities to carefully classify and separate inmates, there are always risks that aggressive inmates will victimize weaker cellmates. Jail officials may be held liable for injuries resulting from inmate-to-inmate violence.

| **BOX 11-5** | ***Anderson v. County of Kern,* 45 F.3d 1310 (9th Cir. 1995)** |

JUDGE POOLE, joined by JUDGES CANBY and RYMER, delivered the opinion of the Court:

In this 42 U.S.C. [section] 1983 action, the district court entered a permanent injunction in favor of inmates at five Kern County jails. The inmates, who are pretrial detainees and convicted prisoners, appeal the district court's refusal to enjoin prison officials from placing mentally disturbed or suicidal prisoners in safety cells. The county defendants cross-appeal the district court's (1) injunction requiring prison officials to develop a policy regarding joint exercise and day room access for prisoners in administrative segregation, (2) injunction requiring prison officials to provide non-inmate translators for Spanish-speaking inmates seeking medical care, and (3) holding that their former dental and vision care policies were inadequate. We affirm in part and reverse in part.

I. SAFETY CELLS

The inmates contend that the district court should have enjoined as unconstitutional Kern County's use of safety cells for suicidal and mentally disturbed inmates. Safety cells are padded cells that are used to temporarily confine violent or suicidal prisoners so they cannot hurt themselves.

The convicted inmates' challenge is evaluated under the Eighth Amendment, and the pretrial detainees' challenge is evaluated under the Fourteenth Amendment. . . . Under the Eighth Amendment, the proper inquiry is (1) whether placement of mentally disturbed or suicidal inmates in safety cells constitutes an infliction of pain or a deprivation of basic human needs, such as inadequate food, clothing, shelter, sanitation, and medical care, and (2) if so, whether prison officials acted with the requisite culpable intent such that the infliction of pain is "unnecessary and wanton." *Farmer v. Brennan* [1994]. . . . In prison conditions cases, prison

officials act with the requisite culpable intent when they act with deliberate indifference to the inmates' suffering . . . *Wilson v. Seiter* [1991]. . . . Similarly, the placement of pretrial detainees in safety cells is "punishment" in violation of the Fourteenth Amendment only if prison officials act with deliberate indifference to the inmates' needs. *Redman v. County of San Diego,* 942 F.2d at 1441-43. . . .

The test for whether a prison official acts with deliberate indifference is a subjective one: the official must "know . . . of and disregard . . . an excessive risk to inmate health and safety; the official must both be aware of the facts from which the inference could be drawn that a substantial risk of serious harm exists, and he must also draw the inference." *Farmer,* . . . 114 S.Ct. at 1979.

The parties proffered the following evidence.

Kern County currently has one safety cell in use [although it had a virtually identical second cell in use at the time of trial]. It is approximately 10 feet by 10 feet, is covered with rubberized foam padding, and has a pit toilet with a grate. If inmates are in the cell at mealtime, they eat their meals there.

Sergeant Bradley, a supervisor, estimated that 40% of the prisoners placed into the safety cell were suicidal. Inmates that are placed on suicide watch in the cell are given paper clothing so that they cannot hang themselves with their regular clothing. Sometimes the inmates destroy this paper clothing and thus are naked or clad only in their underwear. According to Sergeant Bradley, inmates placed in the safety cell are always given paper clothing and are not put naked into the cell. One inmate testified that she was placed naked into the cell because she threatened to choke herself with the paper clothing.

If inmates are violent, they may be shackled to the grate over the pit toilet. According to one nurse, chaining did not happen frequently. According to Sergeant Bradley, during the period

(continued)

July 1987 to January 1991 he observed approximately ten instances of an inmate shackled with handcuffs, attached to a waist chain, leg irons separated with a 12-inch chain, and secondary chains attached from the leg irons to the toilet grate. A supervising nurse testified that sometimes "the kindest thing to do was to restrain [certain inmates] . . . to prevent them from hurting themselves. . . . I've seen inmates bang their heads on the wall [and] . . . on the grate in the safety cell since that was the only metal part in there."

Inmates and prison officials testified about three inmates' experiences in the safety cell. One inmate was placed in the safety cell on several occasions, once after he tried to kill himself and twice after he became violent. On the occasion he tried to kill himself, he was shackled all night to the toilet grate with leather restraints and was given only a paper shirt that prison officials placed over his lap. Another inmate, who was placed in the cell for about three hours after she threatened suicide, was shackled to the grate. A third inmate testified that after he told a deputy that he was thinking about hurting himself, he was placed without restraints into the safety cell for about an hour and a half, which made him feel "awful," "depressed," "claustrophobic," and "degraded." The inmates testified that the cell was dark, scary, and smelled bad, and that the pit toilet was encrusted with excrement and urine.

Dr. Rundle, the plaintiffs' expert witness, testified that the cell was small, dark, dingy, and scary. He also testified that these conditions would be psychologically damaging to anyone and would be particularly damaging to mentally disturbed and suicidal inmates left alone in the cell. He opined that it was inappropriate to secure any prisoner to the toilet grate, but he later testified that it would not be inappropriate to restrain violent prisoners in this manner.

A prison administrator from King County, Washington testified that most prisons attach a device to the wall for shackling in lieu of shackling prisoners to the toilet grate. A former administrator with the Federal Bureau of Prisons testified that safety cells in federal prison

have a bed, a stainless steel commode, and a wash basin.

Evidence was presented regarding the monitoring of the safety cell. California Code of Regulations title 15, section 1055 provides that an inmate

> shall be placed in a safety cell only with the approval of the facility manager or the watch commander and continued retention in such a cell shall be reviewed a minimum of every eight hours. A medical/mental health opinion on placement and retention shall be secured within 24 hours of placement in such a cell or at the next daily sick call, whichever is earliest, and the inmate shall be medically cleared for continued retention every 24 hours thereafter. Intermittent direct visual supervision shall be provided every half hour.

In addition to section 1055's procedures, nursing staff does a screening within 30 minutes after an inmate is placed in the cell, the inmate is checked visually every 15 to 30 minutes, and the shift supervisor reviews the safety cell placement every 4 hours.

On the basis of this evidence, the district court rejected the inmates' challenge to the use of safety cells, finding that nothing suggested that "the safety cells had been inappropriately used as more than a temporary measure to control violent inmates until they 'cooled down' sufficiently to be released from those cells. The experts . . . agreed that the cells could appropriately be used for this purpose." The district court also held that the plaintiffs failed to show that Kern County had an inadequate program for identifying, treating, and supervising suicidal inmates.

We affirm the district court's holding. The safety cell is admittedly a very severe environment, but it is employed in response to very severe safety concerns. There was ample testimony that some prisoners became so violent and such a danger to themselves that temporary placement in a safety cell was needed in order to deprive the prisoners of all means of harming themselves. The fact that some prisoners who are violent or threaten violence to themselves or others may be mentally disturbed or suicidal does not detract from the need. There was testimony that sinks, stand-up toilets, and beds can be and have been used by prisoners to harm themselves by banging against them or by other means. Deprivation of these articles for short periods of time during violent episodes is constitutionally justifiable. There was sufficient evidence to support the district court's factual finding that the safety cell was used to control violent inmates, and that the inmates were confined to the safety cell only for short periods of time. See *Hoptowit v. Ray,* 682 F.2d 1237, 1258 (9th Cir.1982) (in evaluating challenges to conditions of confinement, court may consider the length of time the prisoners must go without basic human needs). The district court therefore did not err in refusing to enjoin the County from ever making use of a safety cell for mentally disturbed or suicidal prisoners.

There was testimony from some plaintiffs that the cell was dirty and smelled bad. Unquestionably, subjection of a prisoner to a lack of sanitation that is severe or prolonged can constitute an infliction of pain within the meaning of the Eighth Amendment. See, e.g., *Gee v. Estes,* 829 F.2d 1005, 1006 (10th Cir.1987) (Eighth Amendment claim established by allegations that prisoner was placed naked in a lice-infested cell with no blankets in below forty-degree temperatures, denied food or served dirty food, and left with head in excrement while having a seizure); *McCray v. Burrell,* 516 F.2d 357, 366-69 (4th Cir. 1974) (prisoner placed naked in bare, concrete, "mental observation" cell with excrement-encrusted pit toilet for 48 hours after he allegedly set fire to his cell; prisoner had no bedding, sink, washing facilities, or personal hygiene items, and he was not seen by a doctor until after he was released), . . . ; *Gates v. Collier,* 501 F.2d 1291, 1302 (5th Cir.1974) (punishment of prisoner by confinement in small, dirty cell without light, hygienic materials, adequate food, heat; prisoner also was punished through administration of milk of magnesia); *LaReau v. MacDougall,* 473 F.2d 974, 978 (2d Cir. 1972) (prisoner confined for five days in a strip cell with only a pit toilet and without light, a sink, or other washing facilities). . . .

The plaintiffs here have not shown, however, that the sanitary limitations imposed upon them were more than temporary. More important, they have not shown why possible sanitation problems required that the County be enjoined permanently from *ever* making *any* use, however temporary, of a safety cell for mentally disturbed or suicidal prisoners. That a safety cell needs more frequent cleaning, or that its toilet needs more frequent flushing, does not establish that the cell must never be used at all.

In addition to their failure to establish that temporary imposition of the conditions of the cell constituted an "infliction of pain" in violation of the first part of the *Farmer* test, the plaintiffs also have not satisfied the second part of the test: prison officials' deliberate indifference to the inmates' suffering. *Farmer [v. Brennan].* . . . Prison officials have to have some means of controlling violent or self-destructive inmates temporarily until the episode passes, and as the plaintiffs' own expert testified, it is difficult to distinguish between violent, mentally healthy inmates and violent, mentally disturbed ones. Similarly in an emergency, prison officials are not culpable when they put an inmate who imminently threatens or attempts suicide temporarily in a place where he cannot hurt himself. In light of the safety concerns underlying use of the safety cell, the plaintiffs' evidence is not so sufficient to compel an inference that the defendants are "knowingly and unreasonably disregarding an objectively intolerable risk of harm" and will continue to do so in the future. . . . The plaintiffs accordingly have failed to establish the subjective as well as the objective components of an Eighth Amendment prison conditions claim for injunctive relief. . . . We therefore affirm the district court's refusal to enjoin the use of the safety cell.

II. JOINT EXERCISE FOR INMATES IN ADMINISTRATIVE SEGREGATION

The defendants contend that the district court erred by ordering them to develop a policy allowing prison officials to determine whether certain prisoners housed in administrative segregation

(continued)

can safely exercise or have dayroom access together.

. . . [T]he hardship associated with administrative segregation, such as loss of recreational and rehabilitative programs or confinement to one's cell for a lengthy period of time, does not violate the due process clause because there is no liberty interest in remaining in the general population. *Toussaint v. McCarthy,* 801 F.2d 1080, 1091-92 (9th Cir. 1086) (applying *Hewitt v. Helms),* . . .

Kern County has various classes of prisoners in administrative segregation, including inmates (such as former police officers, former correctional officers, and persons accused of notorious crimes) who might be subject to attack by other inmates, other protective custody inmates, security risk inmates, combined protective custody–security risk inmates, and general population inmates who require temporary administrative segregation. A prison official testified that administrative segregation was a last resort for people who, either for their own safety or safety of other inmates, cannot be around one other person without direct absolute control of their movement and behavior. And that even means being out in the dayroom with other folks, even one other person. The potential could be there that they can either be harmed or they're going to harm someone else.

Inmates in administrative segregation retain all inmate privileges such as family visits, tele-

phone access, and exercise. They are all single-celled, however, and have no contact with any other inmate, either for exercise, day room access, or otherwise. The inmates presented some evidence that isolation has adverse effect upon the inmates.

Here, the inmates contend that a policy that does not give prison officials discretion to allow certain ad seg inmates to exercise or use the day room together constitutes deliberate indifference to the inmates' needs. This contention fails.

First, as this court held in *Toussaint,* administrative segregation, even in a single cell for twenty-three hours a day, is within the terms of confinement ordinarily contemplated by a sentence.

Second, prison officials have a legitimate penological interest in administrative segregation, and they must be given "wide-ranging deference in the adoption and execution of policies and practices that in their judgment are needed to preserve internal order and discipline and to maintain institutional security." *Bell v. Wolfish* [1979] . . . see *Turner v. Safely* [1987]. . . .

Confinement in a cell for most of the day is not pleasant. And the relief ordered by the district court was extremely reasonable and deferential to prison officials. These factors make it somewhat difficult to reverse the district court's injunction. But the confinement at issue here does not rise to the level of deliberate indifference. As this court observed in *Wright v.*

Equally difficult, but less well recognized by the general public, is the problem of jail suicides. People can become frightened, disoriented, bewildered, and depressed when they are arrested and locked in jail. They may feel embarrassed and humiliated to find themselves incarcerated. They may feel fearful and depressed because of the atmosphere in which they find themselves. They may be coming back to their senses after being high on drugs or alcohol. They may have histories of mental problems that contributed to the behavior, whether criminal or not, that led police to place them in a jail cell. There are many reasons why detainees may try to kill themselves, often within the first few hours of incarceration, and jail suicides thus are a significant problem.

As you read *Hickey v. Zezulka* (1989), which is excerpted in Box 11-6, ask yourself how this case—and others like it—put pressure on sheriffs and other jail administrators to show concern for inmates' health and safety.

Rushen, "[c]ourts must diligently ensure compliance with constitutional requirements and with statutes designed to improve prison conditions. But courts may not institute reform programs on their own under the guise of correcting cruel and unusual punishment." 642 F.2d 1129, 1135 (9th Cir.1981).

Accordingly, we hold that the district court erred by finding a constitutional violation and by ordering injunctive relief.

III. NON-INMATE TRANSLATORS FOR MEDICAL INTERVIEWS

The defendants contend that the district court erred by ordering them to provide a Kern County employee, preferably a member of the medical staff, to translate for Spanish-speaking inmates who request a translator during medical and mental health interviews.

Jail officials violate a prisoner's Eighth Amendment rights if they are deliberately indifferent to his serious medical needs. See *Estelle v. Gamble,* [1976]. . . . *Jones v. Johnson,* 781 F.2d 769, 771 (9th Cir.1986) (same standard applies to pretrial detainees). The indifference to medical needs must be substantial; a constitutional violation is not established by negligence or "an inadvertent failure to provide adequate medical care." *Estelle.* . . .

The Ninth Circuit has not ruled on the issue of whether failure to provide translators can constitute deliberate indifference. The Seventh Circuit has held that it can:

> *An impenetrable language barrier between doctor and patient can readily lead to misdiagnoses and therefore pain and suffering. This type of language problem which is uncorrected over a long period of time and as to which there is no prospect of alleviation, can contribute to unconstitutional deficiencies in medical care.* Wellman v. Faulkner, *715 F.2d 269, 272 (7th Cir. 1983).* . . .

Here, the district court ordered only that a non-inmate translator, preferably a member of the medical staff, be made available upon an inmate's request. This is consistent with the jail's existing written policy that a medical staff member will translate, and, if a medical staff member is not available, a member of the correctional staff will translate. Inmate translators can still be used unless an inmate requests a staff member. The testimony was undisputed that inmate translation was inappropriate and potentially inaccurate, and even the nursing supervisor admitted she preferred non-inmate translators. Finally, there are nine members of the jail staff who are fluent in Spanish. The district court did not abuse its discretion. See *LeMaire v. Maass,* 12 F.3d 1444, 1451 (9th Cir.1993) (a district court has broad discretion to fashion remedies once a constitutional violation is found). . . .

As indicated by the large sums of money awarded in this case, jail administrators face significant financial risks if they are not especially careful in ensuring the safety of jail inmates. In a case from the early 1990s, the City of Lansing, Michigan, lost a million-dollar judgment in the case of a man who drank automobile windshield washer fluid before he was arrested. Jail personnel believed that he was only under the influence of alcohol when they observed him fall asleep. He died in his jail cell, and the city was held legally (and financially) responsible.

The question of whether government agencies should be held responsible when people take their own lives is hotly debated. Obviously, a jail might be liable if one of its employees injured an inmate by, for example, slamming him or her into a brick wall. It is arguably a different situation when an individual voluntarily acts to end his or her own life. Under such circumstances, the jailers are held responsible for not doing enough to monitor or otherwise prevent the

BOX 11-6

Hickey v. Zezulka, 443 N.W.2d 180 (Michigan Court of Appeals, 1989)

JUDGE SHAMO:

. . . In the early morning hours of October 3, 1982, decedent John Joseph Hickey, III, a student at MSU [Michigan State University], was driving along Harrison Road on the campus of MSU when officers of MSU's Department of Public Safety observed Hickey driving erratically. After Officer Linda Zezulka stopped Hickey's vehicle, she noticed that Hickey appeared to be intoxicated. Hickey did not have a driver's license because his license had been suspended. He was given sobriety tests and then taken into custody.

[Hickey was given a Breathalyzer test which showed a reading between 0.15 and 0.16. Zezulka asked her supervisor for permission to take Hickey to the Ingham County Jail, but permission was denied. Zezulka was told to bring Hickey to MSU's Public Safety Department to be photographed and processed.]

. . . Hickey was advised that he would soon be taken to the Ingham County Jail. Officer Zezulka did not remove any articles from Hickey's person. No one else was placed in the cell with Hickey. Holding cell 171 was one of three detention cells in MSU's Department of Public Safety building. Cell 171 had a nine to ten foot high ceiling and a concrete bench along one side. Above the bench was a heater with a metal mesh that was supported by four metal brackets which extended one to two inches from the wall.

After placing Hickey in the holding cell, Officer Zezulka carried on with her other duties. Zezulka spent some of the time in the processing room which was across the hall from the holding cell. It was Zezulka's responsibility to check on Hickey because no other officer was assigned to watch Hickey while he was in the cell. Zezulka did not check on Hickey until she was instructed to take him to the Ingham County Jail.

At about 3:57 a.m., Zezulka entered Hickey's cell and observed Hickey hanging from the heating device. Hickey had used his belt and socks to fashion a noose and hung himself from one of the brackets on the heating unit. Hickey was pronounced dead on arrival at Sparrow Hospital in Lansing, Michigan.

[Hickey's family filed a lawsuit in the state Court of Claims. A jury found Officer Zezulka, the police commander at MSU, and MSU's public safety director to be negligent. However, only Zezulka's negligence was found to be a proximate cause of the death. In addition, Zezulka was found guilty of violating Hickey's civil rights. The jury awarded a verdict of $1 million against Zezulka. The Hickey family also won a $650,000 award against the University because the building was defective or dangerous in that the location of the brackets and heating device enabled the suicide to take place.] . . .

suicide. Despite the disagreements about whether jail officials and government agencies should be liable for jail suicides, juries do hold officials responsible. In light of that reality—and the threat of severe financial liability that goes with it—jail officials are becoming increasingly aware of the need to create a safe jail environment and to monitor the behavior of inmates closely.

Lawsuits concerning constitutional rights are not the only legal actions that shape the policies and practices of corrections institutions. The threat of significant liability verdicts in regular state **tort** suits—concerning the negligence of jail officials—can motivate sheriffs and other officials to examine and alter their policies. As Chapter 12 will discuss in greater detail, a central issue in contemporary corrections law is the extent to which officials can be held legally and financially liable for rights violations or other harms suffered by inmates in prisons and jails. As indicated by the case in Box 11-6, the threat of liability and substantial financial awards is very real. And this is not a case in which the U.S. Supreme Court is protecting particular rights for incarcerated individuals. Instead, the statutes and case law in a particular state provide the basis for trial judges and juries to hold corrections officials accountable for actions—or inaction—that contribute to substantial harms suffered by inmates.

Now return to the example at the beginning of the chapter. What are the prospects for success in the lawsuit? As you can see, the decision in *Bell v. Wolfish* seems to indicate that there is little likelihood of success for most constitutional rights claims. On the other hand, there may be the possibility of tort liability for any injuries suffered while in jail.

SUMMARY

- The context of jails presents many difficult challenges for jail administrators. Limited resources and a changing mixture of inmates create an environment in which it is difficult to maintain ideal conditions. Indeed, some jails have conditions that are much worse than those in almost any prison.

- Courts apply the Due Processes Clauses of the Fifth and Fourteenth Amendments, instead of the Eighth Amendment, in assessing conditions of confinement for unconvicted pretrial detainees in jails. The Eighth Amendment protects only convicted offenders because they are being legally "punished" within the American criminal justice system.

- The U.S. Supreme Court's decision in *Bell v. Wolfish* (1979) answered many questions about the rights of pretrial inmates. The justices rejected inmates' challenges to double celling, limitations on obtaining books and magazines, room searches, and body cavity searches.

- The Supreme Court looks for unconstitutional practices and conditions in jails by asking whether there is evidence that officials intend to punish rather than merely detain unconvicted inmates. The justices also examine whether the jails' practices are reasonably related to legitimate government interests.

- Because a majority of justices place such great emphasis on the security and order goals of jails, unconvicted and presumably innocent jail inmates have no more rights and liberties than incarcerated offenders convicted of serious crimes.

- Jail officials can be held accountable for inmates' safety through civil liability lawsuits that may produce substantial financial awards, even in cases of jail suicides. These cases often are decided in state courts and guided by state law.

Key Terms

Bell v. Wolfish (1979)   due process of law
body cavity search   tort

Additional Readings

Sorrell, Elisha. 1990. "Arresting Officer Placing Leg Shackles on Arrestee Is Objectively Reasonable Conduct with Respect to Federal Civil Rights Statute and New Jersey Tort Claims Act." *Seton Hall Law Review* 20: 658–659.

Welsh, Wayne. 1995. *Counties in Court: Jail Overcrowding and Court-Ordered Reform.* Philadelphia: Temple University Press.

Ziegelmueller, William. 1993. "Due Process on Drugs: The Implications of Forcibly Medicating Pretrial Detainees with Antipsychotic Drugs." *Journal of Criminal Law and Criminology* 83: 836–867.

Notes

1. See John Irwin, *The Jail: Managing the Underclass in American Society* (Berkeley: University of California Press, 1985).

2. Stephanie Saul, "Mental Patients Dumped: With Hospitals Full, Officials Are Forced to Put Some People in Jail," *Lansing State Journal* (*Newsday* wire service), 1 June 1997, p. A8.

3. Ibid.

4. Lanza v. New York, 370 U.S. 139 (1962).

5. Block v. Rutherford, 468 U.S. 576 (1984).

6. Houchins v. KQED, Inc., 438 U.S. 1 (1978).

7. Strickler v. Waters, 989 F.2d 1375 (4th Cir. 1993).

The Law and Corrections Personnel

Imagine that a close friend has come to you for advice. She knows that you are studying corrections law. She is a new corrections officer at a nearby state prison for men. She is having problems on the job and she isn't sure what she should do.

During her first week on the job, she was stationed at a cellblock on the first floor of the prison. Her job was to monitor prisoners entering and leaving the cellblock, making sure that they moved to different areas of the prison only during the permitted pass period every two hours. She also had to make sure that prisoners were accounted for when they returned to the cellblock at the end of the day and that no prisoners from other cellblocks entered the area. Obviously, she was also supposed to do whatever was needed to maintain order and security in the cellblock.

Your friend tells you that during her orientation period prior to her assignment in the cellblock, she sensed several times that her supervising captain was hostile to her. Although there were other female corrections officers in the prison, she was the only one assigned to this particular wing. She felt that the captain criticized her more quickly and harshly than the other new corrections officers.

During her first week in the cellblock, she had endured—and ignored—a steady stream of insulting comments, sexual gestures, and other harassment by the prisoners. She believed that they were merely testing her, so she resolved to maintain an appearance of toughness and not respond to the prisoners' behavior. One day, two prisoners began fighting at the far end of the cellblock. She called for assistance on her radio and then hurried down the corridor to break up the fight. As she reached the scene, another prisoner jumped her from behind, he put her in a bearhug, and grabbed her breasts.

"I did it! I got her!" he yelled with a laugh.

All of the prisoners nearby laughed, too—including the two prisoners who, as it turned out, had only pretended to fight in order to distract her.

She angrily broke free from the laughing prisoner's grasp, spun around, and punched him in the mouth, knocking out his front tooth. The captain and two other corrections officers came rushing around the corner just in time to see the angry prisoner, with blood trickling out of his mouth, screaming, "I'm going to sue you, you no good . . ."

"Shut up! All of you get to your cells!" yelled the captain. Turning to one of the officers, he said, "Take this guy to the medical center and ask him what happened."

Next, the captain turned to your friend and scowled. "You're relieved of your post. Go to the central office and write a report about this incident. You better make sure you didn't break the skin on your hand and get contact with his blood. He could have AIDS or something. Starting tomorrow, you're going on night shift, and you can spend your time filing papers in the office until I figure out if you can do anything useful."

As the captain walked away, she heard him say to one of the other officers, "I've always said that women can't handle this job. I guess this is another one that I'll have to find a way to get rid of."

Your friend is very interested in a career in corrections. She would like to get promoted and eventually move into administration. Because of this incident, she fears that her career may be over before it even gets started. What would you tell her to do?

CORRECTIONS OFFICERS AS EMPLOYEES

As you think about this scenario, you will recognize that the law affects corrections personnel in a variety of ways. In previous chapters, we have seen how the law affects prisoners' relationships with corrections institutions, including the personnel who work within those institutions. Law and judicial decisions create rules concerning the treatment of prisoners by staff. Law also affects the relationships and interactions between personnel and the institution in which they work. More than 320,000 people work in state corrections facilities, and more than 25,000 work in federal corrections facilities.[1] Thus, laws affecting corrections personnel impact a large number of people's daily lives.

Corrections officers are in a difficult position. They must assert their authority to control the behavior of difficult individuals who have proved that they lack self-control or have little regard for rules. This responsibility creates pressures and leads to difficult—and sometimes dangerous—situations. Corrections officers also face pressures from above. They are monitored by supervisors who may not always understand the quick decisions that must be made in unexpected situations. They must impress their supervisors with their performance in order to gain promotions and favorable job assignments. Just as corrections officers' relationships with inmates are governed by legal rules, there are also rules and regulations that define the relationships between corrections officers and prison administrators.

In Chapters 4 and 5, we examined the Michigan Department of Corrections' policies for searches of both visitors and prisoners. Although corrections personnel are the employees who run the institutions, they also are subject to searches. Box 12-1 contains the actual Michigan Department of Corrections policy regarding searches of employees. How do the regulations for these searches compare to the other search policies? Imagine working in an environment in which you are searching prisoners one minute and then possibly being searched yourself a few minutes later. Although the authority to search everyone inside a corrections institution is essential for safety and security, do you think the application of such authority over employees is likely to have any impact on employee morale or employer–employee relations?

Employment Discrimination

Employment discrimination laws are designed to prevent employers from denying people job opportunities for improper reasons. Congress has enacted employment discrimination laws to cover most employers throughout the country. Most notable among these laws are **Title VII** of the Civil Rights Act of 1964, which prohibits discrimination based on race, gender, national origin, and religion. Additional federal laws prohibit discrimination against people with disabilities (Americans with Disabilities Act) and age discrimination in employment against people age forty and over (Age Discrimination in Employment Act). States also have their own antidiscrimination laws. Sometimes, state laws and local ordinances cover additional categories by barring discrimination based on such things as marital status, political affiliation, and sexual orientation.

Normally, employment discrimination complaints must first be filed with a state civil rights commission or the U.S. Equal Employment Opportunity Commission. If the agencies are unsuccessful in resolving the complaints through mediation or other strategies, then the person may have the opportunity to file a lawsuit in court.

Corrections agencies may establish qualifications for people who wish to work within corrections institutions and programs as custody officers, counselors, teachers, and other essential personnel. For example, they might require a certain level of education (e.g., a high school diploma or associate degree), a certain level of physical fitness (e.g., the ability to pass a medical exam and lift a specific weight), and a clean criminal record in order to become corrections officers

SEARCH OF EMPLOYEES

K. Use of Screening Devices; Frisk and Clothed Body Searches; Search of Property

1. The responsibility to manage and control correctional facilities and prevent introduction of contraband encompasses the authority to search employees and their property while on the grounds of any facility. This is clearly stated as a condition of employment in the Employee Handbook.

2. All employees must submit to the use of a hand held screening device or walk through device, as required. Dogs trained to detect controlled substances may also be used to detect contraband on employees entering the institution. In addition, employees must submit to frisk or clothed body searches which occur as part of a general periodic search of all employees entering a facility during a certain time period or of randomly selected employees.

3. The institution head or acting institution head shall determine whether a frisk or clothed body search will be used and all employees searched shall be subject to the same type of search. These unannounced searches shall be conducted on a random basis by the facility to detect breaches of security.

4. A frisk search may be conducted by an employee of either sex but a clothed body search shall be conducted by an employee of the same sex as the person being searched.

5. An employee who refuses to submit to a search shall be warned that such refusal constitutes grounds for dismissal or other disciplinary action. The employee may also be refused admission to the facility until disciplinary action has been completed.

6. In addition to the above, an individual employee may be specifically singled out and requested to submit to a clothed body search, or a search of his/her vehicle or personal property, if there is reasonable suspicion that the employee is attempting to carry contraband onto facility property or into or out of the facility. Such searches of an employee may be carried out only upon authorization of an employee with the rank of shift commander or above, or in a corrections center, upon authorization of the first line supervisor in charge of the facility or his/her supervisors.

7. An employee may refuse to submit to a clothed body search or a search of his/her vehicle or personal property unless a search warrant has been obtained, but the employee shall be warned that refusal to submit to

responsible for incarcerated offenders. The government agencies that handle corrections—the federal Bureau of Prisons, state department of corrections, and local sheriff's departments—are not free, however, to establish whatever qualifications they wish. If job qualifications will adversely affect categories of people according to gender, religion, or national origin, then it must be shown that these qualifications actually are necessary for the job. Such qualifications are called "*bona fide* occupational qualifications," or "BFOQs." This naturally raises questions about which qualifications truly are necessary.

Box 12-2 contains an excerpt from one of the U.S. Supreme Court's most important cases concerning BFOQs: *Dothard v. Rawlinson* (1977). The case concerned the height and weight requirements that Alabama claimed were necessary for corrections officers. Because many women could not meet these require-

such a search shall constitute grounds for dismissal or other disciplinary action. The employee also shall not be allowed to remain on prison property if s/he refused to be searched and may be refused admission to the facility until disciplinary action is completed.

8. If a search of the vehicle or personal property of an employee is conducted based on reasonable suspicion, it shall be conducted in the presence of that employee or his/her designated representative.

9. Any vehicle or other personal property which is taken inside the security perimeter of a correctional facility shall be subject to search. Reasonable suspicion is not necessary to conduct a search.

L. Strip Search

1. An employee may refuse to submit to a strip search, unless that search is conducted pursuant to a search warrant, but refusal shall constitute grounds for dismissal. The employee also shall be required to leave the facility property immediately if s/he refuses to be searched and may be refused admission to the facility until disciplinary action is completed.

2. All strip searches of employees shall be subject to the following conditions:

a. There shall be reasonable suspicion that the employee is concealing contraband.
b. Prior written authorization shall be obtained from the Warden, or in his/her absence, the acting warden.
c. The search shall be conducted by a person of the same sex as the person being searched. All other persons present shall also be of the same sex as the person being searched.
d. The search shall be conducted in a place which prevents it from being observed by anyone not conducting or assisting in the search.
e. A written report of the search shall be prepared as soon as possible, using CAJ-289, Strip Search/Body Cavity Search Report. The original of the report shall be sent to the Warden and a copy must be given to the person who was searched, subject to deletions permitted by the Freedom of Information Act.

M. Body Cavity Search

1. As required by State law, a body cavity search of an employee shall not be conducted without a valid search warrant. If the Warden, or the acting warden, believes that such a search is required, s/he shall contact the appropriate police agency and ask them to proceed.

ments, the Court was asked to examine whether these requirements were really necessary or merely a means by which women were being denied job opportunities as corrections officers.

As you can see, Alabama argued that the height and weight requirements were BFOQs—despite their impact in excluding most women from employment opportunities—because of the need for a certain level of physical strength in dealing with prisoners. You can understand Alabama's reasoning. Because corrections personnel must deal with difficult and dangerous prisoners, they must be physically strong enough to defend themselves, assist other corrections personnel, and maintain order. Nevertheless, Alabama's argument was unpersuasive, for two reasons. First, officials did not prove what level of strength, if any, is necessary for working with prisoners. They simply claimed that some level is

BOX 12-2

Dothard v. Rawlinson, 433 U.S. 321 (1977)

JUSTICE STEWART delivered the opinion of the Court.

. . . At the time she applied for a position as correctional counselor trainee, Rawlinson was a 22-year-old college graduate whose major course of study had been correctional psychology. She was refused employment because she failed to meet the minimum 120-pound weight requirement established by an Alabama statute. The statute also establishes a height minimum of 5 feet 2 inches.

After her application was rejected because of her weight, Rawlinson filed a charge with the [U.S.] Equal Employment Opportunity Commission, and ultimately received her right-to-sue letter. She then filed a complaint in the District Court on behalf of herself and other similarly situated women, challenging the statutory height and weight minima as violative of Title VII and the Equal Protection Clause of the Fourteenth Amendment. [Her complaint was amended to also challenge state corrections regulations preventing women from holding positions that require contact with prisoners in male, maximum-security institutions.] . . .

Although women 14 years of age or older compose 52.75% of the Alabama population and 36.89% of its total labor force, they hold only 12.9% of its correctional counselor positions. . . . When height and weight restrictions are combined, Alabama's statutory standards would exclude 41.13% of the female population while excluding less than 1% of the male population. Accordingly, the District Court found that Rawlinson had made out a prima facie case of unlawful sex discrimination [i.e., she

had presented enough initial facts to raise suspicions that gender discrimination was occurring and therefore force the state to explain and justify its policies]. . . .

We turn, therefore, to the [prison officials'] arguments that they have rebutted the prima facie case of discrimination by showing that the height and weight requirements are job related. These requirements, they say, have a relationship to strength, a sufficient but unspecified amount of which is essential to effective job performance as a correctional counselor. In the District Court, however, [prison officials] produced no evidence correlating height and weight requirements with the requisite amount of strength thought essential to good job performance. Indeed, they failed to offer evidence of any kind of specific justification of the statutory standards.

If the job-related quality that the appellants identify is bona fide, their purpose could be achieved by adopting and validating a test for applicants that measures strength directly. Such a test, fairly administered, would fully satisfy the standards for Title VII because it would be one that "measure[s] the person for the job and not the person in the abstract." But nothing in the present record even approaches such a measurement.

For the reasons we have discussed, the District Court was not in error in holding that Title VII of the Civil Rights Act of 1964, as amended, prohibits application of the statutory height and weight requirements to Rawlinson and the class she represents. . . .

necessary. It may be the case, however, that discipline and order in prisons are more readily maintained by corrections officers, whatever their level of physical strength, who gain respect through firm, fair, and consistent treatment of prisoners. It also may be true that by learning certain techniques, such as holds and pressure points, even smaller staff members who lack significant strength can learn to physically control much larger inmates.

Second, Alabama did not demonstrate that their height and weight requirements established the proper line for the strength justification. Is it possible that someone who does not meet the height and weight requirements actually might be stronger than someone who does? Alabama needed to conduct tests and show persuasive results in order to establish a minimum strength level and a correlation of that level with a person's height and weight.

Elsewhere in the *Dothard* opinion, a majority of justices accepted Alabama's exclusion of women from contact positions in certain maximum-security institutions for male prisoners. However, most justices emphasized that this conclusion did not mean that other states could deny women employment opportunities in men's prisons. Instead, this conclusion was based on the unique situation in Alabama—illuminated the previous year in Judge Frank Johnson's decision in *Pugh v. Locke* (1976) (discussed in Chapter 8)—in which the prisons were in terrible condition, no classification system existed, and the prisons were using inmates to control other inmates. The Court noted that other states, such as California, successfully employed women as corrections officers in men's prisons. In the two decades since *Dothard,* female corrections officers have been hired in all kinds of corrections institutions throughout the country.

Judicial interpretations of Title VII have expanded its coverage, especially with respect to gender discrimination. Currently, the statute protects not only against denial of employment opportunities based on gender but also against sexual harassment in the workplace. Such claims may be based on unwelcome sexual advances and physical contact or on the creation of a hostile work environment. Employees may file Title VII complaints for sexual harassment against uninvolved supervisors if the supervisors knew about harassment by the victim's co-workers yet did nothing about it.

Employment discrimination laws do not limit their focus to hiring decisions. Such laws also may be used when employees believe that they have been victimized by discrimination in decisions concerning promotions and job assignments. In addition, there are laws that prohibit discrimination in pay based on improper bases, such as race or gender.

Most corrections personnel are government employees. Only a relatively small percentage of corrections personnel work for corrections corporations that run private prisons under contract with various states. As units of government, most corrections agencies have incorporated affirmative action programs into their employment policies. **Affirmative action** refers to a variety of efforts to recruit and promote people from segments of society that previously were subject to discrimination in seeking government employment. Affirmative action programs may include developing recruitment brochures specifically intended to attract women, African-Americans, and Hispanics to careers in corrections, and giving preferences in the employment process to individuals from selected groups (e.g., the federal government's policy of giving military veterans extra points in the civil service application process).

The use of affirmative action often causes controversy because people who do not receive such extra attention and consideration in the employment process may feel that they are the victims of discrimination. In corrections, there are practical reasons for seeking a diverse work force. As indicated in *Pugh v. Locke* in Chapter 8, one source of friction in prisons is the sociocultural gap between rural white corrections officers and urban minority prisoners. Prisons have sought to diminish problems by making their work forces reflect the racial, gender, and other aspects of diversity of society.

In government employment, the U.S. Supreme Court has—thus far—endorsed the use of affirmative action in hiring and promotion decisions. If a lawsuit reveals a history of employment discrimination by a government agency, a judge may order that agency to remedy past discrimination by hiring a certain number of women or minority group members.[2] The Supreme Court also approved giving preference to members of underrepresented groups if they were among qualified finalists for a position.[3] In other cases, however, the Court did not permit affirmative action preferences to overcome an established seniority system when there were layoffs.[4]

Corrections agencies generally have not experienced the clash between affirmative action and seniority for two reasons. First, rather than experiencing a shrinking job market, corrections employment has grown tremendously over the past two decades. Second, most corrections workers are employed by state governments, which tend to have more stable revenues and budgets than local governments, which sometimes lay off teachers, firefighters, and other workers. In addition, affirmative action may cause less conflict in hiring in corrections than elsewhere in the public sector. This is due to the growth in job opportunities and to the fact that most applicants for corrections positions have similar qualifications. That is, they have the minimum educational attainment established for the job; they meet the physical fitness requirements; they have clean criminal records (although some agencies will hire ex-offenders); and they are unlikely to have special expertise in corrections. Thus, it may be easier to diversify a work force when employment opportunities are growing and a large applicant pool exists.

In corrections, the most likely source of conflict about affirmative action is promotion decisions. After people have developed expertise and work records, they may have definite views about their worthiness for promotion in comparison to their co-workers. The application of affirmative action preferences in such situations may produce resentment—and even litigation alleging racial or gender discrimination.

The future of affirmative action is uncertain, especially with respect to actions designed to redress the past history of racial discrimination. Supreme Court decisions in the mid-1990s limited the ability of governments at all levels to use affirmative action programs in awarding government contracts. Thus, the legal rules affecting affirmative action and employment discrimination may change in the near future.

Other Employment Issues

Because most corrections personnel are state government employees, they often are covered by state **civil service laws** that were developed in the twentieth century and that apply to all levels of government. Previously, people typically ob-

BOX 12-3	**Discipline for Corrections Officers**

Eighty corrections officers picketed outside the state's largest prison complex to protest what they regarded as bad management practices. They complained that corrections administrators unfairly enforced a strict discipline system and that several corrections officers with years of experience had been fired as a result. The picketers complained that the state's disciplinary actions directed at corrections officers simply were too harsh. For example, if an officer mistakenly switched two numbers when recording the count of prisoners, the punishment was an automatic three-day suspension without pay. The officers complained that their colleagues actually were being fired for making clerical errors in filling out paperwork. In response, the spokesperson for the state's Department of Corrections asserted that prisoner counts were of extreme importance in order to detect escapes or other problems and that the state was justified in imposing punishment on officers for making errors.

If you were head of the state department of corrections, how would you deal with staff errors like these? What legal issues might factor into your decision?

Sources: "Prison Officers Call State's Discipline System Too Strict," *Lansing State Journal* (Associated Press report), 15 April 1998, p. B3; "80 Jackson Prison Officers Protest State's Strict Rules," *Detroit News,* 16 April 1998, p. D8.

tained government jobs solely based on their political connections to elected leaders. This led to the employment of individuals who lacked any qualifications, who were untrained, and who acted to support political leaders rather than to perform their job responsibilities in a professional manner. By contrast, civil service laws created procedures for hiring government employees through open and competitive application processes. They also protected employees from arbitrary firing by political leaders attempting to pressure government workers to provide political and financial support for election campaigns. Usually, civil service employees can be fired "for cause"—that is, when they have done something sufficiently improper—but they cannot be fired at the whim of officials. Civil service laws and court decisions give civil service employees procedural rights when their agencies attempt to end their employment. They are normally entitled to hearings, in which they may present their side of the story, and to an appeals process before their employment is terminated.

Although corrections officers also are protected against arbitrary actions, they must comply with many more rules and regulations than workers in most other occupations because of the environment in which they work. Obviously, security and safety in corrections institutions depend on corrections officers following proper procedures. And if they do not follow proper procedures, they may be subject to disciplinary action or dismissal. As you read the story in Box 12-3, which concerns one state's corrections system, ask yourself whether corrections administrators were being too harsh on corrections officers in meting out discipline for violations of procedures.

Civil service rules also may provide employee grievance procedures for circumstances in which corrections officers wish to challenge disciplinary actions against them or otherwise question actions by their supervisors.

BOX 12-4

Government Regulations and Employee Religious Rights

Federal law protects workers against religious discrimination. However, workers' free exercise of religious rights may be limited by regulations affecting their jobs. For example, Native American drug rehabilitation counselors lost their jobs and were denied unemployment compensation by the state of Oregon for ingesting peyote as a recognized component of their traditional religious ceremonies.[5]

Many devout Mennonite men believe that God requires them to refrain from shaving. In one state, several Mennonite corrections officers had beards because of these religious beliefs. But the state department of corrections ordered them to either shave their beards or lose their jobs because it was discovered that the gas masks used by the department did not fit properly on bearded faces. The state gave the corrections officers the option of keeping their beards

and their jobs if they transferred to minimum-security institutions, which did not keep gas masks as standard equipment. But, there were no job openings at such institutions. Thus, the corrections officers faced the prospect of violating their religious beliefs by shaving or losing their jobs. The officers complained to news reporters that prison inmates had more constitutional rights than they did with respect to freedom of religion.

If you were the head of the state department of corrections, how would you handle this issue? Would your views be any different if you were a federal judge presented with this issue in a legal action filed by the Mennonite officers?

Source: John Schneider, "Razor or Ax?" *Lansing State Journal,* 29 August, 1995, p. B1.

Because corrections officers belong to unions in some states, rules in the corrections setting also develop through unions' legislative lobbying and collective bargaining agreements. Many states permit corrections officers' unions to bargain for contracts. Through this process, rules are developed concerning work assignments, working conditions, and grievance procedures in addition to the traditional concerns with pay and benefits. These rules have legal force because they are part of contracts that can be enforced by a court of law. Unions also use their political influence to lobby legislators about laws related to corrections. With regard to the situation presented at the beginning of the chapter, consider the possibilities for a union grievance procedure and for a gender discrimination complaint—in addition to the issue of the prisoner's potential lawsuit against the corrections officer.

Like employees in other organizations, corrections officers are affected by other kinds of laws directed at workplace issues. For example, the federal Fair Labor Standards Act affects the payment of overtime for eligible employees, and the Occupational Safety and Health Administration (OSHA) issues regulations concerning safe working conditions. In addition, corrections departments have their own regulations that affect working conditions for employees. How would you address the clash of values presented in Box 12-4?

There are other emerging legal issues that affect the work of corrections officers. For example, officers may be required to administer first aid or cardiopulmonary resuscitation (CPR) to an injured or ill prisoner. Urgent medical interventions raise the risk of contact with a prisoner's bodily fluids, either blood (first aid) or saliva (CPR). Unfortunately, treatment-resistant tuberculosis (TB), hepatitis, HIV, and AIDS are significant and growing problems among prison populations. Because privacy regulations may protect inmates from having their medical conditions made known to the entire staff, corrections officers may not know which prisoners have tested positive for HIV and AIDS. Ideally, corrections officers would use latex gloves and other proper precautions in such situations, but something can always go wrong—for example, a hole in the latex glove. Thus, many officers would prefer to know beforehand which prisoners carry infectious diseases. Should an officer who contracts HIV from administering first aid to a prisoner be able to sue the institution for failing to inform him or her about the prisoner's condition? Should a prisoner be able to sue for violation of privacy rights if officials reveal to the guards which prisoners have HIV? This may be of great importance to the prisoner because he or she may fear mistreatment at the hands of corrections officers and other prisoners if the medical diagnosis is known. And this is but one example of the kinds of issues related to law that may arise in conjunction with corrections officers' employment within prisons and jails.

CORRECTIONS OFFICERS AND LIABILITY

In previous chapters, we discussed the vulnerability of corrections officers and institutions to lawsuits by prisoners claiming violations of their rights. These rights provide the basis for legal actions against corrections officials. As we have seen in the Supreme Court's rulings on issues such as conditions of confinement and excessive use of force, certain legal elements (e.g., malicious intent or deliberate indifference) must be proved in order for a prisoner to win a legal action. For example, according to *Whitley v. Albers* (1986), when corrections officers use force to quell a disturbance, prisoners must show that the force was applied with malicious intent in order to establish an Eighth Amendment violation. In discussing law and litigation in the corrections context in previous chapters, we examined issues from the prisoners' perspective: What kinds of actions can prisoners file? What rights do prisoners have? What do prisoners need to show in order to establish that particular rights were violated? Corrections officers need to be aware of these issues because they may be held responsible for violations that occur. As we saw in Chapter 11 concerning jail suicides, the financial sanctions imposed on corrections officials can be substantial.

Clearly, corrections officials cannot be sued successfully for anything and everything that prisoners feel upset about. There are specific rules and limitations concerning who can be sued and who can be held responsible in light of allegations that corrections officials have violated inmates' rights or caused prisoners' injuries.

Who Can Be Sued?

As discussed in Chapter 2, section 1983—the federal civil rights statute—provides the vehicle for many prisoners' civil rights lawsuits against corrections officials. According to the statute, "any person" who deprives others of their rights while acting under authority of the law may be liable in a lawsuit. In *Cooper v. Pate* (1964),[6] the Supreme Court made clear that prisoners could use this statute to initiate lawsuits.

The reach of section 1983 was clarified in subsequent cases. In ***Monell v. Department of Social Services* (1978)**,[7] the Supreme Court declared that municipalities, counties, and other local units of government could be regarded as "persons" to be sued under section 1983. This decision altered the legal tradition of **sovereign immunity** that historically prevented lawsuits against government unless the government consented to the lawsuit. Thus, for example, the federal government cannot be sued unless the lawsuit is based on an act of Congress, such as the Federal Tort Claims Act, which permits lawsuits for certain kinds of injuries caused by the government. States also continue to enjoy sovereign immunity. According to the Supreme Court's decision in ***Will v. Michigan Department of State Police* (1989)**,[8] a state is not a "person" under section 1983. Moreover, the Eleventh Amendment to the Constitution frequently has been applied to bar lawsuits against states, although its literal language prohibits lawsuits by citizens from different states or foreign countries. In addition, state officials cannot be sued in their official capacity as representatives of the state. If this avenue were available, prisoners might say, "If I can't sue the state, then I'll sue the governor since he (or she) represents the state." Instead, state officials must be sued in their personal capacity based on actions for which they actually were responsible.

Look back at the U.S. magistrate judge's report and recommendation in Box 3-2. The opinion addressed the issue of whom a prisoner can sue by examining the naming of the sheriff as a defendant in the section 1983 case. The magistrate judge recommended dismissing the claim against the sheriff because there was no allegation that the sheriff personally acted to violate the prisoner's civil rights. Take note of the statutory basis for the lawsuit described in Box 12-5. If state and local officials were responsible for what happened to Hyatt, what kind of claims, if any, could be raised in a section 1983 lawsuit?

Even though state officials, such as corrections personnel, are sued in their personal capacity, attorneys for the state usually will defend the case, and most states will assume responsibility for any financial damages awarded. Payment of damages by the state on behalf of an employee is called **indemnification**. The primary exception would involve cases in which a corrections official acted intentionally or maliciously, or committed a criminal act against a prisoner. In such cases of willful rights violations, corrections employees may be on their own with respect to paying legal costs and any damages awarded by a jury.

Certain government officials enjoy **absolute immunity** from lawsuits. For example, because we do not want officials like the president of the United States and prosecutors to be worried about being sued for the decisions that they make, we grant them complete immunity for their official decisions and actions. They are not immune from criminal prosecution if they commit crimes. But they are

| BOX 12-5 | **Lawsuits Against the Federal Government** |

The federal government enjoys sovereign immunity; that is, it cannot be sued without its consent. A primary source of permission for aggrieved individuals to sue the federal government is the Federal Tort Claims Act (FTCA), which enables individuals to seek compensation for injuries or property loss. For example, a man in New York City named Earl Hyatt was arrested by federal Drug Enforcement Administration agents who were looking for a drug trafficking suspect named *Erroll* Hyatt. The actual suspect had lost his left eye, but federal authorities did not include that information in the arrest warrant. Moreover, the name "Earl Hyatt," rather than "Erroll Hyatt," was mistakenly typed onto the warrant. Earl Hyatt spent ninety-nine days in federal detention facilities in Oklahoma, Indiana, Michigan, and Illinois before he gained release by convincing a federal judge that he had two good eyes and that he was *Earl,* not *Erroll,* Hyatt. After his release, Earl Hyatt filed a Federal Tort Claims Act suit.

At a bench trial, a federal judge found that the U.S. government acted in a "grossly negligent" fashion. He awarded Earl Hyatt $297,000—$3000 per day for each of the ninety-nine days of wrongful detention. The payment was for "the loss of liberty" due to "wrongful confinement." Earl Hyatt might have won an even larger award if he could have proved the value of other injuries and losses, such as lost wages or postimprisonment stress.

If this had been a section 1983 lawsuit against state and local officials, could Hyatt have proved that specific individuals were responsible for his loss of liberty? Because the state cannot be sued under section 1983, the claimant must pinpoint specific individuals responsible for an alleged rights violation.

Source: Bill Alden, "'Wrong Man' Jailing Costs DEA $297,000: Judge Faults Agents in Drug Suspect Mixup," *The New York Law Journal,* 15 July 1997 (on-line source at www.ljextra.com).

immune from civil liability lawsuits filed by disgruntled individuals claiming injuries due to actions taken by public servants as part of their official duties. Absolute immunity is primarily limited to the president and to officials in the judicial process; it does not protect corrections officials.

Other government officials, including corrections officials, enjoy **qualified immunity.** They may defend themselves against lawsuits by asserting that they did not ignore or disregard established law that a reasonable officer would have known regarding constitutional or statutory rights.[9] There is no liability if the "conduct does not violate clearly established statutory or constitutional rights of which a reasonable person would have known."[10] An official cannot be expected to anticipate future Supreme Court decisions establishing new rights for prisoners or expanding existing rights. However, officials can be found liable for not knowing the existing definitions of statutory and constitutional rights if their actions violate those rights. Fundamentally, corrections officials are most vulnerable to liability if they act intentionally to harm or violate the rights of prisoners, or if they violate well-established rights of which they should have been aware.

The rise of private corrections institutions has raised new issues concerning prisoner litigation and officials' immunity. In an effort to save money on corrections, several states contract with private corporations to handle incarceration of

BOX 12-6 *Richardson v. McKnight,* 117 S.Ct. 2100 (1997)

JUSTICE BREYER delivered the opinion of the Court.

The issue before us is whether prison guards who are employees of a private prison management firm are entitled to qualified immunity from suit by prisoners charging a violation of 42 U.S.C. [section] 1983. We hold that they are not.

Ronnie Lee McKnight, a prisoner in Tennessee's South Central Correctional Center (SCCC), brought this federal constitutional tort action against two prison guards, Darryl Richardson and John Walker. He says the guards injured him by placing upon him extremely tight physical restraints, thereby unlawfully "subject[ing]" him "to deprivation of" a right "secured by the Constitution" of the United States. . . . Richardson and Walker asserted a qualified immunity from [section] 1983 lawsuits . . . and moved to dismiss the action. . . .

History does *not* reveal a "firmly rooted" tradition of immunity applicable to privately employed prison guards. . . . *Government* employed prison guards may have enjoyed a kind of immunity defense arising out of their status as public employees at common law. . . . Yet, we have found no evidence that the law gave purely private companies or their employees any special immunity from such suits. . . .

History therefore does not provide significant support for the immunity claim. . . .

Whether the immunity doctrine's *purposes* warrant immunity for private prison guards presents a closer question. [An earlier precedent] described the [immunity] doctrine's purposes as protecting "government's ability to perform its traditional functions" by providing immunity where "necessary to preserve" the ability of government officials "to serve the public good or to ensure that talented candidates were not deterred by the threat of damages suits from entering public service.". . . Earlier precedent described immunity as protecting the public from unwarranted timidity on the part of public officials by, for example, "encouraging the vigorous exercise of official authority," . . . [and] by contributing to "'principled and fearless decision making,'" . . .

The guards argue that those purposes support immunity whether their employer is private or public. . . . Since private prison guards per-

convicted criminal offenders. The corporations build and staff their own prison facilities. They gain these contracts by convincing state officials that they can incarcerate prisoners more cheaply than state governments can while upholding the necessary standards for prison conditions. These corporations frequently save costs by having smaller administrative staffs and paying their non-unionized employees less than state corrections officials are paid.

By acting on behalf of the state in incarcerating offenders, private prisons assume responsibility for upholding prisoners' constitutional rights in much the same way that private physicians working under contract with state corrections agencies are "acting under color of state law" in treating (or failing to treat) prison inmates.[11] However, the question remains as to whether private prison personnel should expect to enjoy the benefits of qualified immunity bestowed on state corrections officials. The concept of immunity derives from sovereign immunity, the traditional prohibition on suing the government without its consent. Private prisons clearly are owned by private corporations, and not the govern-

form the same work as state prison guards, they say, they must require immunity to a similar degree. To say this, however, is to misread this Court's precedents. The Court has sometimes applied a functional approach in immunity cases, but only to decide which type of immunity—absolute or qualified—a public officer should receive. . . . Indeed a purely functional approach bristles with difficulty, particularly since, in many areas, government and private industry may engage in fundamentally similar activities, ranging from electricity production, to waste disposal, to even mail delivery.

[The guards'] argument also overlooks certain important differences that, from an immunity perspective, are critical. First, the most important special government immunity producing concern—unwarranted timidity—is less likely present, or at least is not special, when a private company subject to competitive market pressures operates a prison. . . .

In other words, the marketplace pressures provide the private firm with strong incentives to avoid overly timid, insufficiently vigorous, unduly fearful, or "non arduous" employee job performance. And the contract's provisions—including those that permit employee indemnification and avoid many civil service restrictions—grant this private firm freedom to respond to those market pressures through rewards and penalties that op-

erate directly upon its employees. . . . To this extent, the employees before us resemble those of other private firms and differ from government employees. . . .

[Private entities do not need privatization to recruit talented people. They can indemnify employees and have no civil service restrictions to limit pay increases that would offset any risk of liability.]

Our examination of history and purpose thus reveals nothing special enough about the job or about its organizational structure that would warrant providing these private prison guards with a governmental immunity. The job is one that private industry might, or might not, perform; and which history shows private firms did sometimes perform without relevant immunities. The organizational structure is one subject to the ordinary competitive pressures that normally help private firms adjust their behavior in response to the incentives that tort suits provide—pressures not necessarily present in government departments. Since there are no special reasons significantly favoring an extension of governmental immunity . . . , we must conclude that private prison guards, unlike those who work directly for the government, do not enjoy immunity from suit in a [section] 1983 case. . . .

ment. But in serving a function of government—incarcerating offenders—under a contract with the government, these corporations arguably stand in the government's stead in the actions they take regarding prisoners.

The U.S. Supreme Court addressed this issue in ***Richardson v. McKnight*** **(1997).** As you read the case excerpt in Box 12-6, ask yourself whether you agree with the Court's decision. What will be the consequences of the Court's decision for private corrections institutions?

The Supreme Court was deeply split in its decision. The five-member majority focused on the history and purposes of immunity, and found no historical precedent for granting immunity to private prisons. It also concluded that private firms, with their resources and flexibility to respond to developments, were not in the same position as government with regard to needing immunity as an incentive for officials to avoid being timid in making decisions.

The four dissenters, led by Justice Antonin Scalia, argued that history did not definitively answer the question in the manner concluded by the majority.

Moreover, they believed that immunity should be determined by the function fulfilled by the official. Thus, a private prison guard is entitled to the same protections as a public prison guard because each fulfills the same function for society. The dissenters also were very critical of the majority's faith that economic market forces will shape the actions of private prison officials in ways that make immunity unnecessary. Scalia's opinion concluded with an implicit accusation that the majority's opinion would contribute to a reduction in the use of private prisons:

> *Today's decision says that two sets of prison guards who are indistinguishable in the ultimate source of their authority over prisoners, indistinguishable in the powers that they possess over prisoners, and indistinguishable in the duties they owe towards prisoners, are to be treated quite differently in the matter of their financial liability. The only sure effect of today's decision—and the only purpose, as far as I can tell—is that it will artificially raise the cost of privatizing prisons. Whether this will cause privatization to be prohibitively expensive, or instead simply divert state funds that could have been saved or spent on additional prison services, it is likely that taxpayers and prisoners will suffer as a consequence. Neither our precedents, nor the historical foundations of [section] 1983, nor the policies underlying [section] 1983, support this result.*

The Basis for Lawsuits and Liability

We must remember that corrections officers and agencies are susceptible to different kinds of lawsuits. Section 1983 lawsuits allege constitutional rights violations committed by state corrections officials in their personal capacity. That is, the action of the individual official must have caused the rights violation or injury at issue. It is not enough to say that the official's negligence caused the rights violation or injury to occur. The Supreme Court's conclusion that mere negligence by a corrections officer is not a basis for a section 1983 civil rights lawsuit is emphasized in the excerpt from ***Daniels v. Williams*** (1986) in Box 12-7. As you consider the Supreme Court's approach to negligence, ask yourself whether the Court's conclusion provides sufficient protection for prisoners against the harm they may suffer in prison.

Local jails are on different footing than state and federal prisons. Because municipalities and counties, which administer local jails, can be sued under section 1983, there are broader possibilities for litigation. Normally, liability will be imposed only when the rights violation stems from a policy or custom of the local government agency. For example, the U.S. Supreme Court has ruled that municipalities can be found liable for their failure to train their criminal justice officials properly when that failure amounts to deliberate indifference to people's constitutional rights.[12] Note that the Supreme Court is not opening the floodgates to permit lawsuits against municipalities for any harm that may be caused. The failure-to-train basis for liability is limited to a showing of a conscious choice on the part of the municipality. If the failure to train were a conscious choice, then it could be considered a policy of the county that led to the rights violation or injury.

BOX 12-7	*Daniels v. Williams,* 474 U.S. 327 (1986)

JUSTICE REHNQUIST delivered the opinion of the Court.

In this [section] 1983 action, petitioner seeks to recover damages for back and ankle injuries allegedly sustained when he fell on a prison stairway. He claims that, while an inmate at the city jail in Richmond, Virginia, he slipped on a pillow negligently left on the stairs by . . . a correctional deputy stationed at the jail. Respondent's negligence, the argument runs, "deprived" petitioner of his "liberty" interest in freedom from bodily injury; because [the deputy] maintains that he is entitled to a defense of sovereign immunity in a state tort suit, [the prisoner] is without an "adequate" state remedy. Accordingly, the deprivation of liberty was without "due process law" [and therefore actionable under a federal section 1983 lawsuit]. . . .

. . . This history reflects the traditional and commonsense notion that the Due Process Clause, like its forebear the Magna Carta was "intended to secure the individual from the ar-

bitrary exercise of the powers of government." By requiring the government to follow appropriate procedures when its agents decide to "deprive any person of life, liberty, or property," the Due Process Clause promotes fairness in such decisions. And by barring certain government actions regardless of the fairness of the procedures used to implement them, it serves to prevent governmental power from being "used for purposes of oppression."

We think that the actions of prison custodians in leaving a pillow on the prison stairs, or mislaying an inmate's property, are quite remote from the concerns just discussed [as being central to the right to due process]. Far from an abuse of power, lack of due care [i.e., negligence] suggests no more than a failure to measure up to the conduct of a reasonable person. To hold that injury caused by [negligent] conduct is a deprivation within the meaning of the Fourteenth Amendment would trivialize the centuries-old principle of due process of law. . . .

Similarly, in 1997, when a sheriff was negligent in failing to adequately check a newly hired deputy's background, the Court absolved the county of responsibility for injuries the deputy inflicted on a woman during a traffic stop. The county was cleared of responsibility because the inadequate background check was not a *deliberate* county action that was a moving force behind the civil rights violation.[13] The county could not be held liable based on the sheriff's single decision to hire his great-nephew as a deputy despite the man's record of driving infractions and misdemeanor convictions. This single decision did not constitute a policy or custom of the county that could trigger the county's liability.

In another 1997 case,[14] the Court further limited potential liability for counties and complicated the possibilities for some lawsuits against jail officials by declaring that Alabama's sheriffs are policymakers for the state of Alabama, not for the individual counties in which they are the chief law enforcement officers and jailers. The decision is important because the state is immune from section 1983 lawsuits. Therefore, sheriffs' decisions—in their capacity as state officials—preclude holding the state or individual sheriffs liable, unless the sheriffs are sued in their personal capacity. By contrast, if sheriffs were considered county officials, then the county could be held liable under section 1983 for policy decisions made by them. The specific case concerned a man wrongly convicted of murder and sentenced to death who spent six years on death row before it was shown that the key witness against him lied—apparently with the knowledge of some county officials involved in investigating the case. The case hinged on a disputed interpretation of the Alabama Constitution's classification of county sheriffs as state officials. However, it raised the possibility that other state constitutions might be interpreted to regard traditionally county-centered officials as actually making decisions on behalf of the state. Such a result would limit the possibility for section 1983 lawsuits aimed at counties for the alleged violation of constitutional rights in their jails.

Lawsuits also may be filed under state civil rights statutes or state tort law. Again, the issue of sovereign immunity arises, but some states have statutes that permit lawsuits against the state and state officials for certain injuries and rights violations. For example, prisoners (or their families in cases when the prisoner dies) may sue for damages resulting from such intentional torts as wrongful death, assault, and battery. They also may sue under state law for negligent wrongs such as failure to protect an inmate—as in the jail suicide case excerpted in Chapter 11 in which a college student committed suicide by hanging after the arresting officer did not remove his belt and socks before placing him in a cell with accessible ceiling brackets.

The failure to protect inmates also includes protection against assaults by other inmates. Officials may be liable for failing to classify and separate inmates who might pose a threat to other prisoners. There may be liability as well for failing to intervene when an assault takes place or for failing to check for weapons and working to keep weapons from being manufactured in the prison or smuggled from the outside.[15]

To establish liability in a tort case, the plaintiff (the person alleging injury who files the legal complaint) must show that (1) the officials had a duty, such as a duty to protect an inmate from harm, (2) they breached the duty by failing to uphold their responsibilities, (3) their actions in failing their duties were the **proximate cause** of the injury—namely, an action in the chain of events that was immediately responsible for the injury—and (4) the plaintiff suffered an injury for which he or she seeks an appropriate remedy.

The U.S. Supreme Court has declined to recognize all harms as constitutional violations that can serve as the basis for section 1983 actions. Thus, prisoners may be forced to look to state laws, particularly tort law, if they wish to pursue a legal remedy. For example, the U.S. Supreme Court ruled that there was no constitutional violation upon which to base a section 1983 action when prison officials lost a $23.50 hobby kit that an inmate had ordered.[16] As you read the excerpt from *Parratt v. Taylor* (1981) in Box 12-8, consider whether you believe this was a correct decision in light of the Fourteenth Amendment provision, which says states shall not deny people their property without due process of law.

As you can see, the Court's decision focused on the availability of state procedures and remedies (i.e., the existence of due process) in determining that there was no constitutional violation.

This and other limitations on the applicability of section 1983 (e.g., the immunity doctrines) mean that prisoners often must make use of available state laws and procedures to seek remedies for alleged harms. From the perspective of

| BOX 12-8 | *Parratt v. Taylor,* 451 U.S. 527 (1981) |

JUSTICE REHNQUIST delivered the opinion of the Court.

. . . This Court has never directly addressed the question of what process is due a person when an employee of a State negligently takes his property. In some cases this Court has held that due process requires a predeprivation hearing before the State interferes with any liberty or property interest enjoyed by its citizens. In most of these cases, however, the deprivation of property was pursuant to some state procedure and "process" could be offered before any actual deprivation took place. . . .

We have, however, recognized that postdeprivation remedies made available by the State can satisfy the Due Process Clause. . . . [Our precedents] recognize that either the necessity of quick action by the State or the impracticability of providing any meaningful predeprivation process, when coupled with the availability of some meaningful means by which to assess the propriety of the State's action at some time after the initial taking, can satisfy the requirements of procedural due process. . . .

Application of the principles recited above to this case leads us to conclude the respondent has not alleged a violation of the Due Process Clause of the Fourteenth Amendment. Although he has been deprived of property under the color of state law, the deprivation did not occur as a result of some established state procedure. Indeed, the deprivation occurred as a result of the unauthorized failure of agents of the State to follow established State procedure. . . . Moreover, the State of Nebraska has provided [the prisoner] with the means by which he can receive redress for the deprivation. The State provides a remedy to persons who believe they have suffered a tortious loss at the hands of the State. . . . Through this tort claims procedure the State hears and pays claims of prisoners housed in penal institutions. This procedure was in existence at the time of the loss here in question, but the [prisoner] did not use it. It is argued that the State does not adequately protect the [prisoner's] interests because it provides only for an action against the State as opposed to its individual employees, it contains no provisions for punitive damages, and there is no right to a trial by jury. Although the state remedies may not provide the [prisoner] with all the relief which may have been available if he could have proceeded under [section] 1983, that does not mean that the state remedies are not adequate to satisfy the requirements of due process. The remedies provided could have fully compensated the [prisoner] for the property loss he suffered, and we hold that they are sufficient to satisfy the requirements of due process. . . .

a corrections officer, it may make little difference if a case goes to federal court or state court, especially if the state provides an attorney to defend the action and indemnifies the officer if there is an adverse result. Cases that reach trial in either system are likely to be time-consuming and draining for corrections officers, who must sit for depositions, answer interrogatories, and eventually testify at trial. Fortunately for corrections officers, many prisoners' cases are dismissed during pretrial proceedings. Many of these cases do not state a valid legal claim or lack evidence to support a hypothetically plausible claim. Moreover, because prisoners do not have a right to counsel for such legal actions, they often are overmatched by attorneys from the state attorney general's office. And even if they have a valid claim, they are likely to violate proper court procedures in preparing and presenting a case.

SUMMARY

- The law affects and defines corrections officers' relationships with their supervisors, just as it affects their interactions with prisoners.

- Employment law relevant to corrections personnel includes employment discrimination statutes, affirmative action, union collective bargaining agreements, other workplace laws, and emerging issues affecting their workplace context (e.g., interactions with prisoners who have HIV, AIDS, tuberculosis, or hepatitis).

- The concept of sovereign immunity traditionally prohibits lawsuits against the government unless the government consents.

- The Supreme Court has declared that local governments, but not federal and state governments, may be sued under section 1983. Federal and state governments may be sued under their own statutes consenting to lawsuits in specific situations (e.g., Federal Tort Claims Act).

- In section 1983 actions, state officials may be sued in their personal capacity, but not their official capacity as representatives of the state.

- Government corrections officers enjoy qualified immunity against lawsuits for money damages if they take good-faith (well-intentioned and knowledgeable) actions, but corrections officers in private prisons do not have such immunity.

- Officials' actions that constitute mere negligence do not give rise to constitutional claims under section 1983. Similarly, property losses for which the state provides procedural avenues for remedy do not raise constitutional claims.

Key Terms

absolute immunity
affirmative action
civil service laws
Daniels v. Williams (1986)
Dothard v. Rawlinson (1977)
indemnification
Monell v. Department of Social Services (1978)
Parratt v. Taylor (1981)

proximate cause
qualified immunity
Richardson v. McKnight (1997)
sovereign immunity
Title VII
Will v. Michigan Department of State Police (1989)

Additional Readings

Barrineau, H. E. 1994. *Civil Liability in Criminal Justice,* 2nd ed. Cincinnati: Anderson.

Kappeler, Victor E. 1997. *Critical Issues in Police Civil Liability,* 2nd ed. Prospect Heights, IL.: Waveland Press.

Nahmod, Sheldon H., Michael L. Wells, and Thomas A. Eaton. 1995. *Constitutional Torts.* Cincinnati: Anderson.

Notes

1. Kathleen Maguire and Ann Pastore, eds., *Sourcebook of Criminal Justice Statistics—1996* (Washington, DC: U.S. Department of Justice, Bureau of Justice Statistics, 1997), p. 85.

2. United States v. Paradise, 480 U.S. 149 (1987).

3. Johnson v. Transportation Agency, 480 U.S. 616 (1987).

4. Wygant v. Jackson Board of Education, 476 U.S. 267 (1986).

5. Employment Division of Oregon v. Smith, 494 U.S. 872 (1990).

6. Cooper v. Pate, 378 U.S. 546 (1964).

7. Monell v. Department of Social Services, 436 U.S. 658 (1978).

8. Will v. Michigan Department of State Police, 491 U.S. 58 (1989).

9. Harlow v. Fitzgerald, 457 U.S. 800 (1982).

10. Ibid.

11. West v. Atkins, 108 S.Ct. 2250 (1988).

12. City of Canton v. Harris, 489 U.S. 378 (1989).

13. Board of Commissioners, Bryan County v. Brown, 117 S.Ct. 1382 (1997).

14. McMillian v. Monroe County, 117 S.Ct. 1734 (1997).

15. Michael S. Vaughn and Rolando V. del Carmen, "Civil Liability Against Officials for Inmate-on-Inmates Assault: Where Are We and Where Have We Been?" *The Prison Journal* 75 (1995): 69–89; Michael S. Vaughn, "Prison Civil Liability for Inmate-Against-Inmate Assault and Breakdown/Disorganization Theory," *Journal of Criminal Justice* 24 (1996): 139–152.

16. Parratt v. Taylor, 451 U.S. 527 (1981).

CHAPTER THIRTEEN

Conclusion:
Law's Impact
on Corrections

Gone are the days when prison wardens decided for themselves how to run corrections institutions. The walls of prisons and jails are no longer "closed," and outsiders now can examine and evaluate practices and conditions in corrections institutions. Prisoners may use the courts to seek changes in their conditions of confinement, while legislators may enact statutes to shape corrections programs and policies. Thus, the law has invaded territory that formerly stood isolated and secret, beyond the boundaries of society's interests and knowledge.

As demonstrated in this book, the various forms of law—constitutions, statutes, judicial decisions, and regulations—influence the activities and conditions in corrections institutions. We can see how these rules influence the policies established by corrections institutions and why corrections officers must be trained to know and follow the rules. But we also can understand how difficult it may be for corrections officers to get everything right. Prison populations keep growing, and overcrowding creates tensions within institutions. Therefore, corrections officers find themselves in daily confrontations with some of the most troublesome and least cooperative people in society. The rules of law seek to inform corrections officials how they must behave by defining what they can and cannot do. In reality, however, those rules are but one of the influences over corrections officials' actions. They also use their judgment to react as new situations arise.

Although law may not control every decision and action taken by prison officials, the legal rules developed over the past three decades clearly have changed the world of corrections. How might we summarize the various ways in which legal developments have affected corrections? Professor James Jacobs has proposed a series of hypotheses about the impact of law on corrections.[1] More specifically, Jacobs addresses the impact of the prisoners' rights movement that produced judicial intervention into prisons. Although these eight hypotheses will require further research and analysis to say for certain whether they are all true, it appears that they are all supported by the current knowledge about law and contemporary corrections.

1. *The prisoners' rights movement has contributed to the bureaucratization of the prison.* In the old days, prisons were run by the whim of the wardens and other corrections officials, who could make up the rules as they went along. Outside authorities cared only about whether order and security were maintained. More recently, lawsuits forced prisons to develop detailed rules and regulations. You have already seen how court decisions affecting, for example, disciplinary proceedings forced prisons to develop hearing boards and detailed procedures for hearings. The development of rules, regulations, procedures, and paperwork in the aftermath of court decisions changed prisons from the personal fiefdoms of wardens, many of whom were simply political appointees, into government bureaucracies in which civil servants are obligated to follow rules and regulations. Today's corrections administrators likely are college graduates with training and experience in corrections who have risen through the ranks of civil service.

2. *The prisoners' rights movement has produced a new generation of administrators.* Today's prison administrators must be professionals who understand management concepts, human relations, the political system, the law, and the news media. They must know how to run a complex organization while remaining under the scrutiny of judges, lawyers, legislators, and news reporters. By contrast, the wardens of old merely had to know how to give orders. Their actions were not visible to outsiders, and they were not accountable to outsiders.

3. *The prisoners' rights movement expanded procedural protections available to prisoners.* Prisoners no longer are subject to punishment at the whim of corrections officials. Proper procedures must be followed because the courts have imposed the requirements of due process of law on prisons.

4. *The prisoners' rights movement has heightened public awareness of prison conditions.* Prison litigation brings to light allegations about abusive practices and procedures. News reporters and entertainment producers have seized these opportunities to glimpse inside prison walls in order to increase the public's awareness. Stories about prisons are frequently presented on television news shows, such as *60 Minutes* and *Dateline*. Movies and televi-

sion dramas about prison life, including some based on real incidents, continue to be produced. The Robert Redford film *Brubaker,* for example, was based on the reform of the Arkansas prison system.

5. *The prisoners' rights movement has politicized prisoners and heightened their expectations.* When prisoners were not allowed to file lawsuits, they had little hope that anyone would hear, let alone respond to, their complaints. Now, many prisoners are more knowledgeable and assertive about their rights. Many prisoners are quick to complain—and quick to file lawsuits—if they believe their rights are being violated or if they wish merely to hassle corrections officials.

6. *The prisoners' rights movement has made it more difficult to maintain control over prisoners.* As indicated by the discussion of prison reform litigation in Chapter 8, some scholars believe that court intervention into prisons produces violence as prisoners become more assertive and authority figures lose their previous power to use any means necessary to force prisoners to obey.

7. *The prisoners' rights movement has demoralized staff.* Whether corrections officials actually are demoralized and depressed, they certainly are less in control of their institutions. They no longer have unlimited authority to force prisoners to obey. They must be concerned about following rules and regulations. And they must worry about being sued for taking an action that violates a prisoner's rights or causes an injury to a prisoner. Undoubtedly, many corrections officials are angry and distressed when judges, sitting in some faraway courthouse, tell them how to do their jobs.

8. *The prisoners' rights movement has contributed to a professional movement within corrections to establish national standards.* As discussed with respect to changes that occurred in southern prisons, court decisions forced states to achieve common, nationwide minimum standards in the treatment of prisoners. Because the U.S. Constitution applies to the entire nation, any decision by the U.S. Supreme Court concerning prisoners' rights or prison conditions applies with equal force in establishing minimum standards for corrections institutions throughout the country. As educated corrections professionals have replaced old-style political appointees in running prisons, they have been drawn together in professional associations to share research, innovations, and experiences. Out of this process, the development of national standards has emerged as one means to avoid litigation. If the professional corrections community can agree on national standards for practices and conditions in prisons, then corrections administrators will know what they need achieve in order to avoid the expensive, time-consuming, and disruptive process of prison reform litigation.

If Jacobs' hypotheses accurately describe the impact of prisoner litigation on corrections, the law's impact certainly has been tremendous. And additional hypotheses could be added to Jacobs' list, especially if considered from the perspective of prisoners who gained protections and improved conditions. For example, the proper use of force by corrections officials has been defined and limited. The living conditions in some corrections institutions have improved. Prison administrators have gained new incentives to provide training for corrections personnel. The list could probably go on and on.

Although any list of the law's impacts on contemporary corrections would be extensive, that list is not necessarily growing. In light of major changes in corrections through judicial intervention and the professionalization of corrections management, today's judges often seem more reluctant to intervene further into corrections issues. In part, this may be because the worst abuses of the past have been recognized and redressed. In part, this also may be because the U.S. Supreme Court's composition has changed and the high court has begun to limit the expansion of protections for prisoners.

In the majority opinion in *Bell v. Wolfish* (1979), Justice William Rehnquist surveyed the past and guided the future in prison litigation by acknowledging that abuses needed to be corrected but warning that judges should not go too far in intervening into prisons. In time, Rehnquist became chief justice (in 1986) and assumed an even more influential position from which to limit lower courts' involvement in prisons. Apparently, Rehnquist and his like-minded colleagues have succeeded in encouraging—and in some instances, requiring—judges to step back a bit from prison reform litigation. As you read Rehnquist's statement from 1979, think about how it is consistent with later judicial and legislative developments, such as the Prison Reform Litigation Act of 1996, which limited prisoners' opportunities to file civil rights lawsuits and judges' authority to remedy violations.

> There was a time not too long ago when the federal judiciary took a completely "hands-off" approach to the problem of prison administration. In recent years, however, these courts largely have discarded this "hands-off" attitude and have waded into this complex arena. The deplorable conditions and Draconian restrictions of some of our Nation's prisons are too well known to require recounting here, and the federal courts rightly have condemned these sordid aspects of our prison systems. But many of these same courts have, in the name of the Constitution, become increasingly enmeshed in the minutiae of prison operations. Judges, after all, are human. They, no less than others in our society, have a natural tendency to believe that their individual solutions to often intractable problems are better or more workable than those of the persons who are actually charged with and trained in the running of the particular institution under examination. But under the Constitution, the first question to be answered is not whose plan is best, but in what branch of the Government is lodged the authority to initially devise the plan. This does not mean that constitutional rights are not to be scrupulously observed. It does mean, however, that the inquiry of federal courts into prison management must be limited to the issue of whether a particular system violates any prohibition of the Constitution or, in the case of a federal prison, a statute. The wide range of "judgment calls" that meet constitutional and statutory requirements are confided to officials outside of the Judicial Branch of Government.[2]

Rehnquist's call for judicial deference to prison officials and elected legislatures is reflected in Supreme Court decisions limiting opportunities for prisoners to file habeas corpus and civil rights actions. It is reflected in Supreme Court decisions favoring corrections officials' judgments about the need for order and security over the asserted rights of inmates. It is reflected in legislative actions by Congress to limit judges' authority to order remedies in prison reform cases. These developments have not left prisoners unprotected. Prior court decisions have defined rights, albeit limited in scope, that must be respected by corrections officials. In addition, even if the federal courts are less receptive to constitutional rights cases, opportunities for tort lawsuits under state law and the Federal Tort Claims Act still deter officials from harming prisoners.

In the late 1990s, the courts appear to be refining and limiting the rights developed for prisoners in the preceding three decades. This may mean that the era of major changes in corrections law is over because prisons nationwide have already been prodded toward compliance with a common set of minimum standards for corrections practices and conditions. This does not mean that future major changes are out of the question. The composition of the U.S. Supreme Court inevitably will change, and new justices may bring different perspectives to the issues in corrections law. States' current emphasis on long prison sentences may create overcrowded conditions that require judges to make new assessments of the legal standards needed to fulfill the requirements of the Constitution. Also, society's values and viewpoints about incarceration as a means of punishment may change. If so, those changing values may be reflected in the decisions of state judges elected by the citizens, in the verdicts by citizen-jurors in prisoners' tort cases, and in the opinions issued by federal judges appointed by presidents and senators elected by a changing citizenry.

Through legal developments, corrections moved rapidly through a period of change. Today, the pace of change has slowed—some might even say stopped—as judges have become less active in reshaping prisons, in part because there are fewer glaring problems. Law remains an important force, however. It continues to provide rules designed to reinforce and maintain the changes that have occurred. It continues to tell corrections officials what they can and cannot do. And it continues to provide the avenue through which convicted offenders and unconvicted detainees can raise complaints about improper treatment—a crucial avenue when so much of society seems to care so little about what happens to the people drawn into the criminal justice process.

Notes

1. James B. Jacobs, "The Prisoners' Rights Movement and Its Impacts," in James W. Marquart and Jonathan R. Sorensen, eds., *Correctional Contexts: Contemporary and Classical Readings* (Los Angeles: Roxbury, 1997), pp. 231–247.

2. Bell v. Wolfish, 441 U.S. 520, 562 (1979).

The Bill of Rights and the Fourteenth Amendment to the U.S. Constitution

FIRST AMENDMENT (ratified in 1791): Congress shall make no law respecting an establishment of religion, or prohibiting the free exercise thereof; or abridging the freedom of speech, or of the press; or the right of the people peaceably to assemble, and to petition the Government for a redress of grievances.

SECOND AMENDMENT (ratified in 1791): A well regulated Militia, being necessary for the security of a free State, the right of the people to keep and bear Arms, shall not be infringed.

THIRD AMENDMENT (ratified in 1791): No Soldier shall, in time of peace be quartered in any house, without the consent of the Owner, nor in time of war, but in a manner to be prescribed by law.

FOURTH AMENDMENT (ratified in 1791): The right of the people to be secure in their persons, houses, papers, and effects, against unreasonable searches and seizures, shall not be violated, and no Warrants shall issue, but upon probable cause, supported by Oath or affirmation, and particularly describing the place to be searched, and the persons or things to be seized.

FIFTH AMENDMENT (ratified in 1791): No person shall be held to answer for a capital or otherwise infamous crime, unless on a presentment or indictment of a Grand Jury, except in cases arising in the land or naval forces, or in the Militia, when in actual service in time of War or public danger; nor shall any person be subject for the same offence to be twice put in jeopardy of life or limb; nor shall be compelled in any criminal case to be a witness against himself, nor be deprived of life, liberty, or property, without due process of law; nor shall private property be taken for public use, without just compensation.

SIXTH AMENDMENT (ratified in 1791): In all criminal prosecutions, the accused shall enjoy the right to a speedy and public trial, by an impartial jury of the State and district wherein the crime shall have been committed, which district shall have been previously ascertained by law, and to be informed of the nature and cause of the accusation; to be confronted with the witnesses against him; to have compulsory process for obtaining witnesses in his favor, and to have the Assistance of Counsel for his defence.

SEVENTH AMENDMENT (ratified in 1791): In Suits at common law, where the value in controversy shall exceed twenty dollars, the right of trial by jury shall be preserved, and no fact tried by a jury, shall be otherwise re-examined in any Court of the United States, than according to the rules of the common law.

EIGHTH AMENDMENT (ratified in 1791): Excessive bail shall not be required, nor excessive fines imposed, nor cruel and unusual punishments inflicted.

NINTH AMENDMENT (ratified in 1791): The enumeration in the Constitution, of certain rights, shall not be construed to deny or disparage others retained by the people.

TENTH AMENDMENT (ratified in 1791): The powers not delegated to the United States by the Constitution, nor prohibited by it to the States, are reserved to the States respectively, or to the people.

FOURTEENTH AMENDMENT (ratified in 1868):
Section 1. All persons born or naturalized in the United States, and subject to the jurisdiction thereof, are citizens of the United States and of the State wherein they reside. No State shall make or enforce any law which shall abridge the privileges or immunities of citizens of the United States; nor shall any State deprive any person of life, liberty, or property, without due process of law; nor deny to any person within its jurisdiction the equal protection of the laws. . . .
Section 5. The Congress shall have the power to enforce, by appropriate legislation, the provisions of this article.

Forms for Filing Prisoners' Civil Rights Lawsuits

PRISONER CIVIL RIGHTS INSTRUCTION SHEET

If you wish to file a prisoner civil rights case in the United States District Court for the Western District of Michigan you must follow the specific instructions below:

1. A Prisoner Civil Rights Complaint must be *legibly* handwritten or typewritten.

2. The clerk's office will provide a *limited* number of complaint forms on request. You are responsible for any extra copies needed.

3. You, as plaintiff, must sign and date the complaint. If the complaint is being filed by more than one plaintiff, a signature from each plaintiff is required.

4. You are required to furnish the correct name and address of each person you have named as a defendant. You must also provide the clerk's office with one copy of the original complaint and all attachments (if any) for each defendant named *and* one copy for the court. For example, if you name two defendants, you must file the original complaint and three copies.

5. **A filing fee of $150.00 is required.** If you cannot afford the filing fee, you may request permission from the court to have your complaint proceed *in forma pauperis* by completing and signing a financial declaration. You must also have an authorized officer in charge of financial records at the institution issue a certificate establishing prisoner account activity with attached printout. If a printout is not available at the institution, the authorized

officer must complete the certificate located on the financial declaration. Whichever method is used, the authorized officer must first have your financial declaration. *Note:* If the complaint is being filed by more than one plaintiff, a financial declaration must be completed for each plaintiff named.

6. When your case is filed you will be notified of the case number and the name of the judge to whom the case is assigned. If the filing fee has been paid, you will receive a copy of your receipt. If the court has granted your request to proceed *in forma pauperis,* you will receive a copy of the pauper order.

7. If these instructions are not followed, your complaint and all copies will be returned to you with a notation as to the requirements not yet completed.

FORM TO BE USED BY A PRISONER IN FILING A COMPLAINT UNDER THE CIVIL RIGHTS ACT, 42 U.S.C. §1983

In the United States District Court for the Western District of Michigan

_____

_____

_____

(Enter above the full names of all plaintiffs in this action.)

v.

_____

_____

_____

(Enter above the full name of the defendant or defendants in this action.)

Instructions for Filing a Complaint by a Prisoner Under the Civil Rights Act, 42 U.S.C. §1983

This packet includes four copies of a complaint form. To start an action, you must file an original and one copy of your complaint for each defendant you name and one copy for the court. For example, if you name two defendants you must file the original and three copies of the complaint. You should also keep an additional copy of the complaint for your own records. All copies of the complaint must be identical to the original. **The clerk will not file your complaint unless it conforms to these instructions and to these forms.**

Your complaint must be legibly handwritten or typewritten. You, the plaintiff(s), must sign and date the complaint on the last page. If you need additional space to answer a question, you may attach additional pages.

Your complaint can be brought in this court only if one or more of the named defendants is located within this district. Further, you must file a separate complaint for each claim that you have unless they are all related to the same incident or issue.

You are required to furnish, so that the United States Marshal can complete service, the **correct name and address of each person you have named as defendant.** A PLAINTIFF IS REQUIRED TO GIVE INFORMATION TO THE UNITED STATES MARSHAL TO ENABLE THE MARSHAL TO COMPLETE SERVICE OF THE COMPLAINT UPON ALL PERSONS NAMED AS DEFENDANTS.

In order for this complaint to be filed, it must be accompanied by the filing fee of $150.00. In addition, the United States Marshal will require you to pay the cost of serving the complaint on each of the defendants.

If you are unable to pay the filing fee and service costs for this action, all plaintiffs must petition the court to proceed in forma pauperis by completing and signing the attached declaration (pages 6 and 7). If you wish to proceed in forma pauperis, you must have an authorized officer at the penal institution complete the certificate as to the amount of money and securities on deposit to your credit in any account in the institution.

You will note that you are required to give facts. THIS COMPLAINT SHOULD NOT CONTAIN LEGAL ARGUMENTS OR CITATIONS.

When these forms are completed, mail the original and copies to the Clerk of the United States District Court for the Western District of Michigan at any of the addresses below:

U.S. District Court	U.S. District Court	U.S. District Court	U.S. District Court
452 Federal Building	229 Federal Building	B-35 Federal Building	113 Federal Building
110 Michigan St., NW	P.O. Box 698	410 W. Michigan Ave.	315 W. Allegan
Grand Rapids, MI 49503	Marquette, MI 49855	Kalamazoo, MI 49007	Lansing, MI 48933

I. Previous Lawsuits

A. Have you begun other lawsuits in state or federal court dealing with the same facts involved in this action or otherwise relating to your imprisonment?   Yes ☐   No ☐

B. If your answer to A is yes, describe the lawsuit in the space below. (If there is more than one lawsuit, describe the additional lawsuits on another piece of paper, using the same outline.)

    1. Parties to this previous lawsuit:

        Plaintiffs: _____

        _____

        Defendants: _____

    2. Court (If federal court, name the district. If state court, name the county.)

        _____

    3. Docket Number _____

    4. Name of judge to whom case was assigned _____

    5. Disposition (for example: Was the case dismissed? Was it appealed? Is it still pending?)

        _____

    6. Approximate date of filing lawsuit _____

    7. Approximate date of disposition _____

II. Place of Present Confinement

A. Is there a prisoner grievance procedure in this institution?   Yes ☐   No ☐

B. Did you present the facts relating to your complaint in the state prisoner grievance procedure?

                                                            Yes ☐   No ☐

C. If your answer is YES,

    1. What steps did you take? _____

        _____

    2. What was the result? _____

        _____

D. If your answer is NO, explain why not _____

    _____

E. If there is no prison grievance procedure in the institution, did you complain to prison authorities?

Yes ☐   No ☐

F. If your answer is YES,

1. What steps did you take? _____

_____

2. What was the result? _____

_____

III. Parties

In Item A below, place your name in the first blank and place your present address in the second blank. Do the same for additional plaintiffs, if any.

A. Name of Plaintiff _____

Address _____

Additional Plaintiffs _____

_____

_____

_____

_____

In Item B below, place the full name of the defendant in the first blank, his official position in the second blank and his place of employment in the third blank. Use Item C for the names, positions and places of employment of any additional defendants. Attach extra sheets if necessary. **State whether you are suing each defendant in an official capacity or personal capacity.**

B. Defendant _____ is employed as _____

at _____

C. Additional Defendants _____

_____

_____

_____

_____

_____

_____

_____

_____

_____

_____

_____

_____

_____

_____

_____

_____

IV. Statement of Claim

State here, as briefly as possible, the **facts** of your case. Describe how each defendant is involved. Include also, the names of other persons involved, dates and places. Do not give any legal arguments or cite any cases or statutes. If you intend to allege a number of related claims, number and set forth each claim in a separate paragraph. Use as much space as you need. Attach extra sheets if necessary.

_____

_____

_____

_____

_____

_____

_____

_____

_____

_____

_____

_____

_____

_____

_____

_____

_____

_____

_____

_____

_____

_____

_____

_____

_____

_____

_____

_____

_____

_____

_____

_____

_____

_____

_____

_____

V. Relief

State briefly, exactly what you want the court to do for you. Make no legal arguments. Cite no cases or statutes.

_____

_____

_____

_____

_____

_____

_____

_____

_____

_____

_____

_____

_____

_____

_____

_____

_____

_____

_____

_____

_____

_____

_____

_____

_____

_____

_____

_____

_____   _____
Date   Signature of Plaintiff

Forms for Filing
Habeas Corpus Petitions

PETITION UNDER 28 USC § 2254 FOR WRIT OF
HABEAS CORPUS BY A PERSON IN STATE CUSTODY

(If petitioner is attacking a judgment which imposed a sentence to be served in the future, petitioner must fill in the name of the state where judgment was entered. If petitioner has a sentence to be served in the future under a federal judgment which he wishes to attack, he should file a motion under 28 U.S.C. § 2255, in the federal court which entered the judgment.)

PETITION FOR WRIT OF HABEAS CORPUS
BY A PERSON IN STATE CUSTODY

Instructions—Read Carefully

1. This petition must be legibly handwritten or typewritten, and signed by the petitioner under penalty of perjury. Any false statement of a material fact may serve as the basis for prosecution and conviction for perjury. All questions must be answered concisely in the proper space on the form.

2. Additional pages are not permitted except with respect to the facts which you rely upon to support your grounds for relief. No citation of authorities need be furnished. If briefs or arguments are submitted, they should be submitted in the form of a separate memorandum.

3. Upon receipt of a fee of $5 your petition will be filed if it is in proper order.

4. If you do not have the necessary funds for transcripts, counsel, appeal, and other costs connected with a motion of this type, you may request permission to proceed *in forma pauperis,* in which event you must execute form AO 240 or any other form required by the court, setting forth information establishing your inability to pay the costs. If you wish to proceed *in forma pauperis,* you must have an authorized officer at the penal institution complete the certificate as to the amount of money and securities on deposit to your credit in any account in the institution. If your personal account exceeds $ _____, you must pay the filing fee as required by the rules of the district court.

5. Only judgments entered by one court may be challenged in a single motion. If you seek to challenge judgments entered by different courts either in the same state or in different states, you must file separate petitions as to each court.

6. Your attention is directed to the fact that you must include all grounds for relief and all facts supporting such grounds for relief in the petition you file seeking relief from any judgment of conviction.

7. When the petition is fully completed, the original and at least two copies must be mailed to the Clerk of the United States District Court whose address is . . .

8. Petitions which do not conform to these instructions will be returned with a notation as to the deficiency.

United States District Court   District

Name _____   Prisoner No. _____   Case No. _____

Place of Confinement _____

Name of Petitioner   Name of Respondent
(include name under which convicted)   (authorized person having custody of petitioner)

v.

The Attorney General of the State of: _____

PETITION

1. Name and location of court which entered the judgment of conviction under attack _____

2. Date of judgment of conviction _____

3. Length of sentence _____

4. Nature of offense involved (all counts) _____

_____

_____

5. What was your plea? (Check one)

   a. Not guilty   ☐

   b. Guilty   ☐

   c. Nolo contendere   ☐

   If you entered a guilty plea to one count or indictment, and a not guilty plea to another count or indictment, give details: _____

   _____

6. If you pleaded not guilty, what kind of a trial did you have? (Check one)

   a. Jury   ☐

   b. Judge only   ☐

7. Did you testify at the trial?   Yes ☐   No ☐

8. Did you appeal from the judgment of conviction?   Yes ☐   No ☐

9. If you did appeal, answer the following:

   (a) Name of court _____

   (b) Result _____

   _____

   (c) Date of result and citation, if known _____

   (d) Grounds raised _____

   _____

   (e) If you sought further review of the decision on appeal by a higher state court, please answer the following:

   (1) Name of court _____

   (2) Result _____

   _____

   (3) Date of result and citation, if known _____

   (4) Grounds raised _____

   _____

   (f) If you filed a petition for certiorari in the United States Supreme Court, please answer the following with respect to each direct appeal:

   (1) Name of court _____

   (2) Result _____

   _____

   (3) Date of result and citation, if known _____

   (4) Grounds raised _____

   _____

10. Other than a direct appeal from the judgment of conviction and sentence, have you previously filed any petitions, applications, or motions with respect to this judgment in any court, state or federal?   Yes ☐   No ☐

11. If your answer to 10 was "yes," give the following information:

   (a) (1) Name of court _____

        (2) Nature of proceeding _____

                _____

        (3) Grounds raised _____

                _____

                _____

                _____

        (4) Did you receive an evidentiary hearing on your petition, application or motion?   Yes ☐   No ☐

        (5) Result _____

        (6) Date of result _____

   (b) As to any second petition, application or motion give the same information:

        (1) Name of court _____

        (2) Nature of proceeding _____

                _____

        (3) Grounds raised _____

                _____

                _____

                _____

        (4) Did you receive an evidentiary hearing on your petition, application or motion?   Yes ☐   No ☐

        (5) Result _____

        (6) Date of result _____

   (c) Did you appeal to the highest state court having jurisdiction the result of action taken on any petition, application or motion?

        (1) First petition, etc.   Yes ☐   No ☐

        (2) Second petition, etc.   Yes ☐   No ☐

   (d) If you did *not* appeal from the adverse action on any petition, application or motion, explain briefly why you did not: _____

        _____

        _____

12. State *concisely* every ground on which you claim that you are being held unlawfully. Summarize *briefly* the *facts* supporting each ground. If necessary, you may attach pages stating additional grounds and *facts* supporting same.

    CAUTION: In order to proceed in the federal court, you must ordinarily first exhaust your available state court remedies as to each ground on which you request action by the federal court. If you fail to set forth all grounds in this petition, you may be barred from presenting additional grounds at a later date.

For your information, the following is a list of the most frequently raised grounds for relief in habeas corpus proceedings. Each statement preceded by a letter constitutes a separate ground for possible relief. You may raise any grounds which you may have other than those listed if you have exhausted your state court remedies with respect to them. However, *you should raise in this petition all available grounds* (related to this conviction) on which you base your allegations that you are being held in custody unlawfully.

Do not check any of these listed grounds. If you select one or more of these grounds for relief, you must allege facts. The petition will be returned to you if you merely check (a) through (j) or any one of these grounds.

(a) Conviction obtained by plea of guilty which was unlawfully induced or not made voluntarily with understanding of the nature of the charge and the consequences of the plea.

(b) Conviction obtained by use of coerced confession.

(c) Conviction obtained by use of evidence gained pursuant to an unconstitutional search and seizure.

(d) Conviction obtained by use of evidence obtained pursuant to an unlawful arrest.

(e) Conviction obtained by a violation of the privilege against self-incrimination.

(f) Conviction obtained by the unconstitutional failure of the prosecution to disclose to the defendant evidence favorable to the defendant.

(g) Conviction obtained by a violation of the protection against double jeopardy.

(h) Conviction obtained by action of a grand or petit jury which was unconstitutionally selected and impaneled.

(i) Denial of effective assistance of counsel.

(j) Denial of right of appeal.

A. Ground one: _____

_____

Supporting FACTS (state *briefly* without citing cases or law): _____

_____

_____

_____

_____

_____

B. Ground two: _____

_____

Supporting FACTS (state *briefly* without citing cases or law): _____

_____

_____

_____

_____

_____

C. Ground three: _____

_____

Supporting FACTS (state *briefly* without citing cases or law): _____

_____

_____

_____

_____

_____

D. Ground four: _____

_____

Supporting FACTS (state *briefly* without citing cases or law): _____

_____

_____

_____

_____

_____

13. If any of the grounds listed in 12A, B, C, and D were not previously presented in any other court, state or federal, state *briefly* what grounds were not so presented, and give your reasons for not presenting them:

_____

_____

_____

14. Do you have any petition or appeal now pending in any court, either state or federal, as to the judgement under attack?   Yes ☐   No ☐

15. Give the name and address, if known, of each attorney who represented you in the following stages of the judgment attacked herein:

(a) At preliminary hearing _____

_____

(b) At arraignment and plea _____

_____

(c) At trial _____

_____

(d) At sentencing _____

_____

(e) On appeal _____

_____

(f) In any post-conviction proceeding _____

_____

(g) On appeal from any adverse ruling in a post-conviction proceeding _____

_____

16. Were you sentenced on more than one count of an indictment, or on more than one indictment, in the same court and at the same time?   Yes ☐   No ☐

17. Do you have any future sentence to serve after you complete the sentence imposed by the judgment under attack?   Yes ☐   No ☐

   (a) If so, give name and location of court which imposed sentence to be served in the future:

     _____

   (b) Give date and length of the above sentence: _____

     _____

   (c) Have you filed, or do you contemplate filing, any petition attacking the judgment which imposed the sentence to be served in the future?   Yes ☐   No ☐

Wherefore, petitioner prays that the Court grant petitioner relief to which he may be entitled in this proceeding.

_____

Signature of Attorney (if any)

I declare under penalty of perjury that the foregoing is true and correct. Executed on _____

(date)

_____

Signature of Petitioner

Glossary

access to the courts Fundamental prisoners' right that is the key element for enforcement of other rights because it is the mechanism for gaining judicial protection of constitutional rights. The right includes protected contacts with lawyers and provision of legal resources for case preparation.

absolute immunity Complete protection from civil lawsuits enjoyed by the U.S. president, judges, and prosecutors for official decisions they make.

Affirmative action The general label covering a variety of activities involving active steps to recruit and promote people from segments of society that previously were subject to discrimination in seeking government employment.

answer The legal filing by the defendant in a civil lawsuit that responds to the initial claims in the complaint. In prisoner cases, this is corrections officials' first response to legal claims about rights violations.

Antiterrorism and Effective Death Penalty Act of 1996 A federal statute that included new procedures creating barriers to prisoners' habeas corpus petitions.

appellate brief Formal written arguments submitted by each side in a case before an appellate court.

***Bell v. Wolfish* (1979)** Landmark U.S. Supreme Court case concerning the rights of jail inmates in which the majority of justices rejected pretrial detainees' claims because they placed greater emphasis on the jail's interests in order and security.

body cavity search A strip search that includes examinations of bodily openings that might be used to hide contraband after contact visits. The Supreme Court has approved such searches, even for unconvicted pretrial detainees, because of concerns about safety and security within jails.

***Bounds v. Smith* (1977)** U.S. Supreme Court decision requiring prisons to provide law libraries or other legal assistance as part of prisoners' right of access to the courts.

case law Legal rules produced by judges' decisions.

case precedent Legal rules created in judges' decisions that serve to guide judges in subsequent similar cases.

civil disabilities Legal restrictions on rights and opportunities as a consequence of past criminal convictions. Depending on state law, such restrictions may limit the right to vote, hold public office, or obtain certain occupational licenses.

Civil Rights of Institutionalized Persons Act (CRIPA) A federal law setting standards for grievance procedures in state correctional institutions.

civil service laws Statutes that mandate fair procedures for hiring government employees based on qualifications rather than political connections.

***Coleman v. Thompson* (1991)** U.S. Supreme Court decision requiring forfeiture of federal habeas corpus claims if the petitioner's attorney violated any procedural rules in the state appeals process.

common law The legal system that the United States inherited from England, in which judges create law by deciding cases while relying on judges' opinions in prior similar cases.

complaint The initial filing in a civil lawsuit that presents allegations about the defendant's legal responsibility for harms suffered by the claimant.

concurring opinion The opinion by an appellate judge who agrees with the outcome of a case but disagrees with some aspect of the reasoning in the majority opinion.

consent decree A negotiated resolution to a prison reform lawsuit that becomes law as the order issued by the judge.

constitution The fundamental laws contained in state or federal documents that outline the design of the government and the basic rights for individuals.

constitutional rights Legal guarantees, specified in the fundamental legal document of a state or nation, to protect individuals against improper actions by government.

contraband An item, such as weapons, drugs or money, that prisoners are not allowed to possess and that officials seek to discover and seize in searches and mail inspections.

***Cooper v. Pate* (1964)** U.S. Supreme Court decision declaring that prisoners can file section 1983 civil rights lawsuits against corrections officials.

corporal punishment The use of physical punishments, most commonly recognized as beatings and other pain-inflicting punishments, but also including restricted, uncomfortable confinement in a small punishment space.

court of last resort The highest court in a judicial system, either a state supreme court or the U.S. Supreme Court.

***Daniels v. Williams* (1986)** U.S. Supreme Court decision declaring that mere negligence by a corrections officer causing injury to a prisoner does not provide a basis for a constitutional claim under section 1983.

depositions Sworn testimony from litigants or witnesses recorded during questioning by attorneys from both sides prior to a trial.

digital examination A finger probe search of a prisoner's body cavities, which must be justified by reasonable suspicions that contraband is hidden inside the prisoner's body.

disciplinary segregation Isolation cells used to hold prisoners being punished for violating prison rules. Typically, prisoners in segregation for disciplinary reasons lose many privileges and are permitted to leave their cells only once each day for exercise—often by themselves in an isolated exercise pen.

discovery Pretrial procedures to gather information from witnesses and the opposing side.

discretion The authority of corrections officials to make decisions based on their own judgment and not mandated or controlled by specific rules.

discretionary jurisdiction The power of courts of last resort to pick and choose which cases they will hear and thereby to decline to hear other cases brought forward from the lower courts.

dissenting opinion The judicial opinion by an appellate judge who disagrees with the court majority's decision on the outcome of a case.

***Dothard v. Rawlinson* (1977)** U.S. Supreme Court decision rejecting Alabama's height and weight requirements for corrections officers because the state had not proved that these were bona fide occupational qualifications (BFOQs).

due process of law A flexibly interpreted right contained in the Fifth and Fourteenth Amendments to the Constitution that is used to examine jail conditions for pretrial detainees because the Eighth Amendment protects only convicted offenders, and not unconvicted detainees.

en banc **hearing** A hearing in which all of the judges of an appellate court hear and decide a case as a group rather than in three-member panels.

equal protection The right not to be discriminated against, guaranteed by the Fourteenth Amendment and sometimes raised when prisoners from one religion believe they are being treated differently than prisoners from other religions.

Establishment Clause The portion of the First Amendment that prevents government support or endorsement of particular religions.

Estelle v. Gamble **(1976)** U.S. Supreme Court decision determining that the Eighth Amendment protects prisoners against deprivations of medical care based on the deliberate indifference of corrections officials.

executive branch The branch of government headed by the elected president, governor, or mayor that is responsible for carrying out laws enacted by the legislature and managing the programs and agencies of government, including corrections institutions.

Ex parte Hull **(1941)** U.S. Supreme Court decision declaring that corrections officials cannot block or censor prisoners' legal correspondence and case filings.

Ex Post Facto Clause Constitutional protection against *ex post facto* laws whereby the government defines crimes or increases punishments after a crime has already been committed.

facts The events and circumstances that produced a legal case. In a court case, the decision is based on legal facts developed through the presentation of admissible evidence.

federalism An underlying principle of the American system of government that recognizes states' authority to handle many of their own affairs without interference by the federal government.

Free Exercise Clause The portion of the First Amendment that forbids government interference with people's religious beliefs and practices.

Gagnon v. Scarpelli **(1973)** U.S. Supreme Court decision ruling that the procedural requirements for parole revocation hearings established in *Morrissey v. Brewer* also apply to probation revocation proceedings. In addition, parolees or probationers facing revocation have no right to counsel. Counsel may be provided as needed on a case-by-case basis in complex cases or when the accused lacks the capability to present arguments and evidence.

good time Time taken off a sentence that is earned through good behavior and lost through violation of prison rules.

Griffin v. Wisconsin **(1987)** U.S. Supreme Court decision permitting probation officers to conduct warrantless searches of probationers' home under the authority of a state statute or regulation that requires reasonable grounds for such searches.

habeas corpus petition A petition filed by an offender who has been unsuccessful in the appellate process but who wishes to allege that his or her federal constitutional rights were violated during the investigation and prosecution of a criminal case. This petition permits a federal judge to review prior actions and decisions in state criminal cases.

hands-off policy The usual approach of judges to prisoners' rights cases prior to the 1960s because of a widespread belief that prisoners had no rights and that corrections officials were best qualified to run their own prisons and programs.

harmless error Procedural errors or constitutional violations in the investigative and trial processes that an appellate court decides are not serious enough to require the reversal of an offender's conviction.

Helling v. McKinney **(1993)** U.S. Supreme Court decision permitting Eighth Amendment claims about prison conditions that may cause future health problems.

holding The statement of a legal rule in a judicial opinion that will serve as a precedent for later cases.

Hudson v. McMillian (1992) U.S. Supreme Court decision permitting lawsuits charging excessive use of force in prisons even when the prisoner did not suffer a serious injury.

Hudson v. Palmer (1984) U.S. Supreme Court decision declaring that prisoners have no Fourth Amendment protection against searches of their cells.

incorporation The process by which the U.S. Supreme Court applies provisions of the Bill of Rights to state and local governments by including them in the Due Process Clause of the Fourteenth Amendment.

indemnification Payment of legal damages by the state on behalf of an employee found liable for a tort or civil rights violation.

in forma pauperis **petition** A legal filing by a litigant claiming to be too poor to pay court fees and seeking to have the fees waived.

Ingraham v. Wright (1978) U.S. Supreme Court decision declining to apply the Eighth Amendment to forbid paddling and other forms of corporal punishment directed at schoolchildren.

interrogatories Questions requiring written responses that are presented by one side to the opposing side in the discovery process for civil lawsuits.

issue The question of law or procedure being addressed by an appellate court in a legal case.

Jackson v. Bishop (1968) U.S. court of appeals decision barring the use of whipping and pain-inflicting corporal punishments in prisons.

jailhouse lawyers Self-educated prisoners who have gained skills in preparing legal papers. They are also known as "writ writers."

Johnson v. Avery (1969) U.S. Supreme Court decision requiring that jailhouse lawyers be permitted to assist other prisoners if prisons do not provide alternative forms of legal assistance.

judicial activism The claim that certain judges make decisions exceeding their proper judicial authority and thereby assume power that belongs to another branch of government, particularly the executive branch.

judicial branch The branch of government, comprised primarily of judges and courts, that interprets constitutions, statutes, and case law as the result of lawsuits, criminal prosecutions, and other legal processes.

judicial opinion A written document issued by a judge that announces and explains a legal decision.

judicial review The power of U.S. judges to review actions by other branches of government to determine if those actions should be invalidated for violating constitutional law.

jurisdiction The legal issues and territory under the authority of a court.

Kansas v. Hendricks (1997) U.S. Supreme Court decision permitting a state to commit sex offenders to mental institutions after those offenders have served their criminal sentences in prison.

Lewis v. Casey (1996) U.S. Supreme Court decision limiting district judges' power to identify deficiencies in prison law libraries and legal assistance programs except to the extent that specific prisoners can show definite harms caused by particular deficiencies.

McCleskey v. Zant (1991) U.S. Supreme Court decision requiring convicted offenders to present all of their claims in a single habeas corpus petition instead of filing subsequent petitions when they identify additional constitutional claims.

Monell v. Department of Social Services (1978) U.S. Supreme Court decision declaring that municipalities, counties, and other local units of government could be regarded as "persons" to be sued under section 1983.

Morrissey v. Brewer (1972) U.S. Supreme Court decision requiring a two-stage hearing process for parole revocation: a preliminary hearing after arrest to establish probable cause for revocation and a final revocation hearing. Such hearings require notice of charges, a neutral hearing officer or board, an opportunity for the accused to present arguments and evidence, and, in most cases, an opportunity for cross-examination of opposing witnesses.

natural rights theory The philosophy of rights underlying the U.S. Constitution and based on the idea that all human beings, whether good or bad, are entitled to protections against improper government actions.

objection A verbal statement an attorney must make during a trial to note alleged errors if those errors are to be challenged in an appeal.

O'Lone v. Estate of Shabazz (1987) U.S. Supreme Court decision applying the reasonableness test to prison rules that clash with free exercise of religion claims.

parole A status attained by incarcerated prisoners who serve most of their sentence in prison before being granted release into the community. They serve the remainder of their sentence in the community under restrictive conditions and the supervision of a parole officer.

Parratt v. Taylor (1981) U.S. Supreme Court decision declaring that no constitutional claim arises when a state provides postdeprivation procedures to address the loss of an inmate's property due to actions by a corrections officer.

pat-down search A search involving a corrections officer moving his or her hands along the outside of a prisoner's clothing in an effort to detect contraband hidden on the prisoner's body.

Pennsylvania Board of Probation and Parole v. Scott (1988) U.S. Supreme Court decision permitting officials to present at parole revocation hearings evidence that was obtained through an improper search.

per curiam An opinion issued by an appellate court that is not signed by any judge who is the author on behalf of the court. Instead, the opinion comes from the entire court majority.

preliminary injunction An immediate order to prevent corrections officials from taking a certain action until court hearings can be held to determine whether that action would be lawful.

Prison Litigation Reform Act of 1996 A federal law limiting federal judges' power to order remedies for rights violations in corrections institutions and imposing additional requirements for prisoners seeking to file civil rights lawsuits.

probation A sentence served within the community under restrictive conditions and the supervision of a probation officer. During probation, a sentence of incarceration is suspended, but the person may be imprisoned for violating probation conditions or committing a new crime.

Procunier v. Martinez (1974) U.S. Supreme Court decision declaring that censorship of prisoners' mail to outsiders violates the First Amendment rights of those outsiders unless the officials have legitimate reasons for their actions and follow appropriate regulations.

pro se **litigators** People who present their own court cases without the assistance of an attorney.

proximate cause In a prisoner's tort lawsuit, an action by the corrections official in the chain of events leading to the harm or injury that was immediately responsible for that harm or injury.

Pugh v. Locke (1976) The famous and controversial federal district court case in which Judge Frank Johnson issued detailed orders instructing Alabama corrections officials on how to run the prison to meet constitutional standards for conditions of confinement.

qualified immunity Limited protection against civil lawsuits enjoyed by government officials for decisions made and actions taken within the scope of their authority under existing law.

rational basis test One test used to evaluate the constitutionality of some laws and regulations that collide with constitutional rights. The test merely requires that the regulation provide a reasonable, rational method of advancing a legitimate institutional goal. It is also known as the "reasonableness test."

reasonable expectation of privacy The concept that usually provides the basis for Fourth Amendment decisions on the permissibility of searches. In prison settings, the courts have tended to regard it as unreasonable for prisoners to expect that their clothing and cells will receive protection from searches.

reasoning The portion of a judicial opinion that provides justifications for a judge's decision.

regulation Legal rules created by government agencies, including state departments of corrections.

Religious Freedom Restoration Act of 1993 The congressional statute designed to counteract

Justice Scalia's opinion in *Employment Division of Oregon v. Smith* by imposing a higher burden of justification upon government actions colliding with free exercise of religion, including actions in the corrections setting. Although this statute was declared unconstitutional by the U.S. Supreme Court in 1997, many states are considering their own parallel legislation, but they are less likely to include protections for prisoners.

remedial orders Judges' orders directing government officials or other persons on the steps they must take to correct constitutional violations.

Rhodes v. Chapman (1981) U.S. Supreme Court decision rejecting a claim that double celling violates the Eighth Amendment.

Richardson v. McKnight (1997) U.S. Supreme Court decision declaring that corrections officers in private prisons do not enjoy the qualified immunity from liability in civil rights lawsuits that is granted to government employees in other prisons.

Ross v. Moffitt (1974) U.S. Supreme Court decision declaring that convicted offenders who are too poor to hire their own attorneys are not entitled to have an attorney provided for them beyond their initial appeal after trial.

Sandin v. Conner (1995) U.S. Supreme Court decision reducing the recognition of state-created liberty interests to those that imposed atypical and significant hardships in affecting a prisoner's freedom from restraint.

section 1983 Federal statute used by prisoners to file lawsuits against state prison officials alleging that those officials violated the prisoners' constitutional rights.

self-defense The legal use of force reasonably necessary to protect oneself against attack. The level of force cannot exceed that which is needed to stop the attack.

social contract theory A philosophy of rights based on the idea that people lose their claim to society's benefits if they violate society's rules.

sovereign immunity A legal tradition inherited from England dictating that the government (or king) cannot be sued unless it consents to be sued. The doctrine helps to protect the federal government and state governments (but not local governments) from certain kinds of lawsuits.

special master (or **special monitor**) An outsider, often a lawyer, law professor, or retired corrections official, appointed by a federal judge to oversee either the details of the litigation and negotiation process or the details of implementing the remedies for constitutional violations.

statutes The law created by the people's elected representatives in legislatures.

state-created liberty interest An entitlement for prisoners created by a state's own rules that triggers procedural protections under the right to due process.

strict scrutiny test The usual test for the constitutionality of laws and regulations affecting fundamental rights. The test requires that the government bear the burden of showing a compelling reason for its regulation and that the regulation take the least restrictive approach. However, the test generally is not applicable to prisoners' rights.

strip search A search requiring prisoners to remove their clothing and submit to visual examination of their entire body.

Talley v. Stephens (1965) The initial federal court decision by a district judge in Arkansas limiting the ability of corrections officials to employ corporal punishment.

Thornburgh v. Abbott (1989) U.S. Supreme Court case approving regulation of outside publications received by prisoners and clarifying the application of the reasonableness test to inmate correspondence.

Title VII Federal statute that prohibits discrimination in employment based on race, color, gender, national origin, or religion.

tort A civil wrong, typically pursued via a lawsuit seeking financial recovery for injury caused by another person or corporation. Civil liability lawsuits under tort law help to raise jail officials' awareness and motivation to act regarding inmates' safety within the jail.

tort law The field of law that provides the basis of civil lawsuits seeking damages for personal injuries or property damage.

Trop v. Dulles (1958) U.S. Supreme Court decision establishing that the Eighth Amendment prohibition on cruel and unusual punishment shall be interpreted according to evolving contemporary standards.

Turner v. Safley (1987) U.S. Supreme Court case establishing an influential four-part rational basis/reasonableness test for laws and regulations that clash with prisoners' rights. The case also approved bans and censorship applied to correspondence between prisoners, and invalidated a Missouri regulation that prevented prisoners from getting married without a compelling justification.

U.S. circuit court of appeals The intermediate appellate courts in the federal court system that handle initial appeals on cases within a specific geographic region.

U.S. district court The trial courts in the federal courts system.

U.S. magistrate judge Federal judicial officers appointed by U.S. district judges to eight-year renewable terms and authorized by Congress to undertake most tasks fulfilled by district judges. U.S. district judges often delegate prisoners' cases to U.S. magistrate judges.

Vitek v. Jones (1980) U.S. Supreme Court decision applying a Constitution-based right of due process to an involuntary transfer from a prison to a mental hospital, even in the absence of a state-created liberty interest.

Warren Court era The time period from 1953 to 1969 in which the U.S. Supreme Court, under the leadership of Chief Justice Earl Warren, incorporated the Bill of Rights and expanded interpretations of constitutional protections for individuals.

Whitley v. Albers (1986) U.S. Supreme Court decision establishing a difficult standard for imposing liability on corrections officials for the use of excessive force. To win a lawsuit, a prisoner must show that the force was used "maliciously and sadistically for the very purpose of causing harm."

Will v. Michigan Department of State Police (1989) U.S. Supreme Court decision declaring that a state is not a "person" that can be sued under section 1983, and state officials similarly cannot be held liable for money damages in their official capacity.

Wilson v. Seiter (1991) U.S. Supreme Court decision requiring a showing of "deliberate indifference" on the part of corrections officials in addition to a showing of improper conditions in order to establish Eighth Amendment violations for any conditions-of-confinement claims.

Wolff v. McDonnell (1974) U.S. Supreme Court decision applying the concept of a state-created liberty interest to a prison discipline case concerning loss of good time. The decision also established the basic notice and hearing procedures for cases involving the right to due process in a prison setting. Furthermore, it approved prison regulations that permit corrections officials to open legal mail and examine it for contraband in the presence of the prisoner, but not to read correspondence between the prisoner and his or her attorney.

writ of certiorari A legal protection used to ask the U.S. Supreme Court to accept a case for hearing by calling up the case from a lower court.

Index